American Biographer

Irving Stone once stated his ambition "to make the biography as dramatic and deeply moving as any novel or play, and at the same time make it a clear and penetrating portrait." He has pursued his goal with remarkable success. Lust for Life first popularized the name of Vincent Van Gogh in America. His biographies of Jack London, Sailor on Horseback, Jessie Benton Fremont, Immortal Wife, Mary Todd Lincoln, Love Is Eternal, have met with critical and public acclaim. Of CLARENCE DARROW FOR THE DEFENSE, *The New Yorker* said: "An excellent job, fluently written and exhaustively documented!"

Books by Irving Stone

LUST FOR LIFE

THEY ALSO RAN

IMMORTAL WIFE

PASSIONATE JOURNEY

THE PRESIDENT'S LADY

LOVE IS ETERNAL

CLARENCE DARROW

FOR THE DEFENSE

A BIOGRAPHY BY
Irving Stone

AUTHORIZED ABRIDGMENT

bantam books, inc.
new york

FOR JEAN STONE (MY GOOD RIGHT ARM)

I may hate the sin, but never the sinner.
—CLARENCE DARROW

CLARENCE DARROW FOR THE DEFENSE

*A Bantam Book / published by arrangement with
Doubleday & Company, Inc.*

PRINTING HISTORY

Doubleday edition published October 1941

2nd printing.....October 1941	7th printing........April 1951
3rd printing...November 1941	8th printing........April 1953
4th printing........May 1943	9th printing........April 1956
5th printing......March 1949	10th printing...November 1956
6th printing........April 1950	11th printing........April 1957

12th printing.............November 1957

Literary Guild edition published November 1941
2nd printing...........................May 1942

Garden City edition published July 1943
2nd printing..................May 1944
3rd printing...............November 1944
4th printing..................May 1945
5th printing..................May 1946

Abridgment appeared in OMNIBOOK *December 1941*

Bantam edition published September 1958
2nd printing............September 1958
3rd printing............November 1958
4th printing..................May 1959
5th printing.........February 1960
6th printing............November 1961
7th printing
8th printing

*Bantam Books are published by Bantam Books, Inc. Its trade-mark,
consisting of the words "Bantam Books" and the portrayal of a bantam, is registered in the United States Patent Office and in other
countries. Marca Registrada. Printed in the United States of America. Bantam Books, Inc., 271 Madison Ave., New York 16, N. Y.*

Contents

THE MAIN sources of this biography were Clarence Darrow's private correspondence, family documents, manuscripts, legal briefs, notebooks and unpublished memoirs, sold to me by Mrs. Darrow; the back files of court reports, congressional reports, newspapers, magazines and privately printed pamphlets; the personal contributions of more than two hundred of Darrow's lifelong friends, partners, associates, and the untiring efforts of the Darrow family, in particular Mrs. Clarence (Ruby) Darrow and Paul Darrow, to enrich and authenticate every phase of Clarence Darrow's life. No restrictions were imposed upon me by the Darrows as to what I might write or publish.

It would be ingratitude indeed if I did not acknowledge at this point that A. Kroch is the godfather of the project; that Justice Francis S. Wilson has worked indefatigably to document it; that Maurice Berkson has read every line of manuscript in an effort to keep it free from legal errors.

The entire collection of Clarence Darrow's private papers, as well as all correspondence with the author, is in the possession of Leo M. Cherne, of the Research Institute of America, 292 Madison Avenue, New York City, where it may be seen or studied by anyone who is interested.

IRVING STONE

February 27, 1941

A Lawyer Comes of Age

IT WAS only a short distance down the hall from the legal department, with the roar of the elevated trains pouring in on a level keel from the open third-story windows, and up two flights of stairs to the office of the president, but if he traveled those few steps they must prove the longest journey he had undertaken in his thirty-seven years.

He strode down the hall, his massive shoulders hunched forward, musing that he would make a mighty poor opponent for an industry that attempted to control the national Congress and the courts, to elect governors and mayors, to buy state legislators and city councilmen. True, he owned his modest home, but he had only a few hundred dollars in the bank; he was a quiet, bookish fellow who loathed discord; what business had he in this mess?

Marvin Hughitt, president of the Chicago and North Western Railway, was seated behind his desk at the far end, in front of a row of windows that gave a commanding view of the Chicago River and the passenger station on its opposite bank. Though it was a hot July day, Hughitt was dressed in a heavy dark suit, his iron-gray hair and long beard giving him the appearance of an Old Testament prophet. A man who rarely smiled, Hughitt's eyes twinkled slightly when Darrow came in, coatless, his broad black suspenders holding shapeless blue trousers, the black satin necktie wiggling down his white shirt front like a cork-screw, his big head telescoped into wide shoulders, his fine brown hair falling from a part on the left side over a high, rounded brow.

Clarence Darrow admired Marvin Hughitt because he had a sense of justice; only the year before he had risked his position and reputation by joining with Darrow in a plea to Governor Altgeld to pardon the four anarchists convicted of a conspiracy to throw the fatal Haymarket bomb. On his part, Hughitt liked Darrow's simple manner of handling and settling what other lawyers might have turned into complicated cases; if he cost the company a few extra dollars he justified the expenditures by earning good will and keeping them out of the courts. Hughitt and the other officials knew

1

Darrow to be an intellectual liberal, sympathetic to the underdog, but he made no attempt to proselytize within the company, and he did his job better than anyone else they could find.

"You look hot, Clarence. But tomorrow's the Fourth; you'll be able to cool off."

"Nobody's going to be cool in Chicago tomorrow," he said in a tight voice. "I just finished reading the injunction the Circuit Court served against the strikers this morning. It not only makes it a criminal act for a man to go out on strike, but it becomes a prison offense for one man to suggest to another that he strike."

"That injunction will save bloodshed and the destruction of property," replied Hughitt soberly.

"I thought this was supposed to be a free country? I thought men had a right to stop work when they didn't find conditions satisfactory? If their own elected government tells them it's illegal to strike, that they must work under any terms the employers see fit to grant them, then they're no better than slaves. If this is really a democracy we live under, that injunction is illegal."

Hughitt had begun as a telegrapher in the Civil War and by sheer force and conviction had become one of the railway leaders of the country. Though he was autocratic in his methods, his employees respected him for his ability to fill a tough job.

"It's perfectly legal, Clarence, under both the Interstate Commerce Act and the Sherman Anti-Trust Law. We have a technical justification too. No body of men can obstruct the United States mails."

Darrow shook his head. "Only three days ago the Chicago superintendent of mails wired Washington that no mails have accumulated here and that almost all regular trains are moving nearly on time—except those carrying Pullmans."

"But surely, Clarence," replied Hughitt, "you cannot justify a sympathy strike. Debs and his A.R.U. have no grievance against us. They went out only because they were sympathetic to the striking Pullman shop employees."

"Eugene Debs and the other American Railway Union officials are certainly not going to obey this highhanded injunction. Mr. Hughitt, I've watched your General Managers' Association control wages on the twenty-four lines operating out of Chicago; I've watched you depress wages uniformly on all the lines, so the men couldn't quit and find better jobs elsewhere; I've watched you blacklist good workmen whose only offense was that they thought labor should have better hours and wages; I've watched your agency supply

2

men to struck member lines, to break those strikes. Why do you think Debs formed the American Railway Union? To fight your conspiracy. Within a few days Debs and the boys will be in jail for contempt and conspiracy. Don't you think that in the spirit of fair play the heads of your General Managers' Association should keep them company in jail?"

There was silence in the sun-filled room.

"I'm giving up my job here, Mr. Hughitt, to defend Eugene Debs and the American Railway Union."

Hughitt regarded Darrow sternly. The traditional role of the lawyer was to serve big business against any and all comers, to accomplish its purposes by any and all means. Darrow was a freak, a renegade, but he was a good man even if a misguided sentimentalist.

"They haven't a chance, Clarence; this injunction is a Gatling gun on paper. Why give up a good position for a hopeless cause? These unions can't pay you anything; when the case is over you'll be stranded, without clients or a future, and every businessman in Chicago avoiding you as a radical. Stay with us; we can put you on top, make you governor or United States senator, get you a Cabinet post——"

"Like Attorney General Olney," commented Darrow bitingly.

"Yes, like Olney. There's fame and fortune for the asking——"

"Then I guess those are not the things I'm asking for. I believe in the right of people to better themselves, and I'm going to throw in my ten cents' worth to help them.

"When a member of the United States Cabinet like Olney, who is an old-line railroad lawyer, appoints Edwin Walker special assistant attorney general at Chicago, knowing that Walker is at the very same time the lawyer for the General Managers' Association, and Walker as a representative of the United States government persuades two Federal judges in a Chicago Circuit Court to enjoin the workers from striking, that's too much. I gotta fight."

Hughitt leaned across the desk, his hand extended.

"After we've wiped out the American Railway Union we want you to come back."

Darrow stared. "You want me to come back!"

"Well, not full time—if you don't want to. Say half time: handle our cases that don't involve labor or personal injury."

Darrow grinned, shook hands with Hughitt. Back in his office, he stuffed some papers into a brief case, and walked out on his job as counsel for the Chicago and North Western Railway.

3

Chapter One

What Goes into the Making of an American?

Amirus Darrow, Clarence's father, was the son of a New England farmer who had emigrated to the pioneer country of Ohio around 1830 in an effort to improve himself. He did not better himself materially; no Darrow was ever blessed with the special gift of making or retaining money. Amirus went to a good school in Amboy. In one of his classes he met Emily Eddy, whose parents had also emigrated from Connecticut and whose father had likewise served the Underground Railway. The couple fell in love, married very young and moved to Meadville, Pennsylvania, where Amirus, athirst for knowledge, attended Allegheny College.

Amirus soon realized that his greatest joy would always be in contemplation and that he must manage to earn his living from the spoken word and the printed page. Theology being the only apparent field in which one could subsist on the earnings of a scholar, Amirus entered the new Unitarian school in Meadville. He was the first to be graduated. With a comfortable life assured him, with innumerable hours of the day and night available for his reading and thinking, Amirus abandoned theology because his studies led him to doubt. "The end of wisdom is the fear of God; the beginning of wisdom is doubt." He was equipped neither by training nor temperament to do anything else; already knowing the privations of poverty, the young couple walked fearlessly into a dark uncharted world rather than be dishonest to their convictions and beliefs.

They returned to Farmdale, just two miles from Kinsman, where they found themselves always the opposition and always the minority: the lone free-thinkers against rock-ribbed religionists, the lone Democrats against Ohio's solid Republicans, the lone free traders against the high-tariff tradition, the lone intellectuals in a tiny valley of farmers. Amirus Darrow enjoyed this role of the opposition, not only because it kept his mind alert, but because it enabled him to be a teacher, to bring ideas from the world beyond the mountains, to plead for open-mindedness, variety in thought, tolerance, the love of the naked truth.

"In all the country round," said Clarence, "no man knew so much of books as he, and no man knew less of life. The

5

old parson and the doctor were the only neighbors who seemed able to understand the language he spoke. . . ."

To her everlasting glory, Emily Darrow, who had to bear eight children and raise seven of them, cook for them, wash their dishes, scrub their clothes and necks and feet, nurse them when they were ill and train them when they were well, who had to make each dollar fulfill the obligations of two, never reproached her husband for his impracticality or tried to change his nature or way of life.

Clarence Seward Darrow was born on April 18, 1857, in a white frame cottage in Farmdale. In 1864, when he was seven, his family managed to buy a house just a half mile from the town square of Kinsman.

Kinsman was a valley town planted alongside a small river on whose banks the original settlers built white frame houses and planted corn, potatoes, hay. The settlers remained within the citadel formed by the two flanking ranges. Neither their legs nor their thoughts roamed past the protecting wall of hills, for life was primitively ample in Kinsman. The settlers were content, and their children remained after them, content. All except the Darrows, whose father "looked to the high hills to the east and to the high hills to the west and up and down the narrow country road that led to the outside world. . . ."

There is an old saying that "every pot finds its cover." The nonconformist Darrows, who served as the town agnostics and intellectuals, stumbled onto the one eccentric and nonconformist house in the countryside, an octagonal-shaped structure with a wide wooden pavilion running around seven of its eight sides.

At the long-anticipated age of six he was entered in the one-room district school. In Clarence's McGuffey readers every manifestation of virtue earned its immediate and grandiose reward, but not one story told that any profit "might come from willfulness or selfishness or greed." By observing the savage conduct of their playmates and the business ethics of their elders, the children rejected their teachers and books. In most of their minds was destroyed the faith in the printed word, the truth to be found in books, the value of an education.

After passing six years in the district school his first pair of long trousers was given to him, and he was sent up the hill to the public academy. His estimate of his high-school years is best delineated by the consternation he caused when he was invited to address the 1918 graduating class of the Nicholas Senn High School in Chicago.

"Our glassy-eyed, pompous principal had us five hundred

graduates thoroughly numbed and awed by the recital of our great responsibilities. Darrow patiently sat it out, playing with a watch chain and looking up at the ceiling as he sprawled in his dinky folding chair. Finally he was lavishly introduced with the usual long hot-air harangue of noble phraseology. Darrow ambled over to the big rostrum and leaned against it comfortably in that stooping way he had. He looked like a big easygoing janitor in the wrong place with all those ramrod stuffed shirts around. He looked us over, turning his head in dead silence, and finally he began to chuckle.

" 'Look—let's you fellows down there relax now. That was as fine a lot of bunk as I ever heard in my life, and I know darned well you youngsters didn't believe a word of it. You're no more fit to "go forth and serve" than the man in the moon. You're just a bunch of ignorant kids full of the devil, and you've learned practically nothing to show for the four years you spent here. You can't fool me, because I once spent four years in just such a place!'

"The parents were shocked; the faculty purple with rage, but we were ecstatic. It was the only good sense we had heard in months."

From his father Clarence learned that tolerance is something more than an opportunistic demand made on other people to persuade them to endure one's views. As an agnostic, Amirus would have no part of the church on the hill, yet every Sunday morning the seven young Darrows were scrubbed with soap and brushes in iron tubs heated on a wood-burning stove, dressed in their best clothes and shoes and led up the hill to services—by Mother—while Father retired to the sanctity of his study. Amirus contended that merely because he was unreligious was no justification for forcing his opinions on his defenseless children. After they had participated in the ritual of the church and been grounded in the history of world religions at home, they would be free to form their own preferences to fit their particular natures. The contest was doubtless not an even one, for the church strove to stifle any joyful religious impulses of the young.

"The Sabbath, the Church and religion were serious and solemn matters to the band of pilgrims who every Sunday drove up the hill," wrote Clarence. ". . . I could not understand then, nor do I today, why we were made to go to church; surely our good parents did not know how we suffered, or they would not have been so cruel or unkind. I could not have sat through the interminable prayers but for the fact that I learned to find landmarks as the minister, his white face circled with a fringe of white whiskers, went along. At a certain point I knew it was well under way;

7

at another point it was about half done, and when he began asking for guidance for the President of the United States it was three quarters over, and I felt like a shipwrecked mariner sighting land."

When Clarence was fourteen his mother died. Emily Eddy Darrow was only forty-four, but she had already done the work of two lifetimes. Not until he reached his full maturity did her son Clarence understand how kind and strong and good his mother had been; how overworked and harassed and unappreciated.

At sixteen, lanky and gangling, he was sent off to Allegheny College to follow in the footsteps of his father, even though his father's education, to all external appearances, had seemed to do him more harm than good. Young Darrow had not the faintest notion what he wanted to do. Yet his father and his older brother Everett and older sister Mary, who had already graduated from college and were teaching, believed passionately that if only Clarence would subject himself to education all obstacles would be removed, an open, shining road would be revealed. Nor was this mouthy talk with the three older Darrows: they scrimped and saved and denied themselves the ordinary comforts that they might garner the few dollars to send Clarence to college. Here he majored in baseball, added to his dislike of Latin and Greek, stonily refused his father's plea to study Hebrew, "got by" in geometry and scratched his first spark of interest in the natural sciences.

At the end of his freshman year he returned to Kinsman torn between apathy and disgust with higher education. If not. for the panic of 1873, Darrow might have completed his studies at Allegheny.

Charles A. Beard relates, "Once a bright reporter asked Darrow to what he owed his success. Gently protesting against the use of the word 'success' in connection with his life, Darrow replied: 'To hard work.' When the reporter looked pained at this chamber-of-commerce reply, Darrow explained, 'When I was a boy my father set me to work on a hot summer day, hoeing potatoes, and after I had worked hard for a few hours I ran away from that hard work, went into the practice of law and have not done any work since. . . .'"

At the beginning of the fall, to his astonishment, Clarence was offered the job of teacher in the district school at Vernon, three miles from Kinsman. Opposition to his appointment arose on the ground that he had been subjected to unfortunate influences which he might communicate to the children; but by now a number of years had passed, and because of their exemplary life folks thereabouts had come to the charitable conclusion that the Darrows were almost as good Christians as they would have been if they had attended church. Besides, the wage was so low that no full-grown man would take the job.

Those fears proved well founded: he promptly set out to revolutionize district-school teaching. Having been slapped by his teacher the first day he had entered school, he abolished corporal punishment. The McGuffey readers were thrown out, as was the system of teaching in terms of moral precepts; he taught from books borrowed from his father's study. Resolving to make his pupils happy instead of wise, he utilized the teaching tools of humor and sympathy, lengthened the noon hour and recesses, joined in their sports, coached their baseball team, tried to make them understand that as their teacher he was a friend and not an enemy. For his efforts he was paid thirty dollars a month, most of which he turned over to the family, and was received as a guest in the home of a different pupil each school night.

The Darrows were always anti, and in Saturday night debates Clarence liked the tart sensation of getting to his feet, after his opponent had received an ovation which shook the kerosene lamps, and facing four or five hundred people whose expressions were compounded of aversion, incredulity, disbelief. There was no exhilaration equal to that of standing alone against the field, beaten before he started, fighting for a hopeless cause. These good people liked young Clarence, but while he was on the platform fighting against the things they believed in, he became the enemy, the infidel, the apostate, the turncoat. Though he never succeeded in winning a debate, occasionally he had the pleasure of puncturing one of their ideological bubbles with a pinprick of satire or good sense.

After the debate had been settled, the benches were cleared away, and the square dances and reels began.

Clarence was fond of dancing, but most of all he liked to dance with Jessie Ohl, who was the best dancer in the crowd, an expert at calling the reels. Jessie had a trim figure, amply curved for a sixteen-year-old girl, and an honest, forthright face with the glowing skin of youth. They made a pleasant couple.

After a year of teaching the eighteen-year-old boy found his interest turning more and more to the lawbooks in his father's study.

He was drifting, not knowing that he wanted to become a lawyer. The only thing he knew for sure was that he wanted to earn his living by the spoken word, the formulated idea, the expressed thought. Since the Church was out of the question, there remained only two fields: teaching and the law. He saw by now that he enjoyed conflict, the clash of mind against

9

mind in the fight for what each conceived to be the right and the truth, and often he was fired by thinking of the cases in which he would battle to help justice triumph. But of what the practice of law actually involved he knew little.

"The law is a bum profession, as generally practiced," he was to write many years later to a young man who contemplated entering law school. "It is utterly devoid of idealism and almost poverty stricken as to any real ideas."

When Clarence was twenty and had been teaching for three years, it was obvious that he could not continue at the district school at thirty dollars a month. He had all the prerequisites of a lawyer: he liked books; he had a natural fluency of speech, was able to think clearly and to the point; he had a personality which inspired confidence. Everett, teaching in Chicago, and Mary, teaching in Champaign, insisted that he go to the law college at Ann Arbor, Michigan; they would send him enough money for his keep.

Once again he spent an undistinguished year in college. He was not impressed by his teachers, their method of instruction or the books in the library to which he was assigned to brief cases. He liked to teach himself, to work alone, to ferret, accept, reject, come to his own conclusions.

He did not return to Ann Arbor. Instead he found a job in a law office in Youngstown, twenty miles from his home, where he did odd jobs around the office, and read the lawbooks. A few weeks after his twenty-first birthday he presented himself to "a committee of lawyers who were chosen to examine applicants. They were all good fellows and wanted to help us through." He passed the simple test and was embarked upon a legal career, which was to cover six decades and implicate him in nearly every conflict at the core of expanding American life.

In the meanwhile his friendship with Jessie Ohl had deepened. He had liked her since he was seventeen and had apparently been attracted by no other girl—though in the innocence of his youth and the innocence of the age he seems to have done no experimenting to test his emotion. They were well suited to each other; they were both kindly, easygoing, forthright and simple in their tastes. There could be little doubt but that Jessie would make a good wife.

He asked Jessie to marry him, and Jessie agreed most heartily. It was a better match for Clarence than it was for Jessie; the Ohl family was solidly entrenched, while he was penniless. And there was always the danger that he would be too much his father's son, spending his life in genteel poverty, his nose in a musty book.

They were married in the home of Jessie's brother in

Sharon, Pennsylvania, and went directly to Andover, Ohio, a sleepy but prosperous farming center of about four hundred people, ten miles from Kinsman. Here they rented a flat above a shoestore, with a bedroom, parlor and bath. The bedroom faced the long flight of stairs and was turned into an office, Jessie spending part of her wedding money to buy lawbooks with which to impress the potential clients. The first couple of months the young lawyer took in less than the thirty-dollar wage he had earned as a school-teacher.

After a year of practice he found that he was taking in fifty and sixty dollars a month, which even enabled Jessie to save a few pennies. The climax was reached on the night he dashed into the kitchen, slapped his knee excitedly and exclaimed to his wife:

"I made twenty dollars today!"

The Darrows spent a pleasant three years in Andover. The young couple loved each other; they got along well, and Jessie never interfered in Clarence's way of life. On December 10, 1883, a son was born to them, named Paul; this event stirred Clarence sufficiently to get him to move to Ashtabula, a town of five thousand people.

He was no stranger, he had journeyed here several times to try cases for Andover folk and had come off pretty well. He had a fund of what the farmers called horse sense; he grasped situations quickly, thought through them logically in terms of right and justice, talked the simplest English, never attempting to hide his ignorance behind a barrage of legal phraseology. Once believing his client to be right, he fought with an emotional intensity that transcended the small fees or properties involved.

It was Darrow's technique in a lawsuit to unhorse his adversaries rather than to shout them down. When the opposing attorney tore off reams of bombast he made the rhetoric sound silly by stating quietly and simply the point at issue; when they wandered far afield he poked gentle fun at their meanderings; when they took shelter in abstruse technicalities he appealed to the common sense of the judge and jurors. All his life he remained a country boy at heart; his understanding of the farmer's psychology served him well.

He remained in Ashtabula for four years. He made a comfortable living, was well liked and was on his way to becoming one of the leading lawyers of the county. Evenings he played poker with his cronies, the game he loved best next to baseball; over a few bottles of beer or highballs the men would tell tall tales, play for low stakes and high excitement. For the first time Darrow had fun.

He had already passed thirty before the role of country lawyer played itself out. Having saved five hundred dollars,

11

he and Jessie decided to buy a home. They found a suitable one for sale for thirty-five hundred dollars. Darrow drew up a deed with the owner which provided for the payment of five hundred in cash and the balance in monthly payments. The next day the owner turned up without his wife's signature on the deed, the implication being that she did not think young Darrow could meet the monthly payments.

"All right," fumed Darrow, "I don't want your house because—because—I'm moving away from here."

The following afternoon he met a woman of whom he was not specially fond. "And how is our prominent lawyer today?" She asked.

"Oh, fine, fine," replied Darrow. "I just got a big case."

"How nice. Here in Ashtabula?"

"No-o-o-o," stuttered Darrow, "in—in Chicago."

"That's just lovely. When are you going to try it?"

"Why—as a matter of fact—tomorrow."

"The next day I had to go to Chicago, because if the woman saw me on the streets of Ashtabula she would have told the whole town I was a liar—which I was."

Having nothing better to do, he went to see his brother Everett who had been working on his younger brother to move to Chicago.

His nature drew him back to the books. A banker of Ashtabula introduced him to Henry George's *Progress and Poverty*, which excited both his imagination and his critical faculties, starting him on the jagged, boundless road toward economic justice. A police judge by the name of Richards gave him a copy of *Our Penal Machinery and Its Victims*, by John P. Altgeld, which turned his mind to thinking about crime and prisons. He consumed the works of Walt Whitman, who was anathema in Ashtabula, as were the European novelists with whom he felt a kinship of spirit: Flaubert, Turgenev, Zola. He wanted to discuss free trade and free thought, socialism, paganism; he wanted to hear theories built up or torn apart by educated minds. He wanted to meet people who knew the outside world, who could lead him to new books and philosophies, who argued from logic rather than prejudice.

He was slowly, awkwardly, painfully, coming of age. If he had been content in Ashtabula he would have found another house to buy with his five hundred dollars down.

Darrow went into Chicago hungry for intellectual and literary companionship; he wanted to see a great city in action, but what he wanted for himself he did not know. He hoped to do a good job and an important job but his ambition did not include the making of large sums of money. He simply wanted to find his place in the world, do his share of its work, think his share of its thoughts, feel his share of its feelings, know his share of its knowledge.

He installed his family in a modest apartment on the south side near his brother Everett, was admitted to practice in the state of Illinois, then rented desk space in a law office. Coming from a small town, dressing like a country lawyer, talking in a lazy drawl, almost naïve in the open simplicity and sweetness of his manner, he made no impression on the train-shunting, skyscraper-building, hog-killing, steel-blasting city. He knew no one, months passed; the savings dwindled.

He started on a new tack: since clients could not find their way to him, he would find his way to the clients. His first step was to join the Henry George Single Tax Club. After he had attended a few of the weekly meetings, he ventured to speak. His personality was warm and lovable, his voice low, musical, rich in tonal contrasts, and he did not rise to his feet until he had formulated precisely what he had to say. His combination of logic and good-natured humor helped the group accept his arguments even when he disagreed with certain of their theories. After the meeting he joined in the informal discussion; and at midnight the group adjourned to Mme. Gali's Italian restaurant for a steak and a bottle of beer, for pipefuls of tobacco and spirited, intelligent talk.

He also joined the Sunset Club, whose hundred members formed the rallying point of the literary renaissance in Chicago. Here he was even more at home than at the Henry George Club, where he could not help but be critical of their economic panaceas. In the Sunset he could read aloud from Omar Khayyam, hear lectures by visiting authors, discuss Tolstoy, debate the literary values of the realism of *L'Assommoir*, *Germinal*, *Crime and Punishment*.

He had been in Chicago only a few months when he was asked by the Democratic committeemen he had met at the Henry George Club to campaign in the 1888 election. He accepted, hopeful that someone in the hall would be impressed and bring him a case the next day. But he always found himself just one of an interminable string of ambitious young lawyers striving to make an impression. Living off Everett's savings, able to find only an occasional real-estate abstract to examine, he became increasingly discouraged and sorry he had left his practice in Ashtabula.

Then suddenly, but naturally, his opportunity came.

The Henry George Club staged a Free Trade Convention in Chicago which attracted speakers from all over the country, including Henry George himself. Because Darrow had been a faithful worker for the club and was one of its best speakers, he was put on the program of the closing session in the Central Music Hall. He worked for days on his paper, sound in its economics, constructively critical of the single tax in its weaker links and written with a lyrical lucidity. He committed it to memory and set out for the meeting.

Henry George was scheduled to speak first. His long, strongly idealistic talk was so good it not only gripped and thrilled the assemblage but also left them completely satisfied. When the applause died down the audience rose and began to leave the hall. Darrow begged the chairman to introduce him quickly; his few friends clapped as loudly as they could when he came forward. The departing throng turned its head momentarily in the aisles to see what was going on. Darrow struck out boldly, thinking hard and fast and clear as he adapted his speech to supplement what Henry George had said, stimulated, as always, by the presence of an audience. People began slipping back into their seats; soon the aisles were clear, and for the first time in his life Darrow felt that he had his listeners entrapped in his words, that he could move them as he willed.

When he had finished he received an ovation. Henry George wrung his hand and assured him that he had a brilliant future. Newspaper reporters crowded about. Friends pounded him on the back; strangers came up to shake his hand.

The next morning his name and opinions were on the front pages of the Chicago newspapers. But no new business arrived on the flood of publicity. However, new friends came into the office to urge him to speak in favor of DeWitt Cregier for mayor. Having learned something of political tactics, Darrow picked his own hall, the best in town, and spoke alone. Reporters quoted him with moderate accuracy in the morning papers.

Though his first year of practice had brought him only three hundred dollars in cash, the prospects for the next year looked good. He rented a house, the upper floor of which Jessie sublet, thus earning back the better part of their rent.

During his first year in Chicago the most important thing to happen to him had been his meeting with another lawyer, John Peter Altgeld, author of the book *Our Penal Machinery and Its Victims*, which the police judge had handed him in Ashtabula. John P. Altgeld had had ten thousand copies printed at his own expense and sent out inscribed to every legislator, judge, warden, minister, educator, writer, lecturer, social-service worker and club president on a mailing list. He

14

had attempted to show in his book that poverty, slums and the lack of opportunity which resulted from the unequal distribution of wealth lie at the base of the major portion of crime; that the brutal treatment afforded to the merely accused, and later to the imprisoned, was a second crime committed by society against the individual whose obsolescent surroundings had been one of the contributing causes of his original criminality.

One of Darrow's first acts in Chicago was to go to Altgeld with a copy of the book under his arm and tell him what a courageous and penetrating work it was. Altgeld had been so delighted to find his book reaching young lawyers, he had forgotten his restraint in meeting people, and had welcomed Clarence with warm affection.

A deep friendship developed: both had come from small farming communities; both were plain, down to earth, detesting pretension, hypocrisy and deceit. Both were gentle-souled, desirous of avoiding discord, yet so intensely stirred by injustice and human suffering, they were willing to endure strife, contumely and ostracism to fight against them.

Altgeld was the profoundest influence in Darrow's life. He buttressed in him his love of study, of acquiring all the facts no matter how distasteful they might appear, of clinging to the truth even in the face of such tempests as were nearly to destroy both men. In return Darrow was able to bring to the childless Altgeld some of the good things brought by a son: love, an eagerness to learn, an hour spent in the warmth of confidence.

During his second year in Chicago Darrow managed to clear expenses by carrying on the general run of minor law business. His evenings he spent at the various clubs and homes of members, debating socialism, discussing modern poetry, formulating plans to help young labor unions to earn recognition. He wrote articles for the liberal and labor press. But mostly he liked to lecture on literary subjects.

Darrow made a profound impression on his audiences because his magnetism leaped out and engulfed people, made them feel warm inside, made them feel good, made them feel happy, made them feel soft and friendly, sympathetic and generous and clearminded, brought out the best in them. He became one of the leaders of the cultural life in Chicago because he was so gentle and genuine and honest, because his love for books and thinking shone through everything he said, because he had the gift of the bold, striking phrase, the delicious chuckle, because he could dramatize literature and knowledge, bring them to life with tenderness and a wallop. He had passed the point of hoping to find business through this kind of activity; it was self-expression for him and gratified the inherent Darrow love of teaching, of communicating to others the joys he had found.

He had been in Chicago two years when he received a note from Mayor Cregier, asking him to call. He promptly ran to the mayor's office, where he was astounded to be offered the position of special-assessment attorney for the city.

"But, Mr. Mayor, how do you happen to ask me to be special-assessment attorney when you never met me before?"

"I heard you make that speech that night with Henry George."

Since the salary was three thousand dollars a year, Darrow accepted the offer and was on the pay roll before he stumbled down the steps of the city hall. He trotted all the way to Altgeld's office.

"But I haven't sufficient experience in big-town law."

"I'll see that you get the proper instruction," replied Altgeld with his quiet smile. Darrow did not know it was his friend's recommendation to the mayor that had helped secure his appointment.

He was given an office in the city hall, with a big desk, a library, a secretary and a law clerk, and without preliminaries was plunged into work. His duties were to pass on matters of assessments, taxes, condemnations, licenses; to advise city officials who wanted legal justification before they went ahead. Because the city officials wanted opinions right away, right now, without waiting for him to look up the law, Darrow found himself swimming in the middle of a wide, wide ocean. With Altgeld's help he evolved a *modus operandi* which was to serve him all his professional life: he thought through a problem on the basis of its facts, then came to the conclusions which he thought to be right, logical and just. If upon looking up the matter in the casebooks he found precedent against him, he did not abandon his stand.

"This is the sensible and honest way for such a matter to be decided," he would exclaim. "Somewhere, in some lawbook, there must be a precedent to sustain me." And nearly always he found a decision that upheld him.

Three months after Darrow had been serving the assistant corporation counsel resigned. The politicians liked Darrow—a sentiment he did not always return—so he was promoted to the office of assistant corporation counsel, at five thousand dollars a year. His job was to represent the city in court in all contested cases. Here he acquired his first experience in court procedure, the relation of the law and the client to the judge and jury. In addition he was in constant conference with the mayor and aldermen and came to know all the judges.

The thirty-three-year-old Darrow had held office only ten months when he was promoted to be corporation counsel of the most tumultuous city in America. One of his assistants writes that in the preparations for the Columbian Exposition "to open in 1893 . . . the railroads opposed the city's efforts to open streets across their rights of way to offer greater access to the Exposition grounds, and efforts were made to block condemnation proceedings and to enjoin the opening of streets. The railroad employed many of the leading lawyers of the Chicago Bar, but Darrow won the litigation and the streets were opened."

After four years of working for the city the offer had come from the Chicago and North Western Railway, inspired in part by the trouncing he had given their "leading attorneys of the Chicago Bar" in the right-of-way litigations. On the advice of Altgeld, against his own inclinations, he had accepted. He repaid his debt to Everett, bought a comfortable home for himself and Jessie on the north side, had continued to read and lecture and debate, making friends with socialists, labor leaders, anarchists, skeptics, freethinkers of all breeds. He remained ambidextrous, serving the railroad with his right hand and the liberals with his left. Life was interesting. He had no conception of what the future held for him.

Then the workers of the Pullman Palace Car Company had struck; the American Railway Union had gone out in sympathy, and an injunction had been issued, for defiance of which Eugene Debs would be thrown into jail.

Chapter Two

A Liberal Gets a Liberal Education

THE NEXT morning, July Fourth, he rose at six-thirty, had breakfast with his wife and son Paul and rode downtown. He checked the satchel he was taking with him to Springfield, where he had been invited to take supper *en famille* with John Peter Altgeld, who had been elected governor of Illinois two years before; this done, he walked toward Lake Michigan, then strolled a couple of blocks south on Michigan Avenue with the sun on his face.

Suddenly his attention was caught by the sound of tramping feet. In the distance, coming north on the boulevard, soldiers marched four abreast, the guns on their shoulders glistening. As they came closer he saw they were Federal troops, Companies A and C from Fort Sheridan. Then as he heard the commanding officer bark, "Column right," and watched them wheel onto the bare lake-front next to Convention Hall, where Abraham Lincoln had been nominated for President only thirty-four years before, break ranks and pitch their tents, he realized they had not been ordered into Chicago for anything so innocent as a Fourth of July parade. They had been sent here by the secretary of war to carry out the injunction against the strikers; they were the enforcing half of what Marvin Hughitt had so neatly termed "a Gatling gun on paper."

Just the day before, Eugene Debs, president of the American Railway Union, had confided to him, "I do not believe in socialism, but I am forced to the conclusion that government ownership of railroads is decidedly better for the people than railroad ownership of government."

He had looked up the law; he knew that the order to send troops into Chicago violated one of the Constitutional guarantees of states' rights. No units of the Federal army could be sent into a state until the state governor had officially asked for them. Governor Altgeld had not asked for military aid; Mayor Hopkins of Chicago had made no request of Governor Altgeld for troops. There had been no trouble in Chicago, no hostile gatherings, no violence, no attacks on property, for the American Railway Union had pledged itself to keep the strike peaceful, to protect the Pullman shops and railroad property. From the day they had gone on strike, three hundred strikers had guarded the Pullman shops so constantly that the Pullman executives themselves had never asked for police protection. The Chicago police had patrolled the many miles of railroad track without clashes or disturbances; Superintendent of Police Brennan had reported only the night before that everything remained peaceable.

Clarence crossed Michigan Avenue and watched the soldiers make camp, ruminating on the irony of Federal troops being sent to break a people's strike on Independence Day! It was a bare hundred and eighteen years since the colonial farmers and merchants, craftsmen and mechanics, laborers and clerks, had rid themselves of the economic and political yoke of the English monarchy at the cost of misery, starvation and sudden death, to free themselves from an economic despotism that controlled their lives without giving them a voice or a hearing.

Now the descendents of these patriots were ruled at home, where they could be ruled more efficiently and comprehensively. Where the General Managers' Association, an illegal organization, could unlegally use its influence on the attorney general of the United States to extralegally appoint the General Managers' Association's attorney as assistant attorney general in Chicago and then illegally order him to demand an injunction be issued. Two Chicago Federal Circuit Court judges, Grosscup and Woods, would then meet with the newly appointed Assistant Attorney General Walker and assist him in drawing up an airtight injunction—with no representative of labor allowed to be present to defend the interests of the workers. To complete the cycle the United States Army would then illegally be ordered into Chicago to smash the strike.

Riding out to gather data in the town of Pullman, where all the trouble had begun, Darrow took from his pocket a pamphlet he had picked off his desk that morning. It was called *The Story of Pullman* and had been distributed by the Pullman Company to visitors to the World's Fair. He read, "Imagine a perfectly equipped town of twelve thousand inhabitants. . . . that is bordered by bright beds of flowers and green velvety stretches of lawn; that is shaded with trees and dotted with parks and pretty water vistas and glimpses of artistic sweeps of landscape gardening; a town where the homes, even to the most modest, are bright and wholesome and filled with pure air and light; a town, in a word, where all that is ugly and discordant and demoralizing is eliminated and all that inspires to self-respect, to thrift and to cleanliness of person and of thought is generously provided."

Presently Darrow was walking down the main street with its bright red flower beds in the center and rows of tall green trees lining the walks, the houses of neat red brick with trim lawns in front. Why should any workman privileged to live in this utopia want to strike against such a benevolent employer?

To answer his own question he dropped into the library that Pullman had erected for his workers. There the annual dues to borrow the books Mr Pullman had selected for his employees to read were so high that only two hundred and fifty families out of the five thousand families living in the town availed themselves of its privileges. Yet the deserted library was well peopled compared with the padlocked parsonage alongside of the imposing church edifice, where Darrow stopped next; the parsonage had never known human occupation because the sixty-five-dollar rent Mr Pullman asked for the cottage made it unobtainable for any of the Protestant clergymen who had been called to preach in the church.

Knocking at random at the doors of several of the red brick houses, Darrow introduced himself as the attorney for the American Railway Union. Some of the men were at the shops on guard duty; others talked to him freely, their wives and children behind them. It took only a tour of inspection to convince him that the town of Pullman was a false front, designed to impress the casual visitor: the houses were of the cheapest construction, the rooms small and dark and airless, the equipment of the most rudimentary type. Each house had only one faucet, generally in the basement, where it cost the least to bring in pipes. Despite Pullman's boast that in his town "everything that inspires to cleanliness of person is generously provided," not one house had a bathtub.

For these dwellings the Pullman employees paid twenty-five per cent more rent than had to be paid for similar housing in neighboring communities, but no man could have a job in the Pullman shops unless he rented a Pullman house. The rent was deducted from his check by the Pullman bank before he was handed his wage. If any repairs had to be made to the house before the worker moved in, the Pullman Company advanced the money to repair it, and the total sum was taken out of the worker's wages. In the lease which the worker had to sign before he could get his job there were provisions that he must pay for all repairs but that he could be evicted upon two weeks' notice. Every family Darrow visited told him they had to take in roomers.

Darrow walked into the back part of town where visitors were never taken. Here he found lawless tenements with four and five families crowded into each railroad flat, all the families using one toilet. Again the rent of seventeen dollars and a half paid by each family was from twenty-five to thirty-three per cent higher than similar accommodations in neighboring districts, where they could have had privacy, sunlight, a lawn, flowers and a back yard for their children. Behind the tenements he found wooden shanties that had cost only one hundred dollars to erect, occupied by marginal families who had eight dollars a month taken out of their wages, a return of from forty to fifty per cent to the Pullman Company on its investment.

Going from family to family, most of whom he found to be second-generation Americans, Darrow became profoundly dejected at life in Pullman, where "all that is ugly and discordant and demoralizing is eliminated and all that inspires to self-respect is generously provided." The inhabitants were constantly spied upon, everything they said being reported back to the company. When the men went out of town their every move was watched; with the first attempt of a man to join a union he was fired, his family turned out of their home, his name entered on a black list and sent to every railroad in the country. Any attempt to discuss, protest or better any condition brought immediate dismissal. The company gave free medical care to men injured in the shops, but only in return for a liability release signed by the injured workman;

if he brought suit the company doctor testified against him. All savings had to be deposited in the Pullman bank; no saloons or resorts were allowed so that the men might enjoy an hour of fun or escape. The workmen complained that even in the sanctity of their own homes they couldn't go to the toilet without Mr Pullman knowing about it.

George Pullman, proclaiming to the world that he had built a "perfectly equipped town, built out from one central thought to a beautiful and harmonious whole," had created for himself a feudal village where he could be the lord and his workmen the serfs; where he could take back in rent the better part of the wages he paid them. The families lived under a reign of terror, afraid to trust neighbors or friends, afraid to think or talk or show their feelings except behind shuttered windows and locked doors.

But all this had not caused the strike of May 11, 1894, now almost two months old. A depression following the panic of 1893 had seized the country, and Pullman had found it difficult to secure contracts for his shops to build new passenger or freight cars. In order to keep his plant working, he had accepted, at an estimated loss of fifty thousand dollars, building contracts to cover the first few months in 1894.

He had then cut wages. When he saw that these cuts were not going to be sufficient to absorb the fifty-thousand-dollar loss that the thirty-six-million-dollar Pullman Company would sustain, he changed the wage scale from a day wage to a piece wage, at the same time cutting the piece rates to speed up production. By February expert veteran workmen who had been earning $3.20 a day, were down to $2.60 a day, then $2.20 a day, then $1.80 and $1.20 a day, and were forced to turn out more work by the piece scale to earn their $1.20 than they had had to turn out to earn their $3.20. By March skilled mechanics were drawing for two weeks' work, after their rent had been deducted, sums ranging from eight cents to one dollar, on which they had to feed families of four and five and six for the following two weeks. After their meager savings were gone able-bodied but starved men had to stop work every hour and sit down to gain strength to carry on. Conscientious workmen fainted at their machines and were carried out by their fellows. In homes the mothers searched their empty larders frantic to keep their children from developing rickets.

Yet George Pullman refused to lower rents. "The Pullman Land Company has to earn its three-and-a-half per cent," he said. "The Pullman Land Company has no connection with the Pullman Palace Car Company, so I can do nothing about rents." When it was pointed out that Mr Pullman also owned the Land Company, that his rents had always been twenty-five per cent above prosperity prices, that now rents in surrounding towns had been reduced twenty and thirty per cent, Pullman replied by so distributing work that every inhabitant of a Pullman house could earn just enough to cover his company rent debt: a pattern for starvation so ingenious that only the mechanical brain of George Pullman could have invented it.

There is a starvation level below which not even the most abject laborer will permit his family to sink, for it will do him no good: they will be destroyed in either event. The Pullman employees organized; they sent word to the company to ask if a delegation would be received to present their grievances and if the company would promise not to discharge their delegates. The company promised. Forty-three delegates were elected. They told their story to Mr Wickes, the vice-president, after which George Pullman stormed into the room and informed the men that he had nothing to discuss with them. The following morning all forty-three of the delegates were discharged, their families given dispossess notices.

That was when the workers struck. They asked Mr Pullman to arbitrate. Pullman declared that he had nothing to arbitrate. "The workers have nothing to do with the amount of wages they shall receive; that is solely the business of the company." Mayor Hopkins of Chicago announced his sympathies with the strikers; Jane Addams of Hull House urged Pullman to meet his workers; the mayors of fifty-six American cities telegraphed Pullman, urging him to arbitrate. Pullman folded his arms and stood like a colossus above his shops, his village and his workers, a medieval king who ruled by divine right, whose will was sacrosanct.

It was, thought Darrow, walking to the train with the background material he needed for the preparation of this case, an almost unparalleled instance of brutal greed and callousness. If Pullman had been as farsighted and resourceful in building his town as he had been in building his revolutionary sleeping car he would have been revered as the designer, not merely of a railroad car and a railroad system, but of a humane civilization.

In his train seat Darrow speculated on why it was that America was bringing forth the greatest mechanical geniuses in history. Why was it that they were rarely interested in the welfare of humanity? Did interest in the machine preclude interest in people? Why had America developed so few men whose rich, resourceful and inventive minds conceived of the machine as the liberator of all men, rather than the producer of wealth for the initiate?

He picked up his valise and walked quickly to the Chicago and Alton station, where he bought half a dozen Chicago and Eastern newspapers before boarding the train. In several of them were pictures of George Pullman, his hands stretched out in front of his chest in clerical gesture, all five finger tips touching; under the photographs were encomiums of the patriot and benefactor who was being attacked and undermined by the striking "anarchists." Within the same pages were cartoons of Governor Altgeld, standing on the supine bodies of President Cleveland and the Democratic donkey, an incendiary torch in one hand, the flag of anarchy in the other: Altgeld, the "fomenter of lawlessness, the apologist for murder, the encourager of anarchy, rapine and the overthrow of civilization, the lunatic . . . who has not one drop of true American blood in his veins."

John Peter Altgeld, one of the least attractive-looking men in public life ("If I had to depend on my looks I'd have been hung long ago!"), with a harelip, an impediment of speech, coarse hair that grew forward on his skull like a mat, with heavy features and a thick torso on stubby legs; the man who had risen from the most abject poverty, from the enslavement of a brutish peasant father, who had been badly fed, badly clothed, worked into exhaustion as a child, who was without formal education, who had been despised and ridiculed and had endured the humiliations and sufferings of the underdog, had become the first Democratic governor of the state of Illinois.

He had been elected by the working people of Illinois because he had worked for their rights and protection in the form of industrial legislation. Altgeld believed in capitalism, but the kind which would bring to actuality the promise of industrial democracy implicit in the line of the Declaration of Independence which says that "every man is entitled to life, liberty and the pursuit of happiness." Pullman, in refusing to recognize or deal with a union, said, "We deal with our men individually as a corporation, and we expect them to deal with us individually as workmen." Altgeld felt that if it had been true politically for the thirteen colonies that "In Union there is strength" then it was also true economically for the tens of millions of workers that the more their union brought them strength, the more would it enstrengthen the nation.

At dusk the train reached Springfield, and Darrow walked to the governor's mansion. Mrs Altgeld, a lovely and sedate woman, led him upstairs to the governor. From the open door of the library he observed the older man writing hurriedly at his desk. Altgeld looked up, then rose and gripped his visitor's hand.

"Well, Clarence, I hear you resigned from your job to defend Debs. Son, there's little but grief in this martyr business."

Darrow answered, "You know, Governor, most men do things through a desire to escape pain. Did you ever stop and watch a blind man begging on a street corner? A man passes by hurriedly and suddenly stops still. He goes back and drops a coin in the blind man's cup. The sight of the helpless man standing forlornly at a corner hurts him, makes him feel a sense of social responsibility, and so he buys ten cents' worth of relief from social pain. It hurts me too much to see Debs and men like him faced with the possibility of spending years in prison, so I am buying relief too."

Altgeld smiled, put his hand on Darrow's shoulder, then returned wearily to his desk.

"I'm just drawing up my protest to President Cleveland for sending Federal troops to Chicago. Right this very moment I have stationed in Chicago three regiments of infantry, one battery and one troop of cavalry, but neither Mayor Hopkins, the police, nor the county sheriff felt there was any need for them. Then how can the United States Army move in?"

"Railroad politics: the railroads make it appear that you refuse to protect private property, then have Attorney General Olney misrepresent to President Cleveland and send in Federal troops. That gets you out of the way, and they have complete control."

"There's more to it than that, son. By peacefully refusing to move trains carrying Pullmans, the strikers are on their way to victory; their demands are just, and the public is with them. The only thing that can defeat the strike now is violence. The railroads know that by bringing Federal troops in here they can outrage the workers and start them fighting. The newspapers will blame any disorder on the workers, and the people of the country will turn against them."

Altgeld asked, "Would you like to hear the protest I am sending to President Cleveland? . . . 'Waiving all questions of courtesy, I will say that the state of Illinois is able to take care of itself. Our military force is ample. . . . To ignore a local government, when the local government is ready . . . and . . . able to enforce the law, not only insults the people of this state by imputing to them an inability to govern themselves, but is a violation of a basic principle of our institutions. I ask the immediate withdrawal of the Federal troops from active duty in the state.' "

Darrow took the paper. "If Cleveland has any regard for the laws under which he is supposed to rule——"

Altgeld shook his head. "He won't withdraw the troops. The Eastern papers are screaming that a state of insurrection

24

exists in Chicago. Olney is showing him frantic telegrams from Edwin Walker crying for more troops to quell the riots. Clarence, if you want to get a clear picture of what will happen to you if you defend labor leaders and fight for social justice, just watch the flood of invective poured on my head in tomorrow's papers for protesting this inexcusable violation of the Constitution. . . . It's their final insult because I pardoned the anarchists; they want to repudiate me as a Democrat so the Republicans can't say, 'We told you the Democrats favor anarchy and the destruction of property.' "

As Darrow bade him good-by after dinner, Altgeld murmured, "We're partners now, son, and there'll be bad days ahead for both of us."

The next morning Darrow alighted cramped and stiff from the coach in which he had sat up all night, had breakfast and rode a streetcar into South Chicago. When he reached the point where the tracks of the Illinois Central and the Rock Island paralleled each other, he found the tracks heavily guarded by men with revolver holsters strapped about their waists, thirty-six hundred of them having been sworn in as deputy marshals. Walking among the newly sworn deputies, stopping here to share a cigarette and there for a chat, he saw that they had been recruited from the dregs of the Chicago tenderloin: gangsters, hoodlums, toughs, petty criminals, sharpers, loafers. These were the men who now wore the badge of the United States government, who were going to defend society against the revolutionary strikers. The headlines that had alleged Chicago to be in control of incendiary anarchists had indeed come true; these deputized representatives of the Federal government, armed and paid for by the railroads, fitted neatly into what the terrorized public had been bludgeoned into believing the anarchists were: miscreants, who would burn and destroy a city for pleasure and pillage.

By midmorning he had made his way to the stockyards. He halted abruptly as he saw United States soldiers attempting to move a cattle train out of the yard, astounded at the boldness of the General Managers' Association in committing this most obvious illegality of them all: Federal troops had been sent into Chicago by President Cleveland to protect property, and here they were acting as strikebreakers. The assembled workers and their sympathizers, as had been expected, were not liking this idea; each time the soldiers tried to move the train the track ahead was blocked by overturned empty freight cars and spiked switches. Darrow watched; by night the army had moved the train six blocks.

Learning that the General Managers' Association was determined to prove they could bring a Pullman train into Chicago over the Rock Island road, early the following morning Clarence hurried south to Fifty-first Street. A through train was coming slowly down the track, United States soldiers stationed on its cowcatcher. A protesting crowd collected; the engine slowed; the soldiers jumped down, charged into the men and dispersed them. There was jeering; a few stones were thrown. When the train reached Fortieth Street it was blockaded by overturned freight cars; only through the combined efforts of Mayor Hopkins, Superintendent of Police Brennan and a railroad superintendent with a crack crew which righted the freight cars was the Pullman able to move the next thirty blocks by the end of the day. The railroads were paralyzed; foodstuffs and machinery could be moved neither in nor out of the city; the workers had won. Nevertheless, the overturning of the strike was implicit in the overturning of the cars, for contrary to the orders of Eugene Debs, the first railroad property had been manhandled.

That night violence broke loose. Standing above the yards, Darrow watched a number of freight cars—and the strike with them—burst into flame and vanish in smoke. The next morning the newspapers of the country informed their readers that Chicago was in a state of insurrection. The railroads demanded further protection; Mayor Hopkins wired Governor Altgeld, who promptly provided six companies of state militia.

Human blood once again flowed in the streets of Chicago. The police spent a considerable portion of their efforts restraining the newly appointed United States railroad deputies from shooting into the crowds, arresting numbers of them for drunkenness and thievery. Mayor Hopkins, fearing that the railroads might sue the city to collect damages on the grounds of inadequate protection to property, gathered forty depositions to prove that agents of the railroad companies had set fire to the cars. By afternoon huge crowds collected along the tracks and in the yards: some few hotheaded strikers who could not be restrained by Debs's orders, thousands of sympathizers, the interested and the curious, the wild boys, the foreign-speaking population, which inhabited those sections, and the entire underworld of Chicago came out to watch, to see what they could get out of it.

They milled about; the excitement rose; angry names were called; fists flew. At three-thirty in the afternoon they charged into the police and militiamen who were trying to disperse them. The soldiers fired. Three men fell dead of bullet wounds. Many others, including women, were bayoneted and clubbed.

By dinnertime Debs had been arrested on charges of criminal conspiracy and of violating the Federal injunction and
26

was lodged in the Cook County jail. Darrow's four-day observation period of America in the making was over. He was now just a lawyer whose one and only client was behind prison bars.

The guard unlocked a cell door. Darrow stepped inside; the iron clanged behind him. A tall sinewy man with a long, plain face stepped forward to clasp his hand. In the cell were five strangers, waiting to be tried on petty criminal charges. Some were "stripped to the waist, scratching the bites inflicted by all manner of nameless vermin, the blood trickling down their bare bodies in tiny red rivulets. Sewer rats as big as cats scurried over the floor."

Darrow sprawled onto the hard bench. "You know, Gene, finding you in the same cell block leads me to think maybe there's something to this anarchism business. Men like Parsons, Spies, Fischer and Engel believed that in America the capitalist monopoly was maintained by the state. That forced them to the conclusion that government was an enemy of the people. The events of the past few days would seem to bear them out."

From the street newsboys shouted: "Railroad strike broken; read all about the Debs Rebellion!"

"Debs Rebellion," murmured Darrow acidly. "You're in rebellion against the existing form of government and are out to burn civilization to the ground."

"There may have lived sometime, somewhere, a kindlier, gentler, more generous man than Eugene V. Debs," Darrow always said, "but I have never known him. Nor have I ever read or heard of another."

No two men in American history were to earn more bitter enemies than these two sitting side by side on a prison bench, their legs hitched under them to avoid the rats scampering beneath their feet; few would be more vilified in the press, from the pulpits and school platforms; few would have more splenetic hatred heaped upon them—and always for identical reasons. Both would suffer endless persecution, overwork, illness, ingratitude, and both would live long and fruitful lives.

"Go get a good night's sleep, Clarence, and don't worry about me," said Debs, the client comforting his lawyer. "We'll come out all right. If not this time—next time."

During the following days Darrow worked frantically to have Debs released on bail while the battle continued to be waged on both the political and economic fronts. After a sharp interchange of letters President Cleveland silenced Governor Altgeld.

Cleveland was greeted with salvos of praise; the attacks on Governor Altgeld for fighting for the principles of states' rights and local self-government, to which his and Cleveland's Democratic party were pledged, grew increasingly bitter. *Harper's Weekly* reflected the tone of the daily press when it called Altgeld "the most dangerous enemy to American institutions of all the ruffianly gang which has broken out of the forecastle of the ship of state and attempted to seize the helm."

On the labor front the pattern of violence entirely replaced the pattern of peaceful strike. Everywhere Darrow went he found freight cars overturned or burning in their yards. Several of the remaining Exposition buildings were set afire; three hundred thousand dollars' worth of railroad property was destroyed by young boys, vandals, the unemployed, a portion of the railroad men who, knowing they had been beaten, wanted to get in their blows of retaliation. Seven men lost their lives. Then the violence had run its course; the crowds dispersed, and the last manifestations of the strike were over. Only then was Eugene Debs granted bail and released from his cell. Attending the last bitter meeting of his industrial union, he asked, "Has anyone ever heard of soldiers being called out to guard the rights of workingmen?"

Disorganized, whipped, humiliated, without funds and with serious charges against their leader, abused by the press, the pulpit and the government, men and women began drifting back to work: to the Pullman shops on the same wage scale against which they had struck—but not until they had turned in their A.R.U. cards; to the railroad yards on any terms. Anyone who had had any voice in the strike was refused work and black-listed; for the next decade derelicts of this industrial war drifted over the face of the continent, seeking a chance to work at their trades, in disguise, using false names, torn from their wives and children and homes; wounded veterans of internecine strife, with no government hospitals or veteran bureaus to which they might turn for help.

While they were in the depths of defeat and despair President Cleveland appointed a Senate Investigating Committee to get at the truth underlying the strike. Since his client would soon be called to trial for conspiracy, Darrow attended the sessions, gathering material for his case. Before this committee, under the leadership of Carroll Wright, scientific economist and first head of the United States Labor Bureau, paraded hundreds of witnesses: Pullman officials testifying that "three hundred strikers were thrown around the closed Pullman shops to protect them, and that from May 11 to July 3 there was not the slightest disorder or destruction of property"; police officials testifying that there had been no disorder in Chicago and no need for Federal troops; newspaper reporters affirming they had seen almost no strikers in the violence mobs; Debs and other union officials revealing why organization was needed to combat the General Managers, and lastly, George Pullman, who avowed that "we recognize that the working people are the most important element which enters into the successful operation of any manufacturing enterprise" and was then forced into the staggering disclosure that for the depression year of August 1893 to July 1894, when he had slashed wages below the subsistence level and refused to lower rents, his company declared a profit dividend of two million, eight hundred thousand dollars!

But George Pullman had known that you can't give in to your workingmen. When asked by the commission whether he didn't think that workmen who had been with him for so many years, who had helped build his shops, his prestige and his fortune, were not entitled to some consideration—in this case a reduction of a dollar or two of dividends on each share of stock—Pullman had replied publicly: "My duty is to my stockholders and to my company. There was no reason to give those workingmen a gift of money."

The hearing concluded, Darrow threw himself into the history of criminal conspiracy, the law which says that if two people agree to do something together which either of them could legally do alone, then both may be deemed guilty of an illegal act; the law against which he would fight for the next forty years. The Senate Investigating Committee had observed, "Some of our courts are still poring over the law reports of antiquity in order to construe conspiracy out of labor unions." This, Darrow knew, was precisely what his clients were up against.

During the fall months of 1894 Darrow rented a small office, surrounded himself with lawbooks, history and economics books and mapped his defense of Debs and the A.R.U. Slowly he evolved a plan. He would not stand on the defensive; he would not go into court as the counsel for the wrongdoer and the guilty, pleading for justice or, at best, mercy. No, he would go in and attack. He would indict the General Managers' Association for criminal conspiracy, revealing to the country their illegal agreements to control rates and service as well as wages, thus eliminating the benefits of the competitive system. He would indict and try George Pullman for antisocial conduct, inimical to the well-being of his country, dangerous to democratic principles. But most important of all, he would place on trial in that Chicago courtroom the industrial oligarchy under which twenty per cent of the people enjoyed comfort and security

29

while the other eighty per cent suffered uncertainty, intermittent unemployment and want, with no discernible share in the democracy which Andrew Jackson and Abraham Lincoln had imagined was created for the betterment of all.

True, he could not convict George Pullman. He could not send the General Managers' Association to jail, nor could he persuade the judge to reconstruct the economic machinery even if he proved it guilty. He realized that in cases of this nature he could not be a trial lawyer. He would have to be a teacher, an educator. His clients might be convicted and sent to prison, but in the meanwhile he would be making every effort to damn the convictors in the mind of the general public, that inert, formless, seemingly powerless mass which, if ever sufficiently educated and aroused, might rise up in its wrath to reshape its civilization.

Words were wax bullets; dollars were dumdums. But words were the only weapons he had at hand.

On the morning of January 26, 1895, Darrow led his eight clients into the courtroom of Judge Grosscup, one of the two Federal judges who had issued an ex-parte injunction to Edwin Walker, with no representative of labor present because labor had not been informed by the court that the hearing was to be held. The eight accused were Eugene V. Debs, George W. Howard and Sylvester Keliher, officers of the A.R.U.; L. W. Rogers, editor of the A.R.U. newspaper; William E. Burns, Martin J. Elliot, Roy M. Goodwin and James Hogan, directors of the organization.

At the defense table with Darrow sat S. S. Gregory, one of the best lawyers Darrow had ever known. "He was emotional and sympathetic; he was devoted to the principles of liberty and always fought for the poor and oppressed. In spite of all this, he had a fine practice, and his ability and learning were thoroughly recognized." The country, already upset by the idea that a railroad lawyer had resigned his position to defend the obviously guilty Debs, was even more confused to find Gregory, a former president of the American Bar Association, also working for the accused. The presence of these two men, coupled with the findings of the Senate Investigating Committee, provoked certain portions of the public to ask, "Is there more to this case than we are permitted to read in our morning paper?"

The courtroom was jammed with spectators who wanted to see the murderous beast Debs, who, like Altgeld, had been portrayed by the press as the most dangerous anarchist and ruffian of his times. "They sat back in frank disappointment when Gene was pointed out to them. This was no long-haired fire-eater; on the contrary, Debs was nearly bald, mild appearing, with candid blue eyes behind gold-rimmed spectacles. He wore a high white collar, a black-and-white scarf, a gray tweed suit, a boutonnière."

The prosecution opened the case with a searing indictment against Debs. He was guilty of murdering the seven men who had been shot by the troops; he was guilty of inciting riots; he was guilty of destroying three hundred thousand dollars' worth of railroad property; he was guilty of a conspiracy to starve the country, paralyze its industries, wreck its economic structure. He was also guilty, parenthetically, of the charge on which he had been brought into court: persuading railroad workers to remain on strike.

Darrow, "who always sat slumped far down in a chair, as though sitting on the back of his neck," slowly pulled himself upward, walked toward the jury box and stood facing the twelve men. They wondered what he could possibly say to defend these men who had so palpably broken the law. But when he began speaking in his low, musical drawl, as though really wanting to find true words for true thoughts, they were astounded to find that by some curious twist of reasoning he had become the prosecutor.

"This is a historic case which will count much for liberty or against liberty. Conspiracy, from the days of tyranny in England down to the day the General Managers' Association used it as a club, has been the favorite weapon of every tyrant. It is an effort to punish the crime of thought. If the government does not, we shall try to get the General Managers here to tell you what they know about conspiracy. These defendants published to all the world what they were doing and in the midst of a widespread strike . . . found time to counsel against violence. For this they are brought into court by an organization which uses the government as a cloak to conceal its infamous purposes."

For a solid month, backed and advised by Gregory, he reviewed the history of labor unions and conspiracy laws. He exposed the conditions at the Pullman plant, revealed the activities of the General Managers' Association and finally presented to the nation Eugene Victor Debs. In order that the American people might learn how so villainous a character could be produced under such a salutary economic system, he led Debs through the story of his life.

Eugene V. Debs was born in Terre Haute, Indiana, on November 5, 1855, of Jean Daniel Debs and Marguerite Marie Betterich, both recently arrived from Alsace.

At the age of fourteen he went to work for fifty cents a day, scraping paint off the sides of old railroad cars. Then one day he was picked out of the shop by an engineer whose fireman was drunk, and put on a freight engine, shoveling coal. He soon found a steady job on the Terre Haute and Indianapolis Railroad at a dollar a night; during the day he robbed himself of sleep by attending a private school and burrowing in the encyclopedia a book agent had sold him on the installment plan.

Even after he reluctantly went to work in a wholesale grocery house, he never ceased to think of himself as a railroad man; he attended meetings of the union, did their clerical work and, when the Terre Haute lodge of the newly formed Brotherhood of Locomotive Firemen was formed, was chosen secretary. For the next seventeen years Gene Debs *was* the Brotherhood of Locomotive Firemen. He drew no pay for his work; he wanted none. In his spare hours he prepared meticulous reports to national headquarters, edited the *Locomotive Firemen's Magazine* and wrote articles for it; in bad years he contributed as much as nine hundred dollars, out of the fifteen hundred he earned, to keep the union and the magazine going. When strikes and depressions depleted the membership he met the challenge by working all night writing hundreds of letters to members who had fallen off, telling them that they must come back into their union; organizing meetings throughout the Midwest trying to infuse courage and unity—a man possessed, a man inspired. "My grip was always packed; to tramp through a railroad yard in the rain, snow or sleet half the night, to be ordered out of the roundhouse for being an agitator or to be put off a train were all in the program."

With the passage of the years he made himself that rarity among union leaders: an educated man, well equipped to compete with the managers on their own ground. For sixteen years the brotherhood grew under his guidance, securing ever-better wages and hours for its men, safer working conditions on the line.

In 1892 Eugene Debs had one of the great social visions of his century: The General Managers' Association had combined all the railroads within the system to control hours, wages and working conditions for the industry. Then, reasoned Debs, we must also organize all labor within the industry to cope with it. It is not enough to have only the highly skilled trades unionized, for they represent probably not more than twenty per cent of the working people of the country. Every last job within an industry, no matter how unimportant or menial, must be organized and joined in a union as big as the industry itself; an injury to one group then would be an injury to all. As soon as the railroads were organized they could go to the other key industries, until every workingman in the country belonged to his union as to his industry; a solid wall of labor to confront the solid wall of management.

After a stormy session with the Brotherhoods of Locomotive Engineers, Brakemen and Firemen, which wanted to confine union strength to the skilled trades, Gene Debs resigned and formed the American Railway Union, which would take in all workers within the industry. In spite of opposition he built his American Railway Union to a membership of a hundred and fifty thousand. Then on April 1, 1894, when James J. Hill cut the wage of his common labor from a dollar and a quarter to a dollar a day, the American Railway Union helped organize the Great Northern workers, stopped all service on the line and, with the aid of the St Paul Chamber of Commerce, forced Hill to restore the wage cut. With this unprecedented victory of unskilled labor, his conception of industrial unionism was justified, and the membership soared. The delegates came confident and flushed with success to their first convention in Chicago in June 1894. There they had encountered the Pullman strike.

The A.R.U. had helped organize the Pullman shops. When the Pullman workers had found it impossible to live on the wages being paid them the A.R.U. had urged arbitration and attempted to achieve it. But Pullman had stood firm that workers had nothing to say about their wages, that he had nothing to arbitrate. Against the advice of the A.R.U. the Pullman workers had struck; their delegates told harrowing tales of starvation, oppression, injustice, despair. Debs and the A.R.U. officers had remained firm: their union was too young to stage a sympathetic strike, they did not have a sufficiently large membership or enough money in the bank. Then in the midst of their denials a girl had come into the convention to tell of how her father had died, owing the Pullman company some sixty dollars in back rent; of how the company was now letting her work for two weeks, then deducting a portion of her father's debt before handing her a few pennies as wages.

The A.R.U. workers had known unemployment, uncertainty, hunger, want, despair all their lives. All they could do was to vote the sympathetic strike and refuse to move Pullman cars.

They had stayed at home and remained peaceable; they had woven for the country a design of industrial unionism. Then the railroads took over the government, and now Debs was a criminal on a witness stand, the strike broken, the workers in disrepute, industrial unionism effectively smashed for four full decades.

Satisfied by the look and feel of the jury that Debs had

gone a long way to acquit himself, Darrow made his next bold move: he would juxtapose George Pullman to Eugene Debs and let the country draw its own conclusions. He subpoenaed Pullman to come into court and reveal the details of the two-million-eight-hundred-thousand-dollar dividend distributed in the preceding depression year and the twenty-six millions in cash of undeclared dividends in the company at the same time that the men who had helped him earn this money were fainting of hunger at their machines.

But George Pullman had fled. The subpoena could not be served. Darrow made the most of this flight, portraying Pullman to the jury and to the world as the true insidious enemy of society. The shoe was neatly on the other foot; the prosecutors were being prosecuted. Pulling his master stroke, Darrow now announced that he was going to subpoena every last member of the General Managers' Association, whom he would then proceed to convict, not only of criminal conspiracy to depress wages, but further, of a criminal conspiracy to take over and use the Federal government for their own conspiratorial purposes.

But Clarence Darrow had planned too well; his first big case promptly blew up under his hand. The next morning only eleven jurors took their seats. Judge Grosscup set forth that, "Owing to the sickness of a juror and the certificate of his physician that he will not be able to get out for two or three days, I think it will be necessary to adjourn the further taking of testimony in this case."

He was on his feet like lightning, demanding that another juror be named, that the record of the case be read to him. Judge Grosscup denied the motion; the case was put over until May.

That Darrow had acquitted his clients of the criminal-conspiracy charges was clear; the government never again called the case for trial. However, Debs and his seven associates were now cited by the Chicago circuit court for "contempt" in having refused to obey the injuction first issued. Darrow was aghast at this move, for in the Federal Court the defendants would not have the benefit of a trial by jury. Judge Woods, the second of the two Federal judges who had granted the injunction, heard the evidence and sentenced the union officials to six months in jail.

In the midst of his bitterness Darrow persuaded Lyman Trumbull to join him in his appeal to the United States Supreme Court. It was Lyman Trumbull who, as the senator with the deciding vote to cast in the impeachment trial of President Andrew Johnson, in 1868, with his reputation, his profession and his life threatened by the political ruffians who were seeking to remove Johnson for their own purposes, defiantly voted to acquit Johnson and thus helped to save his country from an international disgrace. Trumbull had been a Supreme Court of Illinois judge and his appearance in the Debs case further confounded the public.

The Darrow-Trumbull brief was simple and direct. It attempted to show that not since 1824 had there been any statute in the United States making it a crime to organize labor unions or go out in peaceable strike. Therefore, the accused were guilty of no crime under the common law, but even if they had been, both the criminal law and the Constitution provided that the trial of all crimes shall be by jury; a court of equity, such as Judge Wood's court, had no jurisdiction over criminal- or common-law cases. Consequently the Grosscup and Woods courts of equity had assumed jurisdiction illegally when they issued the injunction, and they were now further illegally depriving persons of their liberty without a trial by jury.

Darrow was confident the Supreme Court would throw out the contempt conviction. This was his first major error in judgment: he had failed to go back to the beginnings of the Supreme Court, to trace its consistent efforts to defend and entrench property rights over personal rights in the development of American life. Caught thus off guard, he was astounded at the decision and even more at its basis for reaching that decision.

Ignoring the fact that there had been no obstruction of the mails, the Supreme Court justified sending of Federal troops into Chicago and the violation of states' rights by claiming that "among the powers expressly given to the national government are the control of interstate commerce and the management of the post office. There was in existence a special emergency, one which demanded that the court do all that courts can do; the jurisdiction of the courts of equity to redress the grievance of public nuisances by injunction is clearly established; having this right, the court must also have the right to punish those who disregard its orders." And thereupon refused to set aside the contempt conviction.

There was nothing more Darrow, Trumbull or anyone else could do. Debs once again packed his bag and with his associates went to jail in Woodstock, Illinois. Governor Altgeld had been defeated by President Cleveland. Eugene Debs and the American Railway Union had been defeated by the General Managers' Association. Clarence Darrow had been defeated in his first big case by the Circuit and Supreme courts. The more he studied the Supreme Court decision the more he became convinced that it was based on class prejudice rather than on the Constitution. "Debs

35

really got off easy," he commented. "No other offense has ever been visited with such severe penalties as seeking to help the oppressed."

With Debs and his companions safe behind iron bars, the case was apparently ended, the apotheosis of the struggle of the nineteenth century to build into the structure of American life the insuperable law of property. But for Clarence Darrow this was only the beginning.

If the nineteenth century had solidified the law of property to keep pace with the growth of property, then the twentieth century, he sensed, must develop the law of persons.

In this development he was ready to play his part.

Chapter Three

Darrow Sprinkles Salt on the Tail of Truth

THE STORY THAT Clarence Darrow had given up a lucrative job to defend Eugene Debs spread the legend that a phenomenon, a sport, had arisen within the legal profession: a capable lawyer who would fight for the poor. His modest office in the Reaper Block promptly became a one-man legal clinic. On the hard benches of his waiting room sat endless lines of clients in well-worn, unfashionable clothes: the disinherited who could bring him little but their grief, workingmen who had lost an arm or leg at their job and had been cast off without compensation, wives whose husbands had been killed at their work or in other accidents, unemployed families about to be dispossessed, gullible victims who had been defrauded of their savings, mothers from the slums whose children had run afoul of the law.

When he finished with one client he would walk into the waiting room in his shirt sleeves and say to the next in line, "All right, you can come in now." His office girl was instructed never to turn anyone away; no one was ever told he was too busy; everyone who came could sit and wait his turn. No matter how late it got, he never sent anyone home, to come back again the next day. When people with jobs wanted to see him he let them call after six o'clock. He saw even the crackpots, the lunatics, though briefly. He was a sap, a sucker, a sentimentalist, but he was no fool: he could smell an impostor as far away as an outhouse.

In 1895 he joined the organization of a new firm, Collins, Goodrich, Darrow and Vincent, with offices in the Rookery Building. Lorin C. Collins, the head, had been a judge of the Circuit Court and former Speaker of the Illinois House of Representatives; Adams A. Goodrich was a former state judge; William A. Vincent had been chief justice of the Supreme Court of the then territory of New Mexico—all of which put him in illustrious company. The new firm was "organized for the distinct purpose of . . . representing corporations, including banks and railroads." Almost immediately a sensational murder was committed in Chicago, and Darrow ran afoul of the firm's avowed policy.

"A poor, half-witted, religious zealot" by the name of Pendergast, who earned a meager living by selling newspapers and "whose mentality is disclosed by the fact that in order to come closer to God and nature he used to mingle in the pastures with cattle and browse with them," forced his way into the office of the newly elected mayor, Carter H. Harrison, Senior, and insisted that Harrison had promised to give him an important political appointment in return for electioneering. When the mayor tried to ease the unbalanced man out, Pendergast pulled a gun and assassinated him.

"Mr Darrow volunteered to defend the man, without a fee, paying the costs himself. His so doing was upon his expressed thought that if the law declared that an insane or mentally incompetent person should not be convicted of such a crime, then Pendergast was entitled to the benefit of that law, regardless of the fact that his victim was a man of great prominence." It was Darrow's first murder trial and the only one he ever lost—for Chicago, in the grip of one of its recurrent blood lusts, demanded Pendergast's execution.

The most valuable use of his ability to get his hands on the core of a man was exercised in the selection of juries. He spent weeks examining prospective jurors, oblivious to the passage of time, his other obligations or the size of the fee involved.

"Darrow always picked common people," said a Chicago lawyer; "he didn't want big businessmen. He had a farmer's way about him that appealed to common jurors. He talked to a plumber as though he, too, were a plumber; to a grocery-man as though he, too, were a groceryman. He knew Chicago so well he could divine how the juror would react to his theories by the part of the city he came from. He was a great reasoner. When you opposed him you had to try the case the way he wanted it tried. He would shift his position logically on a moment's notice; we all had to imitate his methods. He was never arrogant or contemptuous with other

37

lawyers and never quarreled with opposing lawyers before a jury. The district attorney's office hated it when Darrow was to defend; he was so resourceful. A marvel as a cross-examiner, he would never give up examining until he got some comfort out of it. No matter how badly the point went against him, he would work on it and turn it to his advantage."

He worked just as carefully on the judge as he did on the jury. "The most important thing to do is to make the judge *want* to decide things your way," Darrow advised one of his younger partners. "They are human beings, moved by the same things that move other human beings. The points of law merely give the judge a *reason* for doing what you have already made him want to do."

For him wisdom did not consist in facts, which altered with every change in the light, but rather in a sharpening of the tools of logic, in the constant, courageous search for truth. The tragedy of most human minds, he thought, was not so much that they were small as that they were closed. He disliked virginity in any form: if only minds could be opened, they could be impregnated, fertilized, and anything might grow, even—who knows?—tolerance.

He rewrote the adage, "The truth shall set you free," to read, "The pursuit of truth shall set you free—even if you never catch up with it!" It took a bold and vigorous mind to say, "I shall pursue truth even though I can never fully grasp it or settle it for all time; even though truth is such a chameleon that it changes color the moment one manages to pour a little salt on its tail." He was wary of those that saw truth as absolute and unchanging, that accepted as permanent one set of doctrines to the exclusion of all others. That made people feel that anybody who didn't believe in their little package of truth was not only wrong but probably evil. A closed mind was a dead mind. Shut minds constipated progress.

Because it took a tremendous force to open anything that had been long closed, he evolved the method of shock to open heavy and dense minds. If his audience were religious he would speak of the fruits of agnosticism; if the audience were reactionary he would extol the virtues of the planned socialist state; if the audience were socialistic he would plead the virtues of anarchism and the freedom of the individual in an uncontrolled society; if the audience were academic he would laud the imperatives of heresy and incessant mental revolution; if the audience were moralistic he would attack the principles of free will, prove that there was no such thing as sin, crime or individual responsibility; if the audience were sentimental or romantic he would argue the blessings of realism; if the audience were mechanistic he would plead for spiritual values.

Amirus Darrow had taught his son that doubt is the beginning of wisdom, and Clarence had grown up with a robust skepticism: accept nothing merely because it exists and hence appears to be true; believe nothing merely because you would like to believe it. Yet he did not consider it sufficient to be a skeptic for the not inconsiderable pleasure of constituting the opposition. Once the plain had been swept clear one also had to know what materials went into the building of a more intelligent, beautiful and civilized world. For this task one had to think clearly, simply and disinterestedly; above all, one had to be a fighter: life consisted of change; change met dogged opposition; hence life implied eternal warfare.

"The only books he never seemed to care for were textbooks and legal books," said Francis Wilson, his closest friend and most beloved partner. "He had a lazy streak and wouldn't work on a case until the last minute, until he had to. Most of the legal preparation was done by others." However, once he had plunged into a case, "he was endowed with a remarkable memory. He was a quick observer and could retain without outside aids. He hardly ever took a note in a case, yet there was hardly a point that could be used that escaped him."

Nearly everybody in America belonged to something: a church, a political party, a fraternal order, an economic clique. He would belong to that rapidly diminishing brotherhood which owed allegiance to no man, creed or program. He feared set and rigid doctrine, no matter how valid it might look at the moment: its followers would too often oppose or close their eyes to change in the external world rather than be forced to make internal modifications. He knew that too often people accepted creeds, philosophies and panaceas because of their imperative need to believe in something, to belong to something, rather than because they had made a searching examination of its tenets and were intellectually convinced; that was why neither reasoning nor facts had much effect upon their emotional allegiances.

"Darrow often debated and spoke for us socialists. . . . Yet we could never count him as one of us. He poked fun at us. He felt that no positive program could succeed in the face of an unpredictable future and lectured us on the need for a fluid program which would allow for modification."

He was in agreement with Kropotkin and the philosophical anarchists who claimed that the growth of government was a social evil because it curtailed the liberties of man and lent itself to manipulation by those interests which seized control; the seizing of the government by the railroads and the General Managers' Association during the A.R.U. strike was proof that the anarchists had a point. However, he always said: "I think you folks are right—but not altogether right. Your idea of free associations would have worked in a handicraft stage of society, like we had back in Kinsman, but you fail to take into account the growing machine age."

Before the freethinkers of America he committed the heresy of insisting that if they wished to remain freethinkers they had to make constant explorations into the realm of the spirit and that they had to build their freethinking on the hypothesis that they might be wrong. When the Atheists' Society invited him to lecture he dressed them down for being as arrogant and prejudiced as the church: religion insisted that there absolutely was a God, heaven and hell; the atheists insisted there absolutely was no God, no heaven and no hell, and neither could prove their point.

Darrow had been in Chicago only a year or two when he began to perceive that the choice of his youth was not the choice of his maturity. Jessie was a homebody. She did not like to go out nights, in particular, she did not enjoy lectures, debates, forums on social and political subjects, for she did not understand them very well. When they first came to Chicago she had accompanied Clarence to his meetings, but she found it difficult to follow the discussions, and she could not grasp why people should become so excited over matters that hardly seemed to concern them directly.

When she no longer wanted to entertain her husband's friends, Darrow stopped asking people to his home; since his wife did not care to accompany him to meetings, he began to see very little of her. Home became a place where he slept and on Sundays spent a few hours with his son. Jessie had developed into a plain woman: plain-looking, plain-dressing, plain-thinking. Yet he respected Jessie and was grateful for her goodness, but there was almost no point at which their minds could touch, no common ground on which they could be companionable. He was fun loving, but there was little buoyancy in Jessie, who was inclined to be lethargic and slow-thinking. He was rarely interested in eating: he mauled his food around on his plate, lit a cigarette, smoked it halfway down, then crushed it out in the middle of a beef stew or steak—the ultimate affront to a housewife. He cared nothing about sleep: he did not wear himself out with exercise during the day, and so he was rarely tired; when he came home from a meeting at twelve or one o'clock there was always a new book or magazine to be read until three. He was oblivious to clothes, never knowing what he had on, and he was indifferent to his home surroundings.

At his clubs, lectures and debates he was meeting the kind of women he enjoyed: social workers studying the causes and cures of poverty; newspaperwomen fighting against heavy odds to create a new profession for their sex; women who were writing novels, composing music, training for the theater and the ballet; women vibrantly alive, in revolt against the restraints and taboos of the puritanical nineteenth century; women who were vividly aware of their times and the important movements within it.

He took women for the sheer physical delight of them, waking in the morning to chuckle over the delicious dialogue, the deep-throated laughter, the feel of a slender arm crooked about his neck. Women gravitated to him, attracted by his courage and independence and the feel that here was a man; drawn by the low musical voice that hit them in the stomach, by the kindly eyes that withal unmasked them and looked through them, by the magnetism of his personality that put people at their ease, untied the knots in their souls, made them glow. His physical appetites, like his mental appetites, did not mature until his thirties; once they had matured they remained in full flower.

There is an old saying that a couple no longer well mated will remain together just so long as neither of them meets someone who fires their imagination and brings their discontent into focus. X was one of Chicago's first newspaperwomen and one of the most beautiful in that city or any other. "She was the Irish type, with light brown hair, blue eyes and a magnificent figure." She was bright and well read, with an inexhaustible fund of high spirits and the inimitable Irish genius for repartee. She kept Clarence chuckling, kept his imagination jumping apace, kept his blood tingling as though a million ants were crawling inside his veins. She taught him how little he knew about the feminine mind and constantly delighted him by outsmarting him, by thinking swifter and deeper than his fumbling male mind could carry him. They became inseparable, had luncheon together every day, attended meetings together, criticized each other's work, spent their spare hours in each other's company. Their friends say they were as perfectly matched as a male and female animal can be: in brains, in courage, in physical attractiveness. Darrow loved her very much, and X loved him. He went to Jessie and asked for his freedom.

"I knew that Mr Darrow was a man of the world. He had to be away from home a lot, to travel about, and I said, 'Well, Clarence, if you want to be free I won't put a feather in your way.' Darrow replied, 'I don't know, I may be making a mistake, but I feel I must have my freedom.' "

When Darrow asked her to secure the divorce, she answered that it would do him less harm in his profession if he divorced her, an act that was little short of noble.

He did things to hurt himself many times; on a few regrettable occasions he did things to injure society and the causes for which he was laboring, but his separation and divorce are the only instances in which Darrow, so excruciatingly sensitive to the pain suffered by humans in their harrowed flight across the earth and the years, knowingly inflicted unhappiness on another person.

He moved into the Chicago Athletic Club and divorced Jessie. "This was done without contest or disagreement and without bitterness on either side, and our son has always been attached to both of us, and she and I have always had full confidence and respect toward each other." He gave her a home and a liberal allowance, which he maintained all his life. He always spoke affectionately of Jessie, though in his autobiography he fails to give her credit for her many years of service and in particular was unwilling to reveal that when "I took a little office in the village of Andover, borrowed some money to buy some books and flung my shingle to the breeze," the money had been provided by his bride, Jessie.

After a number of years Jessie married a Judge Brownlee of Ashtabula, before whom Darrow had tried a number of cases.

Chapter Four

Who's a Criminal?

AT FORTY Darrow was smooth-faced and hard-stomached. He wore a jaunty black derby on the street; in cool weather his meandering black satin tie was kept within the confines of his vest; his clothing had not yet reached that stage of acute dishabille which occasioned his reply to reporters at the Loeb-Leopold trial:

"I can't understand why you chaps look so different from me. I have my suits made at the same tailors you do. I pay as much for them. I go to the same stylish shops to buy my haberdashery. The only thing I can figure is maybe you dudes take off your clothes when you go to sleep at night."

He had spent two summer vacations in Europe, stimulated

to venture on his first trip because his friend Judge Barnum was taking his family and invited him to come along. The Barnums had been admirers of Darrow since 1894 when they had heard him cry at a giant Populist meeting, "There never was any discontent among the people except for good and sufficient reason. Under the benign administration of the Republican party the aggregate wealth of this republic increased in the hands of the few at the expense of the many. True patriotism hates injustice in its own land more than anywhere else!" For the first two days he lay flat in his bunk, moaning, "Tell them to stop the boat; I want to get off." Recovering from his seasickness he became friends with Gertrude, the judge's comely young daughter who was soon to "flee a vapid society life" to become one of the pioneer organizers of women workers. In Europe they spent many companionable hours together tramping in the Alps. After slogging for several days between rows of ecclesiastical Madonnas in the Italian art galleries he exclaimed, "I can't look at any more improbable mothers of impossible children."

Though Collins, Goodrich, Darrow and Vincent had a substantial practice, "it became evident in the early stages of the partnership, because of Darrow's bent on labor, public and political questions, that the life of the firm would not endure—when you took into consideration the purposes for which it was organized." In 1897 it "fell of its own weight— too many great lawyers, perhaps," and Darrow organized the first firm of which he was to be the senior partner and hence the boss. As juniors he took in William O. Thompson, who had been associated with the former firm, and Morris St P. Thomas, who had been his assistant in the office of the corporation counsel. The three men worked well together and enjoyed each other.

"We did a very considerable business from the outset," writes Thomas, ". . . Much of our business was strictly of a civil nature; the division of fees was on a percentage basis; Darrow had a half, I a third and Thompson the balance. Darrow was always eager to take chances, and many of our cases were on a contingent basis—notably personal-injury cases where he was quite successful in obtaining good verdicts. He was a good business getter, and I well remember his telling Thompson and myself not to trouble ourselves about getting business—he said he would attend to that—and he did. Having obtained a good verdict and judgment, he left it largely to us juniors to sustain them in the courts of appeal. . . ."

In this country people were too often judged by whom they were against, not whom they were for. Darrow would have liked to write across the sky, "Difference of opinion doesn't make the other fellow wrong." It was too easy to be tolerant of the things one liked and understood; real tolerance applied to those modes of living or thinking that one hated, feared and could not understand. If this put him in the anomalous position of having critics say to him, "You're intolerant of intolerance," he was not enervated by the seeming contradiction. For him America was an experiment in co-operative living of groups of folks who didn't agree with each other on all issues but who were willing to accept these differences with good will.

Inducing people to live at peace with those whose convictions they found repugnant was a thankless and endless task. He was called an atheist when fighting the religionists for wanting the free-thinkers gagged; a medievalist when he opposed the free-thinkers who wanted the churches leveled. When the puritans wanted the pagans suppressed he fought for the pagans; when the pagans wanted the puritans laughed at he fought for the puritans. Beyond such ideological differences lay the more crucial issues: racial tolerance, economic tolerance, sociological tolerance. When the whites were against the Negroes, chaining them to their mops and brooms, their poverty and their ignorance, he fought the whites; when shortsighted employers were against their workers, chaining them to their machines and their starvation wages, he fought those employers; when society was against the sick, the mentally incompetent or unbalanced, the errant, the miscreant or the unfit, he fought society. Revenge in the form of criminal trials and penitentiaries was the most brutalizing form of intolerance; always he fought for a humane and scientific form of criminology. Callousness and injustice were the most destructive forms of intolerance; always he strove to secure for the poor and underprivileged the same opportunities for health, education and legal justice as were available to the wealthy. That is what he meant by tolerance.

His living he made from his civil cases. Like all hard-working heroes, he would occasionally get fed up with his virtue and exclaim petulantly, "Who's going to feed me, the birds? I'm no Saint Francis!" Yet more and more his sympathies were drawn to the criminal courts, for there, dramas were played that had social implications. Crime, as Altgeld had taught him, was not a cause, but a result; the prisons were the open sores of a diseased social body. Because of his heretical background, of his almost pathological sensitivity to the suffering of others, his uppermost characteristic was the need to defend: to fight for the individual against the mob.

"I grew to like to defend men and women charged with crime. I sought to learn why one man goes one way and another takes an entirely different road. I became vitally interested in the causes of human conduct. This meant more than the quibbling with lawyers and juries, to get or keep money for a client so that I could take part of what I won or saved for him: I was dealing with life, with its hopes and fears, its aspirations and despairs. With me it was going to the foundation of motive and conduct and adjustment for human beings, instead of blindly talking of hatred and vengeance."

Each client became not a legal case but a highly complex mechanism, the result of thousands of years of evolution, molded into its specific form by the environment in which it was immediately conditioned and over which it exercised no power. Since he could not be defending these afflicted ones for the money they did not have, they knew he came to them in compassion: and so they poured out their stories, their griefs, their incoherencies, in their often stumbling fashion telling him more than they realized they were telling about the weaknesses of the human machine that sometimes breaks down on the assembly line. It was from this early conception of man as a machine, which he evolved as an antidote to the conception of man as a spark of the godhead, that he developed into one of the leading proponents of the mechanistic philosophy in America. It was at base a philosophy of love and understanding, but to people who did not grasp its implications—that you cannot blame or punish a human machine that has cracked, any more than you can blame or punish a steel machine that has broken down; that you repair it without moral judgment or abuse so that it may carry on with its work—this view of humanity seemed fraught with pessimism.

His interest in why individuals came to be what they are drove him inevitably into a study of the forces that make and control contemporary society. First, however, he went back into anthropology and *The Golden Bough*, which shed light on the countless centuries when man was little more than an animal living in the forests, fighting and killing for his food. Once you knew what man came from, once you grasped the thousands of years of painful and not altogether successful struggle to emerge from bestiality into a controlled social order, it was easier to understand why men did the seemingly inexplicable.

"Scientists have so thoroughly established the theory of evolution, there is no longer any room for such a doctrine as freedom of the will. Nothing in the universe is outside the law, whether mineral, animal or vegetable. Free will means that man would live day by day, governed by his transient will, instead of being moved and virtually controlled by every

45

experience of his life. The laws that control human behavior are as fixed and certain as those that control the physical world."

Religion, which was acclaimed to be the approach of love, tolerance and forgiveness, said that man sprang from God, was created whole and responsible; anything he did which was adjudged to be bad was entirely his own fault and his own choosing, arising from the conscious evil which he elected of his own free will to exercise. Consequently no one was responsible for him: since he diabolically chooses to be evil, it is no more than just that he be cast out, punished, his life broken forever. Darrow's philosophy of mechanism, which was accused of being a cruel, inhuman and godless approach, insisted that there must be a cause for every antisocial act, and once that cause was found and either removed or eliminated, the *victim of the cause* could be made well and whole again, just as people with diphtheria or typhoid are made whole and well again once the cause of the disease is determined and then wiped out. In his fight for tolerance Darrow went further, and it was his next step which brought down upon him the wrath of organized society: that it is cruel and wasteful to punish further people who are already ill and that no more blame or moral obloquy should be visited upon the victim of a mental or nervous illness than upon a man with a physical illness. Both should be given the finest treatment that modern science can afford; both should be returned to their families and their jobs.

"What about those social crimes that are not punishable by law," he demanded; "exaggerated and lying advertisements that bleed millions of their wages for products that are useless; manipulation of stocks that rob the uninitiate of their savings; forestalling markets, controlling prices of consumption goods by monopoly control, misrepresentation of all sorts?"

For the crime of stealing food or money when a man or his family was hungry Darrow thought somebody ought to be convicted, but not the hungry man: rather all those who permitted their economic system periodically to starve out a portion of its people when there were quantities of food available for consumption. The tragedy of punishment, when he failed to get his client freed, lay not only in what happened to the person in prison, but in what happened to his family on the outside: the mother forced out of her home, the children taken from school to earn a few pennies, the family life broken up, its innocent victims disgraced, made bitter, antisocial. Darrow, who visited their homes and saw what havoc the convictions wrought, believed if the state saw fit to incarcerate the breadwinner to protect itself, then it was

46

also the duty of the state to support the man's family, clothe and feed the children, keep them in school. For no unorthodox theory was more derisive laughter brought down upon him than for this last.

Darrow had arrived in Chicago in 1887 while the sound of four human necks being broken by the noose was still fresh in the ears of the people who had clamored for their deaths. "Hang them first and try them afterward," Chicago had cried out in its psychotic sweat against the anarchists who, so the papers screamed at them, were ready to dynamite Chicago into the middle of Lake Michigan.

Eight men had been tried for the conspiracy to throw a bomb in Haymarket Square on the night of May 4, 1886, which had killed seven police officers. The state had not accused any one of these men of throwing the bomb; the state had never named anyone as the thrower of the bomb; the Illinois law said that an accessory could only be tried after the guilt of the principal had been proved; yet the eight men had been convicted of "a conspiracy with an unknown" to throw the fatal bomb. Three had been sentenced to fifteen years in the penitentiary; one had blown off his head in prison; four had been hanged. The people of Chicago had forced their execution by the weight of their pressure. Because of this and the legal adage that "who does through another does himself," Darrow believed that every last citizen who had demanded the execution had been, individually, their executioners.

He had gone frequently to the penitentiary to visit with Fielden, Neebe and Schwab, the three men who had escaped the hangman's noose, and had come to love them as good and innocent men, guilty only of the crime of striving to free mankind from its economic shackles. The flaming article in which he demonstrated that the eight men had been railroaded in a corrupt and illegal trial had been his first brilliant paper on social justice.

With the passage of the months and the growing realization that the eight men had been convicted, not of having conspired to have a bomb thrown, but of having been opposed to the type of capitalism practiced by such industrialists as Pullman and McCormick; with the ever-spreading knowledge that the sole conspiracy had been committed by the state—the manufacture of evidence by the maniacal police captain, Schaack; the arrest of innocent men who were offered their release to turn state's evidence; the hand-picking of a jury panel which would be sure to convict, and the refusal to excuse jurors who swore they could not give the accused a fair trial; the lynch decisions handed down by Judge Gary—it became

47

clear that the citizens of Chicago who had cried out for the death of these men were not merely executioners by proxy, but actually murderers of innocent men in a legal crime far greater in its implications than the heinous crime committed by the irresponsible lunatic who threw the bomb. The Haymarket bomb had destroyed seven lives; in Darrow's opinion the trial of the anarchists had bombed the Constitution, the Bill of Rights, the structure of legal justice for all men upon which the people of the New World were trying to nurture a free and intelligent social organism.

The philosophy of the four men who had been hanged and the three who went to prison was for the larger part German socialism, mixed with lesser degrees of trade unionism and anarchism; yet they were universally called anarchists by the press, as all his life Darrow was to be called an anarchist, because that was deemed to be the most effective whip with which to beat the dog. All seven were family men, hard working, honest. All agreed that private property was the source from which flowed the evils of wage slavery, poverty, misery, crime, injustice, war. Since force was used against the workingman whenever he attempted to better himself, force alone could free him. The *Alarm* and *Arbeiter-Zeitung*, which had been edited by two of the executed men, ran frequent articles on the virtues and values of dynamite.

The year 1886 was to have been the great year of liberation for American labor, which had had to work from sixty to eighty hours a week to earn its living. On May first unions all over the country were going out on strike for the eight-hour day. The movement was strongest in Chicago, where "railroad and gas-company employees, iron-mill workers, meat packers and plumbers were out on strike for shorter hours, eighty thousand participants in all." Police and state militia guarded the streets, but May first passed in perfect quiet. Some employers locked out their employees; others agreed to arbitrate and cut working hours.

On May third the locked-out employees of the McCormick plant, who had been on strike since March, clashed with the men who had replaced them as they came out of the plant, the police killing one striker, shooting five or six others, beating many with clubs. August Spies, who witnessed the battle, rushed back to the *Arbeiter-Zeitung* to write up the conflict and to call for a protest meeting the following night in the Haymarket Square.

The following night proved to be cold and dreary. Instead of the twenty thousand workers expected, only twelve hundred showed up, Parsons, Spies and Fielden addressing them from the seat of a wagon that had been left at one end of the huge square. Mayor Carter Harrison was there to make sure no incendiary talk was indulged in; he heard passionate speeches against the injustices of the system, the insecurity of the workingman, the evils of the Pinkertons and the deputies being used to slug workers, the misrepresentation of labor by the capitalist press; but the mayor found the speeches peaceable. At a little after ten, while Fielden was winding up the meeting, it began to drizzle, and within a few minutes only a quarter of the people were left. Mayor Harrison went home. Just as Fielden said, "In conclusion . . ." a hundred and eighty police dashed into the square, led by the sanguinary Captain Bonfield, who had been forbidden by the mayor to bring police to the meeting. Fielden, ordered to break up the already ended meeting, replied, "We are peaceable," and began to descend from the wagon, when suddenly a bomb was thrown from one of the buildings above the square, exploding near the front rank of the police.

That bomb killed not only seven officers, but the socialist and eight-hour movements as well. Chicago insisted that somebody be prosecuted, and led by the Chicago *Tribune*, which was owned by the McCormicks of the harvester plant where the strikers and scabs had battled the day before, the Haymarket Riot was used to discredit labor in general and to railroad its outstanding leaders through "trial by prejudice." When in 1893, by working with thousands of prominent Americans, Darrow helped persuade Governor Altgeld to pardon the only three survivors, he was able to say publicly, "The Bar in general throughout the state, and elsewhere, came to believe that the conviction was brought about through malice and hatred and that the trial was unfair and the judgment of the court unsound."

The people of Chicago, he knew, did not like the feeling of being murderers; that was why they now turned upon Governor Altgeld with fury and venom for pardoning, as innocent of the crime charged, Fielden, Schwab and Neebe, who had already been in the penitentiary for seven years. Since that act of justice was now in process of destroying Altgeld both as a political leader and a man, it was the case of the Haymarket Riot that started Darrow on his lifelong crusade against the conspiracy laws and capital punishment. There had been no way for Governor Altgeld to reprieve the four men who had been hanged by the neck, nor the one who had committed suicide, and there was no way to reprieve the bloodthirsty Chicagoans who had demanded their death. Altgeld had turned them into official murderers? Then destroy Altgeld; make him the foulest human that ever lived, the destroyer of civilization.

Because of his love for Altgeld and his distress at the abuse heaped upon his friend, Darrow consented to run for Congress in the 1896 campaign on the same ticket with Altgeld, who was seeking re-election and a vindication of his political and economic liberalism. He had little liking for professional politics, in which he had had a laboratory course while city counsel; he preferred to remain outside the arena so he could choose his own battlefields. But he was overjoyed to see Governor Altgeld rise once again in his full vitality and intelligence, after the eclipse and illness he had suffered for the 1893 Haymarket pardons. The Pullman strike had become one of the issues of the campaign: Altgeld was out to wrest control of the Democratic party from Grover Cleveland, who had defeated the working people by sending Federal troops into Chicago in 1894; Darrow was out to indict "government by injunction."

However, the major issues were Free Silver and Free Golden Oratory. Both Darrow and Altgeld embraced Free Silver, Altgeld because he wanted to defeat gold-standard Cleveland, Darrow because he thought it would be a good vote catcher for a program which was the most progressive ever offered to the American public. But they were neither of them so delighted when they found they had to embrace, along with Free Silver, the gaseous form of William Jennings Bryan, boy orator of the Platte.

Bryan, who was a member of a contested delegation to the Democratic convention, was invited to Chicago by Altgeld, expenses paid, because Altgeld wanted to stop him from splitting the Free Silver candidates and from making a nuisance of himself by begging and conniving for votes. Yet four days after his arrival, when the Illinois delegation convened at the Sherman House, to Altgeld's disgust there was Bryan, "buttonholing all the delegates."

"Tell Bryan to go home," Altgeld finally snapped; "he stands no more chance of being nominated for President than I, and I was born in Germany." Bryan had no legitimate role to play at the convention, yet once he got his feet onto the platform as chairman of a debate on Free Silver, almost the first words of his rehearsed Chautauqua sermon cast the mesmeric spell he had hoped for. But when he finished with: ". . . we will answer demands for a gold standard by saying to them: 'You shall not press down upon the brow of labor this crown of thorns; you shall not crucify mankind upon a cross of gold!' " men went mad with emotional joy, threw their hats in the air, shouted and wept. . . . The election was lost and the Democratic party went into eclipse and bondage for almost sixteen years; the cause of liberalism and the working people was shackled to an opportunistic demagogue who embarrassed his fellow liberals by being for the right causes for the wrong reasons.

The next day, when the sonorous Bryan had swept the convention hall like a typhoon, Altgeld asked Darrow, "I have been thinking over Bryan's speech. What did he say, anyway?"

Darrow didn't get a chance to answer that question fully until 1925, during the "Scopes monkey trial," when these two, each representing the convictions of tens of millions of followers, locked horns in one of the most fantastic battles over religion ever waged.

Darrow stumped the state, campaigning for Altgeld, Bryan and the Democratic party. When the votes were at last counted Bryan had been defeated for President, Altgeld for governor and Darrow for congressman.

After the campaign Darrow returned to his practice, which had begun to include a large colored clientele. In Chicago at the time it was almost impossible for a Negro, even if he had a little money, to get a white lawyer to defend him. When it came to people, Darrow was color blind: he didn't feel sorry for the Negroes; he didn't pity them; he didn't think of them as a racial problem. He liked them as human beings, probably because they had the same childlike quality with which he had been endowed. Every New Year's Eve he went to services in a colored church.

The colored people sitting shoulder to shoulder with the whites on Darrow's undiscriminating benches were nearly always clinic cases. "The wife of a young Negro came to him and told him that her husband had been arrested and charged with murder. She brought humble Negroes to testify to the fact that he was innocent. The family had no money. The woman was pregnant with her third child. She sat in his office, mute, and with her eyes pleaded that he defend her husband. He undertook the case—but it took a long while; witnesses had to be found, detectives employed. Darrow defrayed the expenses of the investigation. The date for the trial was postponed time and again, and the young wife was threatened with eviction. Darrow paid her rent and supported the family—until he got an acquittal for the husband."

Shortly after the Loeb-Leopold case Darrow lectured at the psychiatrists' convention in Richmond, Virginia, after which "a small group of attorneys tendered him a dinner at the Commonwealth Club, sitting up and chatting with him until three in the morning." One of the lawyers exclaimed:

"Mr Darrow, I do not understand how a man of your standing could advocate an equality of the races."

"Why, I don't see why that should worry you. I enjoy the company of intelligent Negroes."

"But what about the purity of the Anglo-Saxon race?"

"Purity of the Anglo-Saxon race," snorted Darrow; "the greatest race of sons of bitches that ever infested the earth. Mind you, if there is such a race, I am one of them, because my ancestors lived in this country for nearly three hundred years. But I do not brag about it; I apologize for it."

Darrow took the routine cases that came to him and did his best with them. Then suddenly a case would flash on the horizon, a case which might prove to be the gateway into the bright future of the twentieth century.

In the town of Oshkosh, Wisconsin, three men were arrested for having organized a strike. The leader of the strike was Thomas I. Kidd, an old friend of Darrow's and general secretary of the Amalgamated Woodworkers' International Union, whose office was in Chicago. Kidd had consulted Darrow frequently on legal matters pertaining to his union and sent other workers to him who wanted to draw up constitutions or arbitrate with their employers. The men were accused of criminal conspiracy; in a very definite sense it was a continuation of the Debs conspiracy case; through his studies in connection with the Debs case Darrow knew more about conspiracy laws than any lawyer in America.

George M. Paine owned a lumber company in Oshkosh which distributed sash and doors throughout fourteen states. The plant employed sixteen hundred workers and, in Paine's figures, "was worth a million dollars." The average wage of the sixteen hundred workers for a ten-hour day was ninety-six cents; skilled mechanics, who had been with him from eight to ten years, received for operating dangerous saw machines a dollar and a quarter a day. Contravening the Wisconsin law which made it a crime to employ children under fourteen, Paine had the hunger-driven fathers sign false age affidavits, thus enabling him to employ children from ten years up. Since he could get these children for sixty-five cents a day and women for eighty cents, he was gradually discharging the men and replacing them with their wives and children; each replacement made him an additional profit per worker of from thirty to forty cents a day, and as a good businessman he knew that a profit was a profit. Though the Wisconsin law made weekly wage payments mandatory, he paid his men once a month, thus operating three quarters of the time on their withheld wages.

Each morning when Paine's employees were all inside the factory, the gates were locked behind them. No one could leave his work to go to the toilet without express permission, and no unnecessary talking was allowed. When the workday was over the gates were unlocked so that the workers could go home. Darrow observed that the main difference between the Paine Lumber Company and the Wisconsin penitentiary was that the workers were not allowed to sleep on the premises. The sixteen hundred Paine employees lived in a jungle slum of shacks and tenements beside the Oshkosh railroad tracks. The efforts of the fathers to feed, clothe, house, educate and keep healthy their families of from three to eight were Herculean and had brought a daily toll of hardship, suffering and deprivation. Paine admitted that his company was making a considerable and consistent profit.

Sitting with these undisputed facts before him, Darrow asked himself the question: "Who's a criminal?"

Was a criminal the hungry man who broke into a grocery store? The young desperado whose unbalanced mind had been inflamed by stories of gunmen? The lover who killed out of jealousy? Or was it a responsible man like George M. Paine who daily kept bread from the mouths of some six thousand human beings, who daily committed acts of fraud against the state of Wisconsin? It was possible to measure the amount of damage done by a criminal who held up a bank at the point of a gun, who killed a guard, but where was one to find a yardstick with which to measure the suffering and misery, the illness and deprivation, the hundreds of thousands of hours of fatigue and frustration of the stunted bodies and stunted minds of the people who made it possible for George M. Paine to earn his riches?

Darrow did not want to see Thomas I. Kidd, George Zentner and Michael Troiber go to prison, but the issue was bigger than that. He did not want to see labor unions wiped out by the star-chamber conspiracy charges, but the issue was even bigger than that. The issue could be put in a few simple words, words that struck to the vitals of the national problem: was America going to develop into an economic democracy or into an industrial slave state? Were conscienceless men like Pullman and Paine to be permitted to destroy the dream of the New World?

He packed his bag, moved to Oshkosh, contacted two local attorneys and selected his jury. By quiet but relentless cross-examination he brought to light the simple and to him familiar facts of the case. When one quarter of the men in the Paine plant had been replaced by their women and children, the workers had organized and sent a letter to George Paine with four requests: he was to stop replacing men at the machines with women and children; he was to obey the Wisconsin law and pay his workers once a week; he was to grant a raise in wages, and he was to recognize their union. Paine threw the letter into the wastebasket, called a meeting of the Oshkosh Manufacturers' Association, of which he had been president. It was agreed that they would fight the union co-operatively.

When Paine failed to answer the letter sent him a committee of employees visited him and asked him why. Paine replied, "Because your letter was unbusinesslike." Notwithstanding the decision of the Manufacturers' Association to fight the union co-operatively, Paine told the men that any worker who had anything to request was to come to the office, where his demands would be considered. Two of his oldest workmen took him seriously; the next day they went to his office to ask for a raise. The first was told:

"You get out of here or I'll give you a raise in the pants!" The second was told, "Go to hell, God damn you. I can get a damn sight better man than you are for a dollar and a quarter a day."

The men struck. Paine replaced as many of them as he could with non-union workers, then appealed to the courts of Oshkosh to grant him an injunction against the strikers, which would force them to return to work. The court replied that in America workmen had a right to cease work, even in concert, when they chose. The workers called upon Kidd to come up from Chicago and show them how to conduct their strike.

In the fourteen weeks of the strike there was no attempt to injure the Paine property. Only two non-union men were molested. Paine brought in Pinkerton labor spies, and the mayor asked for state militia. In the one disorderly scene of the fourteen weeks the strikers clashed with the militia by a gristmill, and one worker was killed. Winter was coming on; the union's funds were gone; the workers were penniless; Paine's plant was still operating; the strike was lost, and the men returned to work under the best conditions they could get. Determined that there should never again be a strike in his plant, and encouraged by the fact that Darrow had not been able to set his precedent against criminal-conspiracy charges in the Debs case, Paine persuaded the district attorney of Oshkosh to arrest Kidd, Zentner and Troiber on charges of "conspiracy to injure the business of the Paine Lumber Company." Once again with the eyes of the industrial world upon him, Darrow was face to face with the greatest weapon against the freedom of the American people.

He rose to present his closing argument without a paper in his hand, nor did he once in the two days of summary consult a note, yet his address to the jury, in effect a funeral oration on the passing of the nineteenth century, is one of the outstanding social documents of its time, enunciating

54

in such logical terms the rights of persons over the rights of property that it helped lead the way toward a new ordering of life in America. Darrow touched greatness for the first time in his appeal; he was to touch it several times more in his long and turbulent life.

Darrow's technique in his closing argument was once again that its appeal was educative rather than legal, aimed at the millions of the public rather than the twelve jurors in the box, designed to change the thinking of the nation rather than the mere keeping of his clients out of jail.

His first step was to show that the state of Wisconsin was not the complainant, but that Paine, the wealthiest man in Oshkosh, had prevailed upon the district attorney to file the complaint. "Paine has used almost everything else in Oshkosh, men, women, little children. And now the district attorney has made an assignment of the state to him." He then moved to strip away the pretenses in the case, and, as in the Debs case, to indict the prosecution.

". . . Ordinarily men are brought into a criminal court because they are bad. Thomas I. Kidd is brought into this court because he is good; if he had been mean and selfish and designing, if he had held out his hand to take the paltry bribes that these men pass out this case would not be here today. Kidd is a defendant in these criminal proceedings because he loved his fellow men, and this is not the first case of the kind in the history of the world, and I am afraid it will not be the last. *It is not the first time that evil men, men who are themselves criminals, have used the law for the purpose of bringing righteous ones to death or to jail.*"

Darrow took the jury through the history of the conspiracy laws as they had developed from the earliest days in England and as he had painstakingly tracked it down for the Debs defense. With this picture clearly outlined, he painted the conspiracy that had been entered into between the Paines and the district attorney. Nathan Paine, son of the owner, had said, "Kidd is the one I want!" but since even in Oshkosh they could not indict Kidd for conspiring with himself, the prosecution had dragged in two obscure men who had been captains of pickets—and had forgotten to prosecute them. Paine had then secured the appointment of a lawyer and Sunday-school teacher by the name of Houghton, at fifteen dollars a day, to act as special prosecutor, and Houghton had sent for employees of the Paine plant, demanding of them as they walked in his door:

"Are you here to convict Kidd?"

Houghton produced a witness by the name of Jones, who testified that he had heard Kidd say in a public meeting,

"If scabs went to work in Chicago as they did in Oshkosh, they would find themselves in the hospital the next day." Not one workman, not even those threatened with the loss of their jobs, could corroborate this "inciting-to-violence" statement, nor could the secretaries sent by Paine to take records of everything said at the meetings. Darrow laid the blame for this perjury on the shoulders of Houghton rather than Mr Jones.

"There is a conspiracy, dark and damnable, and I want to say boldly that someone is guilty of one of the foulest conspiracies that ever disgraced a free nation. If my clients are innocent, other men are guilty of entering the temple of justice and using the law, which was made to guard and protect and shelter you and me and these defendants, for the purpose of hounding innocent men to a prison pen. It is an ancient law that a man who conspired to use the courts to destroy his fellow men was guilty of treason to the state. He had laid his hand upon the state itself; he had touched the bulwark of human liberty. When George Paine raised a hand to strike a blow against the liberty of Thomas Kidd he raised a hand to strike a blow against your freedom and mine, and *he conspired to destroy the institutions under which we live.* There are criminals in this case, criminals who . . . have not been guilty of the paltry crime of conspiring to save their fellow men, but criminals who have conspired against the liberty of their fellows and against the country in which they live."

It was Darrow's good fortune that the opposing attorneys made tactical blunders which outraged the sensibilities of the American public. Houghton reached the height of his legal virtuosity when, seeking to establish a precedent for the conviction, he went back a hundred years to the case of a man who had been convicted for writing a poem lauding Thomas Paine and his *Rights of Man.*

"How Brother Houghton's mouth would have watered," said Darrow in mordant sarcasm, "if he had been given a chance to convict Thomas Paine for daring to proclaim the rights of man!"

Houghton should never have been in the case at all, for the district attorney's office was equipped to handle the case without special appointments. Darrow rubbed Houghton's nose in the fifteen dollars a day he was getting for this prosecution until the man should have become so housebroken that he would never again wet the penal code in his uncontainable excitement at the prospect of making some extra money.

Then he plunged into the essence of the conflict: shall

workingmen be allowed to combine to better their conditions or shall they be convicted as criminals for these activities?

"I take it that in a free country, in a country where George M. Paine does not rule supreme, every person has a right to lay down the tools of his trade if he shall choose. Not only that, but in a free country where liberty of speech is guaranteed, every man has a right to go to his fellow man and say, 'We are out on strike. We are in a great battle for liberty. We are waging war for our fellow men. For God's sake, come with us and help.' Has it come to that point . . . under the guarantee of the freedom of speech and under the Constitution, that a free man cannot go to his neighbor and implore him not to work? If a jury or a court should write a verdict like that, it would be the death knell to human liberty."

Throughout he kept weaving his elemental lesson in economics: "Paine is not supporting these people; these men, women and children are supporting him." All along he kept enunciating the heretical notion that the jury could not convict Kidd, Zentner and Troiber because they were not on trial at all—that the jury system was on trial and that they could convict only the jury system by a verdict of guilty!

Then, for the first time, in this woodworkers' conspiracy case, Darrow utilized the most powerful contradiction of his philosophy: he excoriated the prosecution until they wanted to crawl inside their skins and pull their skins in behind them —after which he pleaded with the jury to forgive them, for they, too, were innocent victims of their heredity and environment.

Once again Darrow had his jury of businessmen and farmers leaning forward in their seats. In closing his case he brought into focus the historical perspective by showing them the part they were playing in fashioning the future of their people.

"Men do not build for today; they do not build for tomorrow. They build for the centuries, for the ages, and when we look back it is perhaps the despised criminal and outlaw . . . who has lifted the world upward and onward toward the blessed brotherhood which one day will come. Here is Thomas I. Kidd; it is a matter of the smallest consequence to him or to me what you do, and I say it as sincerely as I ever spoke a word. No man ever entered this struggle for human liberty without measuring the cost, and the jail is one of the costs that must be measured with the rest. I do not appeal for him; that cause is too narrow for me, much as I love him and long as I have worked by his side. I appeal to you not for Thomas Kidd, but I appeal to you for the long line—the long, long line reaching back through the ages and forward to the years to come—the long line of despoiled and downtrodden people of the earth. I appeal to you for those men who rise in the morning before daylight comes and who go home at night when the light has faded from the sky and give their life, their strength, their toil to make others rich and great. I appeal to you in the name of those women who are offering up their lives to this modern god of gold, and I appeal to you in the name of those little children, the living and the unborn. . . ."

The jury brought in a verdict of "not guilty"; with the weight of the centuries on their shoulders they could do no less.

Chapter Five

"Let Me Speak for the Children of the Poor"

SHORTLY AFTER his return from Oshkosh Darrow began one of the most pleasant periods of his life. He joined forces with Francis S. Wilson, a young cousin of Jessie's who had been born and raised just thirty miles from Darrow's home in Ohio. Wilson was short, husky, handsome, jovial, and made a delightful companion. Together they rented bachelor quarters close to Hull House.

"The Langdon Apartments had just been erected as model tenements on the corner of Des Plaines and Bunker streets in the ghetto of Chicago," says Wilson. "We were among the opulent tenants and had two three-room flats made into one, as a result of which we had two bedrooms. . . .

"Our guests were mostly writers, painters and social-service workers who liked to sit at Darrow's feet. They were bohemianish, inasmuch as they preferred to come in through the windows rather than the door and sit on the floor rather than chairs. Darrow's books were scattered around in a miscellaneous fashion . . . Frequently of an evening he would read aloud from Nietzsche or Marx or some Russian author, and I would make my exit shortly after for the purpose of seeking younger companionship."

The Langdon Apartments became known as a "Co-operative Living Club. Distinguished artists, writers, professors, scientists, musicians, labor leaders and liberals from Europe and America came to dinner in the common dining room and discussed public affairs. His closest neighbors were Gertrude Barnum and Helen Todd, daughter of a wealthy Minnesota miller who, through Darrow's intervention, became Chicago's first factory inspector for child labor. Darrow and Helen

Todd became intimate friends. His most frequently uttered sentiment to her as she wove incessantly from ottoman to chair to sofa, from job to job and social theory to social panacea, was the epitome of his criticism of most social workers from above:

"Light, Helen, light!"

Gertrude Barnum says, "There is nothing in my life of which I am so proud as of Clarence Darrow's faith and friendship. While there never was any romance between us —I was frightened by his theories of free love and, because of his dirty fingernails and rather greasy hair, found him unattractive physically—he surely made all the men of my set look like pygmies and had much to do with my remaining a spinster. My contributions to labor organization, Americanization and adult education had no more generous or faithful backer; he never once refused my appeals for funds for needy individuals or worthy causes. No matter how small or despised the groups who appealed for his educational talks, he never refused."

The anomalous part of Darrow's leadership at the Langdon was that he was opposed to the work being done at Hull House. "Jane Addams spent forty arduous years appealing to the more fortunate to share wealth and opportunity with the 'underprivileged.' Darrow supported and defended the downtrodden in their own self-help organizations to improve their conditions by collective bargaining and strikes, ever urging them to scorn the stigma of philanthropic aid, to rise in their own strength and take what was rightfully theirs; in short, to cease being underprivileged."

Partly because of the confining influences of his first marriage, but mostly because he was a leader of the general revolt of the day, one of whose chief planks was free love as a road to individual liberty, Clarence openly avowed that he wanted no more of marriage. He preached ardently against his young friends allowing themselves to be caught in its mesh—possibly diverting a few. X had also believed in free love; she and Clarence had entered their pact with the clear understanding that they would remain together only as long as they desired, that they would not permit themselves to drift into marriage and that each would be free to terminate whenever he wished, without apologies or explanations. He had rented a room in the home of X and her mother, ostensibly as a boarder, but after a few months he learned that free love was not particularly free when he had to come home every night. He found that X was emotionally incapable of living up to their bargain; she loved him with a terrifying intensity which made her, against her own will and better judgment, jealous and possessive. She insisted that he account for every moment of his time spent away from her, showed up unexpectedly at places where he had gone without her, gave him the feeling that he was being spied upon and ended by causing tearful and hysterical scenes when he went out with other women. For Darrow this possessiveness soon became oppressive.

Though he had moved into the Langdon Apartments to recapture his bachelordom, he and X went to plays and meetings, often had dinner together and on week ends would accidentally meet at the same resorts in the country. He did not feel any necessity of being faithful to her, for if he had to be faithful he might as well have married. While social-service workers were not the most delectable prey, he favored them because he could enjoy a little intelligent conversation before he got around to feeling amorous. He had matured since the days when he took women for their sheer physical pleasure; his friendships were now confined to those in whom he found an emotional sympathy. Gertrude Barnum insists there was nothing of the philanderer about him. "People worshiped the ground he walked on, men and women and children alike." With the men he loved he fought for liberal causes, worked and studied; with the women he loved it seemed only natural that their love should be completely expressed. One of his associates remarks, "There was never any such thing as conscious seduction on his part; the women always showed themselves open and willing."

After he had been indicted in Los Angeles he was greatly depressed by a report that the district attorney was going to introduce into evidence a photograph purported to have been taken of him as he left the house of a beautiful Pasadena widow at dawn. One of his friends consoled him by saying, "Don't be downcast, Clarence; your enemies will believe the worst of you, even without photographs, and your friends will know it is a fake. They will know that if you had spent the night in the home of a beautiful widow you wouldn't leave at dawn. You would stay for breakfast."

Each morning the roommates walked the two miles to the office, stopping on the way at Race's Fish House for breakfast. Wilson tells that Darrow was full of boyishness and had a most delicious chuckle. He liked to laugh for the sake of laughter. He was fond of limericks and had the Midwest farmer's zest for bawdy jokes. A woman who was late for a dinner appointment explained that she and her husband had been detained because her son had dropped one of his balls out of the window, and she had had to go out in the dark to hunt for it.

"What a terrible accident," murmured Darrow. Every time

he met the woman after that he would inquire solicitously, "And how is the little boy now?"

By this time he had already grown what his friends called "inordinately fond and proud" of his son Paul, an open-faced lanky lad of sixteen who resembled Amirus. He took the boy with him for companionship on many of his trips. At sixteen, when he had graduated from high school, he worked for a short time for A. C. McClurg, the publisher, where most of the men were Dartmouth graduates. They sold the father the idea of sending his son to Dartmouth. At the opening of the school year Clarence took the none-too-complaisant Paul to New Hampshire, saying, "You stay until Christmas, and if you don't like it you can come home and take a job." When he left Paul behind he gave him only one piece of advice:

"Never get into a poker game unless there is a limit."

Like most parental advice, it was precisely the kind the father himself was unable to follow. His parting shot was, "If you ever get into difficulty of any kind, you had better tell me, because I don't think you can get into anything I haven't been in."

For a man who has once been married, bachelordom, no matter how exciting, is an interregnum. One night in the spring of 1899 Darrow went to lecture on Omar Khayyám at the White City Club, which was made up of artists, writers and musicians. After the lecture he was introduced by his friend John H. Gregg, originator of the shorthand system, to a young woman with auburn-colored hair, a pink-and-white complexion, wearing a wine-colored jacket trimmed with baby lamb and a pert hat to match.

"Of course you've met Mr Darrow," said Gregg.

"Sorry," replied Ruby Hamerstrom, "but I haven't."

Struck by the sparkle and alertness of the young woman's eyes, Darrow asked Miss Hamerstrom to make an appointment for dinner. She declined. He continued to block her way, talking to her; when the caretaker had turned out the lights he held her hand in the dark, refusing to let her go until she agreed to meet him again or at least give him her address. Miss Hamerstrom finally slipped past him to join the Greggs, who were waiting for her on the sidewalk.

Smitten, Darrow sat before his fireplace and composed messages to the auburn-haired girl which he sent through the Greggs, begged his friends to get another appointment for him and ended, man-fashion, by accusing Mrs Gregg of not delivering his messages. Ruby Hamerstrom was engaged to a New York stockbroker at the time. She went to her fiancé, who was visiting in Chicago, and said, "If you think I should,

I'll go to dinner with him just once with the Greggs, in order to tell him that it's not Mrs Gregg's fault that I have made no appointments with him."

"I can't see any harm in going to dinner with him—just once," replied her fiancé.

Ruby Hamerstrom was born in Galesburg, Illinois, where Knox College is located. Her mother was a "Swedish beauty with black hair who wrote nice things for the religious magazines." Her father was in charge of the blacksmith shops of the Chicago, Burlington and Quincy Railroad. Ruby dropped out of high school at fourteen to take care of her bedridden mother and six younger brothers but found time to read widely in the Knox College library. She did some writing, but her mother burned what she wrote, saying, "Anything that isn't religious is sinful." At eighteen she resigned from the Lutheran Church. "She took her small savings out of the bank and left for Chicago to become a newspaper woman . . . two long braids of auburn hair dangling down her back."

Ruby was twenty-six and was on the woman's page of the Chicago *Evening Post* when she met Darrow, who was then forty-two. She had a fast, well-informed mind, steadfastness of character; though she was not beautiful she had a colorful and charming personality.

"I lived on the west side," said Ruby, "and I planned with Mrs Gregg who was going to have dinner with us, that I should stay over with her so that Darrow wouldn't see me home. When he met us in a Loop restaurant that night he said,

" 'I have to lecture over west tonight, and if you don't mind coming to hear me speak I can take you home after the meeting.'

" 'Oh no,' replied Ruby, 'I'm staying with Mrs Gregg tonight.'

" 'I don't see any reason why you shouldn't go to the meeting with Mr Darrow,' said Mrs Gregg.

"Finally I capitulated. We took Mrs Gregg home. Then in the middle of the Rush Street Bridge, with the wind and the rain blowing in our faces, Darrow stopped, took off one of my gloves and stuck my hand with his into his overcoat pocket.

" 'I've never known anyone I liked so much—right from the start,' he said; 'that's why I think I ought to tell you. I've been married. I never intend to marry again.'

" 'That's fine,' answered Ruby, 'because I'm leaving in two weeks to be married myself.'

" 'You're not! Well, we'll have to devise ways to break

your engagement. People who like each other as much as we do shouldn't be separated.'

"I had fallen in love with him that first night when he lectured on Khayyám," said Ruby. "That was why I didn't want to see him again. But it was four years before I dared to marry him."

In 1900 Darrow persuaded the now ill and nearly destitute Altgeld to join his firm in the place of Morris St P. Thomas, who had retired. After his defeat in 1896 Altgeld had not wanted to return to the practice of law. "He had come to rather despise that profession; he felt that its strongest men sold themselves to destroy people, to perpetuate and intensify the poverty of the oppressed and enlarge their burdens." Darrow made him titular head of Altgeld, Darrow and Thompson. This was a gesture of courage and love on Darrow's part, for not only could Altgeld bring the partnership no business, but his name attached to it would keep certain corporation business away.

The turn of the century was a happy time for Clarence. Frankie Wilson was a gay home companion; he had Altgeld next to him in his office; he was growing ever more enchanted with Ruby.

He lectured to ever-growing audiences on scientific and literary subjects; he would not only lecture without compensation, but he would pay his own expenses to get to an audience in a neighboring city, a type of monetary indifference which made him a plague to professional lecturers.

His law business prospered; as always, many of the cases had social implications. And he continued to try negligence cases, such as streetcar accidents, in which his percentage might be as high as five to fifteen thousand dollars. His conduct in money matters was still erratic:

"The head of a Polish family was permanently injured in the Illinois Steel mills of South Chicago. I arranged with Darrow to take the case for a contingency fee of fifty per cent, the usual method. Darrow's handling it induced the company to settle for twenty thousand dollars without court action. After the check was sent in I was knocked off my pins when Darrow said that ten dollars was all he could really charge, because most of the work was done over the phone and in a personal conference with one of the mill lawyers. He also saw to it that the victim invested some of his money in a home and arranged to safeguard the balance. . . . I doubt if he ever discussed this matter. . . . He wanted no backslapping."

There is a saying that in the breast of every lawyer lies

buried the wreck of a poet. This was particularly true of Clarence Darrow, who confided to Wilson, "The one thing I want most of all to be is a writer." In 1900 Hearst invaded Chicago; he hired Darrow to incorporate the *Evening American*. So ardent were the established newspapers to spread the one and only truth, they sent out men with clubs to beat up vendors of other papers. As general counsel for Hearst, Darrow soon had his hands full instituting suits. The Hearst account was profitable, but its importance lay in the fact that it afforded Darrow the one further activity necessary for his full expression.

His first essays, later published under the title of *A Persian Pearl, and Other Essays,* are appeals for the realistic and critical approach to life. Written in an age when Whitman and Khayyám were condemned as immoral, unfit for the eyes of innocent youth, they remain to this day lucid, forceful and courageous. Writing of the philosophy of Khayyám, he was able to state by indirection his attitude toward scientific criminology. "Every son of man travels an unbeaten path—a road beset with dangers and temptations that no other wanderer met. His footsteps can be judged only in the full knowledge of the strength and light he had, the burden he carried, the obstacles and temptations he met and a thorough knowledge of every open and secret motive that impelled him."

When, after Altgeld's death, Darrow ran for the state legislature feeling he must carry on Altgeld's fight, "he advised the voters that he did not need the job. In his whimsical way he told the audience not much could be done, except that he might be able to unlock the prison doors and set some of the inmates free." When the votes were counted he had received more than all the opposition combined.

By now, having reached forty-five, Darrow began to think of himself as approaching middle age. His accomplishments thus far had been meager: he had published a book of literary essays, a few short stories, a number of controversial pamphlets that had been transcribed from his lectures. He had failed in his efforts to defeat government by injunction and save the American Railway Union from destruction at the hands of his former employers, but in defending the woodworkers' union he had been successful in trying extortionist-capitalism before the bar of public opinion. Yet his efforts were unfocused: aside from his general campaign for tolerance he had consecrated himself to no one task. His enemies among the employer-church-moralist groups called him "a radical, argumentative, opinionated, anarchistic busybody who muddied the waters of everything he touched. . . ."

When, of all the attorneys in the United States, he was chosen by John Mitchell, president of the United Mine Workers, to lead the anthracite-coal miners' fight for existence, the fact was announced calmly at the tail end of a long newspaper column. By the time the hearing before President Theodore Roosevelt's commission was in full swing the name of Clarence Darrow was being blazoned in headlines across the continent, and America had set up a new idol to worship —and at whom to fling offal.

Darrow was elated at the invitation to take charge of the miners' case in this greatest industrial crisis in American history. It was the first strike in which the entire public participated, for had not coal been proven to be as much of a public utility as water or gas? The strike in the anthracite fields had been called in May 1902; though it was now only October, industry was verging on collapse; railroad schedules had been cut to a basic minimum; in spite of the sharp rise in the price of coal, in spite of the imminent misery of a heatless winter, the public was solidly in sympathy with the coal miners and was expressing that sympathy in audible and concrete terms.

To Darrow the most hopeful aspect of the upheaval was that for the first time in industrial disputes the operators had agreed to accept the decision handed down by the commission. The Senate committee investigating the railroad strike of 1894 had been empowered only to listen to evidence and submit recommendations to the President. The Coal Commission of 1902-03 had the power, ceded to it by the operators in their last moments of desperation, not only to hand down a decision, but to enforce its awards. This seemed like coming forward eight hundred years in eight; at last industry was to be made responsible to the government.

Not that the operators had ceded with good grace: only four days before their capitulation their spokesman, George Baer, president of the Reading Railroad, of the Philadelphia and Reading Coal and Iron Company, of the Lehigh and Wilkes-Barre Coal and Iron Company, of the Temple Iron Company, etc., etc., had taken the most hostile attitude toward President Theodore Roosevelt, who was attempting to avert a disaster for the public and to send the miners back to work on a settlement satisfactory to both sides.

"The duty of the hour is not to waste time negotiating with the fomenters of this anarchy and insolent defiers of the law," said Mr Baer, "but to do what was done in the war of the Rebellion, restore the majesty of law and re-establish order and peace at any cost. The government is a *contemptible fail-*

ure if it can only protect the lives and property and secure the comfort of the people by compromising with the violators of law and the instigators of violence and crime."

Somehow, neither President Roosevelt nor the Congress nor the Supreme Court nor the voting citizens enjoyed hearing themselves called a contemptible failure. Yet this was the mildest of the four immortal phrases minted by George Baer, four phrases which were to do more to bring about industrial democracy in America than the heroic flailing of Darrow and his fellow liberals.

Darrow saw that although the discovery of the anthracite-coal beds in Pennsylvania had proved a source of great wealth to American industry and a boon to consumers who needed a cheap fuel, it had from the outset been a curse to the miners who drew it from the veins of the earth. It became the most difficult and dangerous industry in which men could earn their living, for six men out of a thousand were killed every year; hundreds were maimed by explosions and cave-ins; few escaped the ravages of asthma, bronchitis, chronic rheumatism, consumption, heart trouble. By the age of fifty the miners were worn out and broken, good for little but the human slag heap.

If a miner were killed in the mine the company paid nothing to his family, and his neighbors chipped in to pay for his burial. If he were injured in an explosion, his legs or back broken, the company would not provide medical care—unless the injured man signed a company release.

In spite of their dangers and difficulties, Darrow perceived that miners were known the world over as one of the most courageous and independent craft of men to be found. They were courageous because only courageous men could descend, day after day, into the dust-laden blackness. They were independent because a majority of them were either "contract miners" or worked for contract miners who were paid by the carload of coal delivered to the operators and over whom, in the endless dark labyrinths of a mine, it was impossible to exercise the kind of supervision and discipline maintained over workers in a factory. With these attributes of courage and independence, miners could have made the highest quality of citizenry; instead they were kept in a continuous state of ignorance and inescapable debt which made them a potential source of peril to the continuation of a democracy. "Why?" Darrow asked.

Was it imperative that these hundreds of thousands of people be kept in a state of destitution? Was it economically inescapable? The figures at his elbow did not seem to indicate so. The anthracite mines, which were confined to a small section in Pennsylvania, had been bought up by the competing Pennsylvania railroads who thus made sure of getting their haulage —and a return of as high as forty-five per cent on their investment.

Through his work for the railroads Darrow had learned that combination in industry generally resulted in a combination to control prices. With these railroad-owned mines combination also involved a restraint of labor, for the banks owned the railroads which owned the mines; thus the billions of national wealth could be mustered to keep the mineworkers from wresting some iota of power from the hands of the operators; nor was any distinction drawn between good or responsible unions and bad ones.

"We spent four million dollars breaking the last strike, and the union along with it," publicly boasted a coal-mine owner. "It was the best investment we operators ever made!"

After several days of intensive study Darrow packed his valise and set off for the coal towns, to visit the collieries and the rows of unpainted shacks on the flanks of barren mountains in which the miners and their families lived, their only trees or vegetation the piles of black slate that had been segregated from the coal by breaker boys. Some of the shacks were propped up from either side by poles to be kept from caving in. Though their total valuation could not exceed ten dollars, the miners who had to live in them to get work were charged two dollars and fifty cents a month. Each shack contained two or three iron beds, a bureau, a stove, a wooden table and chairs; these constituted the worldly possessions of the families that worked in the mines year after year. And people talked their hearts out to him because he was such a plain and simple cuss, looking and feeling like any other mechanic.

All miners traded at the company stores or they lost their jobs, yet the company store charged from twelve to a hundred per cent above the sum charged by neighboring stores. What most outraged the miners was the practice of charging them two dollars and fifty cents a unit for the explosives necessary for their work and for which the company paid ninety cents, with a similar profit margin superimposed upon all other work equipment. Thus the operators made a profit not only from the miner's work, but from his wage as well, a practice known as "mining the miners." By such ingenious devices the miners, who were alleged to receive the "composite" wage of four hundred and eighty dollars a year, actually received the equivalent of about two hundred dollars' worth of house, food, clothing, coal and work supplies. This afforded them about twelve dollars a month to feed, clothe, medicate, educate, cultivate and make happy their families.

The companies had devised other subtle ways of "mining the

miners." The contract men were paid a fixed sum for delivering a car of coal, but the companies kept increasing the size of the car without increasing the payment. The companies kept their own dockers to check on the quantity in any one car of slate or other waste, with no miners' inspectors allowed to be on hand and no protest possible; these dockers arbitrarily took as much payment out of the miner's wage as they saw fit. The men were paid once a month instead of the twice which the Pennsylvania law demanded; they were paid in lump sums, with no detailed accounts available. The firemen and pumpmen, who received a dollar seventy-five a day, worked a twelve-hour shift and twenty-four hours in a stretch every other Sunday, when the day and night shifts interchanged. They were not allowed off on the Fourth of July, Thanksgiving or Christmas; each year they worked three hundred and sixty-five days, except in leap year—when they worked three hundred and sixty-six.

Schools were provided, but by the time the boys were eleven or twelve they had to climb to the breakers to earn their mite.

"As a school director of Wilkes-Barre, what percentage of the children that went to high school would you say were miners' children?"

"There was no percentage of miners' children," replied Mr Shea. "They got out before they got there."

The little girls could not be used in the mines, but the owners of textile mills, knowing that coal-mining areas were centers of poverty in which they could buy labor for a few pennies a day, set up their mills close to the mines and employed girls from ten years up. In this practice they were encouraged and aided by the railroads that owned the mines, because they could then get the textile business, sell their coal to the mills and, in addition, have the mills feed wages into the miners' families. *The girls were paid from three to seven cents an hour and worked a twelve-hour shift.*

What Darrow found in his researches in the Pennsylvania coal fields was a social philosophy in action. The operators, who wanted a large and docile supply of labor from which to choose their workers, contracted with steamship companies to send agents throughout central Europe to round up families on the promise of a good job and high wages in America, the golden land of opportunity. The eager immigrants were given "free" transportation, the fares being deducted from their subsequent wages; when they reached New York they were loaded onto coal cars and carted like cattle out to Pennsylvania, moved into a company shack and given credit at the "pluck-me" store. From that hour onward a large proportion of them were bound to their jobs as the serfs had been bound to the

68

earth, for any attempt to move on to another locality, another industry, meant imprisonment for skipping these debts. It was not uncommon for families to work from the beginning of the year to the end without ever receiving a dollar in cash.

George Baer proved himself to be a master at *reductio ad absurdum* when he said, "We refuse to submit to arbitration before the Civic Federation, because they are to decide not whether the wages paid are fair, but whether they are sufficient to enable the mineworkers to live, maintain and educate their families in a manner conformable to established American standards and consistent with American citizenship. More impractical suggestion was never formed. It would require many years of examination to determine just what those standards are and to determine whether it meant that a man should earn enough money to send his son to Yale or Harvard or to some modest college like Franklin and Marshall, where we keep down expenses."

Though a number of the earlier mining families had come from Ireland, Wales and Germany, the greater portion of them now were central Europeans: Poles, Austrians, Hungarians, Slavs, Italians, who had made the difficult wrench from the homeland, from their friends and relatives, and had taken the plunge into the unknown to find a better life for themselves and their children. They were for the most part of good racial stock: hard working, independent; despite the fact that some of them had been at odds with the religious, political and economic structures of the country they had left, they were reverent and law abiding. A questioning of the operators revealed few complaints against the miners prior to the strike: they still wanted to take off European holidays; sometimes their propping was so hastily put up, in their scramble to get out the coal, that the roof collapsed and killed everybody under it. The operators did not appear to believe this to be intentional.

The hopes of these venturesome Europeans had been rudely blasted in the Pennsylvania coal mines, where life was harder, uglier, more bitter and more enslaved than the life they had come from. They had had no way of knowing that they had been imported for the very reason that they were accustomed to poverty, because they could subsist on the smallest possible quantities of food, because they could be worked hard for small wages.

"They don't suffer," cried George Baer indignantly when confronted with their plight; "why, they can't even speak English!"

Darrow had been in Wilkes-Barre and the vicinity for only a few days when he perceived that something more than a

69

wage strike was at issue in the coal fields. He determined to present this "something more" to the eagerly waiting public, to present the issue simply and clearly on its broadest sociological base: was it possible for America to become an authentic democracy, to achieve the hopes and promises of its founders, when millions of powerless ones were kept in bondage, forced backward through the centuries until they cowered on the very periphery of animal life? Was not democracy founded on individual justice, on a consideration of certain inalienable human rights? Could a free state continue to grow and prosper, achieve the national unanimity necessary for a nation to become strong and great, when it had a slave state eating at its vitals?

For Clarence Darrow the answer came almost immediately in the form of the Jeddo evictions which proved a tactical blunder of catastrophic proportions.

Despite the promises of the operators to President Theodore Roosevelt that they would not refuse work during the arbitration to former employees on the grounds of union activities, "twelve men were selected from their fellows by mine operator John Markle as men whom he absolutely refused to re-employ at the close of the strike. No definite charge was made against any of these men, whose names sound like a cross cut of all the nations and creeds that helped found America: Nahi, Keenan, Poucun, Polack, Jacquot, Gallagher, Kanyeck, Coll, Dunleavy, Helferty, Demchock, Shovlin. At midnight Sheriff Jacobs was roused from his sleep by an agent of the Markles and told that the evictions must take place the next day.

"A cold drizzle set in early in the morning and continued at intervals until late in the afternoon, when a heavy rainstorm set in. It was almost seven o'clock when seven teams, owned by the Markle Company, set out, carrying non-union men to do the drudgery. They were attended by a company of militia equipped with rifles and a corps of heavily armed Coal and Iron police.

"The stroke caught everybody unprepared. To an appeal that was made by a tenant for a few hours' grace there came a curt refusal and an order to the sheriff to proceed immediately with the work. Houses were stripped bare of their poor furnishings. Women and little children, in spite of their pleadings and tears, were hurried out of the places that had been their homes. A bedridden woman, blind and more than ninety years old, was carried out into the storm. The wife of Henry Coll, a woman of fragile frame and of most delicate health, was not exempted from the rudeness of the evictors and the elements. As a direct consequence of the exposure and shock of that day, so says Henry Coll, she died soon after.

"It was evening when . . . the belongings of the last household . . . had been . . dumped on the highway a quarter of a mile distant.

"Then we drove home with the teams."

"How far was it," asked Darrow, ". . . to the nearest place where they might rent houses?"

"Only about two and a half miles."

"It rained heavily that evening, did it not?"

"Yes, quite heavily."

"Do you know how many children, infants in arms or how many sick persons were among those you evicted?"

"No. I did not see any."

"Did you think of the people you had made homeless as the storm came up that night?" continued Darrow in a rage of scorn. "Did you think of their entire store of personal possessions exposed to the wind and the rain?"

The man who had helped with the evictions could find no answer. But deep in its heart the people of America found one, an answer compounded of pity and terror.

Side by side in nearly every miner's shack hung two unframed pictures: Jesus Christ, who would help them in the next world, and John Mitchell, who was helping them in this. To an extent unknown to any labor leader before him, he enjoyed the respect and confidence of workers, government officials and the general public.

Mitchell had come out of Braidwood, Illinois, the son of a bituminous-coal miner who himself went down into the mines at the age of thirteen. He had spent his spare hours studying, trying to understand the pattern of the world as he found it. When he was twenty he was involved in the 1889 permanent lockout of striking bituminous miners at Spring Valley, Illinois. The strikers' families had suffered from hunger, cold and disease, a brutal tragedy having been averted only when Henry Demarest Lloyd, author of *Wealth against Commonwealth*, arrived with carloads of food and medicine that had been subscribed in Chicago.

John Mitchell was not merely honest; he was incorruptible; he was fearless even in the face of the shocking brutality of the armed Coal and Iron police, and nearly everyone agreed that he was intensely devoted to the cause of the miners. During the heat of the strike, when the operators were hurling brickbats at everyone from President Roosevelt down, the worst they could find to say against Mitchell was that, having come from the bituminous fields of Illinois to the anthracite fields of Pennsylvania, he was consequently an alien and unauthorized to speak for the anthracite miners; that he encouraged European aliens to violence against scabs and nonstrikers.

71

Mitchell writes, "The spring of 1897 found the total number of members of the United Mine Workers reduced to less than nine thousand, there being practically nothing left of the organization in the anthracite field. The bituminous men sought relief from their hard and grinding conditions in a general strike. After a stubbornly fought contest a compromise settlement was made which, while giving the miners only a slight advance, lent an impetus to the organization. . . ."

Dealing with the railroad-owned anthracite mines was another matter, for the anthracite mines maintained a force of Coal and Iron police, armed and ever present, and so effective a black list that a man merely suspected of being interested in a union could never again find work for himself or his family. Nevertheless, the organizers succeeded in setting up a union structure and in holding a convention. The operators would not meet with the delegates to discuss a new scale of wages, because by so doing they would be acknowledging the existence of a union. Though the union had less than eight thousand members when it called the strike in 1900, over a hundred thousand men walked out. Because a presidential election was coming, Senator Hanna, chairman of the National Republican Committee, prevailed on the mineowners to compromise so that he could tell the country that everything was peaceful, and consequently another Republican ought to be elected as President.

This was the kind of political reasoning the operators could follow. They posted notices on the bulletin boards announcing a ten-per-cent raise in wages. Suspecting that the raise would be revoked the day after the election, the men refused to return to work. Under pressure from the Republican machine and its allied bankers and industrialists, the operators posted a second set of notices, agreeing to keep the ten-per-cent raise in effect for a year, to obey the law by paying wages semi-monthly and to cut their charge for powder. The miners accepted. Though securing only a small fraction of their demands, they believed even this partial victory in the toughest labor field in America would bring into the union every man in the anthracite mines. It did.

In 1902 a thirty-per-cent rise in the cost of living having wiped out the benefits of their raise, the miners now asked for a twenty-per-cent increase, an eight-hour day for outside men, their own dockers, no further extensions of the elastic-coal car, observance of the Pennsylvania law which made it illegal to force workers to buy at a company store, the recognition of their union. Taking a leaf from George Pullman, the operators repeated, "We have nothing to arbitrate!"

John Mitchell called his strike.

With the approach of winter, after five months of rising coal prices for the consumers and relief kitchens for the miners, meetings were held throughout the country demanding that the operators yield to President Roosevelt's request for arbitration.

The operators sent J. P. Morgan to the President with their acceptance of arbitration. The miners went back to work jubilantly, assured that all decisions of the commission would be retroactive to the day they began work. President Roosevelt named the able Carroll D. Wright, who had been chairman of the Senate Investigating Committee in the railroad strike, as secretary, then appointed a mining engineer, a brigadier general, a judge of the United States Circuit Court, the grand chief of the Order of Railway Conductors, the former owner of a coal mine and a Roman Catholic bishop to make up the committee. The operators named a panel of twenty-three attorneys who would present their case; the miners named Clarence Darrow, James Lanahan and the O'Neil brothers, "well-equipped lawyers who had worked in the mines and were familiar with all the terminology as well as the method of work."

The commission went into the Pennsylvania coal fields to do some firsthand investigating; so did Darrow, Lanahan and the O'Neil brothers. On their first mine tour of inspection two members of the commission could stay down only an hour and twenty minutes because of the "uncomfortable conditions of the mine and the dampness." The committtee reached the Clifford mine a few hours after a Hungarian had been killed by the falling of a roof. They were not told about the accident.

Preliminary hearings were held in Scranton, but the commission quickly adjourned to the Federal Courthouse in Philadelphia for the big show.

Darrow was too sound an economist to make his appeal solely on the basis of the humanities. He set out to prove to the commission, and hence to the nation, one of his fundamental convictions, that economics can be not only an exact science, but is also the basic science by which a man's life is conditioned: his health, his longevity, his surroundings, the well-being of his family, his leisure, his education, cultivation, intelligence—the very freedom of his brain and body and spirit. If a "composite" workman cost the industry two hundred dollars a year, and after deducting the prorata cost of material, management and other overhead, this same composite worker returned to his industry a profit of a thousand dollars, where then was the economic necessity of keeping this workman on a subsistence level so low that his children had to be sent into the breakers and the textile mills?

This move to force industry to bring its books into the court of public opinion was for the mass of American working people almost as great a revolution as the one that had taken place in 1776. Up to this moment industry had been responsible to no one; it had been free not only to despoil the health and happiness of millions of its neighbors but also to plunder and squander the natural resources of the country, its timber, minerals, oil, earth. It had been free to mulct public funds, to absorb public savings by fraudulent manipulations and waterings of stock, to sponge up the wages of the eighty per cent of the people who worked for their living by monopoly-rocketing prices.

"God in His infinite wisdom," cried George Baer, when refusing to meet in the same room with union delegates, "has put the control of business into the hands of Christian gentlemen."

The newspaper accounts showed the public that this man Darrow was raising startlingly basic questions, going far beyond the immediate question of whether the miners were entitled to a raise. *Could the coal mines pay a living wage and still earn a sufficient profit to justify remaining in business? Which was of greater importance, to maintain a living wage for workers or a dividend for stockholders? When business fell off, which should be cut first, wages or dividends?*

Darrow had clearly shown in both the Pullman and Paine cases that a raise in wages would have made but a slight diminution in the profits and would have been offset by a stronger, healthier, happier and hence more loyal working force. Was this not even more true in the coal fields where supervision was impossible? A secure, healthy labor force must help build a prosperous nation, but the coal barons weren't interested in anything so abstract. Their job was to get out as much coal as they could at the lowest possible cost and then sell it at the highest possible price.

Mr Baer asked, "Are you going to increase the rate of wages and attract still more people there to sit down and wait in the hope of getting enough money in a day to support them for a year?"

This was a sophistry made to order for Darrow's lampooning humor. "What average did you put down there that the miners got in Indian Ridge?" Darrow demanded of a company comptroller.

"Five hundred and fifty-six dollars."

"How many miners got above that?"

"Twenty."

"How many got less?"

"Four hundred and seventy-six."

"Then there are only four per cent of the men in Indian

Ridge colliery who got as much money as you set down as the average earnings of the whole colliery? And ninety-six per cent got less? Is not that true?"

"I presume it is."

Under Darrow's method of gently leading witnesses as he would a horse to the watering trough, hundreds of persons from every walk of life paraded before the commission. First he brought on the crippled and maimed and sick miners to testify about conditions in the mines, then doctors to verify their plight with evidence on industrial diseases.

Aware that the hearing was going against them, the operators made a flanking movement: the unions were organizations of violence and lawlessness, hence the miners didn't need a raise and weren't justified in demanding one. Suddenly the hearing flashed into focus, stripped of its evasions, the operators were only mildly concerned over a possible raise in wages; their purpose was to destroy the United Mine Workers and unionism.

"We deny," declared T. P. Fowler, president of the Scranton Coal Company and the Elkshill Coal and Iron Company, "that union of workingmen tend to the improvement of their physical, mental or moral conditions and to the preservation of friendly relations between employer and employee."

A separate group of lawyers was engaged by the operators to represent the non-union men of the coal fields. These men told how they had been beaten up by union men when they tried to go to work, how their families had been intimidated and boycotted, stones thrown through the windows of their homes. Darrow sat with his chin on his chest as he listened to these stories, for in spite of Mitchell's constantly reiterated plea that "the person who violates the law is the worst enemy the strikers could have," hotheads among the hundred and fifty thousand strikers had used their fists, clubs and stones to keep other men from working.

Nor was it the first time that there had been bloodshed in the Pennsylvania coal fields. From 1867 through the bitter strike of 1875, years in which a depression had reduced wages to six dollars a week for a twelve-hour day, the Irish members of the Ancient Order of Hibernians, whose ancestors under the name of the Molly Maguires had fought evictions from the English landlords in Ireland in 1843, founded the American version of the Mollies in the six anthracite counties. A secret organization, their members first worked co-operatively to beat up and run out of the state strike-breakers who had been imported by the Coal and Iron police. Since violence, like a narcotic, must be used in increasingly larger doses to achieve similar results, the Mollies attracted an element of the illiterate Irish who loved force for its own sake. Superintendents were found mysteriously slain; the gangsters and terrorists came to control the Ancient Order of Hibernians.

The president of the Philadelphia and Reading Coal and Iron Company called in Allan Pinkerton, able head of the first private-detective agency in America. To smash the Mollies, Pinkerton selected twenty-nine-year-old James McParland, who had the honor of being one of America's first "labor spies." Disguised as a poor and shabby laborer, McParland now went into the Pennsylvania coal fields, made friends with the Irish miners by his jolly singing and playing of the guitar, his handy manner with his fists, the steady flow of drinks he bought with money which he alleged he got by counterfeiting. He ingratiated himself with the Mollies and after a year was taken into their secret organization, where he worked himself up to the position of general secretary. When he was at last discovered to be a detective he fled, and murder charges were brought against the head Mollies of the six counties. The leading witnesses against the men were James McParland, who claimed he never knew of the murders in advance but always heard of them immediately afterward, and a self-confessed murderer by the name of Kerrigan, whom McParland persuaded to turn state's evidence on the promise of immunity.

In all McParland succeeded in getting fourteen men hanged, some of whom were guilty, some innocent. As a reward for his services, James McParland was promoted to the head of the Pinkerton agency in Denver, Colorado, where the hard-rock miners were making their first efforts to organize. Here McParland remained for thirty years, until he tangled with Clarence Darrow in another murder charge against miners —a charge whose purpose once again was to hang the leaders and hence destroy the Western Federation of Miners.

The problem of the scab and non-union worker presented one of America's most nearly insoluble dilemmas: what were the millions of workingmen who were willing to suffer the privations of a strike and risk of black list, to deny their families the necessities of life in order to better their lot for the future, to do about their neighbors who were too timid or too frightened or too brutalized to care about bettering the lot of their families, particularly since these men who contin-ued to work would share equally in the advantages gained by the sacrifices of their fellows? America was a free country; it was as bad for a union to use force to make a man join their ranks and their strike as it was for the operators to use force to keep men from joining a union or a strike. Yet Darrow felt impelled to agree with John Mitchell that "a man who works during a strike has no moral right to work if his work destroys the hopes of his fellow men."

The operators charged union men with rioting against state troops; Darrow countered by putting Mitchell on the stand and dramatizing for the country the now-infamous "Shoot to kill!" order given by General Gobin to stop the small boys from throwing rocks at the troops as they marched through coal towns.

Mitchell having shown that since the sheriff had not asked for the troops, they had been sent in illegally, Darrow now made clear how it followed that responsibility for the deaths of the two workmen and two troopers who were killed in the clashes fell directly on the shoulders of the governor and not the workmen. The history of strikes in America established that when no disorder arose it was profitable for the employers to bring in Pinkertons, scabs and deputies to incite fights, riots and the destruction of a small amount of property in order to win the sympathy of the public and the courts and have public support to "put down the anarchists."

"Shoot to kill!" General Gobin had ordered his troops.

"Shoot to kill—whom?" asked a badly frightened citizenry. "The people of Pennsylvania? Is this a war?"

Darrow finger-combed the lock of hair from his right eye and patted the cigarette ashes into his gray coat with his other hand before turning to George Baer as his greatest asset in the hearing.

"The unions are corrupting the children of America," cried Baer, "by letting them join their illegal organizations."

Darrow leaped to his feet. "If the children had not been at work in the mines they could not have joined the union!"

Explaining to the commission that capital could not share its management with labor because "God in His infinite wisdom had bequeathed the management of industry to Christian gentlemen," Baer evolved another phrase which, along with his other two, became for the American workman a counterpart of that rallying phrase of the Revolution "No taxation without representation."

"We cannot interfere," proclaimed the patriarchal-bearded Baer, "with the divine right of stockholders."

To Darrow these phrases fell like manna. For centuries the rulers of Europe had built their thrones upon the phrase, "the divine right of kings," persuading their people that any hand raised against a king was a hand raised against God, that God would protect the kings he had appointed and destroy all those who opposed them. The nineteenth century had dissipated the divine right of kings. What was to be the fate of the divine right of stockholders in the twentieth?

After two months the hearings came to a close; each side girded for the final appeal. Darrow wandered the streets aimlessly for an hour before entering a workingman's restaurant. He sat slumped in the hard wooden chair, unable to swallow a bite of the food before him. He had worked hard; he had worked well; he felt that victory would ultimately come to his cause, yet just before one of the greatest single efforts of his life he was seized by a shattering depression. The hearings had forced him to the heartbreaking conclusion that, left to its own conscience, industry's alleviation of the evils it had itself created went forward with the speed of a worm burrowing through a stone wall.

The next morning the final pleas were opened. S. P. Wolverton fired the final salvo for his twenty-two legal colleagues by a "sand-in-the-eyes technique" of avoiding the consequences of the elicited testimony. "Who demands the shortening of the hours of labor?" demanded Mr Wolverton. "Is it the strong, industrious, ambitious young man who desires to succeed in the race for life, or is it the indolent theorist? The young man who has his own fortune to make has no time for theory. One who inherits a fortune or has it thrust upon him by some kind testator has time to theorize upon sociological problems, but to the young man who has his fortune to make for himself [on the breakers?] life is real. Great care should be taken in making any raise in wages that the laborer himself is not injured.

George Baer, in closing for the operators, won the sympathy of the commission and of many of the listeners by a well-thought-out statement: "These are problems that the 'antediluvian' captains of industry in these days must consider—how to increase the wealth of the community you are serving by increasing its prosperity—because only in that way can you add to your revenues; how to return to your stockholders a just payment for the money they have invested, and how to give honest wages, fair and full wages to the men you employ. These are burdens. You may think they are light, but to the man who is charged with responsibility they become terrible realities."

Then Baer launched into the more practical and concrete business of thwarting the miners' demands. "There are some trades where eight hours is enough, but there ought to be no limitation on work in the collieries. Who has ever refused to bargain? . . . We offer them work and we tell them what we will give, and they say what they are willing to take for it, and an agreement is made between man and man, and he goes to work and works honestly on that contract. The man works contentedly and receives his pay, and that system, we are told, is one-sided and slavery. Who enslaves the men? There is plenty of work in the country."

On the afternoon of the third day Darrow rose to speak for the workers, and a hush fell over the courtroom. He stood in the silence for a moment, his face lined, his eyes somber, the fugitive clump of hair falling over his right eye, fully conscious of the burden he had now to carry. "As he started to speak a young lawyer deferentially handed him a bulky sheaf of notes, but he impatiently waved the man aside. Squaring his hulking shoulders and swinging his long arms before him, he delivered his address." He spoke for about seven hours.

". . . If the civilization of this country rests upon the necessity of leaving these starvation wages to these miners and laborers, or if it rests upon the labor of these little boys who from twelve to fourteen years of age are picking their way through the dirt, clouds and dust of the anthracite, then the sooner we are done with this civilization and start anew, the better for the humanities. I do not believe that the civilization of this country and the industry of the East depends upon whether you leave these men in the mines nine hours or ten hours, or whether you leave these little children in the breakers. If it is not based on a more substantial basis than that, then it is time that these captains of industry resigned their commission and turned it over to some theorists to see if they cannot bring ruin and havoc a good deal quicker.

"This demand for eight hours is not a demand to shirk work, as is claimed in this case. It is a demand for the individual to have a better life, a fuller life, a completer life. I measure it from the standpoint of the man, from the standpoint that the interests of the government, the interests of society, the interests of law and all social institutions is to make the best man they can. That is the purpose of every lawmaking power. It is the purpose of every church. It is the purpose of every union. . . . There is only one standpoint from which you have the right to approach this question, and that is, what will make the best man, the longest life, the strongest man, the most intelligent man, the best American citizen, to build up a nation that we will be proud of. Whenever he has turned his attention to improving his condition man has been able to do it.

"The laborer who asks for shorter hours asks for a breath of life; he asks for a chance to develop the best that is in him. It is no answer to say, 'If you give him shorter hours he will not use them wisely.' Our country, our civilization, our race, is based on the belief that for all his weaknesses

79

there is still in man that divine spark that will make him reach upward for something higher and better than anything he has ever known."

When the applause had died down the commission retired to pore over its ten thousand pages of evidence. On Saturday, March 21, 1903, the awards were published. All contract miners were given a ten-per-cent raise and by means of a sliding scale were to benefit from increased coal prices when they went over four dollars and fifty cents a ton. Engineers and pumpmen were put on an eight-hour day, with Sundays off. Company employees were put on a nine-hour day. The miners were permitted to have their own docking bosses and weighmen; the operators had to give a detailed accounting, and any increase in the size of the coal car had to be accompanied by a corresponding increase in wages. Though the commission put no restrictions on the company store, though they soundly castigated the union for the acts of violence on the part of its members and failed to concede that the rate of pay was so low that miners' children were forced into the breakers at a tender age, the decision was an almost solid victory for the United Mine Workers.

To carry out the awards, which were to extend for three years, the commission set up a six-man board of conciliation to handle all disputes. President Roosevelt had conceded to the operators that the final award would not include compulsory recognition of the United Mine Workers, but since the union was to be a party to the six-man board, it had received its recognition in fact if not in name. It was a tremendous step forward for unionism, perhaps the greatest in American history.

Darrow's part in this victory was widely acclaimed. Eager to prove that the prophet was no longer without honor in his own country, Chicago bestowed upon him the greatest honor in its possession: he was asked to become Mayor Darrow!

The accolade of supremacy in his field was draped about his shoulders toward the end of the hearing when, telling how the operators had all the advantages, he said, "Their social advantages are better; they speak the English language better; they can hire expert accountants; they have got the advantage of us in almost every particular," and Judge Grey, glancing over at the battery of twenty-three corporation counsels, murmured with a faint smile:

"Except the lawyers!"

Chapter Six

Can a Lawyer Be an Honest Man?

BY APRIL of 1903, after three months on the anthracite case
and another three months in Springfield, the year previous having been elected to the Illinois legislature as an Independent,
to carry out the dead Altgeld's fight against Yerkes' traction
lobby, Darrow found that his Chicago law practice had pretty
well evaporated. After the death of Governor Altgeld the firm
had been foreshortened to Darrow and Thompson; it was
further foreshortened when Thompson resigned. Darrow now
found himself not only without a business, but without a firm.
As a consequence he formed a partnership with Edgar Lee
Masters.

They met through the accident of having offices on the
same floor in the Ashland Block. It is difficult to imagine a
sharper contrast between two men: Darrow despised the human race but loved people; Masters loved humanity but hated
people. Darrow was warm, informal, generous, tolerant, lovable; Masters was cold, intellectual, brittle, self-centered. Darrow admired Masters' objective legal mind and piercing briefs.
In the firm of Darrow and Masters there were now harbored
the wrecks of two poets.

In July Clarence and Ruby were married by Mayor Dunne
in the home of John Gregg. Darrow's friends were thoroughly
shocked at this apostasy by a man who had been preaching
the virtues of free love and damning the confining influences
of marriage; the few who had been deterred from marriage
by his eloquence were perhaps justifiably piqued.

The couple went to Europe for a two and a half months'
honeymoon "through Holland, Germany, France, Switzerland,
dawdling and happy, up and down countless Alps, over mountain passes, through interminable tunnels and over the Channel
back to England." While on this trip he wrote *Farmington*,
the recounting of his childhood in Farmdale and Kinsman.
The story is now an American classic which has gone through
many editions.

The Darrows returned to Chicago in mid-September. Ruby
"found an apartment on Sheridan Road. . . ." Darrow's en-
tertaining had been informal; when he had invited a lot of
people to take supper with him he would say to the waiter,

"Bring enough beefsteak and potatoes for the crowd, and if anybody doesn't like it they're out of luck."

Ruby changed all this. "We brought home with us the Sheffield steel, ivory-handled knives and forks, . . . that he had always wanted. . . . We served caviar as appetizer, delicious soups, meats, potatoes, desserts, almonds done in olive oil, after-dinner coffee in tea-sized cups. There were daintily colored and arranged bonbons, fine liqueurs in most enticing Old World glasses . . . either a low, large bouquet or low, wide bowl of many-colored fruits. . . ."

Ruby Hamerstrom had taken to herself no small task when she took on Clarence Darrow as husband, but she was more than equal to it. "He had a limited taste for foods and an incurable aversion to things that most people consider the choicest. He never ate fowl or lamb or veal or onions or cabbage, while celery, tomato, radish, green beans, were words to make him shudder." His aversion to vegetables enabled him to originate a line to fortify generations of helpless children: "I don't like spinach, and I'm glad I don't, because if I liked it I'd eat it, and I'd just hate it."

Having rescued her husband from the toils of free love, Ruby was inclined to be a trifle suspicious of Clarence's former lady friends, some of whom encountered "a wall of ice" when they were first invited by Darrow to his new home. Perhaps because he knew that whatever quarreling he did with Ruby was over externals, he made no attempt to postpone their arguments until they were alone; their intimates report spirited clashes, for Ruby could talk faster and more indefatigably than her husband. Clarence teased her a good deal by advising other people never to exchange their freedom for the shackles of matrimony. One of his favorite comments was that "getting married is a good deal like going into a restaurant with your friends. You order what you want, and then when you see what the other fellow has got you wish you had taken that." Though Ruby's love for Clarence rose to planes of the sheerest idolatry with the passing of the decades, she always fought back, never taking his guff in public. Before long it became clear to everyone that they were a good match, that they loved each other and that their relationship would endure.

A short time after Darrow formed his partnership with Masters, Francis Wilson was made a partner. For the next eight years the firm of Darrow, Masters and Wilson was one of the most successful in Chicago, clearing from twenty-five to thirty-five thousand dollars a year for each partner, exploding only when a bomb blew up the Los Angeles Times Building, killing twenty men and wrecking Darrow's career as the country's most brilliant defender of the rights of working people.

Darrow had a large office with a private entrance off the elevator hall, while Masters selected for himself a corner office at the inner and most inaccessible end of the suite, where he is reputed to have spent a considerable portion of his time writing Greek tragedies and other poems.

Darrows' rule of never giving up a cross-examination until he had some comfort from it is exemplified by the blowup of the doctor who was used by the streetcar company in personal-injury suits because he could think faster than most lawyers in Chicago. The doctor had a list of twenty hospitals with which his name was associated; when a tiny hospital opening somewhere in the suburbs invited him to put his name on their staff he consented because the addition would make his titles seem more imposing to credulous juries. Darrow in examining him droned through the list of hospitals, asking the doctor where each of them was—a method of questioning apparently without purpose. Finally he came to the bottom of the list and asked where the new hospital was located. The doctor almost bounded out of the witness chair.

"Jesus Christ, Clarence," he exclaimed, "you got me!"

In Chicago at the time, such a large number of massage parlors were being used as fronts for houses of prostitution, the word "massage" had come to be used as a synonym for a four-letter word which could not be bandied about in polite society, while to give someone a "massaging" stood for the present participle of its more vigorous Anglo-Saxon counterpart. As part of a reform movement all massage parlors in the city were closed up, thereby depriving a lot of honest and hard-working masseurs from earning a living. Their association sent a committee to Darrow, asking him to secure an injunction against their closure. Darrow's sarcasm in court was so excoriatingly funny that when he had finished the state's attorney rose and muttered:

"Clarence has a way of 'massaging' all of us." The ordinance was revoked.

Chicago lawyers who watched him work over a period of years say it was magnificent to see the slow, mesmeric manner in which he broke down hostility and aversion, his warmth and love permeating with kindliness courtrooms in which bitter, acrimonious contests were being waged. Rarely did he attempt to convert the courtroom merely to the innocence of his client; rather he converted them to a mellow and tolerant philosophy of life in which all mankind was innocent as charged. Before long opposing attorneys, witnesses, jurymen and judges were sweating in a glow of brotherly love.

He had progressed from the role of the gadfly, which stung

people into thinking, to the point where he was now one of the country's most effective antidotes, an antidote to the poisons of stuffiness, moralism, lethargy. Watching his audiences, he found that he had to transpose his adage of "The truth shall make you free" to read, "The truth shall make you mad." But he did not mind making people mad; he was not afraid of their anger, resentment, hatred. Perhaps if he could make them mad enough he might make them mad enough to start thinking for themselves.

He was no respecter of sacred cows: the more sacred the cow, the more he believed it needed to be shot at, for every time a man accepted a sacred cow he closed off still another portion of his brain.

In Washington Darrow was met on the street by an acquaintance who was excited because President Taft was going to address a joint session of the Senate and House that afternoon.

"Tickets are practically impossible to get, Clarence. By a stroke of good fortune I have an extra one. You must come along."

Darrow recalled that it had been Judge Taft who had issued the first local injunction against the American Railway Union strikers in 1894, establishing a precedent for the Federal Court in Chicago, and agreed to accompany his friend. Taft received a tremendous ovation before launching into his message. The friend watched Darrow eagerly for some reaction, but he remained stony faced. Toward the end of the speech Darrow nudged his friend, who leaned closer to catch every word.

"Fat son of a bitch, ain't he?" asked Darrow.

Darrow and a college professor named John had debated frequently, "always kidding each other in a humorous vein on the platform. Darrow knew of the professor's inclination to step out of an evening. After his death Darrow and a friend called to pay their respects to the widow, who had placed her husband's ashes in an urn on the mantelpiece. When she left the living room for an instant Darrow gazed up at the urn.

" 'Poor John,' he murmured, 'you'll have to stay in nights now.' "

A good-looking young man asked Darrow to defend him against a charge of robbery. Darrow inquired when he could get a portion of his fee. "I can get some of the money for you tonight," replied the young man. "No-oo," murmured Darrow, "I don't care to accept money that has been stolen —so recently."

Toward more serious problems he turned an acid irreverence. Invited as a criminologist to address the prisoners of the Cook County jail, he gave them a lecture on Altgeld's revolutionary theory of the economic base of crime. "There is no such thing as crime as the word is generally understood. Nine tenths of you are in jail because you did not have enough money to pay a good lawyer. While some of you men might pick my pocket because that is your trade, when I get outside everybody picks my pocket—by charging me a dollar for something that is worth twenty-five cents. If every man, woman and child in the world had a chance to make a decent, fair, honest living there would be no jails and no lawyers and no courts."

When he had finished a guard asked one of the prisoners what he thought of the speech. "He's too radical," replied the prisoner.

To his mind one of the most virulent poisons that had been pumped into the vitals of American life was its Polly-annish God's-in-His-heaven, all's-right-with-the-world blind faith. Because of his determination to antidote this creeping paralysis he was accused of being a futilitarian, a pessimist.

Frank P. Walsh said of him: "Darrow is a wonderful man with a fine mind, a big heart and a great social vision. But . . . he is never happy except at a funeral, and not then unless it was where the deceased had committed suicide."

What people called his pessimism was the recoiling of a sensitive nature from the unnecessary suffering in the world. The man who sees all this suffering, and thinks he has a cure effected is rarely called a pessimist. But Darrow's discerning logic tore holes in every one of what Bertrand Russell was to call the *Proposed Roads to Freedom.* Taking his stand with no one ideology, but insisting upon scrutinizing with relentless logic and accepting what was valid from each social philosophy, he was the man on the raft in the wide, wide ocean. He expressed his credo to Abram Adelman, a neighboring attorney, in one sentence which might serve as his epitaph:

"I can say with perfect honesty that I have never knowingly catered to anyone's ideas, and I have expressed what was within me, regardless of consequences."

Charles Edward Russell writes of him, "The complement of his intense and boundless sympathy for the individual sufferer was a good-natured contempt for all efforts to raise man in the mass. Man was a monkey, always had been a monkey, always would be a monkey, and all efforts to make him anything else were but lost motion. Despite his belief that a socialist state might be superior to a predatory capitalist state, "he looked upon socialists as well-meaning, interesting and utterly futile folk who were wasting their time gesticulating at a chimera. He could not see that bloody revolution, which some of his friends believed to be the universal panacea, would help, since men would still be monkeys when they had ceased to blow one another up with dynamite. Yet . . . he was too sensitive to keep out all faith."

He was a sentimental cynic. He was a gullible skeptic. He was an organized anarchist. He was a happy pessimist. He was a modest egocentric. He was a hopeful defeatist. And was perhaps aware of the various contradictions he was housing under one dome.

As the business of Darrow, Masters and Wilson became more profitable Darrow spent a larger portion of his time traveling for his lectures and debates. Since his primary motivation was to give any and all ideas an airing, he employed the architectural method of batter, or purposeful leaning over backward, to provide correction for the mass of people who were leaning so far forward in obeisance that they were lying on their faces. When debating Rabbi Kornfeld in Toledo on the subject, "Is There Something in Man above the Animal?" he wired his sponsors, "I shall contend that man is simply a machine and that there is nothing in him that cannot be found in a dog, an auto or a tree. I care nothing about winning the debate. I only want to give the ideas a hearing. I'm sure that the great majority of the crowd will be on the rabbi's side. If they are not, I'll be sure I'm on the wrong side."

Newspaper reporters sent to interview him found him to be hot copy, for he had a vivid sense of the theatrical, furnishing them with apostasies that made electrifying banners for their columns. An associate says, "I recall that following the decision in the Scopes evolution case he received a number of reporters at my office and expressed to them very strong opinions in respect to various public questions, such as the treatment of Negroes and defense of criminals, and in every case made strong pronouncements without qualification. After the reporters had left I reminded him that he had discussed those very same questions with me at length and that his views on the subject had been qualified in much the same way as that of other citizens who were not regarded as radical and cynical.

" 'That's quite true,' replied Darrow. 'But when you want to get anything before the public you must decide what is the thing you most wish to emphasize at the time and then state it strongly, forcefully, without qualification, and your view will then attract public attention to the particular thing which you wish to emphasize—it will be news. If you qualify your main point the thing you wish to emphasize loses its news value; it loses its interest to the public.' "

He had his blind spot: he held a low opinion of the political capacity of women. George Briggs, the single taxer, met

Darrow one Sunday morning at an atheist-science service and accompanied him and three of Darrow's women friends to the Auditorium Hotel for luncheon. At the end of an afternoon of intense discussion Darrow turned to Briggs and, indicating his three women admirers commented:

"These women have laughed in the right places; they have nodded their heads in the right places; they've asked the right questions—but none of them knows a damn thing of what we've been talking about."

Another friend relates, "I remember making some remarks about the desirability of women having the same rights, privileges and duties as men. Darrow replied:

"'I'm not so sure. We notice that nature makes the least differentiation between the sexes in her lowest orders. As we rise in the scale the differences become greater until, when we reach the human animal, it is greatest of all. I think possibly it is better that way.'"

He confided to Gertrude Barnum that "votes for women would put progress back fifty years"—but voted for suffrage anyway.

A lawyer by the name of Abner Smith approached Darrow, suggesting that he help finance a bank with a new operating idea: they would sell stock to druggists, in return for which they would make the drugstores depositories or branch banks. His son, Paul, was to be given an important job in the organization. Darrow, a poor businessman under any circumstances, was at this moment doubly susceptible because he wanted to see Paul well placed; he invested ten thousand dollars, almost the total of his savings. He also persuaded friends to join him in the venture, chief among whom was his partner, Masters. The Bank of America opened its office on the second floor of the Ashland Block, a few doors down the hall from Darrow. His business judgment for once proved sound; within less than three months the bank had three hundred thousand dollars on deposit and was spreading fast.

"Then the officers started grafting and putting in bad loans," said Paul. "I advised Father what was going on. He closed them up."

The next morning Darrow had an early session with the Chicago Clearinghouse, which was anxious to avoid a failure. The clearinghouse offered to lend him twenty-five thousand dollars on his personal note if he would open the bank that morning and pay all depositors who demanded their money. By ten o'clock father and son were established behind separate teller's cages with cash before them, meeting all comers. The clearinghouse money, plus the cash on hand, was sufficient to meet the immediate needs; since a fair portion of the collateral was good, the stockholders got some of their money—all except Darrow and Masters.

No one knew better than Darrow that lawyers are janitors who have to clean up all sorts of dirty legal messes. Darrow mopped up his share, for at least half of his time now was devoted to corporation law. He was criticized by the liberal groups of Chicago for consorting with the enemy. Then, as ever afterward, people thought he earned enormous sums of money, a misconception which boiled to a rage of indignation when he was accused of prostituting his talents in defending the Loeb-Leopold murderers to earn a million-dollar fee. Yet it is attested by all his partners that Darrow never knew his worth to his clients. "He charged them five thousand when they were prepared and willing to pay thirty thousand for valuable services rendered." To conduct the defense in the Paine case, in which the trial alone lasted several months, "he received the nominal fee of two hundred and fifty dollars."

Nine years before, in 1895, he had first been attacked with charges of taking corporation gold when he helped an electric company push through an ordinance which the mayor had vetoed. The attack had been made by an estimable woman friend at Hull House, who charged him with betraying the people of Chicago. Darrow's answer to "My dear Miss S." pleads moral guilt and portrays a confused, tortured young man struggling upward through the darkness of an acquisitive society.

He makes an outright statement to Miss S. of the *modus operandi* which was to serve him all his days. When he had come to Chicago in 1887 his attention had been called "to the rights of labor and wrongs of the world" by an idealistic friend. But "I determined to get what I could out of the system and use it to *destroy* the system. I have since sold my professional services to every corporation or individual who cared to buy. . . . I have taken their ill-gotten gains and tried to use it to prevent suffering. My preaching and practicing have ever been the same: I have always tried to show a state and a way to reach it where men and women can be honest and tender. I have defended the weak and poor, have done it without pay, will do it again. I cannot defend them without bread; I cannot get this except from those who give it and by giving some measure of conformity to what is."

The only way he could conceive of unhorsing himself from the dilemma was to live frugally and put aside enough to retire. He wanted to devote his entire time to writing because he felt would be able to reach a larger audience and educate on a wider ideological front. Twice before he had saved a tidy sum, only to lose his money in bad investments. This time he was more cautious: he bought railroad stocks and bank stocks and became partners with the dependable banker Lutz of Gardner, Illinois, in the ownership of the Black Mountain gold mine in Mexico. This Black Mountain mine "was believed to be one of the richest, safest mines ever opened, boasting the most elaborate, expensive and up-to-date equipment of any gold mine." In a very few years it would make him independent for life. Then he and Ruby could roam the world while he wrote all his beautiful and trenchant stories of the idealist. The first case he gave to George H. Francis, who later became a junior in his office, was a routine foreclosure for a real-estate corporation. A widow had been sold a restaurant in downtown Chicago, in return for which she had given a mortgage on her forty-thousand-dollar home. The night before the matter was to go into court the widow called at Francis' home. He perceived that she was a woman of integrity.

"You are a young man," said the widow. "You cannot be long in the law business."

"As a matter of fact," replied Francis, "this is my first case."

"Then you should not commence your legal career with such a dishonorable affair on your conscience. The real-estate people misrepresented when they sold me the restaurant. My home is the only asset my husband left me, and if you take it away from me I shall be destitute."

"I really know nothing of the background of the case," said Francis. "It was handed to me as an office foreclosure by Mr Darrow. I'll be glad to tell him what you said."

"Then the matter will rest between God and Mr Darrow."

"I'm afraid the connection between the two may be rather remote."

"God will intervene," replied the woman calmly, thanked him and left.

The next morning, when Francis reported the meeting to Darrow, he picked up his telephone, made a few pointed inquiries and learned that the real-estate corporation had twice previously sold the restaurant to professional restaurateurs, both of whom had failed in that location. Darrow did not believe in *caveat emptor,* let the buyer beware; he summoned his client.

"You will return to this woman the deed to her home," he announced, "and call the whole deal off."

"But we can't do that, Clarence," exploded the president of the real-estate concern. "We've paid commissions, incurred other expenses . . ."

"I hate to do your thinking for you, but that's exactly what you're going to do."

"My study mate," says one of his students at the Illinois College of Law, "was Richard, a preacher's son who rode his bicycle all the way from Denver to Chicago to enter law school. Richard and I used to discuss whether one could be a successful lawyer and still maintain the Christian principles. One evening Richard propounded our problem.

" 'Professor Darrow, I respect your ability and I value highly the instruction you give us, and I should like your opinion on the question as to whether or not one can be a successful lawyer—I mean financially successful, make a great deal of money, a million dollars—and do it without resorting to sharp practice, taking advantage of the technicalities of the law or injuring the other fellow.'

"Mr Darrow's answer was given without hesitation: " 'No.'

" 'Well, Professor Darrow, you are a successful lawyer and have earned a great deal of money. Then you admit that you are crooked?'

"Mr Darrow answered like a father explaining to a child.

" 'They say I am a successful lawyer, but I am not financially successful. The persons I represent are for the most poor people. My clients are not people of money; they are the downtrodden.'

"He then dismissed the class, took his hat from a chair and walked slowly from the room, his head down, thinking —thinking."

Thinking, perhaps, whether a lawyer could work for corporations and remain honest? Were not his powerful clients demanding more and more of his energies; would not he perforce grow away from the poor wretches whose defense was his only justification? What good were his speeches if he himself knew he was not an honest man?

Bouts of introspection were rare with Darrow; this one not only had a salutary effect, but came at a particularly opportune moment. On the sage and dust prairies of far-off Idaho an ex-governor opened the gate to his cottage and was blown up by a bomb that had been connected to its hinges. That explosion was the climactic salvo in one of America's most sanguinary wars. In addition to killing ex-Governor Steunenberg, it also shattered to a thousand fragments Clarence Darrow's dilemma.

Chapter Seven

Who Will Prosecute the Prosecution?

IT WAS ANOTHER of life's ambiguous jokes that he who had just published a book called *Resist Not Evil* should be called upon to defend the most militant union in America against charges of murder, a defense which must of necessity include a partial justification of force and violence in the industrial wars of the West.

The trouble with the Western Federation of Miners, those hard-rock drillers of Colorado, Montana and Idaho who went deep into the earth to blast out great fortunes in gold, silver, copper and lead, was that they somehow hadn't gotten around to reading Darrow's little book. At least, they hadn't quite been converted to his doctrine of nonresistance. Many of them were acquainted with the lines from Matthew upon which it had been based, "But I say unto you, that ye resist not evil, but whosoever shall smite ye on thy right cheek, turn to him the other also." They also had been told in their churches that the meek would inherit the earth, but by some obscure machinations the mineowners had inherited the earth and all its riches; the workers had inherited the twelve-hour day, the seven-day week, the marginal-subsistence wage and working conditions so dangerous that hundreds of their comrades perished each year under mountains of rock.

For fifteen years now the miners had fought back: with fists, clubs, bullets, guns, dynamite: those who earn their living from dynamite are acquainted with its uses. In the heat of a strike local unions had shot it out with Pinkertons, deputies and non-union workers; they had used their guns to take possession of mines being operated by scab labor, and they had twice blown up mines and mills in the Coeur d'Alene region of northern Idaho. The last explosion had taken place in 1899, six years before, yet as a direct result the officers of the Western Federation of Miners were now in jail in Idaho, charged with murdering Idaho's ex-Governor Frank Steunenberg during the Christmas holidays of 1905.

Darrow found himself in much the same predicament as the Western miners: even after he had finished his book he had not been able to convince himself that nonresistance could serve any purpose. "At its best the doctrine of nonresistance can only be held by dreamers and theorists and

91

can have no place in daily life . . . every government on earth is the personification of violence and force." The better to prove him right, the government of Colorado had in effect seceded from the Union in order that they might, in the words of their militia head, General Sherman Bell, "do up this anarchistic federation."

In the open and publicly avowed warfare between the state of Colorado and the Western Federation of Miners from January 1, 1902, until June 30, 1904, forty-two men were killed, a hundred and twelve injured, thirteen hundred and forty-five arrested and seven hundred and seventy-three deported from the state. The tragic part of this warfare was that it had been caused in its entirety by the refusal of the state government to live up to and obey the laws of its state. It was because the unions had fought back that Darrow was now on a fast train from Chicago to Denver at the request of John Mitchell, whose United Mine Workers were then conducting a strike to secure the same conditions for the coal miners of the South and West as had been earned for those of the East; any injury to the hard-rock miners would necessarily injure the cause of the coal miners. Darrow would not merely defend the federation against the killing of Frank Steunenberg, but against allegations of conducting the most fantastic murder ring ever charged to "an inner circle of terrorists" in American history.

The workingmen of Colorado who had long been brutalized and exhausted by the twelve-hour day in the mine, smelter and mill had labored hard to get an eight-hour law passed in the state. By an intensive program of education they had at length succeeded in getting the legislature to pass their law. But the state Supreme Court had promptly declared it unconstitutional. "It is unconstitutional," observed Darrow, "to pass a law which won't permit Guggenheim to take twelve hours out of the hide of his men. If this is true, then what is the constitution for, except to use for the rich to destroy the laws that are made for the poor?"

This blow would have discouraged a less hardy group, but the miners set to work to amend their constitution so that it would permit the eight-hour law. "Their amendment was adopted by a majority of nearly forty-seven thousand. A legislature pledged and duty bound to enact this amendment was elected." Then the mine and smelter owners stepped in, exerting such power over the legislature that it refused to pass the amendment which they were legally bound and obliged to pass.

The miners struck, and "certain mining camps in Colorado became little short of hells on earth, owing to the contest of the desperate strikers with the men who had taken their places." Non-union workers were clubbed, shot, run out of the Cripple Creek and Telluride sections: the miners had believed in the efficacy of the vote; they had squandered their years, their strength and their funds to get laws passed; when they found that the owners could make a farce out of a political structure in which the government was pledged to operate according to the will and with the consent of the governed, they saw no way to gain their ends except through force. Force had prevailed; the miners had succeeded in their strikes, had won the eight-hour day and gone back to work under good contracts.

But the men who worked in the smelters were still on the twelve-hour shift, with twenty-four hours straight every other Sunday. The miners belonged to a federation, and federation meant all trades within their industry. When the smelterers went on strike and were being defeated because the absentee smelter owners sent in deputies, Pinkertons and scabs, the miners stopped work to keep ore from being provided to the smelters. The mineowners were impelled to call in non-union miners; more blood was shed, and Governor Peabody, declaring the Cripple Creek section in a state of insurrection, ordered out the militia.

The commander of the militia was General Sherman Bell, who had been a Roughrider in Cuba with Theodore Roosevelt and had been working for one of the mine companies at five thousand dollars a year when Governor Peabody offered him the job of adjutant-general. The Boston *Transcript* reported that since this job paid less than the five thousand he had been earning, the Mine Owners' Association agreed to pay him the difference. In addition, as Ray Stannard Baker wrote in *McClure's*, "The mineowners even advanced money to pay the soldiers." The *Army and Navy Journal* cried out, ". . . That arrangement virtually placed the troops in the relation of hired men to the operators. It was a rank perversion of the whole theory and purpose of the National Guard and was more likely to incite disorder than to prevent it."

General Bell, proclaiming publicly that his purpose was the extermination of the miners' union and its affiliates, now played the role of Roughrider over the citizens of Cripple Creek. He seized a private building to use as his military headquarters, marched his troops on the city hall, where he informed the mayor and chief of police that unless they obeyed military orders their city hall would also be seized. The sheriff, county assessor and treasurer were forced to resign. Every workingman in the vicinity who belonged to a union was arrested, thrown into a military bull pen and held incommunicado for weeks. When the editor of the Victor

Record dared to criticize his usurpation of power, Bell established a military censorship of the paper, arrested the entire staff and marched them to his prison, where he kept them for twenty-four hours without food. Women and children voicing criticism were also lodged in the bull pen. In answer to the demand of the hundreds of prisoners for their right of habeas corpus, or their right to be charged with a specific crime and given a public hearing in court—the foundation of the American legal system, which Blackstone called "the second Magna Charta"—General Bell declared that the writ of habeas corpus had been suspended! Judge Seeds of Victor, outraged, ordered the general to bring his prisoners into court. Bell surrounded the courthouse with troops, put Gatling guns in the streets, sharpshooters on the roofs of the surrounding buildings and lined up his prisoners in the courtroom. When Judge Seeds handed down a decree that all prisoners be surrendered to the civil courts General Bell laughed and marched his union men back to the bull pen.

General Bell had precedent in Colorado. When Charles H. Moyer, president of the Western Federation of Miners had gone to Telluride to help the miners in their strike and was seized by the military on the grounds that he had desecrated the American flag by printing on it the complaints of the miners held in the bull pens, Judge Stevens had issued a writ of habeas corpus for Moyer. The general had flatly refused to turn him over to the court, and Governor Peabody had sustained his general by proclaiming, "We have suspended the right of habeas corpus." Federation lawyers had appealed to the state Supreme Court, but the Supreme Court had upheld the governor. When told that he was violating the Constitution, Judge McClelland had replied, "To hell with the Constitution; we're not following the Constitution!"

Darrow had sent a sharp protest to President Roosevelt when this decree was handed down, but Roosevelt had said nothing. Colorado had stepped out of the union. The miners were abandoned. Henry George, Jr., an eyewitness, telegraphed to the New York *American,* "The astounding situation here in Colorado is that instead of bending all their efforts to putting down what they declare to be a state of lawlessness, Governor Peabody and the higher authorities, using the military arm of their government, are devoting practically all their attention to putting down the law. The prime insurrectionist against the constitutional order . . . are the governor and his soldiers, acting with various citizens' committees, inspired and influenced by. . . . all-powerful railroads, mining and smelter interests of Colorado. It is bayonet rule against the rule established by the ballot."

Then on June 4, 1904, a small railroad depot at Independence was blown up, killing fourteen non-union men. The bomb was set off by a smooth, round-faced man named Harry Orchard, who had worked in various mines for a total of eleven months in the previous five years, carried a union card, but for the six months immediately preceding the explosion had been, by his own confession, working for the Mine Owners' Association as an informer, reporting federation meetings to private detectives Scott and Sterling. Five witnesses had seen Orchard climb the back stairs of the boardinghouse in which Scott and Sterling lived no less than twenty times in the days immediately preceding the explosion. When bloodhounds had picked up Orchard's trail the man who owned the dogs was called off the job by Sterling, who told him, "Never mind, we know who blew up the station."

The federation was instantly charged with the crime. Citizens' Alliances, sponsored by the Mine Owners' Association, seized control of the region. Almost eight hundred men, many of them owning homes and businesses in the Cripple Creek area, were deported from the region at the point of bayonets. "In one instance all the union employees of a certain mine were loaded into a train and under military escort were taken across the line into Kansas and dumped on the prairie like so many cattle."

A howl of protest went up throughout the nation. Ex-Senator John M. Thurston of Nebraska, classed as a strong Republican and friend of the corporations, said in the *American,* "The act of the Colorado militia in driving out of the state members of the Western Federation of Miners was purely an exercise of despotic power. In Russia this sort of thing would go unnoticed, but we will not countenance it in the United States. The attempt of the militia to deport miners is a crime against the United States government. . . ."

The Colorado operators were not impressed. General Bell arrested greater numbers of workingmen, sent troops to search their homes without warrants, committed unbridled acts of vandalism against the property of the local unions. The Pittsburgh *Dispatch* said of him, "The despotic manner in which . . . upon the mere fact of being union miners, citizens were deported and dumped, starving, upon contiguous states will remain as a disgraceful record for Colorado long after Bell has vanished," while the Cleveland *Leader* excoriated Governor Peabody editorially, and President Roosevelt maintained a disinterested silence.

Though large sums were offered for the arrest of the culprits, though Orchard could have been picked up by the Pinkertons at any time, no one was ever tried for the Independence explosion.

This was the setup; these were the men Darrow would

have to meet in the Idaho courts; these the men the billion-dollar mining-and-smelter interests would employ; these the methods with which they would try to hang the three union officials. For Governor Gooding of Idaho had declared, "These men will never leave Idaho alive!" and Darrow knew that millions would be spent to make good that threat.

In Denver Darrow was received by Edmund Richardson, tall, lean, dark, bald, one of the most forceful and fearless attorneys of the Northwest. Richardson had long been the attorney for the federation. He was hard, fast, pyrotechnic, a fierce cross-examiner; Darrow was gentle, slow, persuasive, a pleader. Richardson had already made one trip to Idaho for the preliminary hearings. As he detailed the circumstances of the killing and the arrest of the federation officers Darrow shook his head in sadness and consternation.

On the evening of December 30, 1905, Frank Steunenberg conferred until late with the officials of the Caldwell Bank, of which he was president, then walked over to the Saratoga Hotel to sit in the lobby, read the paper and chat with friends. Watching him from a corner of the lobby was Harry Orchard, who had been in and out of Caldwell for five months, masquerading under the title of Tom Hogan, sheep buyer. At six o'clock Steunenberg rose to go home for his supper; Orchard ran up to room nineteen, picked up the bomb he had prepared there and hurried across the snow-covered fields by a back route to Steunenberg's house. He attached his bomb to the gate, stretched a string near ground level which Steunenberg must kick as he entered his grounds. His work done, he ran as fast as he could in the direction of the hotel. When he was a block and a half from the Saratoga there was an explosion "that rocked the supper dishes on the tables of Caldwell and could be heard miles away at Palma." Orchard hurried into the bar, called upon the bartender for a drink and engaged him in conversation as to the possible cause of the explosion.

The bomb tore a hole in Steunenberg's side and back. He was carried into his home, where he died within the hour. The only words he spoke were, "Who shot me?"

"Who was Steunenberg?" Darrow demanded of Richardson. "What was his background? Why should Orchard want to kill him?"

Frank Steunenberg was a big, solidly built man with the face of a Roman senator; by nature he was plain, phlegmatic, unassuming, bluff, a family man; his only idiosyncrasy was that he would never wear a necktie and would never permit anyone to ask him why he wouldn't wear one. He had come out of Iowa where he had served as a printer during the winters on the Des Moines *Register* while working his way through the agricultural college at Ames. Later he joined his brother in Caldwell, Idaho, where they published the Caldwell *Record* with moderate prosperity. In 1896 he was nominated for governor by the Democratic party because they couldn't agree on any one of their professional politicians; since he had been a union printer and had been made an honorary member of the Boise Typographical Union, the labor vote came out for him solidly.

His first term was pleasant, but in 1899 the Coeur d'Alene miners went on strike, with the bitterest friction in the Bunker Hill and Sullivan mines, which had imported strikebreakers and was using armed Pinkerton operatives out of Denver and Spokane to guard them. The miners had met in their union hall in Burke and, against the counsel of their president and cooler heads, voted to blow up the Bunker Hill mine. They took possession of a freight train, rode to Gem, where they picked up more men and dynamite from the depot, and proceeded a thousand strong to Wardner, where they blew up the mine.

The local authorities were few in number; the state militia was fighting in the Philippines; Governor Steunenberg saw no recourse other than to ask President McKinley for Federal troops. It was a difficult decision to make: he had been elected by the labor vote, yet a forbearance of this crime could bring destruction to the state. Within four days troops had occupied the territory and martial law was in effect. Once again every union man in the region was arrested, without any attempt being made to separate the guilty from the innocent; more than a thousand men were herded into a bull pen made up of one barnlike structure and a string of boxcars closed in by barbed wire. Here they were held for from four to six months, without trial or any effort made to locate the ringleaders; the sanitary conditions were excremental, the food bad, the families of the men not permitted to see them. A sign was hung out which read THE AMERICAN BASTILLE. Some of the conditions of overcrowding were perhaps unavoidable; a United States Senate Investigating Committee, which summoned Steunenberg to Washington to account for his conduct, gave him a partial exoneration.

It was his next move which had made his name anathema to every workingman in the Northwest: he decreed that all members of the federation were equally guilty and equally criminals; as a consequence he set up a "permit system" whereby no man could work in an Idaho mine or mill unless he were first approved by the general in charge of the troops, by the adjutant general of the state, and unless he first renounced his allegiance to the federation. Hundreds of men who had homes in the Coeur d'Alene, who had relatives and friends and deep roots in northern Idaho, lost their jobs, had to pack their belongings and, like the veterans of the American Railway Union strike, tramp the roads and mountains of strange countries, face an ever-spreading black list, trying to find work to support their wives and children.

The townspeople of Caldwell had quickly gathered about Steunenberg's home when the site of the explosion became known. Within two hours Governor Gooding and other state officials arrived on a special train from Boise, thirty miles away. A Citizens' Committee was at once formed which offered a twenty-five-thousand-dollar reward for the capture of the murderer; the governor offered another five thousand dollars. Many were too shocked to wonder who had committed the cowardly crime; others said at once, "It's the miners getting even for what he did to them in the Coeur d'Alene in 1899." No one suspected Harry Orchard, who was mingling with the crowds at the Saratoga, for the Caldwell men who had become acquainted with him over the five months described him as a "sociable, affable fellow, well liked. The boys enjoyed having him sit in the game of solo or slough. He was a little red-faced, round-faced man with a kindly appearance; he seemed a whole-souled mick who wouldn't hurt anybody—a common-looking, jolly fellow who you wouldn't pick out for any peculiarity."

On the train from Boise had also come Joe Hutchinson, lieutenant governor under Steunenberg during his first uneventful term. Hutchinson found a piece of fish string near the gateway, which he handed to Charles Steunenberg, brother of the murdered man, saying, "This is the string your brother kicked to touch off the bomb." The next morning Charles Steunenberg was passing the Saratoga Hotel with his friend George Froman, who pointed to Orchard sitting in the lobby behind the plate-glass window.

"There's the man that did it," observed Froman.

"Why do you say that?"

"Because he's been hanging around here for months, doing nothing. He's affluent but has no business. A number of times he has asked about your brother, when he was coming back."

Charles Steunenberg told Hutchinson of Froman's suspicions. Hutchinson "asked Lizzie Volberg, a hasher in the hotel, if she could get him into Orchard's room. Lizzie got a key and, while her sister Theresa stood guard at the head of the stairs, let Hutchinson into room nineteen. He found two towels tied together and hung over the doorknob to hide the keyhole. In the chamber pot he found traces of the plaster of Paris from which the bomb had been made. In

98

a suitcase he found another piece of fishline exactly like the explosion." The sheriff, notified immediately, located a check to Orchard's trunk at the railroad depot; when it was opened it revealed a quantity of the explosive used in the Steunenberg bomb, a full set of burglars' tools and changes of clothing which would enable Orchard to assume the apparel of any walk of life.

The clerk at the bar of the Saratoga thought Orchard wanted to get caught. "He impressed me as being a smart Irishman who hungered for notoriety. . . ." Orchard had left himself so wide open that for several days the newspapers refused to take him seriously, claiming that he was only a front for the real murderer whom he was helping to make his getaway. Nor does Orchard in his confession throw much light on this subject:

"I cannot tell what came across me. I had some plaster-Paris and some chloride of potash and some sugar in my room, also some little bottles and screw eyes, and I knew there might be some little crumbs of dynamite scattered around on the floor. I intended to clean the carpet and throw this stuff that might look suspicious away, and I had plenty of time."

However, if Orchard wanted to be arrested he appeared in no hurry. The following morning, January first, he walked unsolicited into a meeting of the Citizens' Committee taking place in the Commercial Bank, over which Sheriff Mosely was presiding. "I understand I am under suspicion," he said. "I should like to clear myself." So calm and assured was Orchard, so sincere and genuine in manner, "so obviously the whole-souled guy who wouldn't hurt anybody," that in spite of the overwhelming evidence piled up against him the committee was convinced of his innocence and let him go.

It was not until late that afternoon that Sheriff Mosely arrested Orchard and lodged him in the Caldwell jail. Orchard's good humor was not perturbed; he appeared unconcerned and sang in his cell and announced that there would be a lawyer to defend him as soon as it became known that he had been arrested.

Newspapers of Colorado, Montana and Washington filled columns with editorials that Steunenberg had been murdered by the Western Federation of Miners. Private detectives hired from the Thiele agency of Spokane, which supplied labor spies, non-union workers and armed deputies, cried, "Conspiracy to murder!" a cry echoed by the mineowners and officials of Colorado and reprinted in the Idaho *Daily Statesman* for home consumption.

Still the people of Idaho resisted the pressure being put upon them to drag the federation into a murder conspiracy.

The state was mostly inhabited by peaceful farmers and small merchants who had no connection with the distant mines and who wanted to forget the outbreaks of 1899. They were anxious to bring Orchard to trial, convict him, and forget it. They were a quiet, peaceful people who shrank back from starting or participating in a class war. For the eighteen days that Harry Orchard remained in the jail in Caldwell even those who said the murder had grown out of the Coeur d'Alene bull-pen days quickly added, "but it was the act of someone who was injured and nursed his grievance through the years."

Then on the twelfth of January someone convinced the ruling officers of Idaho that they should put James McParland, head of the Denver office of the Pinkertons, in charge of the investigation. He promptly set out for Boise to tell the state of Idaho who had killed their ex-governor. "My God!" groaned Clarence Darrow.

Exactly three days after McParland reached Caldwell, Harry Orchard was moved to the state penitentiary in Boise. The law provides that a prisoner may be moved to the penitentiary only if he is in imminent danger, yet the day before, when District Attorney Van Duyn of Canyon County was asked whether Orchard would be left in Caldwell, he had replied, "I cannot see where he would be safer in Boise. Sheriff Nichols has him well guarded." Sheriff Nichols had added, "It's up to me to say whether Orchard can be brought to Boise for safekeeping, and my answer has been 'no' emphatically several times. I will not consent to the man's being taken away from my county." The next morning, when the sheriff relinquished his prisoner, he was red faced and embarrassed. "I was firm in my belief that nothing could change my mind," he told the twitting newspaper reporters, "but the matter was put to me in an entirely different light. The reason for the removal will be made public in good time."

That good time did not take place for thirteen days, thirteen days of a very odd silence on the part of the *Statesman*, thought Darrow as he fingered through the pages and could find no reference to the Steunenberg murder. For ten of these thirteen days Orchard was held in solitary confinement in condemned men's row, with no human being permitted to see him or talk to him or communicate with him. That this maneuver was commanded by McParland is admitted by as implacable a foe of the federation as Charles Steunenberg, for Harry Orchard had worked as an informer and spy against his own union, drawing pay from the Mine Owners' Association. McParland was accustomed to dealing with informers; he knew that any man who will turn against his comrades for pay will make the most profitable bargain he can get. But first he had to be softened up by ten days of silence and loneliness, ten days of being frightened in a dark death cell, terrorized by the realization that the legal processes of Idaho had broken down, that he might easily rot out his life in this cell without ever coming to trial.

For eighteen years, ever since the inception of the federation, McParland had been retained by the Mine Owners' Association to fight the big union; before that he had been employed to destroy the young locals that were struggling to come into existence in Colorado. For more than twenty years, ever since he had been transferred to Denver after breaking up the Molly Maguires, the mineowners had been McParland's chief employer, often his sole employer. He had been paid millions of dollars to provide strikebreakers; to keep every local union infested with labor spies, who were paid by the Pinkerton office to join the unions, work themselves into office by their ability and to do clerical chores and from this vantage point supplied the mine and smelter operators with discharge lists, with information on every aim of the union; disrupted the unity of the men by causing factional strife; confused the records and squandered the funds; forced senseless strikes at times when the employers were in a position to win—as Sirango has boasted of having accomplished in the Coeur d'Alene. McParland's task of fastening the guilt for the killing of Steunenberg would be paid for not only by Idaho, but by the Denver office of the Pinkerton agency as well.

At the end of ten days Orchard was taken out of solitary and led to a pleasant room where Warden Whitney introduced him to McParland and then withdrew, an act which left no doubt in Orchard's mind but that McParland represented Idaho and was authorized to make a deal for the state. In his published *Autobiography* Orchard gives a one-paragraph picture of this first meeting, which for Darrow illuminated the whole story:

"He started in on my belief in the hereafter and spoke of what an awful thing it was to live and die a sinful life and that every man ought to repent for his sins and that there was no sin that God would not forgive. . . . He also told me of some cases where men had turned state's evidence and that when the state had used them for a witness they did not or could not prosecute them. He said that men might be thousands of miles away from where a murder took place and be guilty of that murder and be charged with conspiracy and that the man who committed the murder was not as guilty as the conspirators. *He further said he was satisfied I had only been used as a tool, and he was sure the Western Federation of Miners was behind this, . . . but that their foundation had begun to crumble."*

Luncheon was served to the two men. It was the first good food that Orchard had tasted for ten horrible days. During the afternoon McParland read to him from the Bible —and told him the story of Kelly the Bum who had taken part in thirteen atrocious murders but who, persuaded by McParland to turn state's evidence, had been given a thousand dollars and permitted to leave the country. At the end of the day Orchard was returned to solitary.

It was McParland's next task to make respectable a man who had begun his career of crime by short-weighting the farmers who brought milk to his Canadian cheese factory; who burned down the factory to collect the insurance; who abandoned his wife and six-months-old daughter to run away with another man's wife; who married a third woman without bothering to divorce his first wife, spent the money she had inherited from her husband and deserted her when she had become so destitute that she had to take in washing; who had stolen from his miner roommate the possessions of his trunk; who had robbed mines of their ore; who burned down a saloon for a hundred dollars so the owner could collect his insurance; who had plotted to kidnap the child of a former partner, to rob streetcar conductors, to sweat gold coins; a man who for years had roamed the West, living off the kit of burglars' tools found in his trunk in Caldwell; who had shot and killed a drunken man in a dark street; who admitted nearly every foul crime on the agenda. McParland had to get rid of this moral leper, whose only code for twenty years had been to live as comfortably and excitingly as he could without doing an hour of work, and replace him with another Harry Orchard who would be as credible and acceptable as this pathological liar was incredible and unacceptable. Without this Orchard's confession implicating the Western Federation of Miners would be worthless.

There was only one way to perform this miracle: a religious conversion so complete that the man's soul would be reborn. Then when Darrow would cry out in his towering rage, "How can anyone believe a word uttered by this self-confessed perjurer, kidnaper, thief, firebug and murderer?" the prosecution could answer, "Ah, but you are referring to the old Harry Orchard. This is the new Harry Orchard, who has found God." For Darrow the most strangulating moment of the series of bitter trials came when Prosecutor James Hawley told the jury:

102

"Orchard is everything despicable in a man save in one regard: he will tell the truth!"

During the succeeding days Orchard was brought to McParland's sanctum, where he intermingled passages from the Bible with tales of how men who had turned state's evidence had become national heroes. The *Statesman* relates the inside story, which, like Orchard's confession, revealed more for the historic record than it intended:

"McParland resolved to use his own personal energies in persuading Orchard to make a confession. This was slow work indeed, but the sagacity of the detective, his great ability of reading human nature, *his will power working over that of the prisoner, at last acquired the desired results. Orchard gradually became as clay in the hands of the detective.* At last one day Orchard met his visitor with an expression upon his face that told the detective as plainly as words that the man was about to confess. . . ."

On the day they broke the news of the confession Orchard cried in the headline of the *Statesman,* which had up until this time reviled him as a heinous murderer: "My only hope is to save my soul from hell!" Its lead column reported, "With tears rolling down his cheeks, with bowed head and thoughts of his early religious training, Harry Orchard broke down and made a full confession. . . . In fact, investigations made have proved conclusively that Orchard told the truth."

Orchard's confession is one of the most confounding ever made. He accused the officers of the federation of hiring him not only to kill Governor Steunenberg, but to murder Governor Peabody, General Sherman Bell, Supreme Court justices, mineowners, mine superintendents, private detectives; of plotting every unexplained mine explosion, including the Independence Depot explosion, fire, accident and death that had taken place in the Northwest since the blowing up of the Bunker Hill mine in 1899. Although Prosecutor Hawley swore that when the federation wanted Steunenberg murdered they naturally turned to "their arch-killer Orchard," Orchard himself admitted that after spending years of time and thousands of federation dollars to bump off their foes, with the exception of Steunenberg, the condemned men were walking the streets hale and hearty, never having been hit by a pea-shooter.

"If I had been one of the federation officials," snorted Darrow, "and this bungler had been working for me, I would have fired him on the grounds of incompetence!"

It is an insecurity which threatens the entire juridical basis of justice for a state to offer promises of immunity to a criminal who will turn state's evidence, yet no man ever collected his rewards on earth, on in heaven, more instantaneously. Borah had said at Steunenberg's funeral, "This crime, when fastened upon its author, will place him beyond the pale of human forgiveness." But Borah was wrong, and when he agreed to take part in the prosecution he helped prove himself wrong. The state provided Orchard with whatever small sums of money he requested. Clothing was bought for him, new suits, shirts, collars, ties, shoes. He enjoyed frequent visits from Governor Gooding; within a short time the governor was calling him "Harry," and Orchard was calling Borah "Bill"; when Governor Gooding took him to Boise for luncheon at the best restaurant in town Judge Wood became so outraged, he was on the verge of citing the governor for contempt. Never again was Orchard confined in a cell. Never again was he kept inside the penitentiary. He was moved into a little bungalow outside the walls and fed from the guards' table. "He will be well fed and provided with reading matter and such luxuries as are deemed advisable to let him have," promised Warden Whitney. The nation was treated to a spectacle in which a man who only a few days before had been loathed as the most unspeakable scoundrel and lunatic in the history of the state became by the simple signature of one of his many aliases a hero and petted darling, to whom papers from the big cities of the East were brought every day so that he might feast on his picture and read the glowing accounts of his regeneration.

It was by no means the first time that Clarence Darrow had to cry out, "Who will prosecute the prosecution?" In the long, flat silence that followed his question he perceived the answer: no one would prosecute the prosecution—except himself. Somehow that had become his main job; he would indict the indictors before a jury not of twelve men, but of a hundred million of his countrymen.

Extradition papers were immediately drawn up in Boise against Charles H. Moyer, president of the federation; William D. Haywood, secretary-treasurer, and George Pettibone, who had formerly been active in the miners' union but now ran a supply store in Denver. Not even Orchard had claimed that these three men had ever been in Caldwell, yet since extradition could only be sought if they were fugitives from justice, Idaho made this consciously fraudulent claim. The officials of Idaho then conspired with the officials of Colorado to remove the three men.

"On the night of February 17, 1906, Moyer, I and George Pettibone were arrested," writes William Haywood. . . .

"About eleven-thirty there was a knock at the door. I got up and asked who was there. A voice replied:

" 'I want to see you, Bill.' I opened the door, when I saw a deputy whom I knew. He said:

" 'I want you to come with me.' I asked him why.

"He said, 'I can't tell you now, but you must come.' We went down and got into a carriage. I asked him where we were going. He told me, 'To the county jail.'

" 'If you are arresting me,' I said, 'why didn't you come with a warrant?'

" 'I have no warrant,' he replied.

"They put me in one of the Federal cells. A few minutes later the sheriff came around. I asked him what it all meant. He said:

" 'They're going to take you to Idaho. They've got you mixed up in the Steunenberg murder.'

" 'Are we to have no chance at all? You can't arrest a man without a warrant and transport him to another state without extradition papers.'

" 'It looks as though that's what they're prepared to do,' he admitted.

"About five in the morning I was taken with Moyer and Pettibone into the office. There were a lot of strange men there. We drove along quiet streets, each of us in a separate carriage with three guards. A train was ready and waiting. We were going at terrific speed. The train took on coal and water at small stations and stopped at none of the larger towns along the route. When we arrived at Boise we were again put into separate conveyances. We drove to the penitentiary. There was a sign over the gate, 'Admittance, Twenty-five Cents,' but I was admitted without charge. We were then put in murderers' row in the death house."

When the papers reported the methods by means of which Moyer, Haywood and Pettibone had been brought into Idaho the clerk of the court in which the men were to be tried exclaimed to one of the leading lawyers of Boise:

"That's pretty highhanded methods!"

"What's the difference?" grinned the lawyer, "as long as we've got them?"

The difference, decided Darrow, was that by setting this precedent any man whom a partisan group wished to convict in a trial by passion could be kidnaped by a conspiring of the officers temporarily in charge of the state's legal machinery. When these illegal processes finally victimized the lawyer who had smilingly asked, "What's the difference?"—as it eventually would in some form or other once the legal structure of the

105

country was kicked overboard—he would see the difference—and from his jail cell he would howl for his rights.

"The fact that a wrong has been committed against a prisoner in the manner or method pursued in subjecting his person to the jurisdiction of a state, against the laws of which he is charged with having transgressed, can constitute no legal or just reason why he should not answer the charge against him when brought before the proper tribunal. The commission of an offense in his arrest does not expiate the offense with which he is charged."

The case went to the Supreme Court of the United States, but Darrow was no longer so naïve as he had been in 1894, when he had expected the Supreme Court to keep Eugene Debs out of the prison. He had been studying the decisions of the Supreme Court since that time, and he had come to the conclusion that the majority of justices handed down decisions aimed to preserve the rights of property over the rights of persons, an opinion which the Supreme Court did little to controvert when it declared unconstitutional child-labor laws and the minimum-wage laws. Nor did the Supreme Court disappoint him; stroking themselves with the dead hand of the past, they decided eight to one that nothing was amiss in the state of Idaho.

"No obligation was imposed upon the agent of Idaho to so time the arrest of the petitioner and so conduct his deportation from Colorado as to afford him a convenient opportunity before some judicial tribunal in Colorado, to test the question whether he was a fugitive from justice." Only Justice McKenna dissented, and while America would continue to produce Justice McKennas, thought Darrow, there was some fighting chance for democracy to survive. "Kidnaping is a crime, pure and simple," wrote Justice McKenna. "All the officers of the law are supposed to be on guard against it. But how is it when the law becomes the kidnaper, when the officers of the law, using its forms and exerting its power, become abductors? The foundation of extradition between the states is that the accused should be a fugitive from justice from the demanding state, and he may challenge the fact by habeas corpus immediately upon his arrest."

The prosecution was so arrogant that it did not bother to save face even before the outside world. Though Warden Whitney had promised to provide Orchard with whatever luxuries he could, the electric bulbs were taken out of the cells of Moyer, Haywood and Pettibone and candles substituted. The warden said, "Our power plant of late has not been able to provide all the lights, and the change was necessarily made." When the prisoners wanted to buy warm socks and flannel shirts to protect themselves against the cold the warden would not make the purchases; they were confined to their cells because the warden said he had no authority to allow them exercise. They were denied the right to talk to each other; they were denied the right to send letters without having them censored or to receive letters without having them read; they were denied access to newspapers, magazines, books or any other contact with the outside world. They were denied the right to have visitors unless permits were signed by the governor and Prosecutor Hawley. When all four of the prisoners were taken to Caldwell for the preliminary hearings the three union men were locked in the jail, but McParland protested that the place was too small for Orchard, who was then escorted to the Saratoga. Strangely, the only room available for Orchard was number nineteen.

"I wonder if he found any use for his trusty chamber pot?" mused Darrow.

When a complaint was raised by the defense against the methods being used on men whom the American law declared "innocent until proven guilty," Hawley expostulated, "It is very plain why all this howl is being made. It is the object of the defense to prejudice the minds of all persons possible. They are trying to queer the chance of getting a jury by claiming persecution."

Darrow plunged into the basic problem of the case: what would the federation gain from killing Steunenberg? What motive could they have for the crime? This was furnished in Orchard's confession:

"Moyer said that he thought it would have a good effect if we could bump Steunenberg off and then write letters to Peabody, Sherman Bell and some others that had been trying to crush the federation and tell them that they, too, would get what Governor Steunenberg got; that we had not forgotten them and never would forget them, and the only way they would escape would be to die. Haywood said we would go back to Paterson, New Jersey, and send these letters from there and write them in such a way that they would think it was some of those foreign anarchists that had sent them, and if we got Steunenberg, after letting him go so long, then they would think sure that we never forgot anyone who had persecuted us. Pettibone said this would be all right. Moyer told me to get what money I would need from Haywood. Haywood gave me two hundred and forty dollars and said he hoped I would succeed in getting Steunenberg."

The provocation for Idaho's kidnaping-and-murder charge against the three officers of the federation is based on these five sentences. Yet the simplest analysis of their content shows them to be an invention. Charles Moyer was a highly intelligent and capable executive of the caliber of Eugene Debs, Thomas I. Kidd and John Mitchell; he believed in the power of organization and unity to better the lot of his forty thousand members and their families. He constantly preached against the use of force as a decapitating boomerang for organized labor. Could this man have been so colossally stupid as to suggest that they kill Steunenberg and then send letters to their other enemies, promising them the same horrible death, when the receipt of the very first of such letters would literally convict them of the murder of Steunenberg? There were no labor disputes in Idaho, nor had there been any serious differences since the riots of 1899. The federation was exhausted from the beating it had taken from Peabody and Bell's militia. After Steunenberg's history in the Coeur d'Alene the union leaders would be instantly implicated by its enemies. Their organization would be vilified, their scant resources shattered; they would lose the sympathy and support of the public; their bargaining power with the employers would be hamstrung; their lawsuits in the Colorado courts would be injured; their years of heartbreaking labor and sacrifice to build hospitals, accident and death-insurance funds, to educate their members, to reduce the seventy-hour week to the forty-eight-hour week, to raise wages above the subsistence level, would all be thrown down the hopper.

What could have been Haywood's idea in saying that they would go back to Paterson and make the threatening letters look as though they came from foreign anarchists? If the letters were to terrorize their enemies those letters would have to come from the federation, not from foreign anarchists who lived two thousand miles away. If Peabody and Bell had walked the streets unmolested during the bloodiest class war in America why should they be frightened by threatening letters from foreign anarchists?—or from anyone else?

No, Steunenberg could do them no harm alive; his death could do them no good.

Before he left Chicago Darrow had met Senator Dubois of Idaho and asked him whom he should employ as associate counsel. "I must have a good lawyer, one with a good reputation in the community, one who is prominent but who hasn't been identified with labor unions."

Dubois ran over a list of Boise lawyers, but of each he

commented, "No, you wouldn't want him. No, that one won't do. . . ."

"Isn't there any lawyer in Boise who will fill my particulars?"

"Yes, I know exactly the man to fill the bill, but he's a very high-grade man, and I don't think he'll take the job. His name is Edgar Wilson."

When Darrow reached Boise he checked in at the Idanha Hotel, then went immediately to see Edgar Wilson to offer him the job. When news of this got about, Boise rose in arms: business firms that had been employing Wilson told him he would never get any more of their work; civic organizations threatened that he would be committing political and legal suicide; family friends implored Mrs Wilson not to let her husband associate with those murderers; they would be ostracized if he did—lose their friends, be driven out of Boise. The situation was complicated by the fact that Fremont Wood, who had been Wilson's law partner for twenty-five years, was to be the presiding judge.

Wilson was a fifth-generation American. He went to Judge Wood. "Would it embarrass you if I took this case?" he asked.

"No, it won't embarrass me," replied the judge. "If you think it's right to take it, go ahead and take it."

Wilson returned to Darrow and accepted the association. The one-acre Wilson estate on the edge of town, with its thousands of beautiful flowers, and the Wilsons' warm friendship, became for Ruby and Clarence an oasis in the sagebrush desert of hatred and vituperation in which they perforce spent their next two years.

Yet Edgar Wilson had had his legal and personal life blasted because he worked with Darrow. He was accused of having taken a thirty-thousand-dollar fee to use his influence on Judge Wood, and Wood, who earned himself a place in history by achieving a fair and impartial trial amidst the hysteria of the blood lust, was defeated for re-election by a green young Democrat in traditionally Republican country.

Sometime afterward Judge Wood asked a lawyer friend: "In what way was I censorable?"

"You were censorable for being a damn fool. You should have sworn in Edgar Wilson, then adjourned court and asked the governor to appoint another judge."

"But why? I wasn't afraid of my own honesty."

"It was a question of what people would think."

The reception Darrow received in Boise would have poisoned a less hardy man, one less inured to this kind of universal condemnation, this all-pervading hatred; he would have been forced to flee. When he walked the streets, when he went into public buildings, when he entered restaurants, he found icy faces of loathing turned upon him or eyes of aversion and contempt.

"He is defending the killers," said Boise, "so he must be in league with the killers."

Boise, which had tried so valiantly to remain calm and fair after the shocking murder, was now saddled with a vindictive series of class-war trials which would breed endless dissention and strife, write black pages on the slate of the seventeen-year-old state, spend a half a million dollars of its hard-earned money and so exhaust its treasury that before the trials were over they would have to issue paper warranties to provide them with funds. Their state officials, leading attorneys and leading newspaper had told the people that Moyer, Haywood and Pettibone were guilty of killing Governor Steunenberg; ninety per cent of the citizens wanted the three men hung as fast as possible.

Hysteria gripped Boise. Reports circulated that "every home in Ada and Canyon counties had suffered intimidation from federation men who went from door to door posing as book agents and insurance men who would talk to the housewives. Sooner or later the conversation would get around to the trial:

"Well, you want to pray your husband doesn't get on that jury. I've watched the Western Federation of Miners in Colorado, and when a juryman convicted a union man that juryman was always killed afterward.' "

Rumors swept the town that Darrow had posted marksmen on Table Mountain behind the penitentiary to pick off Orchard as he left the prison and then get Hawley and Borah. Hawley sent word to the defense that: "The second man to be shot will be Clarence Darrow!"

The city became overrun with detectives. Nobody knew for whom they were working. "One of the detectives was an offensive fellow, potbellied, who went around contacting everybody and insulting everybody," relates one lawyer. "He came to my office and offered me twenty-five dollars a day for the simple task of witnessing signatures for a change of venue. When I refused to work for the union he snarled, 'The federation will get you for this.' It was not until 1912 that I learned from my law partner, who had been prosecuting attorney for Canyon County, that this C. O. Johnson had been employed by the Mine Owners' Association to pose as a federation detective. My partner showed me the dossier in which my reactions to the bait of twenty-five dollars a day had been recorded. If I had accepted that employment I would never again have been permitted to practice law in Caldwell."

The *Capitol News* ran articles demanding that the lists of men working for the state and the salaries they received be published. When by repeated hammerings they became successful in this campaign Charles Steunenberg charged, "The *Capitol News* has been reached. We had to fire some of our best undercover men."

One or two detectives shadowed Darrow night and day; often these detectives were shadowed by detectives. His home was watched at night while he slept; detectives watched his house while he was away; his wife was trailed. His wires were tapped, his mail opened, his notes and reports stolen, his telegrams read: a complete system of espionage.

Yet in the midst of the suspicion and hatred the Darrows found a few friends. Mr and Mrs K. I. Perky, who were among Boise's liberals, invited the Darrows to stay at their home until they could find a place of their own. And Boise was scandalized.

Darrow writes, "When I landed at Boise about the first person I met was Billy Cavenaugh. His face beamed with a broad smile as he came toward me, extending his hand. He was a stonecutter employed on a building I was passing and had thrown down his tools to come down and give me a warm handclasp and rejoice over my arrival in town." Every night Billy Cavenaugh waited for him to finish his work downtown, no matter how late it might be, and walked home with him as his bodyguard. When Darrow was too exhausted from a sixteen-hour siege to fall asleep, Cavenaugh would give his charge an alcohol rubdown with his powerful hands.

After a time the Darrows found a furnished bungalow on the outskirts of town, just three blocks from the Wilsons. There was a rose garden, a bright green lawn and an apple tree. "This is fine," murmured Darrow. "On Sunday mornings I shall loll under this apple tree and read the funnies."

But he never got to read the paper under his apple tree of a Sunday morning. Idaho rang in another extradition, another confession and another charge of murder, a charge of murder which he had to go into the icy regions of northern Idaho to defend, not once, but twice, an effort which very nearly cost him his life.

The prosecution realized how difficult it would be to convict the federation officers on Orchard's testimony alone. Orchard had named Jack Simpkins, a member of the executive board of the federation, as his confederate in Caldwell, but since Simpkins had disappeared so completely that not even the Pinkertons could locate him, they compromised on Steve Adams, whom Orchard had named an accomplice in blowing up the Independence Depot.

Steve Adams was working on the hundred and sixty acres he had homesteaded near Baker City, Oregon, when he was arrested by Thiele, head of the private-detective agency in Spokane, and by Brown, the sheriff of the county. "Adams wanted to know what the trouble was, and they said he was charged with the murder of ex-Governor Steunenberg. The next morning Adams said he wouldn't go any further until he had seen a lawyer. Sheriff Brown had been talking to Thiele and said to Adams, 'Steve, they don't think you are implicated in the Steunenberg murder. They don't want you for that, but as a witness, and if you go down and help them corroborate their stories you will come out all right and not be prosecuted.' "

"Adams was never brought before a magistrate or a judge," charged Darrow. "He was never indicted by a grand jury. He was not charged with a crime committed. He was not taken to the jail in Caldwell, as the law demanded he should if charged with a crime in that county, but straight to the penitentiary in Ada County, and there placed in the same cell with Harry Orchard. For five days Orchard worked on Adams, telling him of the horrible things the state would do to him if he didn't corroborate Orchard's confession and of all the good things that would happen if he did. The only person Adams was allowed to see during those five days was Warden Whitney, who told him that he would hang if he didn't help them. In the meanwhile Adams' lawyer, Moore, had come to Boise and seen the governor. At the end of the five days Moore reported to Adams that the governor had said that Adams would hang higher than Haman unless he corroborated Orchard but that if he did this the governor had promised faithfully that he could get out of Idaho, and Moore had been given a hundred dollars to go to Colorado to see the governor of that state to get him to make the same promise."

The morning after Moore's visit Adams was taken to the same room in which Orchard had made his confession; James McParland was waiting there, his Bible on his knee. "During this first interview McParland told Steve that he had enough evidence to hang him many times, that they would hang him and he would never leave there alive unless he helped the state. He said he knew Adams was the tool of the worst set of sons of bitches alive in the United States and begged him to corroborate the story of Harry Orchard and said that if he did he would soon go back to his home in Oregon with his family; if he wouldn't he would either be hung in Idaho or taken back to Cripple Creek and hung.

The following morning Adams saw McParland again, to hear tales from the Bible of the biblical murderers who had been forgiven, the story of Kelly the Bum, his thousand dollars and his freedom. He had been given the choice between hanging and going free; he had no money or friends in Idaho; Adams signed a confession corroborating Orchard on a number of crimes against property purportedly hired by the federation—though in no way implicating either himself or the federation officers in the Steunenberg murder, the crime for which he had been extradited. He was instantly taken out of his cell "and placed in a sunny room in the hospital." His wife and children were brought from Oregon, and the family was set up in a bungalow outside the penitentiary walls. Three meals a day were brought in from the guards' table; Harry Orchard became their boarder. Once again the officialdom of Boise journeyed out to the penitentiary to make calls: Senator Borah, James Hawley, Governor Gooding, who dandled the Adams baby on his knee.

From the fraudulently drawn extradition to the happy family reunion in the Idaho bungalow Darrow was able to point out ten successive illegalities. Yet with the Adams confession in his pocket Governor Gooding might be right when he exulted, "Those federation officers will never get out of Idaho alive." Orchard's confession would put the noose around their necks; Adams' confession would spring the trap. Somehow he must persuade Adams to repudiate his confession. But how, when absolutely no one except the prosecution was permitted to talk to him?

That night Darrow slipped away from the detectives who were trailing him and took the train for Oregon to locate Adams' uncle. It was a long journey, the last hours of which he spent on foot in the mountains. When at last he located the cabin he was tired and thirsty. He knocked on the door.

"Are you Mr. Lillard, Steve Adams' uncle?" he asked. "I'm Clarence Darrow, the attorney who is defending Moyer, Hay——"

"You leave Steve alone," cried Lillard. "What chance has the poor boy got, all the way off in Idaho? They promised they'd hang him, and now they got a confession."

"Those threats are pure intimidation, Mr Lillard. Idaho nor anyone else can hang Steve on a confession obtained through the illegal devices of fear or hope of reward."

"You go on away," cried Lillard. "I'm not taking any chances getting Steve hung just to help your defense."

"All right, I'll go," replied Darrow quietly, "but before I do would you mind giving me a drink of water? I've been walking."

"Well, I guess it won't do no harm to get you a glass of water."

When he returned with the drink Darrow dropped down on the steps to mop his brow and chat quietly of how good spring water was, of the beauty of the Oregon woods and the imperishable mountains—the hidden wealth they contained, the lives of the men who labored to take that wealth from the ground, the work of the unions to pull the men up from the mile-deep pits of twelve-hour days, dollar-sixty-five wages and sudden death, the part played by the Pinkerton labor spies to crush the unions so the men could be forced back to the twelve-hour day, the starvation wage, the sudden death. After an hour he rose, extended his hand and smiled.

"Thank you for your hospitality, Mr Lillard. I guess I'd better be getting back to Boise and my work."

As he turned away Lillard called, with a puzzled expression on his face, "Wait a minute!" Darrow turned around. "You say they can't hang my nephew if he repudiates that confession?"

"They haven't a chance in the world."

"Well—Steve's got no right to peach on his fellows just to save himself. If you promise to get Senator Stone of Mississippi to defend him I'll go see Steve and tell him to fight."

A few days later Lillard arrived in Boise. Not knowing his mission, the warden let him see his nephew. Assured by the first person he had been permitted to see, aside from the prosecution, that Idaho could not hang him as blithely as they had promised, Adams repudiated his confession. The next morning Darrow demanded of the court a writ of habeas corpus which would force the state to show cause for holding Steve Adams in jail. The prosecution was promptly ordered to release him—but not before it had arranged with the sheriff of Shoshone County to be at the gate to handcuff Adams and take him three hundred miles north to Wallace, where he would be tried for the murder of a claim jumper whom he admitted having killed in the catchall confession. The Idaho authorities had known about this alleged killing for six months; they had known about it when they had laughed and joked with Steve and called him their friend.

That night, preparing to leave for Wallace, Darrow told Steve's uncle Lillard:

"Now don't you worry about this. I'm arranging to have Senator Stone defend Steve."

"Don't bother," replied Lillard. "I've been inquiring around and I guess you'll do."

But when Darrow reached Wallace he was refused permission to consult with his client. He cooled his heels outside the jail while McParland sat in Adams' cell, telling him over and over again, "I am your friend. I am here to help save you if you will do as I say. If you do as the lawyers tell you, when you stand with a rope around your neck you will be sorry. But it will be too late."

The prosecution was resolved to get a conviction in the Fred Tyler murder. Moyer, Haywood and Pettibone had been languishing in their jail cells for over a year now, but not even the combined efforts of Darrow and Richardson could force the state to bring the accused ones to trial. First the prosecution would try for the Tyler conviction to hold as a club over Adams' head and make him re-endorse his confession. James Hawley played the lead for the prosecution, a prime piece of indiscretion; if the state were interested solely in convicting Adams for the alleged killing of a claim jumper whose doubtful remains had been discovered in the woods by land prospectors some two years before and thrown none too reverently into a potter's field grave without the formality of an investigation, why was the busy and highly paid Mr Hawley superseding the elected county prosecutor? The tiny mountain town of Wallace was skeptical and a little put out at being used. For Darrow it was a distinct relief to find the people friendly and cordial; he even lectured to them in the evenings.

The facts in the Fred Tyler incident were indigenous to the snow-covered mountains of northern Idaho. Pioneers came in to homestead sixty acres of forested land; by backbreaking labor in the warm summer months they made clearings and built log cabins from the felled trees. In the winter months the men and their families would move to other parts of the state to work in the mines or the mills and save enough money to further develop their homesteads when spring came. While they were away freebooters would be employed to move into the cabins, lay claim to the properties and sell them to the companies, which would then cut down the trees. These claim jumpers were looked upon with the same loathing in the Northwest as were the early horse thieves in the South-west and often were dispatched in much the same summary fashion. The spectators were more curious than interested as the prosecution opened its case.

"The case of the prosecution which charges Steve Adams with this particular offense will rest upon the confessions and admissions of the defendant himself, confessions made in a free and offhand manner and without any unusual inducement. The confessions of the defendant will show that after the deceased, Fred Tyler, left the cabin of his neighbor he was met upon the trail by the defendant and two other individuals, that these persons were armed, that they took him into custody by force, that they took him into the cabin of Jack Simpkins, I think, and kept him there during the night. I am not sure whether they spent the entire night in conversation. The next morning quite early, they took him up on the side of a little mountain there and shot him with a rifle, without any defense being made on the part of the deceased or anything of the kind."

The prosecution was then forced to spend most of its time proving that the bones the prospectors had found were those of Fred Tyler, for no one knew for sure that Tyler was dead; he had simply disappeared. Dressing Mrs Tyler in heavy black mourning clothes, they brought her into court to identify her son from a swollen knucklebone injured by a baseball and from a few strands of hair that had been found upon a piece of bark. They were also hard pressed to show what motive Adams could have had for killing Tyler. He was not a homesteader in the region; he was only there visiting Jack Simpkins, whose claim someone, probably these poor bones, had been trying to jump. Even if the dead man had been successful in acquiring Simpkins' claim, why should Adams commit murder? To please a friend who was perfectly capable of shooting the claim jumper himself?

Why then did Adams confess to killing Tyler? Assuming that this dead man was Tyler and that Simpkins had killed him, Adams may have seen him do it or been told about it. He may have related the story to Orchard, who in turn conveyed it to McParland. The Pinkertons, wishing to implicate as many federation men as possible, had written the story into the Orchard confession. Once Adams had been locked up Orchard might have assured him that when he became a ward of the state the little murder story could do him no harm. Or Adams may have been telling the truth when he admitted the Tyler killing.

For Darrow the guilt or innocence of Adams seemed of far less importance than the guilt or innocence of the state; he fought the case on that basis. "Whether Steve Adams is guilty of murdering an unknown citizen is a matter of small consequence because these isolated acts of violence leave no impression on the state. . . . the state will go on; the law will be preserved. But if the law can be violated, if the officers of the law can take a citizen without charge and without trial, if they can place him in the penitentiary and then turn him over to the tender mercies of every vagabond detective who seeks to entrap him, then you will not maintain the honor of the state which is meant to protect the liberty and life of its citizens from despots and malefactors. It is infinitely more important to know whether this confession was honestly secured than to know whether any man was murdered. . . .

"It is a remarkable case; it is unprecedented in the annals of criminal prosecution. It is not for him, an humble, almost unknown workman, that all the machinery of the state has been set in motion and all the mineowners of the West have been called to their aid. It is because back of all this there is a great issue of which this is but the beginning. Because out in the world is a great fight, a fight between capital and labor, of which this is but a manifestation up here in the hills. You know it; I know it; they know it. There is not a man so blind, there is not a person so prejudiced or bigoted, to believe that all this effort is being put forth to punish an unknown man for the murder of an unknown man.

"Sometime the employers will learn, sometime we will learn, that hatred begets hatred, that you cannot cure conditions with policemen and penitentiaries, with jails and scaffolds. Sometime they will learn, sometime we will learn, that every man you butcher, whether with a gun or a dagger or with a club or upon the scaffold, only adds to the hatred and prejudice of the other side. Sometime these bitter passions will pass away."

When the jury of farmers and ranchers took their first ballot they stood seven to five for acquittal. Two days later the vote was the same, for no man had changed any other man's mind. The judge dismissed the jury but refused to let Adams out on bail. From the flimsiness of the prosecution's case this hung jury was as stinging a defeat as Darrow ever suffered. Technically it was a victory: the prosecution could delay no longer; they would have to try Moyer, Haywood and Pettibone on Orchard's confession alone.

The first break in the conspiracy case Darrow had made for himself when he convinced Lillard that Idaho could not hang Steve Adams; the second break was handed to him by an overzealous prosecution.

From the jury panel selected many men declared that "they could not convict a defendant on the evidence of Orchard, the accomplice." Before sending out the sheriff with additional venires the prosecution moved to remedy the unfortunate situation by buttressing Orchard's credibility. Representatives of a dozen of the major newspapers and news syndicates in the nation were taken by Governor Gooding in penitentiary rigs to interview Harry Orchard.

"Warden Whitney explained that Orchard had consented to be interviewed but that no question must be asked relating to any feature of the case." Not Orchard the murderer, but Orchard the celebrity had consented to be interviewed!

The following morning's *Statesman* glowed with eulogies of Orchard the reformed Christian. A. E. Thomas of the New York *Sun* allowed the *Statesman* to quote him to the effect that "whatever he has said or done since his confinement began has been done or said voluntarily and without coercion or inducements; he gave his word in my hearing. I believe his statements implicitly. . . ." Judge Wood continues, ". . . The court was so impressed with the injustice and unfairness of these publications that it . . . referred the matter to the district attorney of Ada County to make a thorough investigation." He summoned James Hawley, who swore that the interviews had been given without his knowledge or consent.

Up until this time neither the mineowners nor the Idaho prosecution had dared to use Orchard's confession to its fullest advantage since every revelation of the details enabled the defense to assemble controverting witnesses. Darrow had been able to ascertain such a small part of the confession that his defense, even while he was examining jurors, was shaky and perilous. Now the Idaho officials allowed Orchard's confession, which he admitted he had been rewriting and revising with his collaborator McParland for a year and a half, to run in *McClure's* magazine.

As a result of the release of the confession the hysteria that had largely been confined to Boise spread throughout the country. When the police of big cities used force to break up protest meetings the *Statesman* exulted, "San Francisco is to be congratulated on the fact that its police tore down the red flags and cracked the heads of some of the worthless creatures assembled to participate in such a disgraceful attack on the law." Maxim Gorky, who had come to America with his common-law wife, was ejected from his hotel in New York because he sent a sympathetic telegram to the accused men, was refused other accommodations and driven from the country on the grounds of moral turpitude. President Theodore Roosevelt, who had refused to disapprove of General Sherman Bell's insurrection in Colorado, called Moyer, Haywood and Pettibone "undesirable citizens." Tens of thousands of workingmen in every section of America promptly

118

broke out with badges on their shirts and coat lapels which read: "I Am an Undesirable Citizen!"

Eugene Debs, who had been converted to socialism by the imprisonment from which Darrow had been unable to save him in 1894, committed one of the few indiscreet acts of a long and valuable life:

"Arise ye slaves!" he cried in a manifesto. "This charge is a ghastly lie, a criminal calumny, and is only an excuse to murder men who are too rigidly honest to betray their trust .... if an attempt is made to repeat it there will be a revolution, and I will do all in my power to precipitate it." He then threatened to lead an army of workingmen into Idaho if they executed Moyer, Haywood and Pettibone, to which an editor replied, "Let 'em come. We'll meet 'em at the border with guns!"

Revulsion swept the middle classes of the nation, doing the cause of labor inestimable harm—as the prosecution had known it would. But with the enemy's guns fully exposed Darrow at last knew their strength. As much as five thousand dollars apiece from local unions, had been pouring in for the defense; he used this to employ hundreds of investigators to run down every statement in the Orchard confession, to find and interview people all over the West, to issue appeals to everyone who had ever known Orchard to check their memories against his dates, places and actions for any information that would help the defense. If this release of the confession gave Darrow a fighting chance to save his three clients from hanging, that was a price the mine owners appeared willing to pay: they were playing for larger stakes.

The little town of Boise became jammed with strangers who at times seemed to outnumber the residents: detectives, miners, operators, labor organizers, liberals and radicals, newspaper and magazine writers, politicians, observers of all shades of opinion. Heading a long list of prosecutors, most of whom had been hired for the case and whom the Idaho law allowed to be paid out of funds contributed by outside corporations—an officer of the mineowners declared they had raised a million dollars for a prosecution fund—were William Borah and James Hawley. Both of these men had gained their first prominence by acting as special prosecutors in the Coeur d'Alene in 1892; this was to be much the same show.

"When is Borah coming into the case?" Governor Gooding, feuding with Borah, had demanded of Charles Steunenberg.

Charles Steunenberg relayed this message to Borah, who replied angrily, "I'll get in just as soon as the governor clears the way for me to get in, and he knows it!"

William E. Borah had come into Idaho from Illinois in 1891 as a young man of twenty-six, while the territory, too, was still young. His first major opportunity was afforded him when he was called in as special prosecutor in the Coeur d'Alene in 1892. He won his case against the workers; and also won state-wide fame. From here he gravitated to the counseling of the Northwest lumber interests, doing so well that he had been able to put a hundred and fifty thousand dollars in cash into a lockbox. He had just been appointed to the United States Senate and had no real place in the prosecution, for his presence there made it appear as though the Senate were part of the prosecution; yet he had been ever eager from the very beginning to maintain his position as Idaho's first citizen in the spotlight.

The brunt of the prosecution was in the hands of James Hawley, a six-foot-two giant with a walrus mustache who had read law while working in the mining camps and had developed a rough frontier eloquence. Appointed one of the state's first circuit judges, it was he, as far back as 1893, who had suggested the idea of a federation to the struggling local unions and drawn up their first constitution. Because of his ambidexterity Borah paid him a high compliment:

"Jim Hawley has defended more men and got them acquitted and prosecuted more men and got them convicted than any lawyer in America."

The defense included Darrow, Richardson, Edgar Wilson, John Nugent, attorney for the Silver City local, and Fred Miller, of a Seattle firm which had defended the federation in the Coeur d'Alene. Richardson was to handle most of the cross-examination, Darrow would guide the defense and make the final appeal.

The night before the trial was to open Darrow went into the jail to have a conference with the man for whose life he was to be responsible. He knew that Big Bill Haywood had quarreled with Moyer and Pettibone, who were no longer talking to him. Darrow was saddened to find the cell torn by silent dissensions. Big Bill sprang up to meet him at the door and to clasp his hand, for Darrow had been one of his childhood gods. They made a memorable picture standing there in the dim light of the naked yellow bulb, America's strongest voice for tolerance and her strongest voice for war. Darrow, who was uncertain about so much in life, had a tendency to duck his head into his shoulders and shrink his size so others wouldn't think him bigger than they; Haywood, who was positive about nearly everything, had a tendency to tilt his chin into the air and swell up his chest so that people would think him even bigger than he was.

The two sat on the edge of Big Bill's bunk. Darrow knew

that as crucial as any other aspect of the trial was the need to convince Haywood that he must not try to precipitate a revolution from the witness stand; that he must be quiet, restrained and conservative; that he must reason like a trade unionist rather than a socialist, not only to keep from endangering his own life, but so that he would not pull down Moyer, Pettibone and the federation in his roaring wake.

The man whom the state had selected to hang first was just as big, just as strong and just as tough as his prosecutor, Jim Hawley. Big Bill Haywood had been chosen not only because they thought they had the strongest case against him, but because he was one of the most outspokenly militant leaders in the union movement and an active member of the Socialist party. Honest, fearless, smart, incorruptible except by his own flaring emotions, he was an advocate of force and violence as a means of achieving the workingman's revolution, loathing the college professor-preacher-intellectual type of socialist as a wordmonger and armchair theorist; the workers had to take with their fists and their guns what belonged to them, what they had rightfully earned. He was a one-eyed son of the poor who had come out of the mines at Silver City and believed in smacking the other fellow first when the other fellow began swinging his fist.

A strong picture of Haywood was presented in *McClure's* at this time. "Haywood is a powerfully built man, built with the physical strength of an ox. He has a big head and a square jaw. Risen 'from the bowels of the earth' this man has become a sort of religious zealot, and socialism is his religion. He is a type of man not unfamiliar now in America, equipped with a good brain, who has come up struggling and fighting, giving blows and taking them, who, knowing deeply the wrongs of his class, sees nothing beyond. Take a character like this, hard, tough, warped, and give him a final touch of idealism, and you have a leader who will bend his people to his own beliefs. We do not expect to find such a leader patient of obstacles, nor farsighted, nor politic, nor withholding a blow when there is the power to inflict a blow."

To all of which Haywood would have replied, "I ought to know about blows: I went to school to the Mine Owners' Association!"

No philosophy could have been more repugnant to Darrow than Big Bill Haywood's belief in revolution by force, yet they stood side by side in court as comrades in the most important case the infant twentieth century had yet projected. Both men had been started on the divergent journeys which brought them together in this Boise courtroom by the execution of the anarchists for the alleged throwing of the Haymarket bomb. The execution had started Darrow on his lifelong crusade against capital punishment and against the persecution of honest men for their work for the underdog. And the executions had started Haywood on his career of revolution by force.

To more closely knit the pattern, Oscar Neebe, the only one of the three pardoned men ever to come out of voluntary retirement, did so to speak at a mass meeting protesting the conspiracy against Big Bill Haywood.

After many days of questioning, because both sides had exhausted their challenges, a jury of independent ranchers was accepted, including one man who had been a close personal friend of Steunenberg's. The courtroom so small that Darrow, Richardson, Wilson, Nugent, Miller, Borah, Hawley, Van Duyn, Haywood, Moyer, Pettibone and Haywood's mother, crippled wife and daughter all sat so close to each other in a circle facing the judge and jury that anyone could lean out and touch his neighbor. The jury sat facing the circle, with its back to the judge, and Haywood was so close to the end juror, he felt that although they never exchanged a word they came to be devoted friends. Because it was a hot June doors and windows were thrown open, and the crowds on the courthouse lawn could hear portions of the testimony.

In spite of the closeness and intimacy, more ill will was generated than in any case Darrow had experienced. Hawley opened the hostilities by claiming they would "show that the leaders of this organization have been responsible not only for the death of Steunenberg but scores of others, besides," and that they would convict the defendants of all the violence that had happened in the Northwest mining regions in the past decade. Darrow jumped up for the first of a thousand spirited and bitter clashes with Hawley, demanding of the court that Hawley be ordered to stick to the murder of Steunenberg—an order which Hawley disregarded for the eighty vituperative days of the trial.

The prosecution promptly skyrocketed to the climax of their case: Harry Orchard was brought in to confess in open court as thousands of spectators lined the streets to catch a glimpse of him. He was placed upon the witness stand, and the great moment of the trial had arrived. Hawley led him gently through his confession, one so sordid and disgusting that the country was again revolted and, being revolted, saw no reason to doubt its accuracy. Orchard confesssed to lighting one of the fuses which blew up the Bunker Hill mill; to setting a bomb in the Vindicator mine which killed two foremen; to blowing up the Independence Depot, which killed thirteen men; to the attempted killings of Governor Peabody, General Bell, Colorado judges Goddard and Gabbert and, almost paren-

122

thetically, the murder of Steunenberg. Mixed in with the alleged federation crimes were a hundred other crimes committed for himself on his time off.

So convincing was he that Professor Hugo Muensterberg, the Harvard psychologist who came out to hear him, declared that Orchard was unquestionably telling the truth.

George Kibbe Turner, the *McClure's* editor who spent two weeks with Orchard, helping him prepare his articles, was convinced because "only a man with the imagination of a Defoe could make up the stories he tells—and Orchard's mind is absolutely devoid of imagination. He has turned from a career of hideous crime to an unqualified devotion to truth." Nor was it easy to distinguish the part from the whole: the relating of the details of his long string of personal crimes during the twenty years before he ever heard of a labor union not only made credible his later stories of the crimes of the federation but laid the necessary character base for their plausibility.

Each afternoon Orchard was taken by the warden to Hawley's office, where he had conferences with Hawley, Borah and Gooding and then slept on Hawley's leather couch; each morning McParland came to the office for a session with his protégé before he went into court. It took Orchard three days to tell his story. It was almost airtight. The geography of the mining region was given so accurately that those who knew the country recognized it; the timing on dates of explosions and the havoc they wrought were so accurate that those who had seen, heard or read reports of the explosions recognized the authenticity of the descriptions; his occasional criticisms of the militia and the government made him appear an unbiased witness; his willingness to confess personal crimes gave him the appearance of the true repentant, and his accurate knowledge of where his victims were at specific dates convinced others that he had been an agent for murder. What no one was able to tell was how much of Orchard's story was based on McParland's Pinkerton files.

Was Orchard telling the truth? Was his conversion genuine?

One noon recess, when Orchard was lunching at Hawley's office, he met Charles P. McCarthy, young assistant to Senator Borah. When McCarthy asked him how he could have committed all the horrible crimes to which he was confessing Orchard replied:

"When I was a young man in Colorado I thought there was a war. The government and militia were controlled by the mineowners. I felt we were justified in using dynamite because it was the only weapon I could use. They sent me down to kill Steunenberg. Then they caught me and put me in a cell in solitary confinement. It was then I realized it wasn't a war; it was just revenge. They say that McParland got a confession out of me; *without wishing to detract from Mr McParland's accomplishment, I would have talked to a child if he had come into my cell.*"

This single unrehearsed answer, given seventeen months after his conversion, contains one bald-faced lie, one deception and one connivance. When Orchard claimed he committed the crimes because he thought he was in a class war he omitted the arson, perjury, fraud, bigamy, thievery, kidnaping and murder which he had also admitted having committed before he ever became a miner! When he says, "They put me in a cell in solitary confinement, and it was then I realized it wasn't a war; it was just revenge," he commits a deception in that he gives no reason for reaching this sudden and revolutionary conclusion except that he had been caught, was frightened and had been offered the bargain from which he was every day profiting handsomely. When he uses the phrase, "without wishing to detract from Mr McParland's accomplishment," he reveals the same conniving mind that had connived all the vicious crimes from his earliest youth. Would a man honestly converted have thought in terms of McParland's accomplishment? Would he not have thought of God's accomplishment in performing the conversion? Would a man who had found God have been so smoothly and glibly solicitous not to offend or detract from his benefactor, Mr McParland?

Was Orchard's conversion genuine?

He had worked as a strong-arm man for the federation when they made it profitable; he had worked for the Mine Owners' Association as an informer when they made it profitable; he had worked on the side of saloonkeepers who wanted their buildings burned down when the saloon men had made it profitable, and he had stolen his roommate's few possessions when that had seemed profitable. Would Orchard go over on God's side if it could be made to appear profitable? If he could earn his life by helping to hang three other men when he had confessed to killing certain of his victims for as little as fifty dollars?

Charles Koelsche, who, as one of the prosecuting attorneys, ordered the arrest of Dr McGee because the physician testified that Orchard was a liar and perjurer, tells that, "I was in Jim Hawley's office when Orchard was brought there at lunch time during the trial. Governor Peabody of Colorado walked in. Orchard saw him and began blubbering like a baby. When he finally gained control of himself he said, 'You can't know how good it is to see your face alive, when I might have encompassed its death.'" Koelsche adds, "That had to be the truth, or Orchard was the greatest actor that ever lived."

He had abandoned his wife and six-months-old daughter, left them without any means of support and never sent them a dollar of help in all the years, yet when he writes his confession he says, "There was a dear little girl born to us that spring, and thus my dear little wife was no longer able to look after the cheese making as she formerly had. I rented a nice house in town shortly after our dear little girl was born—but my dear wife would often complain and plead with me to stay home." All these terms of endearment come within four consecutive sentences; are they the words of a genuine repentant, or are they the words of a professional hypocrite wallowing in his highly profitable sentimentality?

Was Orchard's conversion genuine? When challenging its sincerity Darrow was accused of being an atheist, an infidel, an enemy of Christianity, who would not accept the possibility of conversion. He replied, "If Harry Orchard has religion now, I hope I may never get it. Before Orchard got religion he was bad enough, but it remained to religion to make him totally depraved. What does religion mean? It means love; it means charity; it means kindliness. If he had got religion it ought to be charity and kindness and forgiveness to other men whose lives are like his. Would you have any confidence in religion if a man was as cruel, as heartless, as he was before? Take Orchard. He was acquainted with Moyer, Haywood and Pettibone. He had worked himself into the confidence of Pettibone. He had been invited to his house. He had eaten at his table. He had slept in his bed. He was his friend. I ask you whether there was the least look of pity, the least sign of regret, the least feeling of sorrow, when this man sought to hand over his friends to the executioners. I want you to say whether religion has changed the nature of this wretch, and I should expect if any of you were interested in religion you would say he hadn't got it. You would have to say that to keep from giving up your own."

That night Darrow tossed on his sleepless bed, tormented by the shattering riddle behind the nightmare:

Why did Orchard kill Steunenberg? For whom—if anybody? There were equal amounts of evidence that he had been hired by the Mine Owners' Association or the Western Federation of Miners, though the evidence in both instances was slight. He said the federation had given him two hundred and forty dollars in August and had given him nothing since, yet in his travel and bounteous living he had spent over a thousand dollars. Who had provided him with the money? He had always been a free-lance speculator; it was possible that he heard wild talk at the Pinkerton or federation headquarters and figured that if he stirred up trouble by killing Steunenberg, either or both sides would pay him. The newspapers had called him a professional killer, though his behavior had been that of a bungling amateur. He may have done it for some disgruntled miner or merchant of the Coeur d'Alene bull-pen days, or he may have been hired by some local union executive like Jack Simpkins, who was a gorilla and troublemaker, working outside the knowledge of the federation. It was possible that he killed Steunenberg as revenge for costing him his one-sixteenth interest in the Hercules mine, which he had deserted at the time of the Coeur d'Alene trouble, but it was not probable. He may have been hired by the cattlemen of Idaho who hated Steunenberg for his sheep activities or by lumber interests operating similar land grabs. Or it may have been an act of a diseased brain without motive or prompting other than that it would bring him notoriety, fulfill his need for activity and self-expression, for suspense and accomplishment. He had lived a long life of crime with complete immunity and was confident that nothing serious could happen to him for still another crime. There would always be a way out.

And indeed nearly everyone had plumb forgot that he had murdered their Governor Steunenberg. After the trials Orchard became foreman of the penitentiary shoeshop, making trips to Portland and Chicago to buy machinery. For twenty years James Hawley worked every means to get him pardoned. As late as 1922, when the Pardon Board was again to consider his case, the ever-vigilant Charles Steunenberg demanded the right to be heard on the appointed day. The board held a closed and secret meeting the night before, at which Orchard's pardon was at last granted. The next morning Steunenberg wrote an article denouncing this act, and the people of Canyon County threatened to shut up their shops and come into Boise en masse to stop the board.

Failing in their efforts to get him out of the penitentiary, Hawley and Gooding did all they could to make his life an easy one. Charles Steunenberg relates, "The penitentiary outfitted a room for Orchard and paid for the electricity used. Private parties gave him the money with which to buy machinery; the state permitted him to use convict labor for his own private enterprise in which he manufactured shoes for prominent people in Idaho and rolled up a cash reserve of ten thousand dollars."

In 1940, at seventy-three, Orchard was still fat and sleek, oily eyed and unctuous. He told visitors to the prison chicken farm that he "just can't bring himself to kill a chicken." To anyone wanting to clear the historic record on the crime

Orchard cried petulantly, "The trouble with you writers is that you never come here to write about me. You always want to use me to write about somebody else!"

Because Richardson had earned the title of the greatest cross-examiner of the Northwest Darrow had agreed that Richardson should cross-examine Orchard. As a result of this agreement the defense suffered its only serious setback, one so severe that Richardson was released by the federation after the Haywood trial. For a solid week he shot questions at Orchard in an attempt to make him contradict himself; he matched his brains, his skill, his training, against the confessor, yet not once did Orchard fall into an important contradiction. So magnificent was his memory that once when Richardson read back some of his testimony from the day before Orchard interrupted to say that two words had been left out by the court reporter and insisted upon putting them in.

Great portions of the country were convinced by Orchard's invulnerability under fire. Day after day the *Statesman* told how Richardson had failed to shake Orchard, what a magnificent witness Orchard was, how true and clear and honest, while Richardson was called "blundering, disastrous, stumbling, clumsy. Richardson is a bungler; he is damaging his own case; his fellow lawyers squirm under his methods. Orchard is determined, courageous, pert, resolute."

While it was true that Darrow squirmed some under his colleague's efforts, he perceived that Richardson had turned up material under cross-examination which would be important in settling the case. *Orchard admitted that he had previously committed perjury in court; that he had confessed before to crimes which he had never committed; that he had first met Moyer, Haywood and Pettibone when he had been sent to Denver by the mineowners' detectives to spy upon the federation.* In any other instance this would have been sufficient to throw Orchard and the indictments out of court.

Up to this point the case against Haywood had been based on four charges. Orchard said, "Haywood wanted to get ex-Governor Steunenberg. Haywood gave me two hundred and forty dollars and said he hoped I would succeed in getting Steunenberg." It was admitted by Haywood that in 1904 he had hired Orchard as a gunman to protect Moyer, who was going into the militia-infested Telluride region. When Haywood asked him if he had a gun Orchard took off his overcoat, unbuttoned his coat and vest and held open his trousers to show a long-barreled pistol.

"That's fine," commented Haywood acidly; "you'll have to get undressed to take out that thing." Moyer was arrested in

Telluride, before Orchard had had a chance to unbutton his pants.

Actually Hawley was trying Haywood on the crimes committed by the federation in the Coeur d'Alene in 1899, at which time Haywood was working as a miner in Silver City.

The prosecution spent from June fourteenth to June twenty-second leading a long line of witnesses to the stand, all of whom had been found and brought to Boise by the Pinkertons to prove that Orchard had committed many crimes of violence, that he had been acquainted with Haywood and, therefore, must have been commissioned to commit these crimes by Haywood. Hawley worked over the witnesses to prove that Orchard was telling the truth about other crimes he had committed and consequently must be telling the truth about the Steunenberg crime. Not one witness could testify that he had any evidence that Haywood had hired Orchard to kill Steunenberg.

When the prosecution finished presenting its case Darrow instructed Edgar Wilson to rise and ask Judge Wood to "give to the jury an advisory instruction for a verdict of not guilty on the ground that under the statute there was no corroborating evidence of Orchard's testimony sufficient to justify a conviction." Thereupon arose the greatest irony of the case: Judge Wood, wanting to instruct the jury to throw the case out of court, was afraid to do so because his former partner, Edgar Wilson, had made the motion! Judge Wood writes, "As I then . . . and have ever since viewed the actual situation as presented by that motion, there was very little legal corroboration upon which a verdict of guilty could be justified, and when the court came to a consideration . . . the appearance of Mr. Wilson in the case was thrust upon the court as an almost controlling factor. Had Edgar Wilson been absent from the case . . . the decision of the court on the motion for advisory verdict might have been different and the trials thereby terminated!"

It was a good thing for the fifty-year-old heart of Clarence Darrow, who had hired Edgar Wilson to aid in the defense, that he could not know why Judge Wood had refused his motion.

Darrow proceeded vigorously with his case, bringing eighty-seven witnesses to the stand to testify that in some one important detail Orchard was lying, that he had manufactured either the crime or his part in it, that he was not where he had said he was on certain dates, that often he had been very far distant and that it was not reasonable that he should be hired as an assassin by the federation officers when they had excellent basis to suspect that he was working as a detective for the mineowners. Five witnesses claimed to have heard him make threats against the life of Governor Steunenberg because of the loss of his interest in the now-valuable Hercules mine, when he had to flee the Coeur d'Alene after Steunenberg had called in the Federal troops in 1899.

Some of these witnesses were union men and union officers who doubtless would have agreed to perjure themselves to save their leader; others among them might have committed perjury for cash. But among the eighty-seven witnesses who testified that Orchard was a liar and perjurer were men and women from every walk of life: doctors, engineers, former mineowners and superintendents, state officers, the former attorney general of Colorado, businessmen, army officers, housewives, women in business. All of these reputable citizens could not have been lying and Orchard alone telling the truth.

Darrow was therefore cast into the deepest gloom when Hawley cried in court, "Wherever Orchard has been contradicted in his testimony it has been by a person interested as a party to this conspiracy or by a person whose testimony has absolutely been proved to be false." In his next move Hawley descended to one of the lowest levels ever reached in an American court. When Dr McGee, who conducted a string of hospitals in northern Idaho, who was considered to be a good doctor, prosperous and well loved in his country, testified that Orchard had lied when he claimed to have blown up a certain mine because he was with the doctor several hundred miles away on the day the explosion occurred, Hawley called Dr McGee's evidence "the hallucination of a disordered mind" and ordered the doctor arrested for perjury. McGee was arrested in his home, to which he had returned after giving his evidence. It is illuminating that this device had been most effectively used by McParland in the Molly Maguire prosecutions as the biographer of the Mollies testifies:

"A highly significant result of the trial for the murder of Yost was the prosecution for perjury of four witnesses in that trial. They—including two women—pleaded not guilty, were convicted and sentenced within a few days—receiving one- to three-year sentences. With witnesses disposed of thus summarily, friends of subsequent defendants were reluctant to testify in a manner contradicting one of the commonwealth witnesses, particularly if he were a detective or a member of the Coal and Iron police."

Dr McGee was arraigned on a perjury charge. The sole witness against him was—Harry Orchard! Released by the judge, McGee was indicted a second time; after the Haywood and Pettibone trials the prosecution was still attempting to press its charges.

129

Staggered by this kind of procedure, Darrow suffered frequent bouts of depression. "I'm through with the law, Rube," he would grouse to his wife as he lay in her arms and let his hot, tired head be stroked by her relaxing fingers. "This is our last case. Black Mountain mine can support us from now on. We'll travel the world—New York, London, Paris, Shanghai. I'll write my books and stories."

Or he would go into the cell occupied by the three prisoners. "Cheer up, Clarence," said Pettibone; "we are the ones who are going to hang."

Pettibone was the only one who seemed to be enjoying the trial, but then, he had been through it before. Charged with participating in the blowup of the Frisco Mill in the Coeur d'Alene in 1892, he had been convicted in Idaho, only to have the conviction thrown out by the United States Supreme Court. Except for his ingrown hatred of mineowners, Pettibone was a kindly man with a child's love of explosives. One day when Orchard was telling of using some of "Pettibone's dope," a fire-spreading chemical which Pettibone had invented, Pettibone said laughingly to the clerk of the court, "Great stuff, that. A man could have a lot of fun with it. You ought to get some for the Fourth of July."

But Darrow's depression was not caused solely by the methods of the prosecution. It was caused in the main by a conflict within himself, a conflict which would grow with the years. For he gradually had come to the realization that he did not like Big Bill Haywood, that he did not approve of him, that Haywood's methods, unless curbed, would go a long way toward destroying the labor movement. Haywood believed in force and had used force; Darrow became certain that he was guilty of many acts of violence against mine property. Though Haywood gave an excellent account of himself on the witness stand, was quiet, sincere and moderate, in his cell he uttered such fierce bellicosity that even his two comrades turned from him and would no longer talk to him. Often he said, "I'd like to blast every mineowner out of the state of Colorado," and it was clear that he would if he could. Darrow was convinced that Haywood was completely innocent in the Steunenberg killing, which fact, he reasoned, would embitter him even more and send him on to greater acts of violence in the hopes of awakening a revolution by force. Darrow did not like to be in the position of defending a man who believed in such methods.

His distress was caused by the realization that his career as a labor defender had taken a turn downward: he was defending a man who, though not guilty as charged, was guilty of other crimes in the same spirit: crimes against property rather than persons, crimes well provoked, but nonetheless

130

crimes which would bring mass bloodshed and destruction if continued. By defending this man it would appear that he had always favored violence, that the unions he had defended in the past had been guilty of it. His defense of Haywood could only cripple him in his future defense of labor, the cause he loved most in all the world. He was distressed by the inescapable knowledge that other officers and members of the federation also had been guilty of acts of destruction, acts which in part had brought down upon them the retaliation and further terror of the mineowners. He did not want his defense of workingmen weakened by the knowledge that they had been guilty of anything worse than wanting to better the lot of themselves and their families. Yet he did no wishful thinking; as ever he was a sentimental realist.

During his bouts with melancholia he turned with ever-growing gratitude to his wife, who kept herself aloof from the melee of black passions. Ruby worked in her garden, scrubbed incessantly to combat the dust blown in on the desert winds, kept the house always cool and neat and filled with flowers: a calm, restful haven. When Darrow closed his front door behind him he could shut out the noisome and bickering world.

But he must not allow his disapproval of Big Bill Haywood to imperil the cause of unionism. If Haywood were convicted as a murderer labor would be convicted as a murderer; the precedent would be set for hanging any and all labor leaders on any and all crooked, illegal charges. Justice would be destroyed; the state and its courts and legal system would be taken over by the controllers of industry; the democracy of the people would be paralyzed. He must carry on the course he had begun in the Debs trial of 1894. His voice must be the voice of peace, the voice of hope, the voice of faith, the voice of the future.

For almost eighty days Darrow battled with Hawley, and gargantuan battles they were, for both men knew how to fling epithets when they thought epithets effective. Judge Wood's daughter, who sat through the trial, says, "The whole procedure sounded as though it were taking place in an insane asylum."

Hawley's summation was nearly solid invective against the federation and based on the assumption that every word Orchard spoke was absolute truth. "There is some mysterious but powerful influence back of this confession," said Hawley, to which Darrow murmured, "Hear, hear!"

When Darrow rose to make his final plea it was a blistering mid-July day. Since it was impossible to wear a coat in that heat he walked up and down before the jury box in his shirt sleeves and suspenders, sometimes with his thumbs locked into the suspender where it buttoned to the pants, at others holding the suspenders stretched back under his armpits; it was a picture for which he was to become famous. Haywood writes, "When Darrow rose to address the jury he stood big and broad-shouldered, dressed in slouchy gray, a wisp of hair down over his forehead, his glasses in his hand, clasped by the nosepiece. When he spoke he was sometimes intense, his great voice rumbling, his left hand shoved deep in his left pocket, his right arm uplifted. Again he would take a pleading attitude; his voice would become gentle and very quiet. At times he would approach the jury almost on tiptoe."

Darrow spoke to the jury for eleven hours. The words he said would fill a two-hundred-page book of normal print. The speech, even more so than the one he had made to the Anthracite Commission four years before, is astounding in its organization and its mastery of every detail that had been elicited in the seventy-six days of examination: for not once did he consult his notes or papers. He carried it in his head: the character of each witness and what he had contributed to the case, what he had sustained or admitted under cross-examination, the history of the mining regions for two decades and their design of violence, the complete genesis of Harry Orchard and his credibility, the history of conspiracy, the history of the labor movement, the history of the operators' oppressions and their use of force, the importance of this trial in the future making of the civilized world, the fundamental issues involved over and above the life of one William Haywood.

"Mr Haywood is not my greatest concern. Other men have died before him. Wherever men have looked upward and onward, worked for the poor and the weak, they have been sacrificed. They have met their deaths, and he can meet his. But, you shortsighted men of the prosecution, you men of the Mine Owners' Association, you people who would cure hatred with hatred, you who think you can crush out the feelings and the hopes and the aspirations of men by tying a noose around his neck, you who are seeking to kill him, not because it is Haywood but because he represents a class, don't be so blind; don't be so foolish as to believe you can strangle the Western Federation of Miners when you tie a rope around his neck. If at the behest of this mob you should kill Bill Haywood . . . a million men will grab up the banner of labor at the open grave where Haywood lays it down, and in spite of prisons or scaffold or fire, in spite of prosecution or jury or courts, these men of willing hands will carry it on to victory in the end. . . .

"There is no way to give Moyer, Haywood and Pettibone

back the eighteen months they have spent in the Boise jail. These are all parts of the premium one gets and has always received for his services to his fellow men. For the world is the same now that it always was, and if a man is so insane that he wants to go out and work for the poor and oppressed and the despised, for the men who do not own the tools, the newspapers, the courts, the machinery and organization of society, these are the wages that he receives today and which he has received since the time the first foolish man commenced to agitate for the uplifting and the upbuilding of the human race.

"I speak for the poor, for the weak, for the weary, for that long line of men who, in darkness and despair, have borne the labors of the human race. Their eyes are upon you twelve men of Idaho tonight. If you kill Haywood your act will be applauded by many. In the railroad offices of our great cities men will applaud your names. If you decree his death, amongst the spiders of Wall Street will go up paeans of praise for these twelve good men and true. In every bank in the world, where men hate Haywood because he fights for the poor and against the accursed system upon which the favored live and grow rich and fat—from all those you will receive blessings and unstinted praise. But if your verdict should be 'not guilty' in this case, there are still those who will reverently bow their heads and thank these twelve men for the life and reputation you have saved. Out on our broad prairies where men toil with their hands, out on the wide ocean where men are tossed and buffeted on the waves, through our mills and factories and down deep under the earth, thousands of men and of women and children—men who labor, men who suffer, women and children weary with care and toil—these men and these women and these children will kneel tonight and ask their God to guide your hearts."

Darrow achieved greatness as a writer only when he was on his feet, his brain working at white heat, appealing not for the life of one man, but of all humanity. In those final hours in Boise he was as great as his cause; no man can be greater.

Although Judge Wood had refused to allow Darrow to charge the Mine Owners' Association and the state of Colorado with conspiracy against the federation, his conducting of the trial had kept it at all times fair, impartial and legal. He had not had the heart to instruct the jury to dismiss the case earlier in the proceedings, but in his long and detailed instructions he continued to reiterate the demands of the law before a verdict of guilty could be reached.

Judge Wood concluded, "The court instructs the jury that if you believe from the evidence that the witness, Harry

Orchard, was induced or influenced to become a witness and testify in this case by any promises of immunity from prosecution or punishment, then the jury should take such facts into consideration in determining the weight which ought to be given to testimony so obtained. Such testimony should be received by the jury with caution and scrutinized with great care."

As the jury retired to its room a newspaper reporter leaned over to Darrow and said, "Well, it takes twelve."

"No," replied Darrow in exhaustion, "it only takes one."

The report quickly spread about town that the best Darrow was hoping for was a hung jury. The faith of the Boise residents that Haywood would be convicted, which had never wavered throughout the trial, now rose to a positive conviction.

Darrow and Ruby went home about ten o'clock, but she could not get him to go to bed. He kept wandering about the house disconsolately, chain-smoking cigarettes. Despite his ideological differences with Haywood, a human life was at stake; the life of the federation and organized labor was at stake, and, most important of all, the legal structure of America was at stake. Every atom of his brain and spirit was in that hot, stuffy jury room through the interminable hours of the night, hours during which he never sat down, never stopped his silent pacing, smoking, worrying.

Just before five in the morning an eavesdropper on the lawn outside the jury room heard the jury take a poll and the foreman announce a vote of eleven to one. He conveyed his scoop to the newspaper, which was on the street in a very few minutes with an extra crying that the jury stood eleven to one for conviction.

"Boise rose up in joy," relates Mrs Edgar Wilson. "The women came out in their finest clothing and jewelry; the men were attired in their gayest suits and ties. The workingmen, the liberals, the poor, disappeared from the streets to make way for the throngs that laughed and sang and cried out to each other as they surged up and down as though it were New Years' Eve. They were all waiting for that last stubborn juryman to listen to reason, and then they would be ready for . . . a celebration that would have lasted for days and been unprecedented in Idaho history."

When Darrow bought a paper and read the news, the best he could hope for now was that the one juror would hold out and hang the jury. At six-thirty, when he was summoned by a deputy because the jury had reached its verdict, he knew it could only mean one thing: the last juror had given in. He hurried through the streets, racked with cramps. The courtroom was deserted, for no one had been notified of the jury's decision except the attorneys. Richardson, Wilson and Nugent were there, and Hawley and Van Duyn. Borah was missing. First Haywood was brought up from his cell, then the jury was led into its box.

"Have you reached your verdict?" asked Judge Wood.

"We have, your honor."

"And what is that verdict?"

"Not guilty!"

There was a flash of silence, then Haywood broke into a tremendous smile. Tears came to Darrow's eyes as he sat limply, collapsed on his hard chair. The jurymen all suddenly relaxed, some with smiles on their faces, others with tears in their eyes. Darrow shook hands with Haywood, then rose and went to the jury to clasp each of their hands. From the foreman he learned there had never been any danger of conviction. The first ballot had stood eight for not guilty, two for guilty and two not voting. The fourth ballot had stood at ten for acquittal, one for conviction, one not voting. At three-thirty in the morning they had taken the fifth ballot, which had remained the same, so they agreed to get a little sleep. At five o'clock they balloted again, and the count now stood eleven to one for acquittal. This was the count the eaves-dropper had heard; it is illuminative of the mind of Boise that, having heard this eleven-to-one count, the eavesdropper could only assume it was for conviction.

The crucial juryman, Samuel W. Gilman, said, ". . . It was the consensus of the opinion as soon as we got into the jury room that we could not find the defendant guilty in the face of the instructions of the court."

It was eight o'clock before Darrow stepped again into the hot, bright sunlight of the Boise morning. A tremendous throng was gathered to hail him, to embrace him, to shout out his name. They caught him on their shoulders and carried him down the street. He saw Borah standing in a doorway, alone, in his hour of defeat.

"Poor Borah," murmured Darrow; "now we must do something for him."

It was three in the afternoon before the crowd released him to go to the victory breakfast at the Perky house. By that time the repercussions had begun. Judge Wood was publicly charged with throwing the case to his former partner. Borah was accused of throwing the case for fear of losing the labor vote. Darrow was accused of bribing jurors. Bailiff McGinty was accused of taking six thousand dollars to let the jurymen be reached. Jurors were accused of becoming suddenly rich. The federation was accused of packing the courtroom to

135

intimidate the jurors. The good citizens of Boise gave every dishonest, illegal and scandalous reason for the acquittal that inflamed minds could conjure up.

In spite of their fine teamwork Darrow and Richardson came to the parting of the ways. Darrow said, "Mr Richardson was very hard to get along with. He was egotistical, arrogant and exceedingly jealous. We could never travel double again." Richardson said, "Darrow was headstrong, heedless and nearsighted when the interests of the clients was being considered. His great fault was that he was a socialist and was inclined to put the interests of the party ahead of the interests of the men on trial for their lives."

Since Richardson and John Mitchell made the identical accusation, only four years apart, the feeling must have been well grounded; yet Richardson missed the cause and motive of Darrow's radicalism. He was not a socialist member; he cared little for the party; he had denied Eugene Debs permission to come to Boise to report the trial for *The Appeal to Reason* on the grounds that he didn't want the added burden of having to acquit socialism as well as the defendants. Again he was the teacher pleading for tolerance, for the broader view, for a chance for humanity to live in security. He wanted to acquit Haywood, but he also wanted to break the pattern of enmity, violence and retribution.

The miners of the Northwest declared a holiday and staged gigantic parades. Haywood was offered fantastic sums to lecture throughout the country and was proposed as the next candidate for President on the socialist ticket. Moyer was promptly released on bail and went back to Denver to resume his duties as the head of the federation. Exhausted physically and emotionally, sure that the state would drop the remaining charges now that it had lost its strongest case, Clarence and Ruby Darrow returned to Chicago to pick up the threads of their life and their law.

He had been home only a few days when he received a telegram from his colleagues to return at once; Idaho was going to prosecute Steve Adams again in another attempt to gain a conviction with which to force him to testify against Pettibone. He took the next train out, the first of many trains which were to carry him across the ensuing months from doctor to doctor, from hospital to hospital, from court to court, in an agonizing journey, for no sooner had he reached Boise than he went down with influenza and "developed a violent pain in the left ear. The physican came to the opinion that I had received some infection and was in grave danger of it developing into a case of mastoiditis. It became impossible for me to get any sleep without opiates. I sent for Dr

Hudgel in the dead of night; he said I had better make ready to go suddenly to California or Chicago for expert treatment and that in the meantime I should not take another case.

"I knew he was right, but what could I do? Adams had turned his back on the state largely through his confidence in me. I had told him I would try his case. If through my failure he should be put to death I could never forgive myself. I knew I was seriously risking my own life to save his—but no one but a lawyer can understand what a sense of responsibility one may feel toward a client."

Darrow was removed from the Idanha Hotel to the St Alphonsus Hospital.

The second Steve Adams case was about to open in Rathdrum in northern Idaho, to which obscure spot the state had secured a change of venue. With the aid of Mrs Darrow, the doctor and two nurses, Clarence managed to get out of his hospital bed, dress and be moved to the railroad station. Here Dr Hudgel handed him a bag of medical equipment and some stern orders: the eardrum was to be kept open; it was to be irrigated every few hours; all of the equipment was to be sterilized each time it was used.

The train trip to Rathdrum was long and arduous. The first night out most of their time was spent in the dining car, where Ruby could keep water boiling in the kitchen; the next day she had to purchase pots, boil her water over a coal stove and perform her ministration in a cold and dirty depot. Coupled with the skull-cracking pain was the even less endurable uncertainty of what had gone wrong with his head, the knowledge that any instant the strange malady might shatter something in his brain and kill him before he had a chance to murmur his good-bys. The agonies that he endured remained fresh in his memory to his dying day.

When at length they reached Spokane and the specialist to whom they had been recommended had completed his examination, he, too, confessed himself baffled: He, too, ordered Darrow into a hospital, for it had been his experience that such infections generated fever, and unless that fever was discovered and checked at once it proved fatal. He repeated Dr Hudgel's admonition that he was risking his life by going into the Adams case, that he could take no responsibility for him if he left Spokane.

Within the hour the Darrows were once again on a train, "for if Adams lost it meant his death or his surrender to the state, which would further imperil the lives of Moyer and Pettibone." The Spokane specialist had been sound in his judgment, but he had figured without one factor in Darrow's life: Ruby, who, no less than Clarence, was a fighter with a stout heart and tender hands.

137

"We were in Rathdrum for two months, two months of agony. There was scarcely a moment in court when I was not in pain. At night I would try to get some sleep with the aid of a hot rubber bag which had to be reheated from hour to hour and which was constantly and devotedly attended to by Mrs Darrow. When the pain was unbearable we had to resort to the hypodermic. I could not possibly guess how many times she went to the kitchen with its coal stove to keep the kettle boiling, refill the bag, prepare the apparatus for injecting the codine and then irrigate the ear. . . . the outfit assembled with sterilized gauze so that no fresh infection would be added. I believe Mrs Darrow suffered as much as I did over this treatment."

The second Adams trial was a replica of the first. The jury voted ten to two for acquittal; since nothing could persuade the men holding for guilty to change their minds, the judge dismissed them. Adams was once again taken to the penitentiary. Darrow, more ill than ever through the added strain of the trial, left for Portland to receive treatment with violet rays, then went on to San Francisco, where the doctors were still unable to explain his malady or provide him with either relief or mental assurances.

Pettibone wa called for trial. Now it was the San Francisco doctor who told Darrow it would be fatal if he went to Boise; Pettibone replied that it would be fatal for him if he didn't. The two days on the train, with their constant hypodermics and irrigations, were endless nightmares of semideath. When he was taken from the train to the St Alphonsus Hospital in Boise, the Chicago papers sent newsmen to get his dying statement. Obituary notices were prepared throughout the country. However, Clarence had always been an ornery critter; he didn't want to die; he wanted to defend George Pettibone. On the opening day of the trial he was able to rise from the bed; the sisters at the hospital had given him magnificent care or he might not have been able to get up.

The main difference between the Haywood and Pettibone cases was that instead of cross-examining Orchard after he once again went through his confession, Darrow gently encouraged him to enlarge upon his personal crimes against his friends, particularly of how he had played on the floor with the child of his former partner, all the while planning how to kidnap the boy for ransom. The jury turned from Orchard as from the carcass of a dead animal.

That was very nearly the last that he could give. He collapsed completely. Even Pettibone suggested he had better withdraw from the case. The next morning he was carried into court in a wheel chair, white faced, thin and stricken, to make his last whispered appeal to the jury. That evening the doctor ordered him to California, even though admitting that there was small chance of his surviving the thirty-six-hour train trip. Billy Cavenaugh, the stonecutter who had acted as his bodyguard, boarded the train on his own idea and his own money; between Mrs Darrow and Cavenaugh Clarence reached Los Angeles alive, to be sped in the waiting ambulance to the California Hospital where a conclave of physicians was held—but they didn't know what to do.

After seven days of constant and shattering pain a telegram was received that Pettibone had been acquitted; Moyer had been discharged, and the whole ghoulish affair was over. The good news made him feel strong enough to move into a little apartment on the top of Angel's Flight, where he had a view of the city and the mountains beyond.

They lived in the apartment for three weeks, three weeks of unrelenting pain. When there was no change in the condition behind his ear and the doctors continued to be baffled, he decided he might as well be miserable at home. Ruby packed their luggage, and late one afternoon they took a cab down to the station. No sooner had he bought his tickets than he felt the swelling behind the ear which the doctors had been anticipating for five months. He dashed to the California Hospital, where he was operated upon at once and the "freak mastoid" drained.

His many months of illness had depleted his strength. For days life hung on the slenderest thread. He could not talk; he could have no visitors; Ruby set up a twenty-four-hour vigil outside his door. The little he was able to swallow could not be digested because of his shattered nerves.

For many weeks a financial panic had been sweeping through the United States; banks closed and investments were wiped out. From Gardner, Illinois, Lutz commenced to wire frantically that Darrow would have to sign certain papers in order that they might pull out of their Black Mountain gold mine. Telegrams, special-delivery letters, hysterical messages of all kinds continued to pour in, showing that his savings were being wiped out, that other investors also were being ruined, that only his signature could enable them to unload and save themselves from bankruptcy.

The doctors had warned Ruby that shock would kill him. She stuck the messages under the mattress of the couch on which she slept while Darrow slept. At last there came a telegram saying that it would be impossible to keep Mr Lutz from committing suicide unless Darrow boarded a train for Chicago at once. No longer wishing to take the responsibility in the matter, she showed the telegrams to the doctors, who assured her that she would be sacrificing her husband.

"So it amounts to saying that, for Mr Darrow, it's your money or your life?"

"We are sure that it's so, Mrs Darrow."

After several weeks, when he was judged able to leave the hospital, Ruby and the doctors told him as gently as they could that his investment was gone, that the Black Mountain gold mine was no more. Darrow jumped out of bed, broke away from the grasp of the doctors and charged like a bull across the room.

"Do you realize what you've done to me?" he cried at his wife. "You've thrown away my dream of retiring. Now I'll have to begin all over again—be a slave to law work—we'll never be able to travel, to write! I'll never forgive you for this —never, never!"

But he did, husband-like, when he learned that she had probably saved his life by letting his money go.

It was now two years since he had left Chicago to defend the federation. The union funds had been so depleted by the four trials that they could not pay him the fee they had agreed upon. He had his railroad tickets, enough money to pay his hospital bill and to return home, but that was all. He could not meet his doctor bills.

The first day he got back to Chicago he went down to his office, his head bandaged, only one eye peeping out. For seven weeks he had to wear that bandage, in his office and in court, but no one commented upon it or thought it strange: for everyone knew that Clarence Darrow had returned from the wars.

Chapter Eight

This Is War!

SEEKING a quiet neighborhood where her husband might recover his strength and serenity of mind, Ruby searched along the South Shore until she found a top flat of a six-story building called The Hunter, on the Midway, which overlooked the University of Chicago, Jackson Park, with its Japanese bridge and pagoda, and Lake Michigan. "It was built by a man who forgot that neither he nor his building would be everlasting," says Ruby, "so every inch of the inside was solid oak. The nine rooms were exceedingly large, with high ceilings and high and wide windows; even the kitchen was wide enough for a small banquet hall, a very great inconvenience. There were five windows across the front, every one affording beautiful views of lake, park, trees, lawn and unbroken distances." Clarence was delighted with its spaciousnes and the sense of being above the tumult of Chicago life, but he declined to sign a lease.

"We'll have to take it on a month-to-month basis, Rube, because I'm not sure enough about my income. We're between ten and fifteen thousand dollars in debt."

Ruby took their furniture out of its two-year storage vault, recovered some of the pieces, then spent four days and nights in fitting the front room with the red carpet from the Sheridan Road apartment. She put flatirons on the gas stove and with them burned red dye into the carpet to brighten it. She then ransacked the furniture marts until she found an oversized brass bed in which big-boned Clarence could roam comfortably, placing it in "the large bow windows across the south end, looking out over five beautiful maple trees and miles beyond, over other people's yards, lawns and trees. What breezes, what sunlight, what space and privacy and quiet there was."

For a year and a half she cooked, scrubbed the nine-room flat, washed the household and personal linen, never spending a cent on anything but food. At the end of that time the Darrows had paid all debts. Only then did Ruby yield and hire a maid. Only then did Clarence sign a lease, a lease which was to run for thirty years, which was to see the rent rise from seventy-five to two hundred and fifty dollars a month as the district became popular and fashionable, drop slowly again to seventy-five dollars as the neighborhood ran its life circle and disintegrated; a lease which was to leave Darrow undisturbed while styles in housing changed and the big flats beneath him were remodeled into six apartments each; a lease which was to terminate only when he died in his roomy brass bed in the bow window at the age of eighty.

What he liked most about his new home was its proximity to the University of Chicago, where so many of the professors were old friends who liked to drop in for an evening. He knocked out the walls connecting the front bedroom, living room and dining room to make one big ell-shaped library, thirty-three feet by twenty-five feet across the front, overlooking the Midway, and an additional twenty feet deep into the ell. The available walls were lined with shelves to house his thousands of heterogeneous volumes. The room now being large enough to hold a considerable group comfortably, he took into his home the Evolution Club, of which he had been the guiding light. The meetings were held once a week; young and enthusiastic instructors from the university gave courses in biology, archaeology, anthropology, paleontology, sociology, comparative religion. Sitting in one of Darrow's favorite rockers in front of the fireplace, they lectured for an hour, then defended their science for another three hours while Darrow, rocking in the opposite wicker chair, guided the discussion with a deft hand, and the members munched on Ruby's sandwiches and drank sour Italian wine.

These evenings became the most pleasant of his lifetime: visiting professors and philosophers, European writers and scientists, when they learned that the Midway library was the most exciting intellectual workshop in Chicago, came to dine with the Darrows and address the club.

"Cruelty is the child of ignorance," wrote Darrow to a friend during this period, "and someday men will stop judging and condemning each other. I am really more interested in this than anything else; I wish I could make the world kinder and more humane than it is."

It was this abstention from judgment, this refusal to condemn on the standard codes of good and evil, that made him a fire to which chilled human beings came to warm their hands and hearts. To the men and women who were struggling against a fear psychosis in a confused and competitive world, living in constant dread of a slip or a mistake, an accident or a failure, of somehow breaking down, not making the grade, of being judged and found wanting, he seemed a tiny spark of the godhead that saw everything, understood and never condemned. When the day's work was done his office would become crowded with young lawyers who wanted to talk to him, to get the feel of him, to grasp what it was that made this sprawling, drawling, inelegant, plain-faced and plain-mannered fellow a whole man in a sea of fractional human beings. They did not come to him because he was an omniscient casebook or crafty technician, for they knew by now that "he practiced law by ear"; they came because they felt what George Jean Nathan so well described in one word: he had "size."

Hundreds of the near great from every walk of life filed through his office, seeking advice or just a friendly word: Elbert Hubbard, Jane Addams, Senator Pettigrew, William Jennings Bryan, Herbert Bigelow, Harold Ickes, Hamlin Garland, Kenneth Harris, Joseph Medill Patterson, John M. Holmes, William Allen White, Sam Jones, socialist mayor of Toledo, Mayor Tom Johnson, who inaugurated municipal railway service in Cleveland. Youngsters from all over the Midwest pushed open his door to ask his opinion of the law, whether it was a good profession, one they should enter. He discouraged them mildly and, when they were on their way out, handed them a copy of one of his lawbooks.

It became increasingly difficult for him to make any progress when walking on the streets of Chicago; so many friends, acquaintances and strangers alike wanted to stop him for a little chat. T. V. Smith reports that when he escorted Darrow to a meeting of the Democratic convention it took them two hours to cover the few blocks between the Illinois Central Station and the convention hall. "It wasn't a walk," says Smith, "it was a reception." People stood about in clusters to share a few words, to be enveloped, if for only an instant, in that healing smile. It was not so much that he had become a celebrity as that he had become a public property.

The odd part of his heartening effect upon people was that he rarely had anything heartening to say about the world's conduct. He was no optimist who encouraged folks by telling them that everything would come out all right; the best he could convey was that the mess was not their fault. "How will things come out? I guess they just won't come out. Men have been hating each other, robbing and oppressing and killing each other for countless centuries; I see little on the horizon to indicate that they won't continue to do so for centuries to come."

Lieutenant Commander L. H. C. Johnson observes, "While Darrow's keen sense of humor and knowledge of world affairs made him very popular with the men, he was a riot with the women. I took him to a birthday party, and when it came time for us to go I couldn't find the chief. I finally found him on the porch, siting in a low chair, surrounded by at least twenty women of all ages. I almost had to insult the females to get him home." Now that he had passed fifty his interest in women had subsided a bit, but he never lost his connoisseur's eye; when he was returning home from a lecture the porter informed him that Miss Cissie Patterson, of the publishing family, had her private car attached to the train and had asked him to breakfast with her. When Darrow rejoined his wife in Chicago "he mischievously asked me why in the world I didn't wear slinky, satiny, thin, clinging bright green pajamas and pink velvet and things a fellow could see through and get a thrill from—and, oh yes, the kind of slippers that have no heels or toes and have continuously to be pushed back on the feet."

The lawyers who thronged to his office tried to get him to talk about his past cases and triumphs, but he could never be persuaded to discuss them. When someone asked him whether Big Bill Haywood had been innocent or guilty he replied, "By Jove, I forgot to ask him." A number of years later, when a group of friends tendered him a birthday banquet and celebrities from every walk of American life made eulogizing speeches about him, "the religionists trying to prove him to be deeply religious, the scientists claiming him to be a scientist, the judges and lawyers pulling for their ranks, Darrow got up and said in the deceptive drawl: " 'I'm the one all this talk's been about. I always thought I was a hell of a fellow, but now I'm sure of it.' "

The firm of Darrow, Masters and Wilson was doing only fair to middling, for Darrow's two-year absence had cost them many of their profitable accounts, and the depression of 1907 had slowed down all business. Darrow, who had been their main business getter, found that his shattering illness and operation had taken their toll: he suffered recurrent spells of fatigue and general malaise that depleted his strength. The lines deepened in his face, making him look more than his fifty years. When the newspaper photographers laughingly offered to retouch the pictures he replied, "Don't wash out the lines, boys. I worked too hard to earn them." Partly because of this lessening of vigor, but also because he had seen so much bitterness and heartbreak in courtrooms, he began urging his clients to:

"Make a settlement. Give a little to get a little. Stay out of court. Court consumes time, money and energy. Take less than you think you ought to have; you'll come out ahead that way."

He gave this advice to people who had damage claims against companies, to private individuals and business concerns that were hell-bent to sue each other, to unions that had claims against their employers and employers who had claims against their workers. "Make a settlement," he told them, and his clients followed his advice. He spent less of his time in courtrooms, earned less money; his clients never got quite as much as they thought they were entitled to, but they were spared the rigors of a trial. Both sides having compromised and shaken hands on their bargain, the ill will and passions that were generated by a public conflict were avoided.

Yet within another year he had built up one of the most diversified practices in Chicago. William Randolph Hearst brought back the accounts of the *American* and *Examiner;* the International Harvester Company consulted him on their taxation problems; he was adviser to the Teachers' Federation of Labor; the Shuberts came to him with their theatrical complications, and in their wake came the actors Richard Carle and Grant Mitchell, who were involved in a dispute with George M. Cohan and Sam Harris. Mayor Dunne offered him the post of corporation counsel and, when he passed it on to his friend, James Hamilton Lewis, appointed him special counsel for the city in traction matters at ten thousand dollars a year. The firemen's union and switchmen's union retained him to present their case before a Federal board; the employees of the Kellogg Switchboard Company employed him to appeal all the way to the Supreme Court the conviction of certain of their members for picketing the plant in the face of an injunction that had been issued by a trial court; Bernarr MacFadden engaged him to represent his physical-culture school.

By 1908 there began a rush of labor cases in which Clarence was pleased to find himself acting not so much as lawyer as arbitrator. Since he was one of the few men in Chicago whom both labor and employers would trust, he was selected by both sides to settle disputes between the National Brick Company and their brickmakers, the newspaper owners and the typographical union, the brewers and their bottlers, the clothing manufacturers and their cutters. He sat at the head of big conference tables, never permitting the employers to range themselves on one side of the table and the employees on the other, as though they were separate entities and conflicting interests, but persuading them to sit next to each other, to rub elbows, tell a little joke, smoke each other's cigarettes, to come to know each other and perhaps even like each other. Then from his position at the head of the table he brought to bear his gentleness and humor, his warmth and understanding, until the antagonistic slabs of ice in the hearts of the contestants were melted, and he shamed them into being just a little kinder, just a little more generous and sympathetic human beings than they could ordinarily achieve. In each instance a strike was averted; the loss of profits and wages was averted; both sides accepted a compromise solution and lived up to the terms of the agreement.

With the money coming in once again, he decided to invest his savings so that he might within a few years be able to retire and achieve his one remaining personal ambition: to write a long novel. The most promising idea on the market at the moment was a new machine which was expected to produce gas cheaper than the regular coal-gas or water-gas plants. Darrow and a group of his friends bought the patent rights from a bond-selling organization for ten thousand dollars, which included an option on the gas plants of Ottawa, Illinois and Greeley, Colorado.

"The gas-making machine was impractical," relates Paul, "and no money was left to handle the plants. It was up to me to look over the two option deals and guess which one could be handled with the money that could be put up and whether it looked as if anything could be paid back. Ottawa had recently lost some of its industries, so I guessed on Greeley, which was in the center of irrigated farming country. The town was growing, so it meant building a new gas plant and putting in an average of a mile of new mains every year for

145

twenty years. It took most of the money I could get from Father and his friends for ten years and a lesser amount for the balance of the time."

Paul's management of the Greeley gasworks made it a valuable property. When the plant was sold in 1928 Darrow found himself for the first time in his life a rich man. Though Paul had not been able to work up any interest in his father's law business, that had not prevented him from keeping his eyes open while walking through the offices. When he left for Greeley he robbed the firm of a lovely dark-haired, fair-skinned, blue-eyed girl by the name of Lillian Anderson. Once again Paul's judgment proved sound; he enjoyed a fine married life, and Lillian Darrow presented her father-in-law with three granddaughters who were to bring him a good deal of joy, in particular the youngest, Mary.

The time he earned by staying out of court he employed to write short stories and articles, the most widely known of which was his deep-cutting and brilliant essay, "The Open Shop," which was circulated in the big cities where unions were trying to bring workingmen into their organization. Twenty thousand copies had been distributed among the workers of Los Angeles during the industrial warfare that preceded the explosion of the Los Angeles Times Building; it was his authorship of this pamphlet which proved to be the determining factor in his defending of the McNamara brothers, a decision which was to wreck his career and drastically alter the external pattern of his life.

To the flat on the Midway came Samuel Gompers, president and founder of the American Federation of Labor. He was in a state of agitation, for he was about to break a pledge made to Darrow by the executive board after the Boise trials: that they would never again ask him to defend a labor-murder case. Gompers paced the library so distractedly that sometimes he disappeared into the ell, and only his voice could be heard. Darrow knew that he had reason to be upset, for one of the most crushing blows in the history of the American Federation of Labor had befallen him. John J. McNamara, secretary of the International Bridge and Structural Iron Workers, and his brother, James B., had just been arrested for the dynamiting of the Los Angeles *Times* and for the murder of the twenty men who had been killed in the resulting fire. Nor was that all: the McNamaras and their union were charged with committing more than a hundred dynamitings between 1906 and 1911, of blowing up bridges, aqueducts, powerhouses, theaters, steel buildings, in every major city in America. The Los Angeles *Times* swore it would hang the McNamaras on the scaffold of San Quentin and that no force on earth could stop it.

"No force except you, Clarence," said Gompers, stopping before Darrow who crouched disconsolately in his wicker chair.

At first glance it looked amazingly like a replica of the Moyer, Haywood and Pettibone affair. There had been a state of war between the National Erectors' Association and the Structural Iron Workers' Union since 1906, when all concerns using steel in their structures had combined and pledged themselves to maintain the open shop. The William J. Burns Detective Agency had been employed by the erectors to trail union men and garner evidence against them; in April of 1911 James B. McNamara and Ortie McManigal were arrested in Detroit on charges of safeblowing, were moved without warrants to Chicago, where they were held captive in a police sergeant's house until extradition papers could arrive from Los Angeles.

After four days of being held incommunicado McManigal had confessed to numerous dynamitings. In the pamphlet called *Ortie McManigal's Own Story of the National Dynamite Plot*, the frontispiece was not a picture of Ortie, the hapless author, but of William J. Burns. In it the uneducated McManigal purportedly had written, "Hindsight is a splendid quality, but how fine it would be if we could reverse its action. I did not realize then that unionism is a serious menace, not only to the existing government, with its glorious and patriotic traditions, but as a menace to all government and all liberty of the individual or even of the masses."

It would have required an even greater miracle than the regeneration of Harry Orchard for Ortie McManigal to have formulated those pontifical sentences. Since one finds the precise phrases and hundreds of their counterparts in Burns's autobiography, *The Masked War*, there can be little doubt of their authorship. Once again some member of the prosecution had been so confident of success that he had not even bothered to save face; once again it seemed clear that the opposition was not merely out to get McNamara and McManigal or to destroy an individual union. This time the war would be waged on a national front.

James B. McNamara had been handcuffed and bundled onto a train for California without an opportunity to fight his extradition in Illinois. Since McManigal had named as the brains and boss of the dynamitings John J. McNamara, he, too, was arrested, in his office in Indianapolis, and shipped out to Los Angeles by such a fraudulent conspiracy that both William J. Burns and Joseph Ford, assistant district attorney of Los

Angeles, were subsequently indicted by the Indianapolis grand jury.

"History repeats itself," mused Darrow; "that's one of the things that's wrong with history."

The war over steel had begun many years before. When the industry was in its infancy the Amalgamated Iron and Steel Workers' Union had been one of the strongest in the country, yet Carnegie's company had earned a net profit of almost two million dollars. Then in 1892 there came a gigantic merger of coal-and-iron lands and steel ovens. Darrow had learned in the Pennsylvania coal fields that mergers, cartels and trusts unfailingly acted as combinations against labor. Since it was in the natural law of industry to combine for purposes of efficiency and economy, so was it equally inevitable that labor wars would extend to ever-widening fronts.

Carnegie retired to his estate in Scotland, leaving the industry in charge of H. C. Frick, a production genius without humanitarian ethics. More as a token of his power and policy than as a money saver, Frick reduced wages during his first meeting with the union. When he refused to come up to what the men considered a living scale, they struck.

Frick hired strikebreakers, ordered three hundred armed Pinkertons to come to Homestead and guard his new workers. When the strikers heard of the move they armed themselves, and prepared to resist what they considered an invasion. Men were killed on both sides—and the state militia was ordered to protect the mills and the strikebreakers who were working them. By winter the union funds had run out; families were hungry and cold and threadbare. The mills were running at full blast. Dispirited, broken, the men deserted their organization and went back to work as non-union men.

For thirteen years there was quiet in the steel industry while labor put in its seventy-two-hour-per-week stint at reduced wages and Frick zoomed profits. The discovery of the Mesaba iron range had reduced the cost of making steel and cities of skyscrapers were beginning to rise; steel rails were pushing railroads to new borders; gigantic bridges, aqueducts, industrial plants, were being built of this safe and durable and light material. And along with the skyscrapers and bridges a new class of workman had come into existence, the structural-steel worker: a crack mechanic, as tough as the material he handled, tireless, fearless, a master craftsman rebuilding the architecture of the nation. They built a strong union, the International Association of Bridge and Structural Iron Workers, which worked at peace with their employers. But it was an era of mergers: in 1905 the American Bridge Company was formed of firms throughout the country with contracts to build bridges, dams, and the like. The following year this was expanded into the National Erectors' Association, which embraced nearly every firm building with steel. Those firms that formerly had been independent and friendly with the union were obliged to participate in the general policy of the association. The structural-steel workers and the structural-steel builders soon split on the rock that was to cause succeeding decades of wrangling and bloodshed and over which the ultimate battle would be fought: the open shop.

Clarence Darrow had spoken for the workingmen of America when he had written, "In reality the open shop only means the open door through which the union man goes out and the non-union man comes in to take his place. The open shop furnishes, and always has furnished, the best possible means of destroying the organization of the men. The closed shops are the only sure protection for the trade agreements and the defense of the individual. . . . To prevent trade unionism from being conquered in detail, to keep its members from being thrown out through the open door, to maintain the best conditions in shop and mill and factory and strive for others better still, to save the workman from long hours of toil, all these need the effort of every union man, and without the right to protect themselves in a closed shop by refusing to work with those whose weakness or stupidity make them unfaithful to their class, trade unionism cannot hold that which it has won, still less go forward to greater victories."

He was thus the most literate and powerful proponent of the closed shop in America; since the McNamaras had been working through the years for the closed shop and anything they might have done against the Erectors' Association was done in their struggle against the open shop, that made Clarence Darrow the inevitable champion of the arrested McNamaras.

So Gompers told him. But Darrow refused to take the case.

His reasons were many and valid. The two hate-laden, fever-fraught years of the Western Federation of Miners cases had almost killed him. He was still by no means well or strong. He was now fifty-four years old and a little tired; he was convinced that younger men should conduct the case, men who had their full strength and vigor. He knew something of Los Angeles, which the workingmen of the country called "the scabbiest town on earth." If the Boise cases had been bitter, they would seem like a Sunday-school picnic compared with the vitriol bath in which he would be immersed in Los Angeles. The McNamaras had twenty indictments against them, one for each of the men killed in the

Times fire; it would take him at least a year to try the first case, and if he earned an acquittal on that he would have to try the other nineteen cases.

When he had returned from Boise he had promised Ruby that he would take on no more labor trials. Ruby had threatened that if he broke his promise she would refuse to accompany him; that would stop him, for Clarence had become dependent upon his wife and would not consent to being separated from her. He loved his home on the Midway; he was getting along well with his practice; he would be able to retire soon to write his long novel.

He said no, he would not take the case. But Sam Gompers refused to take no for an answer. The entire country, labor and capital alike, had assumed it would be "Clarence Darrow for the defense." Unions from every city in America wrote to tell him how happy they were that he was to defend, because he would show up the conspiracy and save the McNamaras; letters arrived from plumbers in Schenectady, brickmasons of Duluth, carpenters of New Orleans, needleworkers in New York, lumbermen of Seattle, coal miners of Scranton, streetcar conductors of San Francisco, each enclosing a dollar bill, assuring him they would stand behind him. A major labor case without Darrow; that was unthinkable!

He spent the next few days in an unhappy state of mind. Ruby made it clear that she thought it suicidal for him to take the case. Masters and Wilson opposed his going with every argument at their command, even vowing to dissolve the partnership. When the executive board of the American Federation of Labor begged him to attend a meeting in Washington he could not turn them down. They offered him a fifty-thousand-dollar fee; they offered a two-hundred-thousand-dollar defense fund, to spend as he saw fit, without an accounting; they offered him the complete loyalty and backing of their press, of their millions of members. Still he refused.

On the following Sunday afternoon Gompers came again to the flat on the Midway, accompanied by some of the strongest voices in American labor. For hours they were quartered in the library, while Ruby waited with sickening anxiety in their bedroom.

"After many hours Dee came to me in the back," relates Ruby, "wearily, sadly, taking my hand and conducting me to a seat beside him, to break to me the news that he was asking me to break my pledge. He did not seem exactly afraid that I would refuse to do as he asked; he had never asked me anything that I had even hesitated about; he ex-

150

plained that the men in the front room were saying that he would go down in history as a traitor to his cause. He asked me to lift my pledge and . . . go along to Los Angeles. I did not add to his dismay and dread of the situation; I offered no objections to having him do as he deemed necessary and best."

"I felt I had done my share of fighting," writes Darrow of this moment of decision. "It was not easy to combat the powerful forces of society in the courts, as I had been doing for so many years, and I was now weary of battling against public opinion. I had fought through so many conflicts that I felt the need of rest from such strenuous work. The very name of Los Angeles was associated with so much misery and suffering that the thought of going back to that place and its painful memories seemed like a foreboding that I could not quiet. Yet hard as it was to give them my yes, it would have been harder to say no."

Masters and Wilson dissolved their partnership. "It would be the international limelight again," said Wilson, "a lure he couldn't resist. And there was always the chance of winning that fifty thousand dollars quickly, in a few months, so that he could retire to write his novel."

Darrow formed a nonactive partnership with a junior in the office, Jacob L. Bailey, so that his name should not disappear from the Chicago legal register while he was away.

Ruby covered her furniture with sheets and towels, packed their bags. "It may be imagined with what dread and distress we went West," she relates. "Enough had been brought out by the prosecution fine-combing for facts and by the relentless newspapers to show what a web of dangers and disasters awaited us. No one had any inkling about the truth, just how the explosion had occurred, what the motive was, who was most, or least, responsible; nothing could be sifted and weighed until it could be investigated in Los Angeles. Mr. Darrow had never even heard of the McNamaras, had no idea what sort they were, what personalities he would find, what mental make-up. He had not the first or faintest reason for judging whether they were guilty. The situation frightened and bewildered him as nothing ever had in my acquaintance with him, and he would have given almost anything to escape . . . . But . . . he could not have borne the cry against him as a traitor to the cause."

"It was with heavy hearts that Mrs Darrow and I drove to the Chicago and North Western station," writes Darrow, "and boarded the train for Los Angeles."

Darrow went straight from the station to the county jail

to meet his clients. He was pleased to find the McNamara brothers clean cut, intelligent, with a quiet and gentle manner. James B., who was twenty-eight, was lean of face and figure, had an amused, bright gleam in his eye and a poetic, almost mystical strain. His brother John J., the secretary of the union, was a year younger; he was broader of face and figure, with a touch of Irish melancholy in his eyes; he had come up from the ranks of labor, had given himself a legal education, was quiet spoken but intense.

He did not ask the brothers whether they were innocent or guilty as charged. "I've heard Mr Darrow say that he placed little value on the statements of clients," tells Mrs Darrow, "that he could do better work if he was allowed to presume his clients innocent."

It was easy to assume the McNamaras innocent because of their straightforward and honest manner. Fletcher Bowron, a reporter of the *Record*, who later became reform mayor of Los Angeles, says, "I talked to the boys frequently in the jail. From their appearance and way of speaking it would have been difficult to think them guilty. I thought they were innocent." Nor did the McNamaras leave many in doubt. When Sam Gompers came to Los Angeles John J. took his hand and said, "I want to assure you that we are innocent of the crime with which we are charged."

That afternoon Darrow went with Job Harriman, who had had charge of the case until Darrow's arrival, to the charred hull of the Times Building, standing on the exact spot in ink alley where the explosion had taken place. Here Harriman re-created the scene for his chief:

Early in the morning of October first, after the editorial staff had put the paper to bed and gone home for the night, there had been an explosion in the roofed-over alley in which barrels of ink were unloaded from the drays and stored until they were needed for the presses. This explosion was followed immediately by a second, which was either the gas main or leaking gas blowing up. One whole wall of the stone building was blown out. The ink in the barrels caught fire at once, and within four minutes the entire building was a sheet of flames, the fire eating up the wooden floors that had not collapsed under the weight of their machinery in the second explosion. There were in the building some twenty telegraph operators, linotype operators, printers, machinists, compositors, pressmen, but the intensity of the fire made rescue work impossible. Those who had not crashed to the basement with their heavy machinery had fought their way through the fierce flames to the windows and doors. Those who jumped to the pavement below were killed; the others were sucked back by the flames, their stricken faces vanishing into the red curtain behind them.

Los Angeles had been awakened by the force of the explosions and the clang of the fire wagons. Within an hour thousands of people were standing opposite the burning building, many of them in their night clothes, fighting with the police to break their lines, to try to help in some sort of rescue. But it was to no avail: twenty men were killed in one of the most gruesome tragedies in American civilian life.

By dawn, while the firemen were still plying their hoses on the flames, a one-sheet edition of the *Times* hit the streets, having been printed in an auxiliary pressroom. An eight-column streamer read: UNIONIST BOMB WRECKS THE TIMES. Harry Chandler, son-in-law of the owner, Harrison Gray Otis, and the managing editor, wrote, "The Times Building was destroyed this morning by the enemies of industrial freedom. The elements that conspired to perpetrate this horror must not be permitted to pursue their awful campaign of intimidation and terror." The men who had been killed were called "victims of the foulest plot of foul Union Labor Ruffians."

The next day Otis cried in his paper, "O you anarchic scum, you cowardly murderers, you leeches upon honest labor, you midnight assassins, you whose hands are dripping with the innocent blood of your victims, you against whom the wails of poor widows and the cries of fatherless children are ascending to the Great White Throne, go look at the ruins wherein are buried the calcined remains of those whom you murdered. . . ."

"But how could he make those charges?" demanded Darrow of Harriman, "when the firemen were still poking around in the ruins and no one could know what caused the explosion?"

"Ah," said Harriman, "you don't know Harrison Gray Otis."

This trial that brought Darrow to Los Angeles in 1911 had its beginnings in 1890, when the four local newspapers threatened a twenty-per-cent cut and the union typographers struck rather than take the reduction in wages. Within three days the *Tribune* and *Express* had settled their differences with the men; by the end of the third month the typographers were back at work on the *Herald*. This left only the *Times* men on strike; they were eager to compromise in order to go back to work. The decision rested in one man's hands, Harrison Gray Otis, a former union printer who had taken part in fifteen Civil War battles and had come out with a captain's commission in his pocket and a taste for warfare in his mouth. The pattern of life in southern California would be formulated by Captain Harrison Gray Otis's blunderbuss.

Between the Civil War and his purchase of an interest in the *Times* in 1882 Otis was a government hanger-on, constantly importuning for appointments. Failing to land the job of collector of the Port of San Diego, on which he had set his heart, he bought a fourth interest in the weekly *Times*, which was slowly dying of attrition in the mud-baked metropolis of eleven thousand souls. By the end of four years, when the first land boom descended upon southern California, Otis had bought out his associates for trifling sums; people poured in; money poured in; the *Times* became a daily; Otis began buying up tracts of land—and was on his way to becoming a multimillionaire and arbiter of American civilization.

"Otis was a large, aggressive man with a walrus mustache, a goatee and a warlike demeanor, resembling Buffalo Bill and General Custer," writes Morrow Mayo in his excellent book *Los Angeles*. "The military bee buzzed in his bonnet. He called his home in Los Angeles The Bivouac, and when the boom was at its height he built a new plant for the *Times*, which resembled a medieval fortress, with battlements, sentry boxes, surmounted by a screaming eagle. He was a natural warrior and not a man to be crossed. He was a holy terror in his newspaper plant; his natural voice was that of a game warden roaring at seal poachers."

Reporters on the *Times* accused Otis of never getting past the third reader, but they underestimated his functional intelligence for getting a specific job done. No man in all American history, not even in the blackest days of the War between the States, could touch Otis for range, power and intensity of vituperation, while a *schimp-flexikon* of the abuse that Otis and the *Times* heaped upon the heads of workers, unions, liberals, progressives and the co-operative movements from 1890 to 1940 would constitute a confounding document. President Theodore Roosevelt wrote about him in the *Outlook* magazine: "He is a consistent enemy of every movement for social and economic betterment, a consistent enemy of men in California who have dared to stand against corruption and in favor of honesty. The attitude of General Otis in his paper affords a curious instance of the anarchy of soul which comes to a man who in conscienceless fashion deifies property at the expense of human rights. The *Times* has again and again showed itself to be such an enemy of good citizenship, honest, decent government and every effective effort to secure fair play for the workingman and -woman as any anarchist could show itself."

Otis declared that no man who had gone on strike could ever work for the *Times* again, that no union member would ever be employed by him in any capacity. Having embarked upon this road, there was no turning back; every step he took plunged him deeper into strife, and the continued strife only convinced him further that he was right. When he imported non-union printers from Kansas City in 1890 he set the tone for the long contest by writing, "These men came to Los Angeles much as the first settlers of New England came from the old country to escape religious intolerance and to gain personal freedom to worship as they saw fit. Like their hardy, selected forebears, these liberty-loving Los Angeles immigrants were pioneers who laid the foundation for the future growth of their adopted land." In 1929, when summing up in a supplement called *The Forty Years' War*, Harry Chandler carried on his father-in-law's tradition by writing, "It has been war, war in which many lives have been lost, millions of dollars of property destroyed, other millions lost through suspension of production. The cost to the city has been great, yet its profits infinitely greater."

There were other costs which the *Times* did not see fit to mention. "Outside pressure was exerted upon the Los Angeles police," writes Jerome Hopkins in *Our Lawless Police*, "by a dominant financial group, fanatically antilabor, which utilized the police as an adjunct to its open-shop industrial policies. Very early the Los Angeles police ceased to distinguish between economic dissenters, strikers, pickets and the criminal. This line of activity, kept alive by hysterical propaganda, has passed through successive phases: assistance in strikebreaking, espionage upon labor-union organizations, suppression of free speech, unlawful beatings, false arrest, brutality with arrest, unlawful detention, incommunicado and the third degree."

To Otis all this was another Civil War; it was his bounden duty to crush the Rebels. Battle was breath in his nostril. When his Civil War II began his cohorts promoted him from captain to general, and he was known as General Otis to the end of his days.

"It is somehow absurd but nevertheless true," laments Mayo, "that for forty years the smiling, booming sunshine City of the Angels has been the bloodiest arena in the Western world!"

By the decision of this one man Los Angeles became immersed in a half century of bloodshed, violence, hatred, class war, oppression, injustice and a destruction of civil liberties which was to turn it into the low spot of American culture and democracy.

155

The incalculable tragedy behind the Otis decision was that its tentacles soon spread to make this war a national affair. While Darrow was fighting for the American Railway Union in 1894 the groundwork for his present battle in 1911 was being laid, for in the midst of the railroad fight Otis called a meeting of the town's bankers, manufacturers and merchants, to form an organization called the Merchants and Manufacturers.

The San Francisco *Bulletin* wrote, "The Merchants and Manufacturers' Association has one confession of faith, one creed: 'We will employ no union man.' The M. and M. has also one command: 'You shall employ no union man.' The penalty for disobedience to this command is financial coercion, boycott and ruin. 'You hire union men and we'll put you out of business,' says the M. and M., and the businessman knows that the oracle speaks. 'You declare an eight-hour day and we'll stop your credit at the banks,' and the M. and M. does what it says. . . . The merchant who disobeys the M. and M. command runs into something which robs him of his business, hampers him in securing raw material for manufacture, holds up his payment for work when it is completed and frightens him out of speech to rebel."

The large flow of workingmen, attracted by the advertisements of all-year sunshine, flowers and beauty, found themselves at the mercy of the employers. The hours went as high as fourteen a day; wages fell to a new low. All workingmen had to pay dues to the M. and M. If anyone protested he was promptly fired, black-listed, put out of his house, run out of the country. This was Otis's "American Plan" for Industrial Freedom.

The unions were harried and weak, but they never gave up trying. While the *Times* called them cutthroats, assassins, robbers, thieves, rascals, lunatics, anarchists, sluggers, ruffians, swine, they kept plugging for shorter hours, better wages, striking whenever they could: teamsters, carpenters, plasterers, laundry workers, brewery workers, dozens of strikes, hundreds of strikes, bitter strikes filled with smashed heads. *Always the unions lost!* "This is war!" cried Otis from the *Times,* and the Merchants and Manufacturers gave no quarter.

For San Francisco, four hundred miles north, the strongest union city in America, where wages were thirty per cent higher, the chaos of Los Angeles created a danger; the workers were afraid their wage would be pulled down to the Los Angeles level; the employers were afraid lest their low-wage competitors underbid them and take away their contracts. Realizing that Los Angeles constituted an infection area for the entire country, the American Federation of

Labor in its 1910 convention voted to establish a unified labor council in Los Angeles and to fight the open-shop issue to a conclusion. Such powerful labor leaders in San Francisco as Tom Mooney, "Pinhead" McCarthy, O. A. Tveitmoe and Anton Johannsen were sent down to Los Angeles to serve as General Staff.

Since the ironworkers were the toughest fighters and had a strong national organization behind them, the San Francisco leaders used them as a spearhead of the attack. A new scale of wages was asked for; when it was refused fifteen hundred men walked out of such big plants as the Llewellyn and Baker Iron Works. Strikebreakers were hauled in from the Midwest; strong-arm squads were summoned from San Francisco to meet them. Deputies beat up the strikers; the strikers beat up the non-union workers; the police beat up the pickets. Blood flowed in a dozen different parts of the city.

General Otis mounted a small cannon on the running board of his car and dashed about the city to direct his police and special deputies. In his editorials he screamed, "It is full time to deal with these labor-union wolves in such prompt and drastic fashion as will induce them to transfer their lawlessness to some other locality. Their instincts are criminal, and they are ready for arson, riot, robbery and murder!" His hysteria rose to such heights in promising Angelenos that their city was about to be bombed off the face of the earth that a considerable portion of the citizens thought he ought to be clapped in a madhouse. At the peak of the insanity Senator Hiram Johnson hired the auditorium to cry out:

"In the city of San Francisco we have drunk to the very dregs of infamy; we have had vile officials; we have had rotten newspapers. But we have nothing so vile, nothing so low, nothing so debased, nothing so infamous, in San Francisco as Harrison Gray Otis. He sits there in senile dementia with gangrened heart and rotting brain, grimacing at every reform, chattering impotently at all things that are decent, frothing, fuming, violently gibbering, going down to his grave in snarling infamy. He is one thing that all California looks at when, in looking at southern California, they see anything that is disgraceful, depraved, corrupt, crooked and putrescent—that is Harrison Gray Otis."

This was the city, this was the opposition, this was the intrastate conflict, this the hysteria multiplied to infinity by the deaths of twenty innocent men, into which Clarence Darrow plunged when he stepped off his train in sunny southern California.

By the end of two weeks Darrow was settled in a comfortable flat on the high hill of Bonnie Brae and had assembled a brilliant legal staff. For his mastery of California law he chose Le Compte Davis, member of a Kentucky family who had come to California in the hopes of cheating death of another consumption victim. Davis had been assistant district attorney, had prosecuted labor for unruly conduct, was known to be a conservative and had an unimpeachable reputation. Next in line Darrow selected Joseph Scott, the leading Catholic attorney of the community, whose presence in the case would swing sentiment toward the Irish Catholic McNamaras. Another wise choice was that of Judge McNutt, former Supreme Court justice of Indiana, who was known to be favorable to labor.

Job Harriman was the fifth member and the expert on the California labor background. A little past forty, Harriman was a bright, eager man, a theorist and idealist who made a good educator but who had failed as an administrator in charge of a socialist-utopia community. Harriman was later accused by Edward Cantrell, a fellow socialist whom Harriman was instrumental in having expelled from the party for causing factional strife, of having known beforehand that the *Times* was to be bombed. Cantrell went unsolicited to the *Times,* the archenemy of his enemies in the party, and gave them an article in which he told of being in San Luis Obispo for a lecture the night the *Times* was blown up and of having Harriman appear at his hotel for no apparent reason. The next morning, when Harriman read of the twenty deaths, reports Cantrell, he became almost hysterical. From these two deductions, that Harriman had joined him in San Luis Obispo merely to establish an alibi and that he had become overwrought when he read of the deaths, Cantrell went before the grand jury to accuse Harriman of complicity in the Los Angeles dynamiting conspiracy. Cantrell, a retired clergyman, was an honest man, but his unconscious motive was revenge against the men who had expelled and hence discredited him. No scrap of evidence ever implicated Harriman in foreknowledge of the explosion.

Darrow rented the major portion of a floor of the Higgins Building on the corner of Second and Main streets, with offices adjoining those of Harriman. He then moved in desks, chairs, filing cabinets, typewriters, secretaries, a publicity man and a staff of investigators under the direction of John Harrington. Harrington had been for many years an investigator for the Chicago Surface Lines, until he lost his job through insubordination. Since Darrow had always thought him a good investigator and needed someone in Los Angeles whom he felt he could trust, he brought Harrington to head his local detective staff. Darrow both liked Harrington and felt sorry for him; since he was without an acquaintance in Los Angeles, the Darrows took him and his little daughter into their home.

The first great obstacle was the Ortie McManigal confession. Before he had left Chicago Darrow had had Harrington bring to his home on the Midway Mrs McManigal and McManigal's uncle, George Behm. Having been successful in getting Lillard, Steve Adams' uncle, to persuade Adams to repudiate his confession, he saw no reason why he should not try to get Uncle George Behm to persuade McManigal to repudiate, particularly since he "promised to defend McManigal if they had forced him to make that confession." Mrs Ortie McManigal was convinced that her husband had made the confession under fear and threats.

"Mr Darrow asked me if I was a union man," related George Behm. "I told him I was. He asked me if I was in sympathy with the labor movement and the McNamara case, and I told him I was as far as I know about it."

He had paid the expenses for Behm's farm hand and given Behm, Mrs McManigal and her little boy enough money to get out to Los Angeles. But Behm was having no luck with his nephew. He told Darrow that "Ortie refuses to recall his confession. He says he is better off in jail than out on the streets where someone would be liable to blow his head off." Darrow sent Behm back to the jail again and again, but nothing could move McManigal, who finally cried in exasperation. "You will have to cut it out, Uncle George, for I won't talk about it at all. I have got my mind made up to tell the truth." And that was his last word about the McNamara case.

It looked to the defense as though the prosecution's case was to be based solely on the McManigal confession. If Darrow could prove that it had been written by William J. Burns, who had been holding Ortie captive at the time, he could free the McNamaras: for although McManigal had admitted placing charges of dynamite under bridges and aqueducts, always at the order of the union secretary, John J. McNamara, he had sworn that he had not been in Los Angeles or had anything to do with the *Times* explosion. Darrow employed almost a hundred investigators who combed the country to check up on McManigal, to see if he had been where he said he had been, to determine just what had caused the explosions in the various cities and whether McManigal could have had anything to do with them, to find people who knew McManigal and might contradict any part of the confession. He also sent out an investigating staff under Harrington to learn what had caused the *Times* explosion, to find the men who had complained of leaking gas in the plant the very night of the accident. He ordered a complete model of the Times Building made, with all interior fittings, which he planned to blow up in court to prove that only gas could have caused the tragedy; he engaged expert technicians to experiment with gas explosions and their results. He hadn't wanted to take the case, but now that he was in it he gave to his clients every last ounce of his energy and resourceful mind.

Once his investigation had started in earnest there began a campaign of espionage and counterespionage. When reports came in from his Eastern investigators Darrow found that the information was in the possession of the district attorney by the following day. He made connections with a deputy in the district attorney's office who informed him that one of his secretaries was a Burns detective and was making copies of everything that came into the office. Darrow put this deputy on his pay roll; he was daily to report back the information Darrow's secretary had passed on to the district attorney! Darrow, Tveitmoe and Johannsen, the two San Francisco labor leaders, concocted a secret code based on the pagination of Webster's dictionary; Joseph Ford, the assistant district attorney and private attorney for William J. Burns, selected Burns men to get themselves hired as investigators for Darrow and decipher the code. The manager of Burns's Los Angeles office came to Darrow in a secret conference and offered to sell him copies of all of Burns's reports, pay rolls and books. When Darrow learned that the district attorney's investigators were also scouring the East to get corroboration of the McManigal confession he hired several of the Burns men who were working for the district attorney to report back to him everything the district attorney's investigators had found in the East. Before long some of the private detectives were drawing three separate salaries, passing around their information in a daisy chain; Darrow, Fredericks, the prosecuting attorney, and Ford knew what each other had had for breakfast.

If the situation had musical-comedy aspects the trickery assumed dangerous proportions. Defense witnesses and relatives of the accused men were so hounded by night and day that they lost their jobs, their homes, were put out of their hotels and boardinghouses. Defense employees were shadowed, threatened, bribed, kidnaped. Anyone helpful to the defense was hauled before Fredericks' grand jury and threatened with indictment unless he retracted. Darrow's telegrams were stolen, his account books copied, his telephone conversations taken on hidden dictaphones. Once when his investigators unearthed a witness whom he considered valuable he moved him to a small hotel and told him to keep out of circulation. The following morning his spy in the district attorney's office informed him that the district attorney's spy in his office had learned of the man's value to the defense. The witness had then been kidnaped from his hotel and was being held prisoner in a barn in Culver City. Dr Atwater, a Los Angeles dentist, tells that "that night I drove Darrow in my buggy to Culver City. We left the buggy a safe distance from the designated barn, approached it quietly and saw two deputies stationed in front. We went around to the back, tunneled under the wall and found our witness lying on a pile of hay in a drugged or semiconscious condition. We pushed and dragged him under the wall, carried him to the buggy and got him away."

Dirty and stupid business for Clarence Darrow to be engaging in? War is dirty and stupid business.

The pressure of work left Clarence little time for social life, but once a week he and Ruby would go to a party given in their honor by Joseph Scott in Pasadena or by the Le Compte Davises for the cream of the Los Angeles intellectuals. He did not care greatly for big and formal parties; he preferred informal chin fests with cronies who loved books and thought that talking about literature was as important a pleasure as there was in life. His friend Fay Lewis came out from Rockford to stand by his side; Billy Cavenaugh, the stonecutter, who was working in Los Angeles as a policeman, gave him alcohol rubs several nights a week; an old pal from the Chicago *Inter-Ocean*, James H. Griffes, who was publishing a little magazine in Los Angeles called the *Everyman*, ran a series of his articles on everything from Robert Burns's poetry to prison reform and acquainted him with Southern California artists and writers.

As the scorching summer heat came on Darrow slowly became depressed and then dejected: his investigators could find no evidence to controvert the Ortie McManigal confession, no evidence to show that the McNamaras had not been guilty of the violence charged. Worse yet, the district attorney's investigators were sending in mountainous piles of proof to sustain McManigal. When McManigal told how they had bought dynamite from a certain well digger that well digger was found and identified James B. McNamara as one of the men who had bought it. When McManigal told of registering at a certain hotel just before the setting of a blast, there was J. B.'s signature on the register and people to identify him from his picture. When McManigal told of renting a house to store the explosives there was the landlord to identify J. B. One day, when his spy in the district attorney's office brought him a copy of a particularly damaging piece of evidence against J.B., Darrow walked into his cell and cried:

"My God, you left a trail behind you a mile wide!"

McNamara did not answer.

That night Clarence spent some wretched hours, torn by the most basic of his inner conflicts. "I never believed in violence on either side; I don't believe in the violence of war; I don't believe in the violence that everywhere abounds on earth. I know who is responsible for this struggle: it is the men who have reached out their hands and taken possession of all the wealth in the world; it is that paralyzing hand of wealth which has reached out and destroyed all the opportunities of the poor. The acts of the poor are protests against their wrongs; yet I don't believe in the violence of the poor and the weak, who think they can obtain their rights by fighting the rich and the strong." Harry Orchard had accused Moyer, Haywood and Pettibone with a hundred crimes, most of which had been uncommitted; McManigal had accused the McNamaras of a hundred crimes, all of which had been committed, most of which the prosecution could prove! True, the McNamaras were not yet charged with these other and distant crimes; they were charged with the bombing of the Times Building, which did not appear to have been bombed at all and on which no implicity for the McNamaras had been found. But how quick people would be to assume that if they had committed a hundred other bombings and the *Times* had been their archenemy, therefore, they must also have bombed the *Times*. It would only be circumstantial evidence, and it was difficult to hang men on circumstantial evidence; but if he managed the miracle of an acquittal the brothers and the officers of the ironworkers' union would be indicted in every major city in America for the property bombings.

In the dark hours of the dark night he became ill with a despair which was rarely to leave him, night or day, for two years; a despair whose seeds had been sown in the days when he had come to understand that in defending Big Bill Haywood he was defending a philosphy of force. Part of his illness in Idaho had been due to this conflict of loyalties within himself, perhaps enough of it to turn an ordinary mastoid into the freak mastoid which had trebled his suffering. The Haywood case had brought him to grips with what he had always known, that in any conflict of force both sides were wrong and both sides must lose; in the unlikely event that either side should win a victory it could only mean that the war would have to start again. Every aspect of the McNamara case confirmed him in this judgment.

If he defended these practitioners of violence, would not

the country be entitled to assume that since he defended sabotage, force, crimes against property, he must necessarily condone the use of dynamite and violence? Would not all his years of pleading for the broader view, for tolerance and sympathy, for co-operation and understanding between apparently conflicting interests, be undone? By portraying the barbarities on both sides of the class war he had been able to establish a kind of justification for force, but he did not want to confirm other firebrands in their belief that they could solve their problems by any number of crimes and any amount of violence, that they could never be brought to bay.

He could not abandon the McNamaras now, he knew. Nor did he pass judgment against them for what they had done. They had been childish and misguided to imagine that they could conquer a billion-dollar industry by random explosions; he thought they had been blind not to see that they must eventually be caught and do infinite damage to the union movement. Yet he understood their motivations. They were guilty of standing up and fighting in a war which they believed had been forced upon them by the National Erectors' Association. They had worked and sacrificed for years to establish their union, and now their efforts would be wiped out. The only property the union man owned was his skill with his hands. He said:

"All right, we'll keep this a war of property. If you blast our property we'll blast yours. So long as you don't slug or club our men we won't hurt your men. You want to make our membership in a union so costly to us that we'll abandon our union; all right, then we'll make your membership in the erectors' union so costly to you that you will abandon your union."

They had kept their word; in all the explosions no man had ever been injured. In one instance where a watchman would have been hurt because his sentry box was close to the scene of the explosion, they had gone to the trouble and danger of setting off a small charge a distance away so that the watchman would run to investigate and not be hurt by the major explosion. He knew the McNamaras would cry:

"They had all the money, all the power. What else was left open to us? What else could we do? We had no way to fight them in terms of peace. If we did nothing we were licked, destroyed. We had to use force; it was the only weapon left to us."

What could he answer them? Should he quote Matthew, "Resist not evil, but whosoever shall smite thee on thy right cheek, turn to him the other, also"?

He suffered an agony of mind over the trap in which he was caught. He had a suspicion that if Le Compte Davis,

Joseph Scott and Judge McNutt were to learn of the overwhelming guilt of the McNamaras in past dynamitings they would feel obliged to withdraw, an act which would convict his clients before they came to trial. Job Harriman, he felt, had known all along, but he did not discuss the piling evidence with him. What made his burden heavy was that labor throughout the country was still passionately convinced that the McNamaras were innocent of any dynamiting or other criminal acts; its press wrote flaming articles against the injustice in Los Angeles. May Day of 1911 was called McNamaras' Day; demonstrations were held in every major city of America at which tens of thousands voiced their protests against the frame-up. Twenty thousand men paraded in Los Angeles carrying banners which read, DOWN WITH OTIS! REGISTER YOUR PROTEST AGAINST THE MCNAMARA FRAME-UP! Every union in the country was contributing funds; thousands of letters poured into the office in the Higgins Building from workmen who wanted to assure him of their loyalty and contribute a further bit from their savings.

He felt like a man with a rumbling volcano in his pocket, trying to hold back the eruption with his naked hand.

Early in the summer a strong socialist movement had begun in Los Angeles to offset the *Times* and the Merchants' and Manufacturers' Association. Eugene Debs was circulating forty thousand copies of his *Appeal to Reason* each week, and the paper was being read avidly as an antidote to the *Times*. Job Harriman was nominated for mayor; a strong ticket was put into the field. Alexander Irvine, a clergyman who had been stripped of his pulpit in New Haven for preaching Christian socialism, was sent out by national headquarters to conduct the campaign. Socialism was on the upswing in America; many socialist congressmen and legislators had already been elected; several cities had socialist mayors, while others were going into the new campaign with excellent prospects. Considering the hysteria of the moment, the socialist platform was moderate: though it demanded the ultimate replacement of the capitalist system it was willing to settle in the meanwhile for woman suffrage, more schools, social centers, public beaches, hospitals and employment bureaus, civil service, an eight-hour law, municipal ownership of utilities. If the socialists could win in Los Angeles it would assure a sympathetic trial for the McNamaras.

In addition to everything else that was being charged against him Darrow was now accused of starting the socialist campaign to take over the city, and of financing its campaign out of McNamara defense funds. He had not started the socialist campaign; there had always been a strong movement in southern California; neither had he contributed more than a few hundred dollars for its literature, but once it was under way he gave it every aid he could, lecturing on those nights when he could break away from his work. Big Bill Haywood came to exhort large gatherings on the blessings of socialism and swore that the McNamaras had been framed just as he had been in Idaho. Harriman went about lecturing to the effect that "the labor unions are the only organized expression of the wageworker's interest within the present system of production, and they can no more be disbanded or crushed out of existence than can the wageworker himself cease to work for wages."

Thus were the McNamara defense and the socialist campaign inextricably interwoven.

The primaries would be held in October, and it appeared that the vote would be close, for the Good Government League of the Merchants and Manufacturers had been exposed in a series of land frauds. The election would come in December; Darrow asked Judge Bordwell to set the opening of the McNamara case over until December. Bordwell decreed the case should open October eleventh.

On the day before the trial Sam Gompers addressed fifteen thousand labor sympathizers in Philadelphia, who shouted in unison their belief of the McNamara innocence. Seventeen thousand people paraded the streets with banners which read: "Down, Down with Detective Burns, the Kidnaper!" The Times rebutted with "Socialism is not anarchy, but it is a halfway house on the road to anarchy. It would prove the inevitable precursor of a condition of lawlessness, of robbery, of riot and murder. Carry Los Angeles for socialism? Carry it for business stagnation, abandoned industries, smokeless chimneys, bankruptcy, ruined homes, chaos of civil government. Carry it for hell!"

This was the temper of the country; this was the temper of Los Angeles when Darrow walked into Judge Bordwell's court on October 11, 1911, to begin his defense. People the world over assured each other that he would expose the frame-up, that he would win another great victory for labor and the common people.

But Clarence Darrow walked into the courtroom a beaten man. He had learned that the McNamaras were guilty as charged.

In the summer of 1910 three men had gone to the Hercules Powder Plant on San Francisco Bay, represented themselves as businessmen from Folsom, California, and ordered a quantity of eighty-per-cent nitrogelatin, a rarely used explosive, for the avowed purpose of blasting boulders and tree stumps.

A few days later they had rented a motorboat called the Peerless, painted another name over the first, picked up their explosive, carried it across the bay to a wharf in San Francisco, where they had loaded it onto a wagaon and carted it to an empty house rented for the purpose. The three men were David Caplan, a San Francisco labor leader, Matt Schmidt, a young and brilliant engineer who had been traveling with James B. McNamara, constructing time bombs for his explosions, and James B. McNamara. All three were identified by the Hercules Powder employees, by the owners of the Peerless, by the landlord of the empty house, by people who had seen the wagon pulled through the streets of San Francisco. The district attorney's office claimed that the day after the *Times* explosion two suitcases had been found, one near Otis's house, one near the house of the secretary of the M. and M., containing time mechanisms made by Schmidt and sticks of the nitrogelatin which Hercules men identified as the explosive purchased by McNamara, Caplan and Schmidt.

And Darrow realized that his journey along the downward trail, which had begun when he defended Big Bill Haywood, who was innocent as charged but guilty of crimes of violence against mine property, had at last brought him into the swamps of defending men who were guilty as charged. He knew too well that the McNamaras were morally responsible for the deaths of the twenty *Times* employees.

This day was one of his blackest, yet even in his despair he did not condemn the McNamaras. They had done what they thought was right; they had been fighting for labor; he himself had been instrumental in showing them that they must battle the open shop. They had fought with the only weapons at hand. He could not abandon them, not even in his mind, yet the knowledge of the indictment that would be brought against labor made him ill. What a field day Otis, the Merchants and Manufacturers, the National Erectors' Association, the Steel Trust would have! And what could he do to stop them?

To further harrow him he found that James B. McNamara and young men like Matt Schmidt, who had started as labor's martyrs, had grown flushed with success because they had operated for years without being caught. In the early days they had lived carefully, had worked cautiously, but their victories had made them contemptuous of both the law and their opponents.

Over and above the excitements there had been the pleasures of the irregular life: freedom from routine, from constant supervision, from responsibilities of the family and the home, the zest of the nomadic life, the constant travel with its changes of scenery, its new faces and cities and ways of life.

The men had been paid two hundred dollars an explosion, in addition to certain expenses; they had lived irregularly; they had lived well, and slowly they had become unable to resist the subtle encroachments upon character that result from such an existence. They fell into the habit of acquiring new women in each successive town, of necessity posing as something they were not; concealing, dissembling, lying and finally of drinking, in their enforced idleness, in their excitement, in the letdown after the tension of placing the bomb and hearing it explode. They had started out as soldiers in a war and not as evildoers; nor were their deteriorations in character known to them; that was why they had grown bolder, defiant, careless. And that was why the McNamaras were now in jail after being responsible for the deaths of twenty innocent workmen. That was why their union would now be wrecked and every union man in the world injured.

J. B. McNamara says, "On the night of September 30, 1910, at 5:45 P.M., I placed in ink alley, a portion of the Times Building, a suitcase containing sixteen sticks of eighty-per-cent dynamite, set to explode at one o'clock in the morning. It was my intention to injure the building and scare the owners. I did not intend to take the life of anyone. I sincerely regret that these unfortunate men lost their lives; if the giving of my life would bring them back I would freely give it."

Slumped behind his desk in the Higgins Building, feeling confused and torn, Darrow asked himself two questions:

"How can I defend the McNamaras? How can they be defended?"

He shambled slowly over to the jail, had the guard admit him to the McNamara cell and sat on a bunk between his two clients. He had sat in many cells many clients, but for him this was the most hopeless meeting of all. . . .

"Why did you do it?" he asked hoarsely of no one in particular.

There was a long silence, during which J. B.'s face looked long and thin and solemn. His feverish eyes gleamed.

"There was a labor parade," he answered in a hoarse, impersonal tone, as though talking to himself. "The police beat up some of the boys. The next morning the *Times* praised those cops for their heroic work. It was more than I could stand."

It was a reason. . . . But to Darrow it was little consolation; he knew with a terrible surety that these two men, warm live flesh that touched him on either side, both under thirty, would be convicted, would be walked up to the scaffold at San Quentin, the ropes adjusted about their necks, the traps sprung beneath their feet, their necks broken in the noose.

The passage of the years, the burden of suffering and of death he had seen, had not made him hard shelled, had not blunted his almost pathological empathy. And of all the brutalizing acts he had encountered, there was none he found more degrading or more injurious to the spiritual fabric of the people as a whole than the taking of a life by the state.

He believed passionately in the sanctity of human life; if the state could take human life for revenge or punishmen, why could it not take it for a thousand other reasons? If every last iota of life was not made sacred, how could the preciousness of life, and hence the human race, be maintained?

Fletcher Bowron, who went up to his office every morning to find if there was any news, saw at once that something crucial had happened to Darrow; his fire was gone; his confidence was gone; his concentration, singleness and clarity of purpose, his grip on the organization of his job, had disintegrated. He was confused, helpless, terror-stricken.

He didn't know where to turn or what to do.

It was during this period that certain questionable acts began to happen around defense headquarters. One of the most damaging witnesses against J. B. McNamara was Diekleman, a Los Angeles hotel clerk who had registered J. B. McNamara as J. B. Bryce a few days before the *Times* explosion. Diekleman had in the meanwhile joined the Harvey restaurant system and been transferred to Albuquerque, New Mexico. The prosecution knew at all times where he was because it kept Burns operatives surrounding him. One day Burt Hamerstrom, Ruby's itinerant-journalist brother, turned up at Diekleman's restaurant in Albuquerque, introduced himself as Mr Higgins (name of the building in which Darrow had his defense offices) and said:

"We are trying our best to save that man. He is innocent. Don't you think it would be right for you to consider the least doubt there is and be on our side?"

"I don't think there is any doubt," replied Diekleman.

"Now you are a valuable witness to us, whatever your price is we will give it. . . . Do you know Rector's Restaurant in Chicago?"

"Yes."

"Well, I think Mr Darrow is interested in that. How would you like to be assistant manager there?"

Diekleman refused to leave Albuquerque. Hamerstrom came back several times, offering railroad fare to Chicago and thirty dollars a week for expense money until the trial was over and a round-trip ticket to Los Angeles. When

Diekleman still refused Hamerstrom assumed that he didn't want to leave his girl friend behind and offered to pay her expenses too. Diekleman agreed, accepted a railroad ticket and left for Chicago on September 19, 1911. The morning he arrived in Chicago he had a meeting with Hamerstrom and Ed Nockels, then wired the district attorney's office in Los Angeles where he was and returned to Albuquerque on the afternoon train. It was a fiasco which was to cause Darrow a deal of trouble, as did the wild ride of Mrs Dave Caplan.

Mrs Caplan's husband was now a fugitive from justice, for he was one of the three men who had bought the nitro-gelatin from the Hercules Powder Plant, and it was his wagon in which the explosive had been hauled from the Embarcadero to the empty house he had rented. When Mrs Caplan was served with a subpoena and told that she would remain under subpoena from October eleventh on, Tveitmoe and Johannsen hired a limousine and chauffeur, picked up Mrs Caplan and had her driven for two nights to Reno, Nevada. The next day Johannsen accompanied her on a train to Chicago.

With the passage of the weary and disheartening days, only one good thing happened for the defense: Job Harriman won the primary runoff by a whopping vote. It was clear to everyone that he would defeat Alexander in the final election. There would still be the same district attorneys, Fredericks and Ford, the same *Times* and Merchants' and Manufacturers' Association, the same Erectors' Association in the East, which was paying Otis to keep up his fight; but at least the city government would be in friendly hands. The election of a socialist government in Los Angeles could not help but have an effect upon the jury.

For therein would lie the solution of his case: the jury.

When the first venire lists were drawn Darrow engaged a man by the name of Bert Franklin to set up an agency which would investigate all prospective jurors. For the five years previous Franklin had been a deputy investigator for the United States marshal's office in Los Angeles; before that he had been for four years in charge of the criminal investigations under Captain Fredericks, before that had been a guard in the Los Angeles jail. He was recommended to Darrow by Job Harriman and Le Compte Davis. Franklin opened an office, engaged a crew of private detectives and set to work.

"Mr Darrow said he wanted to find out the apparent age, religion, nationality, of every prospective juror, what their feelings were toward union labor, their feelings and opinions regarding the *Times* explosion, their opinion as to whether the McNamaras were guilty or not guilty of the crime with which they were charged, their financial condition, their property, their bank. . . ."

The prosecution had a similar investigating staff. As soon as the lists were drawn each side would make a copy of the names, and the investigators would dash out of the courtroom to get to the potential juryman first to investigate him and bring back a report. Each day as his investigators brought in their reports Franklin took them to the Higgins Building and placed them on Darrow's desk. As Darrow looked over each summary Franklin suggested, "Challenge him when he is called up; he is antagonistic to labor. Accept the next fellow; he is a liberal. Get rid of that next one fast; his brother is a member of the M. and M." When the trial opened on October eleventh Darrow would go into court with Franklin's reports and suggestions to use as a basis for questioning prospective jurors. The only difficulty was that everyone whom Darrow would consider acceptable would be thrown out by the prosecution, and everyone the prosecution wanted would be promptly dismissed by Darrow. So complete was their system of checks that over three hundred jurors would be examined before six men could be found who were acceptable to both sides.

On the sixth of October Franklin went to the home of Robert Bain, an elderly carpenter whom he had known for twenty years and who was about to be drawn for jury duty. Although a workman himself, Bain was known to the prosecution to be hostile to the unions and hence would be acceptable to them. When no one answered his ring at the Bain house Franklin went next door, left his card with the neighbor and asked her to please tell Bain to telephone him at his office. Later that day he went back and found Mrs Bain at home. Franklin relates his conversation with Mrs Bain:

"I told her that I would like to have Bob on the McNamara jury, that I was in a position to pay him five hundred dollars down and two thousand when he had voted for an acquittal for McNamara.

" 'Well,' she said, 'you know that Bob is a very honest man.'

" 'Yes, Mrs Bain, I realize that. I have always felt so.'

" 'But that sounds good to me. I would like Bob to consider it.' "

That night Franklin returned to the Bain house. "I asked him what he thought about the matter, and he said he raised some objection when his wife spoke about it but that she had convinced him that it was to the interest of both of them to accept the proposition, as he was getting old and that it would only be a matter of two or three years until he would have to quit his labors. . . . He told me he had but very little money and that he was paying for his place. I then asked him if he would accept five hundred in cash with the promise of two thousand more after he had voted for acquittal. He said that he would. I first asked that the curtains be drawn, then took four hundred dollars from my pocket and gave it to him. Hs asked me what assurance he would have of getting the balance of the money, and I told him that we would be compelled to pay the money; if we didn't he could report it. He agreed, and then I left."

Franklin handed his employer a satisfactory report on Robert Bain. Bain was called into court and accepted by both sides as a juryman, the first to be seated.

The days spun themselves out as Darrow thrashed in his mind to find a tenable means of defense. Hs asked Judge Bordwell for a postponement, but it was refused. He caused every conceivable delay, sometimes for good reason, sometimes for bad. Judge Bordwell seemed hostile; Darrow asked for a change of judge. Bordwell refused to eliminate himself. The people in the courtroom observed that he questioned for hours and days prospective jurors, even when it was obvious that he would dismiss them—killing time, earning the postponement the judge had refused him, waiting for the break or development that would enable him to prepare a telling defense. To the world the McNamaras were still proclaiming their innocence; Gompers and Debs were declaring them innocent; the great mass of workers were declaring them innocent. His defense associates might have gleaned that portions of the McManigal confession were true, but neither Davis, Scott nor Judge McNutt had access to his private files; they could not know that the McNamaras were guilty as charged. And he was afraid to tell them.

In the third week of October another juror was selected, in the fourth week two more, in the first week of November a fifth. It was on the fourth of November that Bert Franklin made another important trip, this time to the small ranch of George Lockwood, near Covina. Lockwood, past sixty, had worked for the police and district attorney's office as policeman, deputy, investigator, guard in the jail with Franklin under Captain White.

"George," said Franklin, in effect, "this is a matter of the strictest confidence, and it might lead to complications. I consider you are my friend, and I know what under no circumstances will you repeat anything that is said to you without my permission."

"Bert, under no circumstances will I do anything that will cast any reflections on you."

"Did you know I was working for the McNamara defense?"

"No, but I am glad to hear you are employed."

"George, you and I are getting old, and both of us have worked hard and accumulated little, and I think it's time when we should use our brains more and our feet and hands less."

"Yes, Bert, I agree with you."

"George, I have a proposition whereby you can make some money and be of material assistance to myself at the same time. Your name is on the list of prospective jurors that might be called at a future date. In the case that you are drawn, upon proper arrangements would you vote for a verdict of acquittal for the McNamaras?"

"Well, I don't know."

"Take your time and think it over, and if you see your way clear I can give you five hundred dollars in cash, and at the end of the case I will give you two thousand more."

"Bert, that is a matter I would want to think over."

While Lockwood was thinking over the deal offered to him by his former associate, before his name was drawn from the county lists, Lincoln Steffens, in his early years one of America's most penetrating muckrakers and fearless researchers into big business's corruption of government, arrived in Los Angeles and went to see his old friend, Clarence Darrow. Thereupon the McNamara case took on a new dimension.

In his popular magazine articles and in such books as *The Shame of the Cities, The Struggle for Self-Government,* Lincoln Steffens had been, along with Henry Demarest Lloyd, author of *Wealth against Commonwealth,* among the first to demonstrate that a political democracy has difficulty surviving under an industrial oligarchy. During the months of Darrow's preparation for the McNamara trial Steffens had been abroad seeking material with which to muckrake England and Europe. Certain that the McNamaras were guilty and having been converted to the stand of Keir Hardie, the British labor leader, that "labor has done it, and capital and the world should learn why," he conceived the plan of selling New York newspaper editors on the idea of sending him to Los Angeles to show why labor was guilty and what lay behind their acts of violence. The editors were so astounded to find a labor sympathizer convicting his men before their trial, they gave him the assignment.

Steffens asked Darrow for permission to see the McNamaras. Not knowing his mission, Darrow gave his approval. Though the brothers did not know Steffens they greeted him warmly as a friend of labor. He then told the boys that he wanted to write a series of articles called "Justifiable Dynamiting," in which he would reveal to the world why labor had been forced into violence. While the McNamaras sat in shocked silence Steffens continued:

"It's a doubtful experiment and a risk for you, but it's got to be done sometime. Why not now? Why not help me dig up on the side, while the legal case is going on, the case of Labor against Capital as a parallel, as a background to the case of California versus the McNamaras? I might be able to show why you turned to dynamite."

John J. McNamara asked sardonically, "Have you seen Darrow about this?" Steffens reports James as saying, "If you could do what you propose I'd be willing to hang," then continuing to his brother, "It's for this that we have been working, Joe, to force attention to the actual conditions of labor. He means to go and get the actual cases of black-listing that have made it impossible for discharged men to ever get work. Why wouldn't I risk my life to get that told? It's what I've been risking my life for right along."

Elated, Steffens walked briskly back to Darrow's office to make the most extraordinary proposal ever made to a lawyer who had clients to defend against a murder charge. A cold sweat broke out on Darrow's brow. He told Steffens to forget it and dismissed him—but he himself was not able to forget it. If Steffens was so positive that the men were guilty, must not others be equally sure about it? If it was as plain as that to people who had no access to the evidence in his file, what chance would he stand in a courtroom? If, as Ruby says, he was frightened and bewildered when coming out on the train, he was now plunged into hopelessness. Every avenue of escape was blocked. He could not withdraw from the case now; that would hamstring his clients. Though sufficiently ill to be admitted to any hospital, he could not sneak out that way.

At odd moments he would think he saw some hope, some chance, then he would realize that it was wishful thinking. His moods changed so swiftly that Steffens reported of him, "At three o'clock he is a hero for courage, nerve and calm judgment, but at three-fifteen he may be a coward for fear, collapse and panicky mentality. . . . his power and his weakness is in the highly sensitive, emotional nature which sets his seeing mind in motion in that loafing body." When someone brought Darrow further bad news, Steffens says, "His face was ashen; he could hardly walk; he was scared weak and did not recover for an hour. He said, 'I can't stand it to have a man I am defending hanged. I can't stand it.'"

That Saturday, November nineteenth, E. W. Scripps invited

173

Darrow and Steffens to spend the week end with him at his ranch, Miramar, near San Diego. Scripps, like Hearst, had founded a chain of newspapers and a great fortune upon liberalism and the cause of the American masses. An astute student and merciless thinker, his grounding in sociology had given him a genuine sympathy for the labor movement. That night as they sat in the patio Darrow outlined to Scripps the strength of the evidence that had come in against the structural-iron workers. Scripps rose, went into his study and emerged with the manuscript of an article he had just written for his papers, an article in which he explained and justified labor's use of force and dynamite.

" 'We, the employers, have every other weapon,' " he read to Darrow; " 'we have the jobs to give or withold; the capital to spend, or not spend, for production, for wages, for ourselves; we have the press to state our case and suppress theirs; we have the Bar and the Bench, the legislature, the governor, the police and the militia. Labor has nothing but violence and mob force."

Darrow remained silent. Then Scripps made an observation which stopped the wheels from churning in Darrow's head. After three months he was to reach his first decision.

"Workingmen should have the same belligerent rights in labor controversies," observed Scripps, "that nations have in warfare. There has been war between the erectors and the ironworkers; all right, the war is over now; the defeated side should be granted the rights of a belligerent under international law."

"I wish the people of Los Angeles could see it that way," Darrow murmured. "I believe it would be to the best interests of the community and also right and just to get rid of this case without shedding any human blood. I wish we could make a settlement."

The next morning while they breakfasted at the Van Nuys Hotel Steffens asked, "Did you mean it when you said you wanted a settlement?"

"Yes, but I don't believe it will be possible. The feeling is too bitter, and the people are not in a reasoning state of mind."

"I think I can convince the businessmen of Los Angeles," said Steffens, hardly able to contain his excitement, "that it would be better all around to avoid the passions of a trial and to accept a plea of guilty from James B. McNamara."

"I am perfectly willing you should do it, but you must make it very plain that it does not come from me or from our side, for if it should get out that we are making overtures

174

it will make it that much more difficult to defend the men and save their lives.

"I will take it up on my account, and if any proposition comes it will come to you, not from you."

"At all events there will be no use to try to get a settlement unless the *Times* people are in favor of it."

That night Steffens returned to Darrow to tell him that he had seen some of the local politicians and businessmen and "that they believed the matter could be put through to permit James B. McNamara to plead guilty, receive a life sentence and end all other prosecutions in Los Angeles." Steffens was afire as he outlined to Darrow how he was going to bring love and brotherhood to Los Angeles, how everyone would forgive everyone else and become friends, and there would be no more labor troubles in Los Angeles. Darrow believed none of this nonsense; he knew his adversaries too well, yet he was eager for the settlement to be arranged.

"I told Steffens that if such a thing could be done it would take a great burden off me, and I thought it would be a good thing both for labor and capital, especially for the defendants and the city of Los Angeles. I did not have confidence enough to present it to any of my associates at the time or even to my clients. . . ."

The next morning, November twenty-second, when Le Compte Davis walked into court he was met by District Attorney Fredericks, Otis's protégé who had been elected to his position by the *Times*.

"Why don't you get those boys to plead guilty and quit your horseplay?" demanded Fredericks.

Taken aback, Davis replied, "I was not hired for that purpose."

"You know you're going to do it; a committee has been consulted about it, and I have been approached."

When Darrow reached court and saw the expression on Davis' face he promptly explained the Steffens' mission and his reasons for wanting to make a settlement: the prosecution had a great mass of evidence to produce and every day was bringing people into court to look at James B. McNamara and identify him; the defense had no contradictory evidence to offer, nor could they let James B. testify on his own behalf; he wouldn't be able to stand up under cross-examination. The trial would be a rout.

"Is J. B. willing to plead guilty?" asked Davis.

"I haven't talked to him yet, but I think I can make him see the reasonableness of it. You are a good friend of Captain Fredericks; will you go to him and work out a settlement?"

"I don't think we have any right to do it without consulting organized labor," replied Davis. "The American Federation of Labor is my employer in this case, and I won't do anything until I have their approval. The money to defend the men has been furnished by labor, and it will ruin you with labor if you do this without consulting them."

"The money was furnished by organized labor," answered Darrow, "but these two men are our clients, and nobody can possibly give us money that can in any way influence us in an action that is due our clients. As far as I am concerned, I have no right to consider myself; all I have to consider are these two men, and if they think it best and we think it best, we should act."

That afternoon Darrow wired Fremont Older, crusading editor of the San Francisco *Call* and one of the most respected men on the Pacific coast, to come to Los Angeles for an important conference. Older arrived and over luncheon Darrow detailed the situation to his old friend and asked for approval of the plan. Older, who had thought the boys innocent as charged, or at least to have a fighting chance in court, was stunned.

"Well, Clarence, you know best—if you think it's the thing to do. . . . It will be misunderstood by a large number of laboring men who never believed that dynamite was placed in the Times Building—but I'll do what I can to make them understand. I suppose you know what this will do to you with organized labor?"

"The lives of my clients come first. The McNamaras have a right to know that . . . they will probably hang. I won't advise them to plead guilty; I will merely tell them their case looks hopeless. They have the right to choose, to save their own lives."

That same evening Ed Nockels arrived from Chicago, listened to Darrow's presentation of the case and agreed that a settlement was the best way out. Darrow sent Nockels to see Le Compte Davis.

After ascertaining that Nockels could speak for the A. F. of L., Davis went to see Captain Fredericks, and Darrow went to see his clients. They listened attentively while he showed them why they had no chance; that a plea of guilty on the part of James would be the best way out, not only for themselves but for their union and their friends. He assured them that he would work to have John J. freed entirely; that he would insist that James be allowed to plead without giving a detailed confession which would implicate other men; that he would secure from the state a promise not to pursue or bring to trial Dave Caplan or Matt Schmidt; in short, that they be granted an honorable surrender.

176

"John, who had done more of the consulting with us than the other," writes Darrow, "said without hesitation that it ought to be disposed of, and he believed organized labor would come to understand it if they didn't at once. He thought there was little chance to save James's life without it, which was the controlling interest with him, and that his own case was also very dangerous. James from the first was willing to plead guilty and take a life sentence but not willing for John to plead guilty at all."

In the meanwhile a Merchants' and Manufacturers' Association committee had received Steffens' proposal with interest. The mayoralty election was only a few weeks off; Job Harriman's plurality assured him of winning. They did not want to give up their trial, but they saw a way to kill socialism in southern California for at least a generation: they would let James B. McNamara plead guilty—provided he did it before Election Day! The confession of guilt would wreck Harriman's chances. Harry Chandler, Otis's son-in-law, thought this was a wise plan, but Otis was adamant: they had the evidence to destroy unionism, and he wasn't going to rest until every last shred of it was brought out in trial and publicized to the world.

Le Compte Davis went to see Otis on the morning of November twenty-fifth. "Take the bird while you've got it in your hand, General," he said. "By his plea of guilty McNamara will give you a complete victory and prove that everything you have been claiming is right. If you take a chance and force them into trial, lightning might strike; an accident might happen; they might get off."

Otis grumbled, barked, swore, "I want those sons of bitches to hang!" and finally agreed—but not until he showed Davis a telegram from the National Erectors' Association, which was helping to finance the prosecution, in which the erectors said that John J., the directing mind behind the dynamiting, was the one they really wanted and that they would accept no settlement unless he also pleaded guilty and received at least a ten-year sentence.

For Darrow the need to accept punishment for John J. and to plead the McNamaras guilty in time to wreck the socialist campaign was a heavy defeat. Since James B. had never been a structural-iron worker or a member of their union, his activities could somehow be interpreted as happening outside the sanction of the body of workers. But John J. was the directing secretary; when he pleaded guilty he thereupon pleaded his union guilty. Further, to sacrifice the Socialist party and their vigorous campaign on the eve of a stunning and nationally important victory was not only to deal his friends a deathblow, but to do it by means of a stab in the back: for Job Harriman, who had been too busy campaigning to take much part in the preparation of the McNamara defense, had not been informed of the plans to make a settlement; Darrow had not told him for fear he would refuse to sacrifice the Socialist party and the election for the McNamaras.

It was a nasty price to have to pay, but it was obvious to Darrow that he could have his settlement on no other terms. He consoled himself by thinking that if socialism were as truly a historical imperative as its adherents claimed it was, it did not need to ride into office and power on the coattails of guilty men.

On the afternoon of Saturday, November twenty-fifth, Darrow took Le Compte Davis, Judge McNutt and Lincoln Steffens with him to the jail to impart the bad news to the brothers. James refused to plead guilty if his brother had to plead with him, and no amount of reasoning on Darrow's part would change the older brother's mind. He sent Davis back to Captain Fredericks to see if the district attorney would reconsider and let John off. The next morning, Sunday, the twenty-sixth, the group reassembled in the jail.

"I'll take ten years. Anything to save Jim's life," John J. said.

James objected. "I won't let them send Joe to prison. Besides, his pleading guilty will have a bad effect on labor. It will have a pretty serious effect on you too, Mr Darrow."

"You needn't bother about that part of it," grunted Darrow. "Neither do I think that labor has any right to be consulted about a lawyer's duty. I don't think you should sacrifice your lives when something better can be done." But James would not be persuaded.

Darrow says, "I was anxious to have it closed up as soon as possible; if they did not plead before the election we could never get the district attorney to accept the plea. . . . and I did not want anything to happen that could prevent the settlement."

He took John J. aside and talked the matter over with him. John said that his brother's consent wasn't necessary; he would save James's life without it: he was not on trial at the moment, and as soon as Darrow pleaded James guilty, he, John, would come into court and accept as light a sentence as possible, but ten years if that was the best he could do.

This same Sunday, while Darrow was bringing the settlement to a head in the county jail, his chief investigator, Bert

178

Franklin went to see George Lockwood, who had not yet been served for jury duty.

"Well, your name was drawn yesterday, and you will be served between now and tomorrow morning. There will be four thousand in it for you, and I want you to have that money," Franklin said.

"Bert, if I go into this I don't want no mistake about the money."

"There won't be any trouble at all. Captain White will be custodian of the money. We both know him, and he is straight. . . . and he will turn the money over to you when the trial is over."

"When the trial is over," protested Lockwood; "why, there might be no one know anything about the balance of the money."

"I can't see any way out of it but Captain White."

That night Franklin went to see Captain White, former head of the Los Angeles jail under whom both he and Lockwood had served as guards but who was now running a jewelry store. Franklin told White of his plan to bribe Lockwood.

"My God, Franklin," exclaimed White, "I wouldn't trust Lockwood as far as I could throw a bull by the tail!"

"Captain," said Franklin, "I believe that if George Lockwood gives his word he will do a certain thing, he will do it."

"If you are satisfied," the captain replied, "why, other people should be."

Franklin then offered to pay White a hundred dollars for his trouble if he would act as intermediary and hold the thirty-five hundred dollars' balance until Lockwood voted for an acquittal. Captain White agreed.

The following morning, Monday, Davis came to Darrow's office to report that he had had a final conference with District Attorney Fredericks and that the settlement would go through on the terms agreed upon in the jail the night before: a life sentence for James, with the possibility of commutation, and ten years for John, who could be freed at the end of seven years for good behavior. Darrow then asked Judge McNutt, Davis and Steffens if they fully approved the plan. Everyone agreed that it was the best way out.

That night in his flat on Bonnie Brae, Darrow slept soundly for the first time in months.

While Darrow slept Bert Franklin had received a telephone call from Lockwood to come out to the ranch.

"Shall I bring the Big Fellow along?" asked Franklin.

"Yes."

When Franklin reached the Lockwood ranch that evening it was well covered by detectives from the district attorney's office. Lockwood led Franklin out to the barn, where a stenographer was planted to take down the conversation, and asked:

"Where is Darrow?"

"Why, George, did you think Darrow was coming?"

"Yes, that is what I understood."

"Well, you was mistaken; I intended to bring Captain White, but he didn't wish to come."

Lockwood expected to be paid his five hundred dollars that night, but Franklin didn't have the money on him. He said, "George, be at the corner of Third and Los Angeles streets tomorrow morning at nine, and I will see you there at that time." He then returned to Captain White's house, where he made arrangements for the captain to meet him at the corner of Third and Main streets the following morning at eight forty-five, where he would give him four thousand dollars in cash, five hundred of which White was to turn over to Lockwood.

The next morning Darrow rose early. Ruby gave him a manicure and cut some of the hair off the back of his head. Happy to see that he was looking better, she laid out a fresh linen suit and a clean white shirt and tie. After a light breakfast he strolled the two blocks to the car line; since there was no car in sight he walked through Echo Park as far as the aqueduct. At the aqueduct he boarded the car, rode to the terminal at Second and Hill streets and walked to his office. He arrived at his usual eight-thirty, sat down to his desk and dug into the work of clearing up his accounts.

In the meanwhile Bert Franklin was meeting Captain White on the corner of Second and Main streets.

"Good morning, Captain," said Franklin. "I have the money."

"This is a poor place to hand it to me," grumbled White. "We'd better go into this saloon."

They went into the saloon, had a drink at the bar, then Franklin handed Captain White a thousand-dollar bill and six five-hundred-dollar bills. The two men left the saloon together, but once on the sidewalk Franklin left White and walked ahead of him to the corner of Third and Los Angeles streets. Here he met Sam Browne, captain of the Los Angeles detectives, with Detective Campbell following him. Franklin exchanged greetings with Detective Browne, slipped down a side street, came back through an alley and entered a saloon on the corner of Third and Los Angeles, where he could watch White pass the money to Lockwood. While Franklin slipped down the alley Detectives Browne and Campbell went up to the second floor of a rooming house where they, too, could watch White pass the money to Lockwood.

A third detective by the name of Home, who had also been trailing Franklin, entered the saloon after him. He saw that Franklin was behind the red swinging doors of the toilet, the open doors making it possible for him to recognize Franklin from the knees down. When Franklin came out of the toilet Detective Home hid himself by turning his face toward the wall behind an icebox, which was some twelve feet away from the toilet. Franklin walked out of the saloon, looked around and came back in. This time a fourth detective, Dana Ong, followed him in, walked up to the bar beside Franklin and ordered a drink. After downing his drink Franklin walked to the swinging doors and looked over the top, as though searching for someone. He returned to the bar, had another drink, walked again to the swinging doors to peer out. Detective Ong followed him to the door to look over his shoulder. They both saw Lockwood come up Los Angeles Street and Captain White cross over to meet him. The two men shook hands.

"What is new?" asked Lockwood.

"Nothing, except a mutual friend of ours has entrusted me with some money to be paid to you on certain conditions. . . ."

"How much money, and what are the conditions?"

"I am to hand you five hundred dollars and hold three thousand for you until such time as a verdict of not guilty is rendered or the jury hung in the McNamara case."

"It don't go. There was thirty-five hundred to be held, not three thousand. Where is Franklin?"

"He just went away from here."

"Well, it don't go at all, because there was to be four thousand."

"Possibly there is in this roll. I haven't had time to examine it."

"Well, go in that store and examine it."

"I ain't got no business in that store. I'll walk up the street a bit and look."

White walked up the block a ways, faced a store window and counted the money. Then he returned, saying, "There is thirty-five hundred dollars aside from the five hundred I am to hand you."

"All right, I am ready."

White handed Lockwood a five-hundred-dollar bill, showing him the other bills as he did so.

"It ought to have been in twos or fives," complained Lockwood. "It's all wrong in a case of this kind; how could a fellow dispose of a five-hundred-dollar bill under these circumstances?"

Before White had a chance to reply a fifth detective, Detective Allison, came down the street on his motorcycle, stopping close to Lockwood and White. Just as he stopped Lockwood dropped his five-hundred-dollar bill to the sidewalk. As he stooped to pick it up Franklin, who was watching from behind the saloon doors, pushed his way out and joined Lockwood and White. After the exchange of a few sentences Franklin looked up, saw Detective Home watching him from behind the saloon doors, turned slightly and saw Detectives Browne and Campbell coming toward him.

"Don't look around," he said to Lockwood. "Let's get out."

Franklin and Lockwood then walked down Third Street, away from the two detectives on foot, but in the direction from which the motorcycle detective had come. White trailed them.

When Franklin and Lockwood had walked half a block down Third Street they saw Clarence Darrow on the opposite side of the street. Darrow saw them and crossed the street. Just he was about to step up on the sidewalk Detective Browne came between Darrow and Franklin, pushed Franklin sharply and said: "Don't talk to this man, Mr Darrow. He's under arrest." And to Franklin he said, "Bert, I want you."

"What for?" asked Franklin.

"You've been a detective long enough to know what for. You know what you've been doing."

Darrow stood in silence, staring at the two men.

"The first thing that entered my mind," says Darrow, "was as to whether it would be possible to carry out the settlement, and if not, whether it would be possible to save these men's lives. I was shocked and broken up over it."

Steffens came into Darrow's office to ask, "Is this going to interfere with the settlement?"

"Not as far as I am concerned. What about your businessmen?"

"I don't see why it should make any difference to them," replied Steffens. "Suppose they should think that you or any of the rest of the lawyers were connected with this: then what?"

"If that question is raised I want you to tell them that under no circumstances am I to be considered in this matter; if there is any man who thinks that I or any lawyer in this case had anything to do with the bribery, you tell them that there will be no bargaining on that case, that they can take care of that when the time comes. All we are proposing to settle is the McNamara case."

"This is quixotic. Why not get rid of them all at once?"

"No. I never have let my own affairs interfere with my clients, and I never will. You give that message to the committee."

Wednesday morning and afternoon were spent in a series of conferences between the lawyers, the businessmen, the district attorney and Otis. By nightfall the district attorney's office had agreed to let the settlement go through, but the two McNamaras would have to plead guilty together. That would make it impossible for Joseph to plead after James had been sentenced. Darrow knew that it would be another difficult struggle with James. On Thursday morning, Thanksgiving, he again assembled his staff at the jail: Davis, Scott, McNutt— and Steffens, who brought the report that industrial warfare was over in Los Angeles: after the McNamaras were sentenced there would be a meeting between capital and labor at which the hatchet would be buried, all differences dissolved.

Darrow again reviewed the case for the McNamaras, showing them the hopelessness of their situation. James was unmoved: he would not permit his brother to go to prison. Each lawyer in turn presented has arguments in favor of the brothers pleading together; he fought them all. It was not until midafternoon, when they had all been defeated and it looked to Darrow as though they would have to go through with the trial, that Davis took a new tack.

"Jim," he said quietly, "I think you're right, and we've been wrong. It's best that you hang. It 'll be better for labor."

J. B. stared at him without speaking.

"It's better that your brother hang too," continued Davis. "Then labor will have two martyrs instead of only one."

J. B. straightened, his face tense. "Is that the way it looks to you?" he demanded. "That they'll hang Joe too?"

"That's the way it looks to me."

J. B. threw himself face down on his bunk and cried brokenly for a quarter of an hour. Darrow and the others sat huddled into themselves, trying not to see or hear or weep. Then J. B. raised himself on one elbow, brushed the tears from his eyes, and said quietly: "All right. I'm licked."

The next morning at the opening of court Darrow and Davis went into Judge Bordwell's chambers to tell him that the McNamaras had agreed to plead guilty that morning.

"Ten years isn't enough for John J. McNamara," said Judge Bordwell. "He'll have to take fifteen."

Darrow had no authority to accept fifteen years for John; though he knew that the prosecution was laying it on now that they had the upper hand, he had no recourse but to hasten back to the jail and tell the brothers the additional bad news. Having resigned themselves to the idea of prison, the brothers had little spirit left. They agreed. Darrow rushed back to Judge Bordwell to tell him that John would take fifteen years. Judge Bordwell ordered the two men brought into court at two o'clock.

The arrangements had been so closely guarded that only those in the conference circle knew they had been going on. The city was overwrought because of the trial, the election and the torrents of abuse being unleashed on both sides. Thousands walked the streets wearing buttons that read: McNAMARAS NOT GUILTY! VOTE FOR HARRIMAN! The majority were passionately convinced that the McNamaras had been framed, that Darrow would excoriate the Otis-*Times*, Merchants and Manufacturers clique, that the trial would be a complete vindication for the McNamaras and for organized labor—and the people would be freed from their bondage.

That very morning, as he had every morning, Darrow found hundreds of letters on his desk, most of them containing money for the defense, all stoutly avowing their loyalty and faith in the McNamaras' innocence. All over America Thanksgiving meetings had been held to voice support of the McNamaras; the labor councils of nearly every major city: New York, Boston, Philadelphia, Chicago, Pittsburgh, Cleveland, San Francisco, were planning gigantic demonstrations "to protest against the dastardly frame-up, to force the capitalist class to release the McNamaras."

At two o'clock on the afternoon of December 1, 1911, Darrow had his two clients brought into the courtroom. The reporters, who had been bored during the questioning of prospective jurors, sat up when they saw John J., for he was not on trial, and it was the first time he had been in court.

When the court opened District Attorney Fredericks rose and said, "Your honor, the defense wishes to address the court."

With that he sat down. Darrow nodded to Davis, whom he had decided was the closest to the court and the best man to speak. Davis rose and said without inflection. "May it please the court, our clients wish to change their plea from not guilty to guilty."

The announcement fell with a flat, sickening thud. Spectators turned to each other wondering if they had heard aright.

Suddenly, as the import of the astounding twist reached the consciousness of the people, "there was a psychic explosion" that was heard around the world. The reporters were the first to recover; they dashed, sprawling over each other, for telephones. A clamor went up; men rushed into the court from the corridors to learn if the news were true; fist fights started; the room filled with a bewildered, questioning, pushing, screaming, mauling crowd. Within a very few moments the extras were on the streets with the biggest headlines in their history: McNamaras Plead Guilty, but the people of Los Angeles refused to believe: they had belonged to a cause; they had been fighting for a cause; they were strong, resolute; they had an army; they would fight unto the death. And now, suddenly, without warning, without explanation, their army, their strength, their cause, had collapsed.

Judge Bordwell instructed the McNamaras to be brought into court for sentencing on the morning of Election Day, then adjourned court. For an hour the crowd milled about, constantly renewing itself, trying to find out if this heresy were true, to learn who was responsible for the debacle. The district attorney, the court officers, left; Darrow's defense attorneys left; slowly the crowd exhausted itself, dispersed and emptied the big room. Darkness fell. Darrow, who had been sitting slumped in his chair during the storm, his eyes closed wearily, tried to rise. He could not. He sat there in the gloom, aching, miserable, alone.

It was the most disastrous day for labor in American history, and Clarence Darrow was responsible for it.

Should he have pleaded the McNamaras guilty?

Two lives had been spared from almost certain hanging. He had obstructed the prosecution from exploiting the full force of its case, forestalled the putting into evidence of material which would have been used against union officials in San Francisco and Indianapolis. He had save millions of peaceful workingmen from implicating themselves further in the fate of men who had betrayed the American Federation of Labor's pronouncement on peaceable methods; quieted a scandal which could reflect no possible credit on the iron-workers, the details of which would have revolted and alienated great sections of the American public. The country could now say, "The McNamaras are guilty; they have admitted their guilt and gone to prison; they are paying the penalty; let's forget about it and go back to work and our normal way of life." A year, two years, three years, would not be spent in whipping up passions, making accusations, spreading factionalism and warfare so wide and so deep that it might never be rooted out of American life. He had saved the union workers hundreds of thousands of dollars that would have been wasted in a futile defense; avoided a bitter and bloody class-war trial; prevented the horrifying precedent of
185

having labor leaders hanged for their part in it; enabled the city to travel more quickly the road toward peace and co-operation.

He knew that if he had tried the case with all his force he might have brought in a hung jury. But could he have brought all his force to bear? No one knew better than he that his greatest effectiveness, not only before judge and jury, but before the country as a whole, had grown out of his burning honesty and conviction that his clients were innocent. Great and epochal phrases had poured from his lips, phrases that had helped to reshape the minds of men and the life of his country; but how would they have sounded from the lips of a man who knew that he was being dishonest, who in his heart repudiated his own clients? He would be a mountebank and a hypocrite; his insincerity would show in every expression of his face, and he would convince no one.

He might have fought for a verdict of second-degree murder, exploded his miniature model of the Times Building, brought in experts to swear that the escaping gas had caused the explosion and the twenty deaths; yet he knew that with twenty men dead no jury would take into account the lack of intent to kill. Perhaps he could have appealed the convictions, used up years of time in the hope that passions would cool and his clients would be spared. But he knew, too, that the appeals could not save the lives of the men once they had been convicted in open court by a jury, and the constant appeals only would have continued to spread the details of their guilt and the ill will in the community.

Perhaps he could have let them hang and become labor martyrs. But if labor had to have martyrs, let them be innocent men. He could not have viewed the trial as a campaign of education, when anything he might have said would have inflamed hotheads to further violence, with everything in his nature crying out against violence. The National Electors' Association had said, "This is war!" Otis had cried in the *Times*, "This is war!" War was cruel, destructive, brutal, senseless, and until it was banished from the earth all barbarities would not only be condoned but approved, if they led to victory. He despaired of such methods, not only because they caused class war, destruction, bitterness and ineradicable ill will between men, but because they were short-sighted and futile, serving only one purpose: to perpetuate the struggle.

"I know I could have tried the McNamara case," said Darrow, "and that a large class of the working people of America would honestly have believed, if these men had been hanged, that they were not guilty. I could have done this and saved myself. I could have made money if I had done this—

186

if I had wanted to get money in that way. But I know if they had hanged these men it would have settled in the hearts of a great mass of men a hatred so deep, so profound, that it would never die away."

He shook his hot and weary head as he recalled how John Mitchell had accused him of wanting to make a plea for socialism instead of better wages and hours for the miners; how Edmund Richardson had charged him, in Boise, with putting the interests of the Socialist party before those of Haywood, Moyer and Pettibone. Now the cycle had been completed: he would be charged by the socialists with sacrificing the party to save his clients.

Sitting alone in the darkness on the field of battle where he had surrendered his cause and his people to momentary defeat, he was completely convinced that he had done right. To the end of his days he never faltered in his belief. Yet after fighting for labor for twenty years, bringing them by his brilliance, devotion and fearlessness many miles along the saber-studded road to civilization, he had now been the indirect instrument of causing them great harm. Labor would never forget—he knew that—and would never forgive him. He had known that his career as a labor defender was finished the day he had learned that he was defending guilty men.

Once again he tried to rise from his seat but could not. From out of the darkness came a friend to help him up. He walked slowly down the long aisle of the courtroom. When he reached the steps of the courthouse he looked down and saw a throng gathered there, waiting for him, standing in stark and sinister silence. In the flickering light of the gas lamps he could see the Harriman and McNamara badges littering the lawn and the gutters.

He shook off his helpful friend, straightened his shoulders and walked slowly down the stops. A murmur rose which grew in intensity as he came closer. When he reached the sidewalk the crowd closed in: workers, union officials, socialists, liberals, intellectuals, men and women for whom he had spent his years fighting. From the outskirts someone called him an evil name. Close by a man spat in his face. The crowd pushed in closer, surrounding him, pressed against him, heaping their frustration, their defeat, their humiliation, upon him in sordid imprecations. He was hemmed in so close now he could not move. Billy Cavenaugh pushed through the mob, caught Darrow by the sleeve and cried, "Come with me!"

Darrow gazed at the ring of angry faces. "No, Billy, I shall go down the street with the crowd. I have walked with them to the courthouse when they cheered me, and I shall go back the way I came."

He took a step forward. A wall of sullen eyes peered into his. He took another step—and the front line fell back. The crowd parted. He walked through it, cleanly, alone. As he went down the street, the crowd at his heels, one cry came out of the night.:

"Traitor! Traitor!"

Chapter Nine

Prisoner's Dock

BY MORNING the full force of the storm had descended upon the McNamaras and their attorney for the defense, Clarence Darrow.

With tears in his eyes and the hand that held the paper trembling, Sam Gompers cried, "I am astounded. . . . We have had the gravest assurances that these men are innocent. We have discouraged acts like these. . . . Those two men must have been crazy. . . ." So outraged was he that in his autobiography he omitted mention of labor's greatest legal defender, in spite of Darrow's monumental work for the American Federation of Labor.

Harry Orchard "could not conceal his joy. '. . . This confession will convince many who bitterly condemn me that I took the right course when I made a clean breast of my connection with the crimes charged against the Western Federation of Miners.' "

Hundreds of local unions hastened to jump off the McNamara band wagon, each local issuing its own renunciatory proclamation to the press.

The socialists repudiated the McNamaras as being trade unionists; the trade unionists repudiated them as being anarchists; the anarchists repudiated them as being terrorists. The sinking ship was deserted as fast as possible, the survivors pausing only long enough to yank off their cap, spit over their shoulder and cry, "Not in my family!" Only Big Bill Haywood stood stanchily by, reiterating, "I'm with the McNamaras and always will be. You can't view the class struggle through the eyes of capitalist-made laws."

On election morning, December 5, 1911, Darrow brought his clients before Judge Bordwell. Lincoln Steffens had had a chat with the judge and had reported to Darrow that Bordwell would handle the McNamaras gently and say nothing further to array class against class. When Darrow stood between the two brothers and heard the judge call them "murderers at heart," his face blanched and he wrung his handkerchief in his hands.

In the midst of the lashing he understood that every promise made in the settlement would be broken. Caplan and Schmidt were to be hunted for five years, captured and convicted in Los Angeles; the evidence that had been gathered against the McNamaras would be paraded before the public, not so much to convict Caplan and Schmidt as to get into the public record the material that had been suppressed when the McNamaras pleaded guilty. Ninety per cent of the Schmidt trial would deal with J. B. McNamara and not Schmidt, so that when Schmidt met McNamara in the yard of San Quentin the first thing he could say was:

"They tried you and convicted me!"

As soon as the McNamaras were hustled off to prison Los Angeles went to the polls to administer its defeat to the socialists. Job Harriman, who had learned about the settlement in the headlines of the afternoon papers of December first, did not show up at his campaign headquarters until the voting was over.

"Where have you been?" demanded Alexander Irvine.

"I couldn't come here," replied Harriman; "they were going to shoot me in the morning."

"That would have been a good place to shoot you. It would have won us the election."

The finality with which the McNamaras were dismissed included their chief counselor, Clarence Darrow. He was now accused of aiding and abetting a conspiracy whereby labor had been deceived into supporting the dynamiters and thus injured. In spite of labor's renunciation he issued a statement in which he took sole responsibility for what had happened. "I have known for months that our fight was hopeless. I never would have consented to their pleading guilty if I had thought there was a chance left. It was intimated to us that we must act promptly; there was danger that what was being considered would get out and make settlement impossible. We were responsible to our clients alone."

He had known when he saw the indisputable proof of the McNamaras' guilt before him on his desk that he had reached the end of his journey as a labor lawyer; labor now confirmed his decision by casting him off.

It was seventeen years since the day he had made his choice behind the counsel's desk of the Chicago and North Western Railway and taken the long walk down the hall to tell President Hughitt that he was giving up his secure, remunerative job to defend Eugene Debs and the American Railway Union. A man who cherished peace, he had ever since been in the center of incessant strife; a man who advocated tolerance, he had spent most of these years in internecine war, a man who believed that the world could survive only if based on good will, he had seen more ill will, rancor and bitterness than anyone of his age. Yet neither his years nor his battles had been altogether in vain: the millions of men and women who worked with their hands to earn their daily bread had had the hard-biting economic shackles about their ankles and wrists eased the tiniest bit because Clarence Darrow had raised his voice in their defense. Altgeld would have approved of his seventeen years.

The last of his papers had been sorted and filed, when Le Compte Davis called at the Higgins Building to see him.

"I'm certain that Bert Franklin is innocent," he said. "His wife came to see me last night. We can't abandon him. We've got to put up his ten-thousand-dollar bond."

When Darrow remained silent Davis continued, "I recommended Franklin to you, and I'll stand responsible for him. Franklin won't jump bail, but if he does I'll make good the ten thousand."

Darrow hesitated; he knew that if he went bond for Franklin he implicated himself in anything that Franklin might have done; then he wrote out the check against the McNamara defense account.

After Davis left, Darrow sat hunched at his desk. From the trail Franklin had blazed in his bribing operations and from his willingness to have the Lockwood money passed on a detective-infested corner, it appeared that he had wanted to be caught. And if he had wanted to be caught it could only have been part of his orders. Darrow's wide-ranging thoughts told him that it was possible that the San Francisco labor leaders had given Franklin four thousand dollars with which to bribe jurors, that if they had been willing to sanction the use of dynamite they would not shrink from bribing jurors. It was also possible that the Indianapolis ironworkers' officials, who were afraid that a conviction in the McNamara case would be injurious to their own cases in the Midwest, would attempt to bribe jurors. Yet how was it conceivable that any of the labor men would use Franklin for this purpose when they knew that Bert Franklin had been a district-attorney investigator for years, that he was being watched by Burns's operatives, that any slip would cause serious damage to himself and to the McNamaras?

Clarence lighted a cigarette off the butt of the last. Then

whose money was it? Whose machinations could this scheme be except William J. Burns? And if Burns had ordered Franklin to get himself caught, not only in attempts to bribe prospective jurors, but in the actual passage of the bills on an open street corner, then surely Burns could not want Bert Franklin. Surely he must be after bigger game!

He sat at his desk in the now-quiet and -deserted suite, letting his thoughts flow freely so that he might fit the parts into a pattern, while Le Compte Davis went to the courthouse, put up the bail and had Franklin released. Franklin went immediately to see Tom Johnson, a lawyer.

"You are friendly with the district attorney, aren't you?" Franklin asked.

"Yes."

"Will you go see Joe Ford and request him that if he will postpone my case and give me an opportunity to find a certain party with whom I had several meetings prior to my arrest but whom I have been unable to find, that if I can find that dark-complected man—there will be something doing; I will find the party who gave me the money with which the bribery was committed?"

Tom Johnson went to Ford but soon returned to tell Franklin that "Ford refuses to continue the case; he takes no stock in this cock-and-bull story about being furnished the money by a man you didn't know; he is securing new evidence every day, and in a short time he will have sufficient evidence to send Darrow to the penitentiary."

"Neither Davis nor Darrow gave me money to bribe jurors," replied Franklin quickly, "and they know nothing about it. I would be a goddamned liar if I said they did. I know I am expected to say that Darrow did it."

Within a week of his arrest Franklin met with Darrow and Davis in Darrow's office.

"Ford sent word to me that if I know anything about any of the local lawyers," declared Franklin, "to forget about it. Ford say the only one they want to get is Darrow."

Clarence looked up sharply. "But why are they so anxious to get me?" he flared. "Why are they more anxious to get me than—than Job Harriman, for instance?"

"I don't know, Mr. Darrow, but I told them that you never gave me a corrupt dollar."

Nor was it to Clarence alone that Franklin uttered such protestations. He stopped with two acquaintances, John Drain, a contractor and former superintendent of streets, and Frank Dominguez, an attorney who had never met Darrow, in the Waldorf Saloon. After a moment or two the conversation drifted around to the jury bribery.

Frank Dominguez said: "It is absolutely inconceivable to me that a man of Darrow's character and reputation as a man of honor would be guilty of such a thing."

"I don't believe it either," agreed Drain. "I think he is too smart for that."

"I never received a dishonest dollar from Mr Darrow," replied Franklin. "He never knew anything connected with this matter. He is too good a man to do anything of that kind. He is the most kindhearted, generous and the best man I have ever known in my life and would not stand for any corruption or dirty work."

Drain reports, "This conversation . . . could readily be heard by everyone around. Thereupon a man whom I did not know came over, took Franklin by the sleeve and pulled him away."

A few nights later Franklin attended a meeting for the Forester Lodge, where he saw an old friend by the name of Hood.

"You are a damned fool, Franklin," said Hood; "why didn't you just take that money and put it down in your jeans and just simply forget about it and tell them it was all fixed and not take a chance of going behind bars?"

"I was being watched too closely," he replied; "the man who gave me the money for the bribery was a stranger to me; he stood only thirty feet from me when I passed the money. I think he came from the East or San Francisco. I never saw him again."

He was arraigned for his preliminary hearing. On his way into the court he met D. M. Willard, telegrapher for the Associated Press, who was chatting with the reporter. Franklin joined them. "I can't talk about my case until it comes up for trial," he announced, "except one thing: Mr. Darrow knows nothing about this affair, and you can make that as broad as you like."

On the same occassion he made similar statements to three other newspapermen, Carl White of the *Express*, Harry Jones of the *Tribune*, and J. L. Barnard, of the *Express*.

The Christmas holidays of 1911 passed bleakly for Clarence and Ruby. Rumor continued to fill the air. Though the district attorney's office was still saying in the newspapers that they had nothing on him, reports reached him constantly of the pressure being put upon Franklin to "confess that it was Darrow or go to San Quentin." He made no attempt to conceal the gravity of the situation from his wife. She did her best to lighten his heart by putting up a small Christmas tree and inviting a few of his friends to a turkey dinner. He wanted to go home and resume his old life, but he knew that he dared not give the opposition the chance to smear him with extradition from Illinois.

Bert Franklin went to the beach town of Venice to see if he could open a private-detective agency there. He met with F. D. Stineman, hotel owner, Jordan Watt, city clerk of Venice, and Peter Pirotte, a policeman. At the hotel bar, Franklin told them:

"If Mr Darrow would give up certain evidence he has against Gompers he would be let off. Gompers is the man they want, because Gompers is head of the union, and Burns wants to break the union up. They want to get Darrow because he has been defending the unions and is a prominent man on their side. Outside parties furnished me with the money, a 'Frisco man; Darrow never gave me any money to fix jurors or anything of the kind."

Then Franklin had two long, secret sessions with the Executive Board of the Merchants' and Manufacturers' Association; the picture thereupon changed for Clarence Darrow.

Within a couple of days Franklin joined Stineman, Watt and Pirotte, to press Pirotte into opening a private agency with him.

"But what about that trouble you're in?" asked Pirotte.

"Oh, I am going to get out of that all right," murmured Franklin. "The D.A. doesn't want me; they want Darrow."

Walking into a haberdashery store, Franklin confided to the manager, Joseph Musgove, "I can't afford to spend much money because I am under a serious charge and stand a chance of going to the penitentiary. But I have many friends in town and I'm playing my cards; before I will go to the pen I will put it on somebody else."

By the middle of January Darrow had terminated his business in Los Angeles, sent an accounting of the defense expenditures to the American Federation of Labor and closed his offices. He was longing to get out of the hostile atmosphere, to return to his home and books and friends and practice. Yet he knew that he could not leave, that any move on his part would be interpreted as flight.

By the end of January Franklin came up for trial. He pleaded guilty and was fined the precise four thousand dollars that had been taken from White and Lockwood on the morning of the arrest. The city of Los Angeles came into possession of the bribe money, and Captain Fredericks called for a meeting of the grand jury.

On January twenty-ninth, while Bert Franklin stood testifying before the grand jury, Clarence Darrow secluded himself in the offices of Earl Rogers, an attorney whom he had engaged to defend him if he should be indicted. At three-thirty in the afternoon a message was brought to him that he was wanted by the grand jury. He hurried to court with Rogers and Judge McNutt.

The proceedings were short and drastic. The foreman rose to inform him that he had been indicted on two charges: of subornation of perjury, of attempting to bribe Robert Bain and George Lockwood, that he would have to stand trial on these charges. Bail was set at twenty thousand dollars. Mrs Le Compte Davis furnished bond for half of the amount; Young, of the beach town of Playa del Rey, the other half. The photographers made him pose again and again; he was now more of a celebrity than ever before.

In spite of an inner dread Clarence had been hoping that somehow the members of the grand jury would not believe him capable of these criminal acts. Their indictment came to him as a fresh blow. When the interviewers asked, "What have you to say about all this, Mr Darrow?"

He managed a small smile. "Just what I have said from the beginning, and that is that I know nothing of this bribery charge, know nothing of any attempt to approach prospective jurors and knew absolutely nothing of this thing at all until Franklin was arrested."

He needed legal brains to defend him. His thirty-five years in the law had taught him that he had better get the very best that money could buy. That was why his mind had turned at once to Earl Rogers. Rogers was one of the cleverest criminal lawyers in the country; his penchant was freeing murderers. He had a sharp, fast, resourceful, pyrotechnic brain, a good deal sharper, faster and more resourceful than Darrow's. When he was sober, which was perhaps a third of his waking hours, he was almost impossible to beat. Tall, magnificently proportioned, with a full head of graying hair, roguishly handsome features, beautifully expressive eyes and a stirring voice, a dandy who dressed in the height of fashion, Earl Rogers had all of the requirements of a matinee idol. That was in effect what he had become, for he used the courtroom as a theater, staged every trial as though it were a play in which he was the leading actor. For him the law was merely a game to play for high stakes, an adversary to be outwitted, a set of props against which he could display his talents and golden personality.

In the legal profession Earl Rogers was at the polar extremity from Clarence Darrow. There was no client too venal for him. Once when he had tricked a jury into freeing a procurer who had murdered his wife, Rogers brushed aside his client's thanks with: "Get away from me, you slimpy pimp, you know you're guilty as hell!" Yet he was terribly proud of this victory. In the days before legal ethics were solidly established Rogers brought fits of apoplexy upon judges and prosecutors by the manner in which he juggled testimony, stole or switched incriminating exhibits, engaged in torrential acts of passion, anger, ecstasy, hysteria, to confuse the issue, divert the attention of the jury and jim up the proecutor's case.

Darrow knew all this; he knew that it was a wry twist of fate that made it necessary for him to engage a clever and conscienceless rascal; yet when he took Ruby to watch Rogers try a case and saw the manner in which he dominated the court, the skill with which he had prepared and then conducted his case, they both agreed that they had no alternative but to engage him. It was an ironic twist that made it possible: Rogers had been engaged by the state in the McNamara case and had been largely instrumental in tacking the purchase of the nitrogelatin onto McNamara, Caplan and Schmidt.

"If the state can honorably employ Rogers," Clarence told Ruby, "then so can we."

Rogers was enormously set up. "I've been slipping somewhat," he told friends, "and I need Darrow almost as much as he needs me. Selecting me to defend the nation's acknowledged premier criminal lawyer will eventually place me in Darrow's class."

For his defense staff Darrow also chose Horace Appel, an eccentric not overly fond of shaving or changing his linen but an expert on evidence. A youngster in the office of Rogers, by the name of Jerry Geisler, was given the job of looking up the law.

Clarence was at once under heavy expense. He had collected in advance only a small part of the fifty-thousand-dollar fee agreed upon by the federation, and a considerable portion of what he had received he had used for living expenses. He had several thousand dollars in the Los Angeles bank, but he knew that this would be a long siege, that he would need every dollar of his savings. Ruby moved them out of their comfortable flat on Bonnie Brae to a small apartment with a roll-away bed in the dining room, reducing their expenses to a hundred dollars a month.

February and March dragged past while the district attorney used the Burns agency to gather evidence. Clarence had little to do; his defense was simple. The strain of waiting in idleness, the cloud under which his name had fallen, the feeling of impotence in the face of the combination against him, served to make him nervous and overwrought. He became thin and ill. Over and over he would mumble: "What a hell of a trap I'm in!"

And at last Clarence Darrow, who had started with fewer illusions about the human race than any of his contemporaries, found himself stripped of that ultimate illusion without which no man can carry on: that there was any hope or reason left for living. The world was a vile place in which greed and injustice had always triumphed and would continue to triumph—what was the sense of struggling further?—nothing could straighten out the vicious mess; his efforts had been futile; nothing would be left of his name or character or work; he was fatigued with life and the world; he had had enough; he was through. . . .

In his despondency during the interminable days of April he began to drink, he who rarely had taken more than two drinks at a sitting. Dr Gerson became alarmed and tried to stop him. Earl Rogers interfered.

"Oh, let him alone, Doc. The liquor is good for him at a time like this."

Finally on May fifteenth the trial opened. Captain Fredericks fired the opening shot by telling the *Examiner,* "The evidence against Darrow is convincing; it is just as convincing as the evidence in the McNamara case." The *Times* revealed its journalistic attitude by stating, "Every effort will be made to prevent a recurrence of the scenes prior to the McNamara confession, when a permanent juror in the trial admitted receiving bribe money."

Clarence said, "I feel bully physically. Mentally I am also in excellent shape." But his appearance belied his protestations. The *Herald* reported that "his face was haggard, and the muscles of his cheeks twitched unceasingly, while the lines around his eyes and mouth told of nights of sleeplessness and worry."

Ruby had dressed that morning in a simple dress of a thin, dark material and a sailor hat trimmed with green ribbon. When she appeared at the door of the courtroom "she shrank visibly even at the effort of walking through the courtroom to the seat within the railing reserved for her." However, she took a grip on herself, smiled and walked through the stares of the spectators. She sat down beside Clarence and put her hand lightly in his; when the proceedings began her smile gave way to tears.

Judge Hutton, a young, good-looking man with a gentle smile and manner, called: "The People against Clarence Darrow."

Rogers rose and said, "Ready, your honor."

Then he looked down and saw that the outstanding criminal lawyer of America had not realized that he must rise to hear the charge against him.

Rogers put his hand on Darrow's shoulder; only then did the older man rise.

"Clarence Darrow, is that your true name?" asked Assistant District Attorney Joe Ford.

"It is," replied Darrow, then turned to glance reassuringly at Ruby. She smiled back at him with more courage than she felt, for this man who stood before her was only a fraction of the attorney she had watched in action these many years. At this, the most crucial moment in his career, "his voice appeared to have lost its resonancy and piercing caliber, and his manner in worming from the talesmen the facts concerning their home, surroundings, associations, was considerably different from that shown during the McNamara case. His arrest upon the bribery charge appeared to have left its indelible imprint upon him."

However, if Darrow were being feeble in his questioning, District Attorneys Frederick and Ford also were having a difficult time. Dozens of talesmen had to be dismissed because they made the outright statement that Clarence Darrow would never stoop to bribery, while an even larger number said that Darrow would never be so stupid as to order the passing of a bribe on one of the busiest corners of the city and then go down to that corner to make sure the bribe had been passed.

By May twenty-fourth a jury consisting mainly of ranchers and orange growers from outlying towns and one or two businessmen was agreed upon.

In his opening speech Fredericks set the tone of the trial by accusing Darrow of being a director of a wholesale bribery plot, by calling him such foul names that Rogers sprang to his feet to accuse Fredericks of misconduct. Clarence had been hoping that his honorable record of thirty-five years before the Bar would have earned for him at least a quiet and courteous trial; he was stricken by Fredericks' outburst. The *Herald* reporter observed that "both Mr and Mrs Darrow were stunned by the withering remarks of the prosecutor. Darrow fumbled and toyed with a cigarette paper, and his face was flushed from chin to forehead."

The following day saw another explosion in the courtroom. An officer of the National Erectors' Association had given an interview to the *Examiner* in which he said, "I shall convict Darrow with my dictaphone." This line was printed in large banners at the head of the interview and the Hearst paper so exhibited in store windows along the jurors' line of travel from the hotel to the courtroom, they could not help but see it. Again Rogers charged misconduct; the jury was sent out of court; hours were spent while Darrow and Rogers tried to learn how and why the National Erectors' Association had become part of the prosecution.

The case of *The People* vs. *Clarence Darrow* took ninety days to try; the testimony and disputes between the lawyers over the admissibility of evidence fills eighty-nine volumes, comprising five thousand pages. Within the course of the days nine private detectives came forward to accuse Darrow of various things, but only one man accused him of the crime with which he was charged. Bert Franklin confessed:

"I told Mr Darrow I thought I could talk to Mr Lockwood, that he was a man in whom I had the utmost confidence, a man of character, and I thought Mr Lockwood's friendship for me would be such if he didn't wish to accept the proposal as offered to him, he would tell me so, and that would be the end of the matter."

Though Darrow was being tried solely on the charge of bribing Lockwood, Franklin accused him of ordering the bribing of five other prospective jurors, the most important of whom was Robert Bain. "I told Mr Darrow that I knew Mr Bain, that I thought Mr Bain would be a poor juryman for the McNamaras, that I thought he was prejudiced against union labor. He then asked me what I thought about Bain. I asked him if he wished me to see Bain along that line, and he said yes and asked me if I thought I could get him. I told him I thought I could, that Mr Bain was the kind of a man if he didn't want to go in that way he would come out and tell me so, and that would be all there would be to it. Darrow said, 'All right, I will give you a check for a thousand dollars.' He turned to his desk, wrote the check and handed it to me."

When Franklin told the court that he had asked Darrow "if he wished me to see Bain along that line," he inferred that there had been a previous conversation in which Darrow had discussed with him the bribing of jurors. Yet Franklin never referred to or recreated this earlier conversation, nor did the district attorney bring it into evidence; its happening is never introduced in the trial.

Of the other four men whom it was claimed Darrow wanted bribed, the third was Guy Yonkin, who ran a cigar store on the corner near the jail and courthouse and whose father had served under Captain White with Franklin and Lockwood. Franklin told Yonkin that he could make it worth his while to serve on the McNamara jury, and Yonkin replied that "he was not that kind of a man." The fourth man was Frank R. Smith, who stated that Franklin came to his house in Covina and offered him four thousand dollars if he would serve on the jury and vote for acquittal. Smith said, "There ain't no use to talk to me 'cuz you haven't got enough money

198

to buy me." The fifth prospective juror was A. J. Krueger, who had been fined three hundred dollars by Captain Fredericks for running a blind pig. Franklin testified that he told Darrow that Krueger would not be acceptable to the prosecution because of his character and the grudge he would bear against Fredericks, but Darrow replied: "Go give him five hundred dollars anyway."

The testimony of Franklin about the sixth prospective juror was the most illuminating in the case, not only as to fact but as to Franklin's character and motives. Darrow leaned forward in his seat as Rogers rose to cross-examine the witness. During some of the more incredible Harry Orchard testimony in Boise he had cried out, "Sometimes I think I am dreaming in this case." The words again came to his lips as he listened to Bert Franklin's convolutions. Earl Rogers' biographers were not exaggerating when they said of him in *Take the Witness* that Earl Rogers reached his peak as a criminal lawyer during this trial.

"When you got in sight of John S. Underwood's place of business you knew it was an ironworks, didn't you, by the sight of it?" asked Rogers.

"I don't remember whether I knew it. I did when I got inside."

"That was before you said anything to Underwood about acting as a juror in the McNamara case?"

"Yes sir."

"After you had found that he was in the iron trades did you ask him if he had any strike on?"

"He told me he had one on."

"Was that before you approached him on the subject of acting as a juror in the McNamara case?"

"I think so."

"After he told you that he had a strike on and you saw that he was in the iron business, you mean to say you went on and approached him about accepting a bribe and acting as a juror?"

"Yes sir."

Darrow looked over toward the jury box and saw several of the jurors smile; he, too, smiled a tiny smile, the first since he had risen to answer the charge against him.

"After you had made an ironworker a proposition to serve on the jury," sneered Rogers, "what did he say?"

"He told me he would not go into anything of that kind under the circumstances, that he could not afford anything of that kind, that he was friendly to Mr Ford—they both belonged to the same church—and he would not do anything to hurt Joe Ford."

"How long had you known Johnny Underwood?"

"About twenty-two years."

"If you were really in earnest in trying to bribe Underwood and not trying to get up a play or performance, why did you congratulate Underwood on the stand he had taken?"

"Because I am always glad to meet an honest man."

"You went up to bribe him, believing him to be an upright man and an honest man and a man of integrity?"

"I never had any reason to believe that Johnny Underwood was anything but a splendid citizen."

"For that reason you went up to bribe him?"

"No, because he was a friend of mine and, being a liberal man, I thought I could talk to him."

The cross-examination having shown him up as either a liar and a knave or a fool, Franklin backed down and admitted that Darrow had not known anything of the attempted bribery of Underwood, Yonkin, Smith or Krueger, that he had not told Darrow before he had approached these men; nor had he told him that he had failed to secure them. He inferred instead that Darrow had simply given him carte blanche to bribe all the prospective jurors he thought necessary. The fact that he had just testified that Darrow had told him to "Go give Krueger five hundred dollars anyway" did not appear to worry him.

As Franklin's final contribution Captain Fredericks, also an able courtroom tactician, led him to tell the events of the morning of November twenty-eighth. This was the moment that the courtroom had been waiting for. At last it would hear how Darrow had gone to the street corner to watch the bribe being passed. Franklin set himself squarely in his seat as he proceeded to tell his story.

"I met Mr Darrow about eight-forty in his office in the Higgins Building," said Bert Franklin. "Mr Darrow and myself were the only ones present. I asked Mr Darrow if he had gotten the money; that I had made arrangements to meet Captain White at Third and Main streets at eight forty-five. He said that he had not at that time received the money but that he would ring Job Harriman up and find out what time he would be in the office with the money. He then took up the phone and rang up someone unknown to me. After hanging up he said, 'Job will be here in ten minutes.' In about five minutes Mr Harriman came into the office of Mr Darrow with his overcoat over his left arm and walked with Mr Darrow into the room immediately adjoining. In about ten seconds Mr Darrow came out and handed me a roll of bills. I . . . went to the elevator, looked to see how much money there was in the roll. There was four thousand dollars, one thousand-dollar bill and six five hundreds. I then went down in the elevator—handed the bribe money to Captain White . . ."

Several weeks were spent by the district attorney in proving what no one denied: that Franklin had actually passed bribe money. The Bains were brought to the witness stand, the Lockwoods, the detectives who had been on his ranch, the chauffeur who had driven Franklin out, Captain White, the detectives who had followed the crime in action. All of the briberies and attempted briberies were re-enacted in full detail in an attempt to prove that Franklin had passed the bribes, and since Franklin was employed by Darrow, he must have passed the bribes at his employer's command.

For Darrow the most disabusing turn of the trial was the defection of John Harrington, whom he had brought to Los Angeles as an investigator because of his need for someone loyal and whom he had taken into his home. Up until the last night before the Darrows were to move to the less expensive apartment Ruby had selected, Harrington and his daughter had had supper in the Darrow home. The following morning Harrington demanded fifteen thousand dollars from his employer for his services, not as an investigator, but as a lawyer. "I'm entitled to what the other defense lawyers got!" he cried.

When Darrow told him that he had no such money to pay him, nor any reason for so doing, Harrington went to the district attorney's office to report that he, too, knew about Darrow's wish to bribe prospective jurors. Once again Earl Rogers in his cross-examination proved the tenuousness of the testimony.

"Mr Harrington, you say Mr Darrow told you he got ten thousand dollars at Tveitmoe's bank at San Francisco and showed you the roll of bills?"

"Yes sir, showed me a roll of bills."

"Just out of the spirit of bravado, to show you he had a roll of bills?"

"I think it was more buffoonery."

"He told you he had a roll of bills to buy jurors with, in a spirit of buffoonery? What do you mean by buffoonery?"

"Just showing how smart he was."

"That he had ten thousand dollars to bribe jurors and show you how smart he was, a kind of joke?"

"I didn't regard it as a joke."

"You mean to say Mr Darrow showed you a roll of bills and told you he was going to bribe jurors with it?"

"He didn't use the word bribe; he used the word reach."

"Was there any reason why he should tell you he was going to reach jurors with a roll of bills?"

"I didn't know but what he might want me to do it. Feeling me out on it."

"Did he suggest to you that you should do it?"

"No sir. I put a damper on that right away. I told him it would be foolish to attempt such a thing; it would be his ruin. Then he said, 'I guess you're right. I won't try it.'"

This was the case against Darrow. Of the million words spilled during the presentation, perhaps six hundred of Franklin's had a direct bearing on the Lockwood bribery charge. A trial that should have been concluded in a week, as protested by the Eastern papers, stretched on to two weeks, three weeks, a month, two months, three months. . . . . The mountains of evidence elicited dealt with everything except the guilt of Darrow in ordering Franklin to bribe Lockwood.

Though the trial was given sensational space on the front pages of most of the newspapers, Darrow knew that whole sections of society were indifferent to its outcome: the mass of working people did not care whether he was acquitted or convicted; they had lost interest in Clarence Darrow. The socialists, anarchists, radicals of all descriptions, also sloughed him off; he was no longer their man; they would not waste their energy fighting for him. The great middle class of liberal educators, churchmen, doctors, lawyers, journalists, were confused and perplexed; the circumstance of his pleading the McNamaras guilty two days after the arrest of Franklin, his chief investigator, looked suspicious. If he had sacrificed the McNamaras to save his own hide, as some of the hostile papers were saying he had, then they did not care what happened to him.

Here and there friends stood stanchly by; scattered individuals who had loved him for his good works these many years protested stoutly, "Darrow wouldn't do a thing like that. Give him a chance to prove his innocence." Yet some of those who loved him best believed him guilty as charged. Sweet Billy Cavenaugh, when giving him a rubdown one night, broke out with, "Mr Darrow, why did you have to go on down to that corner and let yourself get caught? Why didn't you send me; you know you could trust me, and I would have watched Franklin for you."

Clarence felt sick to his stomach to think that Billy, who trusted him implicitly to do the right thing, had convicted him without even waiting to hear the evidence. He tried to formulate an answer in his mind: "Billy, you have known me a long while—how can you——?" But no words would come; how could he protest to an accuser who had instantly assumed him to be guilty? A few nights later, when he was at the

Severance Club chatting with a group of intimates, Dr Gerson commented:

"None of your friends blame you for what you did, Clarence. If you are guilty, what of it? You had to fight the devil with fire."

This, he knew, was loyalty in its broadest sense; yet it was a loyalty that broke his heart, not only because his closest friends could believe him guilty of a criminal act, but because they could assume him guilty of so wantonly stupid and suicidally destructive an act. His breath died in his chest; he hung his head and closed out from his eyes the picture of his friends who were going to be loyal to him to the bitter end.

"My God," he groaned, "I am as fitted for passing a bribe as a Methodist minister is to be a bartender."

A few days later Mrs Fremont Older informed him that Senator Hiram Johnson had accused him, in front of Senator Borah, of having bribed jurors in the Haywood case.

"No, Darrow didn't bribe those jurors," Senator Borah replied; "he frightened them to death."

Though it was good to know that the man he had defeated in Idaho was affirming his integrity, Darrow was stunned that Senator Johnson, bitter enemy of Otis, who had gotten himself elected on a liberal ticket, should be spreading the gossip that it was his regular and established practice to bribe jurors!

If some of his dearest friends and others on whose side he had been working for decades were openly convicting him, what chance did he have of ever clearing his name, of coming out of this scandal whose and clean?

With his friends and comrades abandoning him outside the courtroom and murderous vituperation being heaped upon him inside, Darrow sank to the lowest ebb of world disgust. The fight no longer seemed worth waving. Rogers' biographers report that "time after time Rogers railed at him under his breath because of the drooping chin, the fear-stricken eyes that so clearly told of his trepidation. At times he was absolutely without hope, and only the rough prodding of the Los Angeles lawyer could make him realize that he was providing for the jury a portrait of guilt."

At last Clarence Darrow perceived that his own attorney believed him guilty. Instead of extinguishing entirely his will to be saved, this knowledge awakened in him anger and indignation. Up to this point he had done very little of the cross-examining, sensing that it would have an adverse effect upon the jury; but at this point he decided he would take a stronger hand in his own defense. He had been holding long meetings with Rogers after court each afternoon, sessions in which the two men quarreled over tactics. Though Rogers had accused Darrow of presenting a picture of guilt as he sat glued to his chair, he now refused to allow his client to rise to his feet or share in his own defense.

"Earl wouldn't let any man in his office get credit for anything," says Mrs Rogers, while his daughter, Adele Rogers St John, adds, "He was the most jealous man in the whole world."

Darrow's determination and strength mounted slowly; he insisted upon helping to try the case. Rogers thereupon rushed out of the office and got drunk. He stayed drunk for two days, while the court wondered where he was. When he returned from his binge and his wife asked him where he had been, instead of answering the question, he muttered, "Oh, that son of a bitch has been up to his old tricks again," from which Mrs Rogers deduced that Darrow had been trying to bribe members of his own jury.

Rogers' absence from court did Clarence a deal of good; while cross-examining Burns and other private detectives, while again thinking on his feet, his blood began to circulate more rapidly, his confidence to come back; he grew certain that he would win.

Rogers re-entered the case, but their differences continued. Trouble between the Darrows and Rogerses had started at once and was never to end. Early in their acquaintanceship Mrs Rogers had invited the Darrows for dinner, and Ruby had telephoned to say, "I trust you won't be offended, but Mr Darrow doesn't eat chicken. I thought it would be better to tell you, because everyone serves it to him."

Mrs Rogers, a brainy woman but a purist, had been deeply offended at this breach of etiquette. At dinner she had seated Darrow at her right and noticed wax in his ear. "I never liked Darrow," she maintains. "He always had a hangdog look. He was one of the dirtiest men I ever saw; his nails were dirty; his ears were dirty." When she noticed in court that Ruby was wearing white cotton gloves with the finger tips darned she was confirmed in her dislike for Mrs Darrow, whom she accused of putting on a show of poverty. Now a new and serious difference arose: a difference over money. Rogers was a prodigious spender; it was never possible for him to get enough cash. Darrow's few thousands had been melting rapidly with the paying of court costs, three lawyers and investigators to investigate the Burns investigators. He was far too quickly reaching the point where he would be without funds and without the means of earning a dollar.

"Earl never got any part of his fee from Darrow," says Mrs Rogers, "except maybe running expenses. They were always pleading poverty, right on the verge of starvation. It got so I couldn't pay our bills at the stores."

Ruby says, "Earl Rogers came to us every morning. . . . If we didn't give him money he said he wouldn't go into court that day."

Each night, when Rogers was in his cups, he would confide to friends that he had little respect for Darrow's ability as a lawyer, attributing his success mainly to wide publicity and his wonderful gift in delivering emotional appeals to juries; each morning Clarence would dig down into his pocket for a roll of bills. Each morning he and Earl Rogers would walk arm in arm into court and, along with Horace Appel, present such a brilliant defense that the outside world never knew of their quarrels.

When the heat of June came on Ruby found an apartment in Ocean Park overlooking the ocean, for which they paid thirty dollars a month. Each day, dressed in a gown of some dark, thin material and the sailor hat with the green ribbon, she rode into town with her husband. Through the endless hours of wrangling and accusation she sat next to Clarence, always managing a comforting word when he turned to her. Her fierce loyalty, her confident and courteous manner above the strife about her, soon won the respect and then the love of the newspapermen. Before long every news story carried its eulogizing paragraph about Ruby.

After the long session in court she would ride back to Ocean Park, draw Clarence's bath, lay out clean linen for him, prepare dinner, wash the dishes, straighten the apartment, press a linen suit for him to wear the next day and get to sleep long after midnight.

By the middle of July Ruby suffered a nervous breakdown, not from fatigue, but from the violence in the courtroom.

As the Los Angeles papers were frequently commenting, it was the most violent trial in the history of southern California. Apart from the vicious name calling and conniving, physically the lawyers were forever at each other's throat. Several times all four of the lawyers were fined by Judge Hutton for abusing each other. At one point Fredericks became so enraged at Appel that he picked up an inkwell to hurl at his opponent; Rogers grabbed him but in so doing cut his hand on the glass. Another time Joe Ford picked up the inkwell to hurl it at Rogers. Once when Rogers was given the privilege of paying a fifty-dollar fine for contempt of court or going to jail, he refused to pay the fine or go to jail, had himself released on a writ of habeas corpus. Rogers and William J. Burns came to blows as Rogers accused Burns of calling him a son of a bitch, of coming into court with a gun and a sword cane. Judge Hutton fined them both twenty-five dollars; Rogers borrowed the money from his young assistant, Geisler, muttering that it was worth it. Hardly an hour went by without an uproar; even Darrow found it impossible to stay aloof.

Judge Hutton presided over this torrential maelstrom, an angel of patience. A Christian Scientist, he wanted harmony to prevail; he believed that the truth would emerge, not from this abuse but from a kind of legal harmony in which both sides did their best work but gave fair play. Most judges suffering the insolence that he endured would have fined all four of the lawyers into bankruptcy. Judge Hutton so deprecated the flare-ups, quarrels and outbursts of passion that he went himself to the newspaper editors and asked them to please devote less space to the quarrels between the lawyers and more space to the serious aspects of the trial.

"These outbursts are only the sparks that fly up in any busy workshop," he said.

If the quarreling and violence sent Ruby to bed with a breakdown and Judge Hutton to the papers with a plea for less sensationalism, it also gave a bad time to the twelve jurors who were to decide whether Clarence Darrow was to go to the penitentiary. Hours and days were spent by them locked in their jury room, while the lawyers fought it out before the judge.

Judge Hutton had done everything he could to make the life of the jurors bearable. The top floor of the Hotel Trenton had been reserved for the twelve men, with the partitioning walls broken down to make it a complete suite. There was a social room with a piano, cards, checkers, chess, all the magazines and newspapers—with the material on the Darrow trial cut out. One Sunday Judge Hutton invited the jury to his home in Santa Monica for a swim and dinner. He gave standing orders that every Sunday they were to be taken either to the ball game at Washington Park or for an automobile ride over Topanga Canyon to the beach. But no juror was left alone for more than a minute during the ninety-two days of the trial, not even when he went up on the roof to play soft ball. All incoming and outgoing mail was censored, all telephone calls listened to by a deputy; when one juror hurt his hip and called for an osteopath a deputy stood over them to watch the treatment; when another juror went to his dentist on a Saturday afternoon his deputy stood over the drill.

Every Saturday afternoon the men would be loaded into cars which would take them home. At each stop the juror would kiss his wife, hand over his bundle of soiled linen in return for a package of fresh linen, discuss family business for fifteen minutes, treat his fellows to a glass of orange juice, kiss his wife and be off.

"It was like ninety-two days in jail," says Manley Williams.

Having spent weeks demonstrating that a bribery had taken place, the prosecution launched into its broad-scale attack on Darrow's character to prove that he was capable of the crime with which he was charged, that he was a lawyer without principle or scruple who would employ illegal or criminal methods to win a case. Fredericks and Ford re-enacted in the fullest detail the removal of Diekleman from Albuquerque, the removal of Mrs Caplan from California to Chicago, the bringing of Ortie McManigal's wife, child and uncle to Los Angeles.

Darrow was able to demonstrate that it was entirely legal to use four hundred dollars to bring McManigal's family to Los Angeles, particularly since Mrs McManigal had said in Chicago that she did not believe her husband to be guilty, that the statements Burns had given out were not true, that Ortie had been bulldozed, given a third degree and had confessed under threat, intimidation and promises.

Dozens of witnesses were brought to the stand to retrace Mrs. Caplan's automobile ride from the Santa Cruz Mountains to Reno after she had been subpoenaed, the district attorney accusing Darrow of thus illegally removing a witness. Darrow went on the stand to swear that he had not ordered the removal of Mrs Caplan. He was followed by Anton Johannsen, who testified that Darrow had known nothing about the removal of Mrs Caplan, that he had taken her out of the state to free her from hounding by the Burns operatives. The truth probably was that Darrow had not ordered Mrs Caplan's removal but had known about it and been unable to stop Johannsen; the San Francisco labor leaders had interfered continually in the preparation of the McNamara case.

Diekleman's removal from Albuquerque was also fully staged with many witnesses. Darrow's defense was that he wanted to get Diekleman out of the influence of the Burns detectives who were surrounding him in Albuquerque; that since Diekleman had been offered a job in a public restaurant in Chicago he had not been concealed, and since Diekleman had been given a round-trip ticket to Los Angeles, it could not be claimed he was being kept away from the trial. His removal was not illegal, though Darrow's hope that once he got Diekleman away from the Burns men and into his own sphere of influence Diekleman would become sympathetic to his cause and refuse to identify J. B. McNamara was doubtless unethical. In the five thousand pages of testimony it is the only unethical act proved against him.

The district attorney put on three Burns detectives to tell how Darrow had attempted to buy their information. Guy Bittinger was the star of this troupe. A former saloonkeeper and policeman, Bittinger had been one of the Burns detectives who had arrested J. B. McNamara and Ortie McManigal in Detroit. When he had been introduced to Darrow in Chicago he had said that J. B. McNamara had offered him thirty thousand dollars for his release and, when refused, J. B. had continued, "If you don't take that money Clarence Darrow will take it. I have the American Federation of Labor behind me, and it will be impossible to convict me."

Bittinger now testified that Darrow had thought this testimony so damaging he had offered Bittinger five thousand dollars not to swear to it in an affidavit. Bittinger says he refused because five thousand dollars was not enough. . . .

Arriving in Los Angeles, Bittinger continued, he went immediately to Darrow to tell him that he had twenty-seven hotel registers with the J. B. Bryce or McNamara signature on them. He reports Darrow as saying: "Couldn't you arrange for a couple of my boys to hit you over the head and take them away from you?"

Bittinger replied that he would let him know, whereupon he claimed Darrow promised to pay him a thousand dollars the next morning and that when they met at the bar of the Alexandria Hotel the following morning Darrow said, "I've got that money for you."

"I don't want to take it here," said Bittinger.

"Do it open and aboveboard," replied Darrow. "Suppose you are being watched? . . . . The bolder you do it the less they will think of it."

This type of testimony went on for hour after hour, week after week, until finally Juror Golding demanded of the court if he might ask the witness a question. The permission granted, he turned to Bittinger.

"Do you know," queried Juror Golding, "what the charge is against Mr Darrow?"

It was a question which people all over the country who had been reading the daily accounts of the trial were beginning to ask themselves and, in the asking, slowly—very slowly —edged back toward faith in the accused man.

Nine private detectives, Franklin, Harrington and seven Burns men, had attacked his character. An alien in a foreign city, Darrow wrote to Edgar Lee Masters, requesting him to go to the lawyers, judges and city officials of Chicago and take depositions to the effect that he was not a scoundrel but a man of good character.

Within a few days the depositions started coming in: "I have known Clarence Darrow for twenty years; he is a man of complete honesty and integrity." ". . . He has the highest possible regard for the ethics of his profession." These were typical of the many.

Having spent weeks blackening Darrow's character, Captain Fredericks tried to keep these testimonials from being read to the jury on the grounds that they were immaterial and irrelevant! When Judge Hutton admitted them into evidence Clarence smiled wanly.

June exhausted itself and then July. Ruby recovered her strength and once again took her place by her husband's side. Their friends, Gerson and Blight, persuaded them to join the Severance Club which met every other Saturday night for dinner at Al Levy's restaurant or the Westminster Hotel. Once or twice a week they went to dinner at the house of Peede, the editor of *Everyman*.

The prosecution having finished, it was time for the Darrow defense to begin. Rogers first elicited from Bert Franklin that the day before he was to be let out of his job in the United States marshal's office he had gone to Joe Ford and asked for work.

"What kind of work do you want?" asked Ford.

"I'll do anything," replied Franklin.

And the very next day he had called on Job Harriman to tell him he would like to work for the defense. Within the next two days he also saw Le Compte Davis and Joseph Scott, telling them how much he would like to work for the defense.

Rogers pointed out that each time Franklin had reported Darrow as telling him to pass a bribe no one else had been present. Many persons were on hand, however, when Franklin went to pass his bribes.

"Mr Franklin," said Rogers, "will you tell the jury which it was, whether you was careless and incompetent and was lacking in judgment, was so lacking in good sense as to take people out on bribery expeditions, leaving a trail painted down the middle of the street behind you on every occasion, taking a woman on a bribery expedition whose name you didn't even know, or whether as a matter of fact you were trying to get caught under an arrangement? You endeavored to get corroborating evidence by somebody everywhere you went, by speaking to somebody immediately before you went there, didn't you?"

"If I had been trying to do so," replied Franklin, "I could not have succeeded any better, apparently."

"How is it that a smart detective like you, with your years of experience, could make such a perfect case?"

"According to your statement, I am not very smart, and I will admit it too."

The defense tackled the triple pass of money on the morning of November twenty-eighth. Franklin had testified that he offered Captain White a hundred dollars to act as intermediary, but Captain White categorically denied this; he stated that he hadn't done it for money but had served as an accessory before the fact and committed a felony merely to help an old friend—then admitted that he had not seen Franklin for two years. Captain White further admitted that although he had been arrested and taken to the district attorney's office, once he had handed over the thirty-five hundred dollars he had been holding he was released, never put under bail, never charged with a crime, never indicted, never tried—all this in spite of the fact that, under California law, he was as guilty as Franklin. Nor did the prosecution try to save face by claiming that White had been acting under orders from the district attorney.

Franklin had claimed that when he came out of the toilet of the saloon he had not been able to see Detective Home hiding behind the icebox twelve feet away. The manager of the saloon came into court to testify that this was impossible, and the entire court made the trip down the street to the saloon to see if it were possible.

Then came the series of confounding witnesses against Bert Franklin. John Drain and Frank Dominguez told from the witness stand the story of Franklin's loud protestations of Darrow's innocence. Franklin called these two men liars and perjurers. Hood told of his conversation with Franklin at the Forester meeting, when Franklin described the stranger who had given him the bribe money. Franklin called his brother Forester a liar and a perjurer. Stineman, Watt and Pirotte recounted the discussions with Franklin in Venice and Los Angeles, in which he had said he was going to get out of his trouble because the district attorney wanted Darrow. Franklin called Stineman, Watt and Pirotte liars and perjurers.

Joseph Musgove, former manager of the haberdashery store in which Franklin had shopped, told of Franklin's boast that before he would go to the pen he would put it on somebody else. Franklin called Musgove a liar and perjurer. The four newspapermen, Carl White, D. M. Willard, Harry Jones and J. L. Barnard all went on the stand to repeat Franklin's heated assertions that "anybody says Darrow gave me a cent to bribe a juror is a goddamned liar." Franklin called them liars and perjurers.

Job Harriman denied from the stand that he had even been

in Darrow's office the morning of the twenty-eighth, let alone given him four thousand dollars. Franklin called Harriman a liar and a perjurer. Frank Wolfe, former managing editor of the Los Angeles *Herald,* testified that he had met Darrow on the streetcar on the morning of Franklin's arrest, gone with him to his office and talked to him there until a telephone call had summoned Darrow to socialist headquarters. Franklin called Wolfe a liar and a perjurer.

It was becoming increasingly obvious that someone in the case was a liar and perjurer. The scoreboard read: Bert Franklin versus Drain, Dominguez, Hood, Stineman, Watt, Pirotte, Musgove, White, Willard, Jones, Barnard, Harriman, Wolfe, Le Compte Davis and Tom Johnson, Franklin's own attorney, subpoenaed by the defense testified only after Judge Hutton had forced him to, and Franklin called him a liar and a perjurer.

John Harrington was quickly dispensed with: Fletcher Bowron testified that Harrington had told him he knew absolutely nothing against Mr Darrow, no corruption or bribery. Harrington and Franklin had sworn that they had met only three times since Franklin's arrest, but two secretaries in Darrow's office and the manager of the building said they had seen the two men together every day for weeks. It was also brought out that since Harrington had left the Darrow roof he had been living with three Burns detectives.

Lincoln Steffens, Le Compte Davis and Fremont Older took the stand to tell the story of the settlement that had been arranged prior to the morning Franklin had given the bribe money to Captain White. For eighty-seven packed pages of pleading Captain Fredericks strove to keep the Fremont Older testimony out of the evidence. Judge Hutton admitted Older's testimony as material, relevant and competent.

Breathing a deep sigh of relief, Darrow ran his crumpled handkerchief over his brow and lumbered to his feet for the most critical, colorful and dramatic clash of the trial: between himself and his accuser, Bert Franklin. Darrow framed his questions so that the whole world, and not Franklin alone, would have to answer them.

"You say that on October fifth I suggested to you that we had better take care of the jury and the next day said it was time to get to work on Bain and gave you a check for a thousand dollars for this purpose. Then why is the check I gave you dated on October fourth? If I was sending you out to bribe a prospective juror would I give you a check that could be traced back or would I give you cash? If I wanted prospective jurors bribed would I send you out, my chief investigator whose every move was being watched by Burns operatives, or would I have imported a stranger for the dirty work? Would I send you on this bribery expedition when I knew that you had worked for Captain Fredericks and the district attorney's office for years and would try to go back to work there when the McNamara case was over? If I gave you four thousand dollars on the morning of November twenty-eighth to bribe Lockwood and you didn't tell me where the bribe was to be passed, how would I know where to go to check on you? If I knew you were passing a bribe there would I let myself be seen in the vicinity? Would I have crossed the street to talk to you, after the bribe had been passed, when I saw Detective Browne walking right behind you? If I had ordered that whole arrangement would I pick one of the busiest corners in the city?

"If you told me that the district attorney would never accept Krueger why did I tell you to give him five hundred dollars anyway? Why would I send you out to bribe John Underwood, owner of an ironworks, whose employees were on strike? If you were bribing these men without my specific knowledge how could I find enough millions of dollars to give you carte blanche to bribe the hundred upon hundreds of men on the venire lists? Would I be such a fool as to try to bribe hundreds of men, any one of whom could have wrecked my life and the lives of my clients?

"If you were trying to pass a bribe for me why did you allow it to be passed when you had seen four detectives following and watching you? Why did you lie about not seeing Detective Home or not knowing Detective Ong? Why did you take witnesses with you on every bribery expedition? Why did you try to bribe the owner of an ironworks, whom you knew would instantly report the attempt to the Merchants and Manufacturers and to the district attorney? The district attorney claims the bribe was passed with marked bills; then when could they have been marked, if you say that Harriman brought them to my office from his safe-deposit vault? Were not those markings put on the bills by the Burns detectives before they were handed to you on the morning of November twenty-eighth?

"You testified that when you asked me if the bribe money could be traced I replied, 'No, I got it straight from Gompers.' Knowing the intensity of the steel trust's hatred for Gompers and unionism, would I have so blithely and callously betrayed the cause for which I have given my heart's blood for twenty-five years, put their fate in the hands of a private detective whom I had known for only three months? You testified that when Job Harriman brought me the four thousand dollars' bribe money and you solicitously asked me if there wasn't a record kept at the safe-deposit department where Harriman had withdrawn the money, I replied, 'You don't need to worry about that part of it, because Mr Harriman took five hundred dollars of the money he got at the same time and paid off a mortgage, so that he could account for being at the safe-deposit department that morning.' Was that Clarence Darrow talking? Since when have I become so lip-loose, so wantonly garrulous? If I were participating in a crime would I wreck Mr Harriman's only possible defense, destroy so blithely the life and good works of a fine labor lawyer and the man who was slated to be the next mayor of Los Angeles? Why do you have to call twenty-five of the most reputable citizens of southern California liars and perjurers? Or are all these things details in a gigantic conspiracy to destroy as many of labor's leaders and defenders as possible? Or is your entire testimony against me the price the district attorney made you pay to keep yourself out of prison?"

The world could not answer those questions any more than Franklin, twitching and squirming on the stand, could answer them.

The final pleas were begun August twelfth by Assistant District Attorney Joe Ford, a forceful young man, a scholar and student of Irish folkways and literature and oriental philosophies. Politically ambitious, Ford hoped with his closing plea to win Captain Fredericks' position as district attorney at the next election. One of the jurors commented, "Ford wrote out his speech, learned it by heart, then dressed up in his Sunday best and invited all his friends to hear him. But he laid it on too heavy; he was too bitter. He was vicious and venomous; I hated him; I couldn't bear to look at him."

He called Darrow a coward; accused him of corrupting some of the best men in the city, among them Le Compte Davis; called his entire testimony perjured; accused him of sacrificing John J. McNamara in order to save himself; described Darrow's conduct as viler than that of Judas or Benedict Arnold. He also told the jury that since Darrow had written that there was no such thing as crime, he had encouraged such misguided wretches as James B. McNamara to kill innocent men; that therefore it was Clarence Darrow rather than McNamara who was guilty, not only of the *Times* explosion and the murder of twenty men, but also of the dozens of explosions that had been caused by the dynamiters.

"It is one of the misfortunes of the American Bar," cried Ford, "that some criminal lawyers practice subornation and perjury and use bribery to win their cases. There is really no difference between the men inside the jail and those outside with men like the defendant employed to fight the case."

From Ford's diatribe Clarence Darrow emerged as one of

the arch criminals in history, a shade or two worse than Harry Orchard. During his long attack Clarence sat at the attorney's table, carefully studying the faces of the jurors.

That night he and Earl Rogers had their last quarrel. It had been agreed when Rogers was engaged that Darrow would make the final plea to the jury. Rogers now balked; he did not think Darrow capable; he did not wish to take a back seat and let Darrow wind up the case; he did not wish to relinquish the spotlight. Darrow agreed to let him make a brief final appeal along with Horace Appel. Both men accused the district attorney's office of conspiracy, tearing Ford limb from limb, even as he had drawn and quartered Darrow.

Then in a few simple sentences Rogers stated the crux of the case: "Will you tell me how any sane, sensible man who knows anything about the law business—and this defendant has been at it for thirty-five years—could make himself go to a detective and say to him: 'Just buy all the jurors you want. I put my whole life, my whole reputation, I put everything I have into your hands. I trust you absolutely. I never knew you until two or three months ago and I don't know very much about you now, but there you are; go to it!'"

On August fourteenth Darrow rose to his feet to defend his good name. The Los Angeles *Record* said: "More than one thousand spectators who had fought and struggled with bailiffs in a narrow corridor for two hours listened as the defendant slowly rose and advanced to the jury box. . . . Hundreds of people were crowded into a space of ten feet, and a thousand more pressed in on them in a wild effort to gain entrance to the courtroom. . . . Women fainted and men gasped for breath. . . . Reserves were called from the sheriff's office to quell the crowd, and clubs had to be drawn before it could be handled. Finally the mob surged into the room and filled all the standing space."

They had come to hear America's greatest pleader plead for himself: for a day and a half they heard pour from his lips words that came out of his blood and guts. While cross-examining the Burns men he had appeared weak and uncertain, and Rogers had accused him of being fainthearted —when he had been brokenhearted. But as finally he rose to make the ultimate plea for an end to the rottenness and corruption, hating and killing, he was once again the attorney for the defense.

He thrust his hands deep in his coat pockets and began to speak in a low voice, "Gentlemen of the jury, I am a stranger in a strange land, two thousand miles away from home and friends. I think I can say that no one in my native town would have made to any jury any such statement as was made of me by the district attorney in opening this case. I will venture to say he could not afterward have found a companion except among detectives and crooks and sneaks in the city where I live if he had dared to open his mouth in the infamous way that he did in this case. . . .

"I have committed one crime which I cannot be forgiven. . . . I have stood for the weak and the poor. I have stood for the men who toil. Therefore, I have stood against them, and now this is their chance. I have lived my life and I have fought my battles, not against the weak and the poor—anybody can do that—but against power, injustice, against oppression. Now let me show you the villainy and infamy of the prosecution which reeks from beginning to end with crime and corruption and with bloodlessness and heartlessness to the last degree. I have practiced law a good long time and I tell you I never saw or heard of a case where any American jury convicted anybody upon such testimony as that of Franklin and Harrington, and I don't expect to live long enough to find that sort of jury.

"By all my training, inclination and habit I am about the last person in all this world who could have possibly undertaken jury bribing. Mine was a position which needed to be guarded most carefully, as these events have shown. If you think I would pick out a place half a block from my office and send a man with money in his hand in broad daylight to go down on the street corner to pass four thousand dollars, if you think I did that, gentlemen, why, find me guilty. I certainly belong in some state institution.

"Gentlemen, don't ever think that your own life or liberty is safe, that your own family is secure; don't ever think that any human being is safe when under evidence like this . . . I, with some influence and some respect and some money, am brought here and placed in the shadow of the penitentiary.

"Show me, in all their watching and their spying, show me, with all the money they have spent, with all the efforts of the strong and the powerful to get me—show me in all these long, weary months where one honest man has raised his voice to testify against me. Just one. Just one. And are you ready, gentlemen, in this day and generation, to take away the name and liberty of a human being upon the testimony of rogues, informers, crooks, vagabonds, immunity hunters and detectives? If so, I don't want to live; I don't want to live in a world where such men can cause the undoing of an American citizen."

He spent hours dissecting the prosecution's case, bringing up from his omnivorous memory point after point of the evidence against him, weighing it and placing it in proper perspective.

He retraced the struggles between the Steel Trust and the

215

workers; he said, "I would have walked from Chicago across the Rocky Mountains and over the long, dreary desert to lay my hand upon the shoulder of J. B. McNamara and tell him not to place dynamite in the Times Building. I have loved peace all my life. I have taught it all my life. I believe that love does more than hatred. I believe that both sides have gone about the settlement of these difficulties in the wrong way. The acts of the one have caused the acts of the other, and I blame neither. Men are not perfect; they had an imperfect origin and they are imperfect today, and the long struggle of the human race from darkness to comparative civilization has been filled with clash and discord and murder and war and violence and wrong, and it will be for years and years to come. But ever we are going onward and upward toward the sunshine, where the hatred and war and cruelty and violence of the world will disappear."

In his instructions to the jury Judge Hutton threw out two thirds of the trial, two thirds of the evidence and two thirds of the ninety days of battle when he instructed the jury that "the defendant is not on trial here for kidnaping Mrs Caplan, nor for the removal of Diekleman from Albuquerque, nor for the payment of money to Bittinger."

He put his finger on the most perplexing aspect of the case: if Darrow were innocent, who was guilty? but made no attempt to solve this problem and instructed the jury that "it is not the duty of the defendant to prove who, if anyone, furnished the money to Franklin for the purpose of bribing the juror."

He instructed the jury to acquit Darrow if they believed a conspiracy had been entered into by Franklin, Lockwood and White, to fasten the alleged crime on the defendant.

Then Darrow must have been plunged backward four years to the spasms that were Boise, for Judge Hutton used the identical words that had been used by Judge Wood in his instructions to the Haywood jury: "You are instructed that a conviction cannot be had on the testimony of an accomplice unless he is corroborated by other evidence which in itself, and without the aid of the testimony of the accomplice, tends to connect the defendant with the commission of the offense. The law absolutely prohibits the conviction in a criminal case upon the uncorroborated testimony of an accomplice, although the jury may believe the testimony of the accomplice to be entirely true."

Abruptly the judge stopped. A bailiff gave a signal; the jury rose and marched out of its box. Judge Hutton left the bench. No one else stirred. Darrow sat clasping the hand of his wife, bruising her knuckles by his intensity. The spectators were motionless; there was hardly a breath or a movement in the room.

The jury was taken out at nine-twenty in the morning. At nine-fifty there was a buzz from the jury room.

"What does it mean?" whispered Ruby.

"Maybe they want some instructions," replied Clarence.

But the jurymen were grinning broadly as they filed into their box. Judge Hutton took his place on the bench amid the silence.

"Your pleasure?" he asked.

"A verdict," replied Foreman Williams.

"Read it," ordered Judge Hutton.

"Not guilty!" cried Foreman Williams.

Darrow jumped to his feet and kissed his wife. Judge Hutton rushed down from the bench, embraced him and cried, "There are millions of peope today who will cry 'Hallelujah!' "

The Los Angeles *Herald* tells that "the scene immediately following the reading of the verdict was one of the most remarkable that has ever been witnessed in a courtroom of the West. Darrow rushed over to the jury box where he was received with open arms. Jurors Dunbar, Golding and Dingman embraced him. Other jurors forced their way into the circle to shake the hand and pat affectionately the shoulder of the man they had freed. The spectators, the majority of whom were women, fought their way past the bailiffs to the jury box; some were weeping, others smiling, as they poured forth their congratulations. Some in their eagerness made the mistake of choosing members of the district attorney's staff. Rogers was slapped on the back and shoulders until he was forced to stand against the wall in self-defense. For two hours neither Mr nor Mrs Darrow left the courtroon.

Darrow said, "It has been a long, hard ordeal and, of course, I have a great sense of relief. None of those who knew me ever believed that I was corrupt, and their encouragement and faith has been my greatest help."

But his troubles were far from over. He was now indicted for the Bain bribery. If the motion for the second trial had been asked of Judge Hutton he probably would have thrown it out of court and Clarence would have been free to return home, vindicated; but Hutton was ill and exhausted, and another judge bound Darrow over on the grounds that he could not know what material the district attorney had against Darrow in the Bain case.

Profoundly embittered now by what the wife of the assistant district attorney, Ford, always called "the Darrow persecutions," Clarence underwent the agony of more months of anxiety and depression. Nor did it cheer him to see how

217

little effort the prosecution was making to save its own face, giving Lockwood a job in the information booth of the Hall of Records, a job he was to hold until he was ninety; refusing to charge, indict or try Captain White for his acknowledged implicity in the crime; learning that Bert Franklin stopped Juror Golding on the street and murmured *sotto voce,* "I just wanted you to know that the D.A. made me wash their dirty linen." What comfort were these things when his money was gone, his strength shattered by his great effort, when he was still under indictment for being a criminal?

So broke now that he could no longer maintain the Midway flat, Ruby requested friends in Chicago to sublet it. The rentees stayed for two months, paid no rent and walked out, leaving the apartment in a sorry state. As a final blow, the Darrow's last investment was lost in a bankruptcy.

Yet even in the deepest gloom there came a few lights. A literary club of San Francisco affirmed its faith in him by inviting him north to lecture on Tolstoy. And as an even more important token of confidence the Chicago labor counsel urged him to come back, if only for a few days, to select a jury in the Shea case. Shea was the head of a teamsters' union who had been arrested in a rough strike in 1911; Darrow had undertaken his defense, only to be released to the McNamaras when they were arrested. Shea had been tried and convicted, but the judgment had been set aside. Darrow came East, spending a week of feverish work, avoiding his old friends and returning to Los Angeles the moment the last juror was selected. The money he earned enabled him to meet his own court costs, and the not-guilty decision handed down by the jury he had picked sparked up his energy and courage.

Earl Rogers and Horace Appel withdrew from the second trial; Clarence retained young Jerry Geisler to help him with the law and an elderly attorney by the name of Powers to assist with the admissibility of evidence. He knew that the brunt of the trial would be upon his shoulders; he felt entirely equal to the task.

The attack by Fredericks and Ford was even more vitriolic than it had been in the first case. Since the Bain bribe had been passed on October sixth, six weeks before the settlement arrangements had begun, Darrow was deprived of this important factor in his defense. As he had sensed when hiring another lawyer to defend him in the first trial, it did not sit well with the jury when he left the lawyers' table to take the stand as a witness, then rose as the attorney to object to evidence; it was difficult for the jurors to separate his functions. He felt the hostility of three or four of the jurors who he came to believe were part of Fredericks' professional jury

218

servers, for he had not been able to afford investigators to check on the veniremen.

In his final plea, instead of solely defending himself against the charge of bribery, he again defended the McNamaras for what they had done on their side of the class war. Between his first and second trial a number of the Indianapolis officers had been convicted and sent to prison; he defended them, too, in a fierce attack upon the exploitation of the American trusts.

Entering the jury room, the jury voted eight to four for conviction. After three days of deliberation they reported that they could never agree and were dismissed.

Ford and Fredericks were not yet through. They threatened a third trial. This persistence to "get him" drained him of his physical and spiritual strength. He didn't have ten dollars to his name; he was terribly in debt; he was tired, discouraged, ill; he did not feel he could endure another trial. And then came a telegram from a complete stranger which read:

> HOT SPRINGS, ARK., MARCH 13, 1913
>
> HON. CLARENCE DARROW
>   LOS ANGELES, CALIFORNIA
>
>   I NOTICE FROM THE DAYS PAPERS THAT YOU HAVE EX-
>   HAUSTED YOUR LAST DOLLAR IN YOUR DEFENSE STOP YOU
>   HAVE SPENT YOUR WHOLE LIFE TRYING TO SEE THAT THE
>   POOR GOT A SHOW NOW YOU SHALL HAVE EVERY CHANCE
>   THE LAW AFFORDS TO PROVE YOUR INNOCENCE STOP IF
>   YOU WILL WIRE ME THE AMOUNT YOU REQUIRE I WILL
>   SEND IT TO YOU
>
>   FRED D. GARDNER

Darrow wired back:

>   YOUR KINDNESS IS SO GREAT I CAN HARDLY UNDERSTAND
>   IT STOP MY CONDITION IS ABOUT AS YOU STATE STOP IT
>   WAS SERIOUSLY HANDICAPPED IN LAST FIGHT STOP DONT
>   KNOW YOUR CIRCUMSTANCES AND WHETHER I OUGHT TO
>   LET YOU DO SO MUCH STOP AT LEAST IT SHOULD NOT
>   BE KNOWN UNTIL ALL IS OVER OR IT WOULD ADD TO
>   EXPENSES STOP WIRE ME MORE FULLY AS TO HOW MUCH
>   HARDSHIP IT WOULD BE TO YOU
>
>   C. S. DARROW

In a few days a check arrived for a thousand dollars, accompanied by a second check from Mrs. Gardner, who sent two hundred dollars out of her private savings account.

Frederick Gardner had gone to St. Louis at the age of

sixteen. Looking for a job, he had seen a "Boy Wanted" sign in the window of a casket factory, had taken the job and become the owner of the plant by the time he was twenty-one. The particularly beautiful part of his gift to Darrow, a man he had never met, was that Gardner, who later became governor of the state of Missouri, had had considerable labor difficulties in his casket factory and was by no means sympathetic to the unions.

The generous gesture revived Clarence. He further was cheered when he learned that the attorney general of the United States had publicly accused William J. Burns of having bribed jurors in a Washington case and had succeeded in obtaining a pardon for the man convicted because of Burns's subornation of perjury.

Within a few days the district attorney's office dismissed further charges against Darrow, and he was free to return to his home in Chicago after more than two years of misery in a city where he had never known anything but misery.

In his library Darrow gathered together some of his first editions to sell so that he could have money with which to buy food. As he trudged down the street with his beloved books under his arm he knew only one thing; he was through with the law.

Chapter Ten

In Defense of the Indefensible

IT WAS NO LONGER difficult for him to walk down the street. A few friends stopped him, shook hands, told him how glad they were to have him back, how happy they were that he had been exonerated, but for the most part the people of Chicago felt that he had been responsible for injuring the city's name, that if he had not been guilty of a crime he had been guilty of the prime indiscretion of falling into trouble. And Clarence Darrow saw confirmed the fear he had felt when he sat in the Los Angeles courtroom and heard Joe Ford accuse him of being worse than Benedict Arnold or Judas Iscariot: if you fling mud at a fence some stains will remain after the mud has dried and fallen off.

The only ones to rise to his defense were the liberal and idealistic attorneys who carried on a general practice, defended unpopular causes, gave their services to the poor and sustained the profession of law with honest hearts and high minds.

Edward Maher, a friend of Darrow's, came to him with the suggestion that "a banquet be given by the Lawyers' Association of Illinois in honor of his return to Chicago." Darrow was touched by the display of loyalty and hurt by the intuition that his confreres felt the display to be necessary. A committee was formed to "put over" the banquet—from time to time Clarence would inquire, a trifle wistfully, how the sale of the tickets was going.

It was fortunate for his proper love of self that he had already renounced the practice of the law, for immediately it became evident that Chicago had renounced him as a lawyer. He needed only a few days to learn that no one wanted his services, that individuals and corporations alike were afraid of prejudicing their interests by having as their representative a man who had just come through two criminal trials.

He was not too unhappy, for he had long wanted to be finished with the arduous requirements of the law, to be free to write and lecture. He closed the office door behind him for the last time, boarded an Illinois Central train. When he reached home he found Ruby in the library, on her hands and knees, burning fresh red dye into the carpet; she had spent the intervening days scrubbing the flat and making it livable after their two-year absence. He dropped into a wicker rocker and sat for a few moments with his chin on his chest.

"Well, Rube," he murmured, "it kinda looks like our lawyering days are over."

Ruby picked up another hot iron and went on with her task.

Though he had a good many thousands of dollars invested in Paul's gas plant in Greeley, he not only could not get his money out but had to keep investing more in order to protect what he had already put into it. Lecturing was the only way he could earn a living now. Determined to make a quick test of his standing, he arranged with one of the Chicago lecture managers to engage the Garrick Theatre for a lecture on Nietzsche. Chautauqua managers had always found him a good drawing card; when they met for their convention in Chicago they invited him to dinner. Clarence sat at the head of the long table and talked; the managers were delighted to find that his misfortunes had neither hardened nor embittered him. Sitting next to him was a young woman by the name of Caroline McCartney, who participated in the rapid-fire discussion. Toward the end of the dinner Darrow turned to Professor Foster and said, "This girl thinks as we do; I don't know about the rest of them."

He took two tickets from his vest pocket and said to Miss McCartney, "I'm going to lecture at the Garrick Theater, and

221

I'm going to give you a couple of tickets." Then he added hastily, "But please don't take them just because I'm offering them to you."

Caroline McCartney, who was to become one of his most enthusiastic lecture managers, went to the Garrick a few nights later, as did several thousand other Chicagoans, who gave him a tremendous ovation as he came out on the platform. Inspirited, he delivered one of his most delightful lectures; as a result the Chautauqua managers scheduled him for forty appearances, and the Walt Whitman Club invited him to be chairman of their annual banquet, a gesture which helped greatly in his repatriation.

For years he had wanted to retire so that he might be free to write, study, teach, but he had wanted to retire voluntarily, with money put aside for travel and leisure and peace of mind. It had never been his intention to retire because he somehow had failed, been forced out. He knew the dangers of bcoming an itinerant preacher, baggy in the pants and baggy in the windpipe, talking not because he had something burning or beautiful to say, but hollowly, to earn his bread.

In 1894 a short, squat, bristly-eyebrowed Russian immigrant by the name of Peter Sissman, who had just finished his law course and with whom Darrow had become acquainted at socialist meetings, had asked Darrow to be taken into his office. Sissman could bring the firm no business; he had a thick accent and was not particularly personable, but Darrow had liked the boy's spirit and, as he had said, "We radicals should patronize each other." He had taken Sissman into his office and trained him. Now, almost twenty years later, Sissman found his opportunity to repay the debt. When someone told him that Clarence Darrow had given up the practice of law Sissman went to Darrow and exclaimed:

"You must not. If you remain in Chicago and don't open your office it is a tacit admission of guilt."

"But I have no practice."

"It will take no time for you to build it up again."

Darrow shook his head, thanked Peter Sissman for his kindness.

In the months that followed whenever a lawyer would say to Sissman, "We hear Darrow has quit the law," Sissman would reply, "He must not. He must start over again. I would be overjoyed to start with him if he would want me."

It did not take long for this sentiment to reach Darrow. One afternoon he telephoned Sissman and invited him to the Midway for dinner. Over their cigarettes and coffee Darrow said:

"Peter, I hear you would be willing to join up with me."

"Of course I would be willing," replied Sissman brusquely. "I would be happy, but I'm not sure it would be advisable for you. I have only a small Jewish practice, a small office business. I can't bring you anything."

"You think kindly of me," answered Darrow.

"Ah!" murmured Sissman.

"I am not sure I can earn anything," continued Darrow.

"You must make an announcement that you are back."

"How do you propose we do it?"

"We must keep Bailey in the firm name. Darrow and Sissman is impossible."

"You give me courage, Peter," observed Darrow.

Sissman opened a joint bank account, dug down into his savings and spent a couple of hundred dollars for a desk, chair and carpet for an office for his new partner. But months passed, and no one brought their legal troubles to Darrow, not even the poor, who would have to ask for his services for nothing. He continued to go out on his Chautauqua lectures, which earned him from one to three hundred dollars apiece. Each time he returned he would go to Sissman and ask: "Haven't you anything for me to do?"

"Mr. Darrow," exclaimed Sissman, "can I ask you to sit down and examine an abstract of title? That's not the work for you. You must wait until important things come in."

Then, exactly like the young graduate sitting in his office waiting for the first case to walk in and give him his chance, Darrow listened to Mildred Sperry asking him to defend her against the charge of perjuring herself for her employer, an insurance agent who had burned a building. He won an acquittal and vindication for the girl even while acknowledging her guilt. The case started him on the long road back, earned him two hundred and fifty dollars. He next was given a bankruptcy to handle, which earned him twenty-five hundred dollars. When Police Chief Healy was indicted for malfeasance of office Darrow agreed to defend him and was paid a thousand-dollar retainer fee.

When Darrow and Sissman had formed their partnership Darrow had said, "As to fees, I think we better start even."

"That wouldn't be fair to you," Sissman had replied.

"We better start even," Darrow had insisted. "If I don't uphold my end I won't take my share."

This total of thirty-seven hundred and fifty dollars represented his legal earnings for the first year; when Sissman split the income of the firm he found that he had made a few hundred dollars less than he had the year before, when he had been by himself.

The passing of time slowly healed the wounds in Chicago's

pride. The people saw his shaggy figure go by, saw him smile and wave to friends, heard his drawling, kindly, musical voice, and their faith in Clarence Darrow resurged. The Biology Club met again in his home; groups all over the city asked him to speak; cases began to straggle in. Each victory brought two new clients. As the cases increased in importance the fees began to rise. He would walk into Sissman's office, pull from his pocket a roll of bills and checks, anywhere from five hundred to five thousand dollars, toss the money on Sissman's desk and say:

"Here you are, Peter; deposit it."

The only time he ever mentioned money was when he would go into Sissman's room and ask, "Peter, how does the treasury look?" And Sissman would write him a check. Every once in a while Sissman would hand him a statement and say, "Don't you want to examine the books? Don't you want to see what we made on what?"

"What's the use of two of us doing that work?" he would reply.

By the end of the second year Sissman saw that he had made several thousand dollars more than he had ever earned alone. He took his account books into his partner's office.

"I think you are beginning to get the worst of this," he said.

"What do you propose, Peter?" smiled Darrow.

"In the future I think sixty-forty would be fair."

"All right"—he nodded—"we'll do it that way."

Very little of his corporation and civil clientele returned, but by 1915 criminal cases began flooding into his office. Never in his thirty-eight years of practice had Clarence Darrow thought of himself primarily as a criminal lawyer. Yet he was enough of a poker player to know that a man must play the cards the way they fall. Never had he gone seeking for causes; if ever the day should come when a cause needed him it would find him and rout him out from under the deepest, most meaningless of courtroom procedure.

Once again it was Clarence Darrow for the defense. Every type of case came to him, and he took them all, all except those of the habitual criminals. He gave his clients the best he had in him. The habitual criminal he turned down, no matter how large the sum of money put on his desk; he felt he could do nothing for him.

Many murder cases were brought to him, and he defended wherever he thought the crime had been a result of poverty, circumstance, passion or insanity. In some instances he secured an acquittal; in others he saved his client from hanging by earning him a life sentence. In one case a Greek choked his landlord to death for "screwing up the rents." The man asked Darrow to defend him, placed five thousand dollars in cash upon his desk. Darrow did some investigating, entered a defense, then saw that the case was hopeless and advised his client to plead guilty and accept a life sentence.

"I'm paying you five thousand dollars to get me off," replied the Greek, "not to send me to jail."

Darrow returned the five thousand dollars. The man went to another lawyer, was convicted and executed.

The case in which he thought he did his most astute work during this period was the Eastland case. The Eastland, a lake steamer, was lying at anchor in the Chicago River at the Clark Street Bridge one summer morning, loaded with women and children who were going on an excursion to Michigan. Most of the passengers were standing on the side of the ship next to the dock, talking to friends and relatives, when suddenly the ship tipped downward on its heavy side and sank into the water. Hundreds of women and children were drowned instantly in one of the worst civil tragedies in American history. The genuine need to blame someone was so great that, in spite of the fact that the Eastland had recently been inspected and approved by both city and Federal inspectors, the captain was indicted for criminal negligence. Darrow was summoned to Grand Rapids, Michigan, to defend Captain John Erickson.

The prosecution put upon the witness stand a university professor who described for the jury the building of the boat from the laying of the keel to the applying of the last coat of paint. When this world authority on ship construction was turned over to Darrow for cross-examination the Grand Rapids attorneys associated with him insisted that he break down the damaging testimony. "No, no," replied Darrow, "I shall build him up." Then with his magnificent ability to assimilate technical information, he led the professor through the mechanics of shipbuilding from the beginning of time, plying him with complex and technical questions for days on end until the judge, the jury and the witnesses were not only exhausted but outraged at him for so inconsiderately wasting their time. When the professor had completed his testimony on the mechanics of ship construction and operation, a good part of which had been unintelligible to the jury, Darrow asked simply:

"Professor, is there anyone else in the world beside yourself who knows everything there is to know about ship construction?"

"Only one other man," replied the professor without a trace of false modesty. "He lives in Scotland."

"Then," demanded Darrow of the jury, "if there are only

two men on the face of the globe who know everything there is to know about ships, how could it be possible that the poor captain of a lake steamer could know what was wrong with the Eastland?"

It was this question that led the jury to acquit Captain Erickson.

He was just another criminal lawyer, and yet he was something more. Now that he again was successful, with his name in the papers, the poor came back to his office, crowding his anteroom, bringing their troubles and griefs. He did not hold it against them that they, too, had abandoned him in his dark hours; that was another facet of human nature that one had to understand. He defended people from whose malefactions the public turned away in abhorrence, men so loathed and reviled, so completely abandoned by the human race that they could find no other defender. He would go before judges, juries, and the public and plead for understanding and mercy.

"I do not know anyone who does not need mercy. This weary old world goes on, begetting, with birth and with living and with death; and all of it is blind from the beginning to the end. I do not know what made him do this act, but I do know there is a reason for it. I know that any one of an infinite number of causes reaching back to the beginning might be working out in his mind. If there were such a thing as justice it could only be administered by those who knew the inmost thoughts of the man to whom they were meting it out. It means that you must appraise every influence that moves them, the civilization where they live and all society which enters into the making of the child or the man. If you can do it—if you can do it you are wise, and with wisdom goes mercy."

Peter Sissman gives a trenchant portrait of his partner at the time of the Healy trial. "Darrow impressed on juries that it was not always easy to distinguish between right and wrong, particularly for historical purposes. His skepticism was so genuine that he imbued the juries with it. He would defend anyone who was in trouble, even a capitalist against a labor racketeer. He was consistent in this human philosophy of defense, which forced him into contradictions in his sociological philosophy. He was not committed to any party or permanent creed; that was his greatness and tragedy both. That was why he was essentially a free man, not bound by doctrines; but it is also why he was inconsistent and sometimes antisocial. Though his motivations were different, he sometimes used the same methods as cheap criminal lawyers. It would be all right for other lawyers to do these things; it is part of their job, but Darrow was a fighter for the people;

226

he had a social duty which he sometimes abused to defend individuals in trouble. To call every crook in trouble an 'underdog' was sentimental nonsense, even though Christ would have approved it highly. Darrow was a Christian anarchist; that was the reason he never fulfilled himself; he had no consistent life plan or design; he just drifted along from case to case and year to year. He was a behaviorist. He said, 'No matter what system we will be under men will be essentially beastly. All a fellow can do is preach charity rather than forgiveness, to be tolerant because we will all eventually do something wrong, and what I mean by charity is love.' "

He had returned to Chicago under a cloud; at the age of fifty-six he had had to start all over again; he had come up the hard way, taking those cases with which he felt a genuine sympathy. Yet by 1917 after only four years he could tell one of his juniors to call any attorney, prosecutor, judge or businessman in Chicago and say that something would be done; his word was accepted as final. By the end of the fourth year the firm of Darrow and Sissman had taken in thirty thousand dollars, and Clarence Darrow was called "the outstanding criminal lawyer of the country."

He had completed his comeback.

He plunged into the first of a series of conflicts over radicals which for the next four years, as the war hysterias would give way to the even more dangerous postwar hysterias, kept his a voice crying in the wilderness. Clarence Darrow was to become the greatest band wagon in America: millions who would jump off, call him a traitor, a radical, a lunatic, would climb aboard again when his next case was one with which they could sympathize; those who had stoutly supported him during his pleas for the conscientious objectors, eulogizing him as a true Christian, a defender of democracy, an authentic hero, would, when he defended other rebels, label him an anarchist, a chaos maker, a menace to organized society. What Sissman had termed Darrow's greatest weakness, that he had no cause, no party, no doctrine, no direction, only identification with all human suffering, now became his greatest strength.

The one regret of his professional life was that he had come to Chicago from Ashtabula a few months too late to assist in the defense of the Haymarket anarchists. Now in the crucial case of *The State of Wisconsin* vs. *Peter Bianchi, Mary Nardini, et al.*, he was given another chance to speak his piece; for here, thirty years after the four Haymarket anarchists had been executed, was another anarchist case, which the state of Wisconsin based squarely upon the Haymarket precedent in order to secure a conviction of all eleven of the defendants.

The Haymarket anarchists had been convicted on the ground that "he who inflames people's minds and induces them by violent means to accomplish an illegal object is himself a rioter, though he takes no part in the riot." The eleven Italians of Milwaukee had been convicted, not of throwing the bomb which blew up a police station and killed several officers, but of having in their possession more than a hundred pamphlets, magazines and newspapers which set forth the political virtues of anarchism.

The eleven Italians had already spent one year of a twenty-five-year sentence in the state penitentiary when they asked Darrow to appeal their case. Before leaving for Milwaukee, where the original trial had been held, Darrow began reading in the almost unintelligible translations that had been made for the court of the Italian anarchist literature, jotting down those sentences which seemed to express the crux of their belief: "The governments commit as many crimes as they prevent. The governments feign a desire to want to put a remedy to the evils of the workingman, but how could they put a remedy to it if they are the principal cause of these evils? The capitalists . . . use the workers or else starve them; the financiers steal with a free hand. At the least sign of discontent of the workingmen the government interferes with its soldiers, with its policemen, with its paid judges, and oppresses the oppressed. The government is the servant of the bourgeoisie, the enemy of the workingman, the starver of the people, the pestilence of society."

The fact that these ten men and one woman in the Wisconsin penitentiary were aliens, that they had made no attempt to become American citizens, that they spoke no English, that their public conduct proved them to be emotionally unbalanced, made no difference in the fundamental issue involved: that if America was to survive as a free land it had to be a country where men could be so completely free that they could believe in any erroneous, even crackpot, opinion and be guaranteed the right of expression of that opinion. So long as they did not actually violate the existing criminal code they must be protected in their rights by the hundred million citizens who would thus be protecting their own rights. It was true that these people were not citizens of the United States, but so long as they were not deported, so long as they were allowed to remain in this country, the least of them was entitled to the same rights the greatest American was entitled to. These childish, hysterical malcontents, who could never become an integral part of American life, were the last people in the world who had any claim to protection, yet to Darrow they seemed the first to need protection: if he could erect a defense for those who least seemed to warrant it, that defense would be the stronger for those who warranted it the more.

If he could make a valid defense of the indefensible, then the defensible would be certain of a sound defense.

Darrow took Sissman with him to Milwaukee, where they dug deeper into the case of the anarchists. They learned that August Juliani, connected with the Methodist Church of Milwaukee, had gone with some of his Italian congregation, on a Sunday afternoon in the summer of 1917, to the corner of Bishop and Potter avenues in the center of an Italian district. As their band played "Columbia" a crowd of about a hundred gathered. Juliani then "started to talk patriotically about the war, the draft and the registering in Italian." One of the Italian spectators cried out, "I don't believe in God; I don't believe in priests; I don't believe what you are saying." Another cried, "We don't believe in this war," while a third said, "We don't believe in any government; Wilson is a pig; the American flag is a rag, and this country is a jail." The other members of the little clique echoed, "You bet; you bet!"

The following Sunday afternoon Juliani led his group to the same corner, where a similar disturbance broke up his meeting. On the third Sunday he asked for police protection. Four detectives went along with him. The meeting started peacefully, but after a few minutes the dissenters left their clubhouse a block away, marched on the meeting and again started a row. Paul Wieler, one of the detectives, called out, "If you don't like this crowd move on. They have a permit." When the man he was addressing refused to move the detective began to search him. Someone opened fire with a revolver. Others returned the fire. Two anarchists were killed; two of the detectives were injured. Eleven anarchists were arrested.

Then in November a bomb was placed in the Central Police Station which exploded and caused the death of ten persons, including two of the detectives who had made the arrests on the corner of Bishop and Potter avenues. The eleven defendants held in the jail under charges of assault with deadly weapons had the charge against them raised to conspiracy to commit murder. The trial was rushed, a change of venue denied, even though the populace was violently inflamed against all Italians. District Attorney Zabel, who had been elected on the socialist ticket, charged that anyone having anarchist literature in his possession was equally guilty of the bomb outrage and, as in the Haymarket case, guilty even if the actual perpetrator of the bombing never was found. He read to the jury inflammatory passages from the translated Italian tracts, and the jury had convicted all eleven of the defendants, giving them sentences of twenty-five years each—not for throwing the bomb, not for having ordered the bomb to be thrown, not for knowing who had thrown the bomb, but for being anarchists whose published literature appeared to favor the throwing of bombs.

"These people have a right to believe in the philosophic idea that they can free themselves by force," cried Darrow. "It is only when it can be proved that they have used force to injure people, when they have run counter to the criminal code, that they can be prosecuted. There is no such crime as a crime of thought; there are only crimes of action. It is bad taste for guests in a country to call that country a jail; it is bad taste to call its President a pig, but these are errors of judgment rather than transgressions against the legal structure. If we wish to keep speech free, to keep criticism open and alive, we have to tolerate even such criticisms as these, distasteful as they may be to us."

In his brief to the Supreme Court of Wisconsin Darrow, with the help of Sissman, who made his most brilliant effort in this case, set out to demonstrate that the eleven anarchists had had a trial by passion; that because of an inflamed press and countryside the jury had been prejudiced; that the district attorney's reading of the inflammatory sections of the anarchist literature had deranged the trial; that the presiding judge had shown prejudice and passion in imposing a uniform twenty-five-year sentence without any attempt to vary the sentence according to the degree of participation; that the anarchist literature had nothing to do with the crime with which the defendants originally were charged; that a shocking confusion had been created in that the defendants, ostensibly being tried for shooting the detectives on the corner of Bishop and Potter avenues, were in actuality tried for a conspiracy to explode the bomb that had killed the police officers, and lastly, that no conspiracy or specific intent to assault the detectives had emerged from the evidence.

The appeal was granted. Nine of the defendants who had had no firearms in their possession at the time of the arrest were acquitted in a new trial. The two men who had been carrying guns were convicted of assault. Darrow boarded a train for Madison to call on the governor of Wisconsin. "A grave injustice has been done to these nine innocent persons who had to spend a year in the peniteniary," he pleaded. "The best way we can show our disapproval of these trials by passion and Wisconsin's repudiation of such methods is for you to pardon the two men who have just been convicted."

The governor pardoned them.

He once again was earning from twenty-five to thirty thousand dollars a year. His apartment on the Midway continued to be one of the most pleasant intellectual centers in Chicago; the Biology Club still met there once a week; nearly every evening saw Clarence surrounded by old and new friends with whom he would read and philosophize. Ruby took flawless care of him, too good care, Clarence complained, for often she was more like a nurse than a wife. She no longer permitted him to eat what he wanted or when he wanted; he had to eat what was good for him, though he might detest the stuff, and eat it at regular hours, though he might not be hungry. She told him what clothes he must wear, when he must change them, when he must take his medicine, when he must bathe, when he must rest, when he must sleep, when he must get up, which friends he could have around him and which he could not. There was rarely an instant spent in her company that he was free from her watchful eye, taking orders which were designed to protect his health and preserve his strength but which in effect distressed him, made him cranky and uneasy.

A man who loved personal freedom above all things, he began to grouse that he had no freedom in his own home. He understood that the confining influences arose from Ruby's love for him, from her tremendous and unused vitality, from her need to be important to him, to keep him healthy and alive; for the most part his grumbling was good natured and resigned. Their only serious trouble in thirty-three years of successful marriage arose over claim jumpers, for as Ruby had occasion to learn, American women did not always respect vested interests or property rights when it came to marriage or a desirable male. Age made little difference in Clarence Darrow; he never burned out: at thirty, forty, fifty, sixty and seventy women loved him. This was difficult for Ruby to endure, but what made it more difficult was that a number of them decided they would replace her, become the third and last Mrs Clarence Darrow. There had been one during the Los Angeles trials, a clever and talented woman who was convinced that Clarence was misunderstood by his wife, or at least that Ruby undervalued him, and that she would make a far finer mate. She had caused Ruby hours of anguish, for Clarence was all she had in life; she had abandoned her journalism and other contacts; the thought of another woman cutting her out was wormwood and poison.

Now that Clarence was back on his feet, was again a celebrity, surrounded by crowds wherever he went, the claim jumpers again surged forward. When her husband was pursued by adoring women, as he often was, instead of enjoying the fact that she had the man they apparently wanted, instead of being the queen of the roost, Ruby became racked with suspicions, fears, doubts, jealousies. Clarence found these suspicions and jealousies intolerable, though he was by no means completely innocent of bringing them on: he

231

was not by nature a one-woman man; he enjoyed the company and especially the adoration of attractive women; he enjoyed matching wits against them, savoring of their female humor and logic; he liked feeding his ego with their admiration. Nor is it unthinkable that upon occasion he might have been above a little adultery.

One of the reasons he had married Ruby instead of X was that he had found unbearable X's incessant spying, observing, questioning and accusations. As Ruby, now unhappy and miserable with her fear of losing him to some scheming woman, wept and made scenes, he became angry, upset, off balance. He took more freedom from her than he actually wanted or needed, especially when she refused to invite to their home one of his friends of whom she had become suspicious. There were weeks of estrangement.

But the bad days passed, and the bad weeks. He had never loved anyone but Ruby since he had married her. After a time she came to see that she had nothing serious to fear. He explained; she explained. She apologized; he apologized. And like most soundly based marriages, their relationship had perhaps another dimension because it had been troubled, because they had understood and forgiven.

War years are bad ones for a man with a lust for justice. Even though the United States had not been attacked and was in no conceivable danger, the nation was caught in a paroxysm of fear which suspended all judgment and paralyzed the legal apparatus. Under the Espionage Act of 1917 and the Sedition Act of 1918 almost two thousand American citizens, including editors, clergymen, educators, had been sent to prison for terms of ten to twenty years for declaring that America did not belong in the war, for offering evidence that the manufacturers of war supplies were looting the public funds of billions of dollars, for criticizing an act of the Congress or a departmental bureau. Several thousand other native-born Americans were clubbed, horsewhipped, tarred and feathered, beaten with an iron cat-o'-nine-tails for declining to buy Liberty bonds or subscribe to the Red Cross, for challenging the operation of the draft, for promoting a World Peace League, for making "disloyal" comments in their own homes. Judges and juries alike were caught up in the dementia, and the country suffered its most complete suspension of civil liberties since the War between the States.

Darrow had been convinced that it was necessary to advocate America's entry into the war; he had then been forced to observe in a state of agony and impotence the legal maelstrom which the war caused. But what he had not been prepared for were the even more severe postwar hysterias which were to rack the country with a series of bitter prosecutions when the war between the nations gave way to a civil war between the classes. Against these latter excesses Darrow did not feel impotent, for they were waged on his field of battle, the public courtroom. Against them he raised his voice in some of the finest pleading of his age. Never was good pleading more sorely needed.

The success of the communist revolution in Russia had immediate and drastic repercussions in the United States. The extremists among the American socialists had split off from their party to form the Communist Labor party with an avowal that ". . . the working class must organize and train itself for the capture of the world state; the Communist Labor party of the United States declares itself in full harmony with the revolutionary working-class parties of all countries and stands by the principle stated by the Third International formed at Moscow." Congress passed the Overthrow Act, which made it unlawful for any person "openly to advocate by word of mouth or writing the reformation or overthrow by violence or any other unlawful means of the representative form of government now secured to the citizens of the United States; to publish, issue or knowingly sell any book, paper, document . . . which advocated crime and violence as a means of accomplishing the reformation or overthrow of the Constitution; to organize, aid in the organization of or become a member of any society or association, the object of which is to overthrow the government."

Attorney General A. Mitchell Palmer, in charge of the enforcement of the Overthrow Act, cried, "Like a prairie fire, the blaze of revolution is sweeping over every American institution of law and order. It is eating its way into the homes of the American workman; its sharp tongues of revolutionary heat are licking the altars of the churches, leaping into the belfry of the school bell, crawling into the sacred corners of American homes, seeking to replace marriage vows with libertine laws, burning up the foundations of society. There can be no nice distinctions drawn between the theoretical ideas of the radicals and their actual violations of our national law. The government is in jeopardy!"

He then sent out his Department of Justice agents to perpetrate what Darrow felt to be one of the most sustained series of illegal acts ever authorized by a high government official. Thousands of innocent persons, most of them foreign-born, were rounded up in mass raids, blackjacked, knocked down, kicked, third-degreed and tortured, imprisoned without

233

warrants, held for weeks and months incommunicado, without trials, their property destroyed, their jobs taken from them, their life in the New World shattered.

Clarence Darrow spent his days and nights rescuing bewildered, frightened men and women from prison cells. "My God," he cried, ". . . if the American patriots and businessmen really want a bloody uprising in the United States, Attorney General Palmer and the Department of Justice have found the best possible means of achieving it."

It remained for the town of Rockford to afford him the opportunity to state legally the case for the revolutionist to the American people. When some of his stanchest supporters demanded to know how he could defend these indefensibles he uttered the credo on which his life had been built:

"I am defending this case for two reasons. The first is that I have seldom known a case where I believed so heartily that I am right. The second is because when I entered the practice of my profession years ago I determined that there never should be a case . . . that I would refuse to do my duty and defend that case; and I can honestly say that I have kept the faith; that I have never turned my back upon any defendant, no matter what the charge; when the cry is the loudest the defendant needs the lawyer most. . . ."

He and Ruby left for Rockwood, a factory town of sixty-five thousand people, ninety miles from Chicago, where they were made comfortable in the home of Fay Lewis. He found the community suffering from the same hysteria that he had encountered in Los Angeles when he had arrived to defend the McNamara brothers. Men were meeting on the streets and exclaiming as they shook hands, "Well, now we'll be rid of these agitators for good. So they got the Reds! The damned traitors! We'll send them over the road."

Four Department of Justice agents had swooped down upon the home of Arthur Person, a glass beveler who had come from Sweden at the age of fifteen and who for twenty years had worked in Rockford factories. Person had three children, a wife who was ill, a home he was paying off on monthly installments, an interest in socialism and a score of friends who declared him to be honest, square, peaceable and law abiding. When the Communist Labor party was formed in Chicago Person was asked to join by Dr Oleson, an old-line Rockford socialist who had once been elected to public office in the city and who was attending Person's wife. Person was made secretary of a Rockford branch, held several open meetings in his home. When the raiding party invaded the house they found a collection of dusty socialist pamphlets in his attic, a membership list of seven persons, thirty cents in the treasury, a brown notebook with a notation of a six-dollar bill for a hall and a speaker, which they were unable to pay, and a red-colored pamphlet containing the Communist Labor party's platform. While being third-degreed by his captors in the automobile that was carrying him to jail Person admitted that "I believe in a government for the working people, of the working people."

When Darrow learned that an important part of the state's case against Person was to be based on this comment he exclaimed, "Why, that is almost the exact language Abraham Lincoln used! Lincoln would be under indictment here, too."

A number of other raids were committed until ten working-men and the wife of a prominent businessman were lodged in the jail. Darrow had many friends among the liberals and socialists of Rockford; they turned to him at once for the defense.

The hostility against him was intense, but he gave no sign that he saw it or that it bothered him. He went on his soft, kindly, persuasive way, using every device he could think of to buck up the town's frightened liberals so that he would have enough public opinion behind him to guarantee a fair trial.

The state's attorney agreed to try Arthur Person only and let the result of this trial determine the fate of his fellow members. The charge was advocating the change and over-throw of the government, and he revolved his prosecution about the red-covered platform of the party, picking out such highly combustible words as "revolution," "conquest," "capture," "dictate," "overthrow," "mass action," "collapse of civilization," attempting to show that men who read and approved of such terms would not hesitate to use illegal methods to destroy the existing form of the American gov-ernment. With the town of Rockford in attendance and a corps of reporters gathered to flash the news to all parts of the country, the state's attorney tried to prove that any criticism of the government was treachery to that govern-ment and must be punishable as such.

Darrow had tried to keep the red pamphlet out of the evidence, but the judge had admitted it. Now his answer was simple and direct; he told the state's attorney and the judge, the jury and the country at large, "If you want to get rid of every socialist, of every communist, of every trade unionist, of every agitator, there is one way to do it, and that is to cure the ills of society. You can't do it by building jails; you can't make jails big enough or penalties hard enough to cure discontent by strangling it to death. No revolution is possible, no great discontent is possible, unless down below it all is some underlying cause for this discontent; men are naturally obedient, too almighty obedient."

235

He built his defense upon his conviction that Arthur Person, the simple workingmen who were indicted with him and the thousands of workingmen throughout the country who had joined the Communist Labor party, thinking it to be a sort of reanimated Socialist party which might help them to get a little more wages, to get a little quicker redress of the workingman's grievances, did not and could not understand the implications of the confused language of the communist platform.

For Darrow the essence of the case was contained in his opening appeal. "What could we think of a jury who would deprive a man of his freedom because he does just what every other human being in the world is trying to do; tries to get enough of his fellow men to see things as he sees them, that he may change laws and institutions so that the workers will have a better chance? Now Person may be wild and crazy; I don't know. I am not here to try another man's views; I am not here for that, and neither are you. It may be that there isn't a single plank in that platform that I believe, and there may not be a single article of faith in the Lutheran Creed that I believe or in the Catholic Creed or any other creed ever made by man; but, gentlemen, unless I will stand for the right of every man on earth to accept his own religious faith and his own political creed and his own ideas, whether I believe in them or not, unless I will do that, I am a very poor American. I would be a very poor citizen and I would belong to that class of bigots who in almost every age have piled the fagots around their fellow men and burned them to cinders because of difference of faith."

When he had tried the case of Debs and the railway union, he had evolved the technique of defense by offense. He found that this would serve him equally well here.

"I am engaged in the difficult task of trying to preserve a Constitution instead of destroying it, and I am seeking to save for the people of this country such liberties as they have left. It is hard for me to realize that men of power and some intellect would seek to terrorize men and women into obedience to their opinions. We wiggled along for a hundred and fifty years without this Espionage Law, and we did pretty well. Where did it come from? It came from the people who would strangle criticism; it came from the people who would place their limits upon your brain and mine, and if we give them their way in this world, every man, if he would be safe, should wear a padlock on his lips and only take it off to feed himself and lock it up after he gets through. No man would dare speak above a whisper; no man would feel himself safe to belong to an organization, whether it was for American freedom, Russian freedom, Irish freedom or any freedom, because the word 'freedom' is the most dangerous word that the English language knows. The time will come very soon when America will be ashamed of her cowardly attempt to send men to jail under laws of this kind; ashamed of the suppression of freedom of thought and freedom of speech which is making a madhouse of a once-free land."

It had been his hope that the American way of life would prove that the employer and the employed might work together in common trust and common prosperity, that there was no need for so rich and resourceful a country ever to be ravaged by class war. Yet as he continued to work against the bitterness and hatred of the Rockford prosecution he was forced to acknowledge that the proceeding was a manifestation of class war. With all his strength and persuasiveness he yearned to prove that this was class war, to show the people that they deluded themselves and perpetuated the war by calling it other and false names and that once they had recognized that this was class war they would understand that they must declare a truce, that they must grant a just peace, that they must make permanent a fair distribution of wealth to keep either side from destroying the other.

"The world has just been through a great war. The world has been crazy, all of us. I hate to think that we went through it all for nothing. I have been one of those dreamers who has felt that from the fire and the smoke and the ashes of the battlefield of Europe there might arise a fairer, a better, a juster civilization than this world has ever known; that out of the infinite sufferings of the human race men might grow kinder and more humane and give a better chance to the common man. I have still not lost faith that the poor and oppressed all over the earth will have a chance to try and better their conditions. But money, wealth, greedily as ever, learning nothing by all the sorrow of the world, said, 'No, all of our privileges must remain; nothing shall be gained by the war for all the blood that has been shed, and whenever a man dares to raise his voice for new conditions or for a better world we will send him to jail.'

"Arthur Person is obscure; he is unknown; he is poor; he has worked all his life, but his case is one that reaches down to the foundation of your freedom and mine. If twelve men should say that they could take a man like him and send him to prison and destroy his home, a man who is guiltless of crime and whose only stain is that he loved his fellow men; if twelve men like you should say that they would take him from his home and send him to Joliet and confine him behind prison walls, you should hang this court-house in crape and drape your city hall with black and wear sackcloth and ashes until his term expires."

The jury apparently had no desire to wear sackcloth and ashes: they brought in a verdict of not guilty, though it was never made clear whether Person was innocent of intending to overthrow the government by force and violence, of knowing what the Communist Labor party platform was all about, of transgressing against a law which had no right to be on the statute books of a democracy.

Darrow was elated because he imagined that here he had established a precedent which would throw out indictments held over the heads of other victims of the Department of Justice raids.

His optimism was short lived: he was summoned to return at once to Chicago to defend the sixteen communists who had been arrested with William Bross Lloyd.

He saw at once that this case went beyond the problem of the workingman who did not understand the implications of communism, for the Chicago clique was composed of native-born Americans, well educated, several of them with wealth and social position. William Bross Lloyd's father, Henry Demarest, had married a daughter of the McCormicks, but he and his wife and children had been dispossessed by his father-in-law because he had worked for the pardoning of the Haymarket anarchists. Apparently the grandfather had relented, for "the record shows that William Bross Lloyd is a man with considerable property and that he regularly employs a manager for his estate and financial matters. He maintains an office and an office force in the Tribune Building. . . . He is surrounded with luxuries in his home in Winnetka."

The Chicago group was made up largely of intellectuals, men who did not work with their hands for a living but who were in the forefront of the radical movement, trying to give it voice and expression. Despite the fact that they had repudiated control from Moscow by refusing to join with the Russian Communist party, their members looked constantly to Russia for their ideology and direction. It was intellectuals like William Bross Lloyd who organized the Communist Labor party in America, who financed it, directed it, wrote its literature and attempted to convert to its economic philosophy the mass of American working people. This was to be a case of the agitator, the organizer, rather than the workingman. Unlike Person and the Rockford workingmen, Lloyd and his fellows had openly called for the use of force and dynamite.

238

So vociferous had been the street meetings held by his Chicago clients that the charge against them was "conspiracy to overthrow the government." It would not be sufficient for him to point out that although these men had advocated force they never actually committed an act of force; that they had been guilty only of the crime of talk; that once they used force or dynamite their action would violate the criminal code and the perpetrators then could be dealt with; that it was implicit in the character of a democracy that it had to be patient, put up with harsh and antagonistic words; that the structure of American life was not so weak that it could be blown down by the first gust of wind. No; the Overthrow Act had made it possible for his clients to be arrested and imprisoned before they had performed an act of violence, and the state had only to prove that any one of the group had an "intent" to overthrow the government, and the entire local would go to prison.

Upon what basis then was he to make his defense, his plea for tolerance? He could base it only upon the principle that these citizens had a right to preach the overthrow of their own government because the Constitution guaranteed them the freedoms of speech, press and assembly and that these rights were implicit in a democracy. He would admit to the court that his clients well knew what they were doing but that they had a right to heresy, economic and political as well as religious. He knew that such a defense not only would be courageous, but foolhardy. But if he could achieve an acquittal on the solid basis of American revolutionary precedent, there could be no further prosecutions.

When the prosecution argued that it was men like Lloyd and his associates who had been responsible for the bloodshed and destruction of the Russian Revolution he defended that revolution by portraying vividly the czarist oppressions and barbarous cruelties during the centuries preceding the uprising. "Russia has been the last word in tyranny in Europe for more than a thousand years, a government of despotism tempered by assassination, where all the brave and the liberty-loving people have been killed or sent to Siberia." When the prosecution accused his men of scheming to achieve their ends by means other than the ballot he defended the right to collective action outside the polls. When the prosecution charged that his clients were attacking the Constitution he quoted from Charles A. Beard's *Economic Interpretation of the Constitution* to show how the Constitution had originally been drawn to protect property rights above personal rights and had constantly to be amended to include such personal rights as would enable a republic to function.

His name and character had been reviled, yet all that had

239

gone before was but a gentle zephyr compared with the tornado that was unleashed when Clarence Darrow defended the right of the working people to take control of their own country. As always throughout his career, he was accused of believing in and advocating the theories of the people he was defending. Few would believe him when he said that he was merely acting as a mechanism of defense.

"Why should not the workingman make a conquest of the power of the state?" he asked. "No organization could believe in the conquest of the power of the state unless it believed in the state. Is there any more reason why the workingman should not make the conquest of the state than any other part of society? Every political party in America is trying to do it and are doing it. The Republican party is now very busy making the conquest of the power of the state and doing everything it can think of that they may make the conquest of power. My clients' policy is just like the policy of everyone else, excepting this, they think they would use it for the benefit of the workingman. Perhaps even if these men did make the conquest of the power of the state their dreams would not come true; I cannot tell, but they have a right to try; they have a right to think; they have a right to proselyte; they have the right to their opinion and to make their opinion heard. This is what I plead for, and I am not interested in whether their opinions are right or wrong. If they are wrong the American people under free discussion can find the wrong, and if by any chance these opinions shall convert the United States, then the United States needs converting.

"I do not know whether socialism or communism will work or not. I do know that the present system does not work; that it is a crazy quilt that allows no man to be really honest, that allows no man to be unselfish . . . no man to live without sacrificing his fellow man. I know that it makes men greedy and selfish and mean. I know that it stifles every good motive in man. I know that under the present system no one . . . can be as good as he would be. I know that capitalism does not work and never can work.

"Gentlemen, I cannot tell whether this scheme will work, but it is what they believe. They have the same right to their belief under the laws of this country as you have to yours, and all of you told me over and over again that you would protect the right of another man the same as you would protect your own rights.

"I know that freedom produces wealth, and then wealth destroys freedom. I know that the nation that is not watchful of its liberty will lose it. I know that the individual that will not stand for his rights will have no rights, and I believe the
240

first duty of every American citizen is to protect himself and his country in all the liberties we have and all that we can get.

"You can only protect your liberties in this world by protecting the other man's freedom. You can only be free if I am free. The same thing that would get me may be used to get you, and the government that is not strong enough to protect all its citizens ought not to live upon the face of this earth."

Darrow's plea reverberated around the world. Always juries had gone with him, but this time he had gone too far. In order to accept his philosophy they would have had to undergo a revolution in their own minds which would have been more radical than the one advocated by William Bross Lloyd and his fellow radicals. They sentenced all sixteen of his clients to the penitentiary for one- to two-year terms, a comparatively light sentence, considering the rights that Darrow had demanded for them. Some of his friends were astonished that the jury did not ask for an indictment of counsel for the defense.

He appealed the case to the Illinois Supreme Court, which upheld the decision of the lower court. This made Darrow a little sad. However, he was cheered by the lone dissenting voice of Justice Carter, who insisted upon writing into the record, "Under the constitution of 1870, governing freedom of speech, this Overthrow Statute of 1919 should be considered so vague and general and so clearly against the American doctrine of freedom of speech as to be held unconstitutional."

As Darrow had commented when a single justice of the United States Supreme Court had ruled against the kidnaping of Moyer, Haywood and Pettibone, "There is always one man to state the case for freedom. That's all we need, one."

Chapter Eleven

Even the Rich Have Rights!

THE DARROWS were fast asleep in the early-morning hours of June 2, 1924, when they were startled "by a frightening ringing of the front doorbell, as though the place were afire."

"I hastened out of bed," says Mrs Darrow, "and while I sped through the long hall to the front of the apartment the bell kept ringing frantically. When I threw open the front door I found myself confronted by four men who seemed like masked desperados, clutching at their upturned coat collars. They forced themselves forward. 'We've got to see Clarence Darrow! Is he here?'

" 'Mr Darrow isn't well—he should not be disturbed.' "

The four men insisted upon seeing Darrow and dashed into his bedroom. The leader of the group, Richard Loeb's uncle, flung his arms about Darrow's shoulders, exclaiming, "Thank heavens you are here! No one else can save us. If you had been away we would have been ruined. You must save our two boys!"

Darrow had known the Loebs for years; he had watched the arrest of young Loeb and Leopold for the murder of fourteen-year-old Robert Franks with sickened amazement. "But they are not guilty. You have your nephews, the Bachrach brothers, defending them; their innocence should not be difficult to prove."

"No, no!" cried the uncle, distraught. "Dickie and Babe confessed this afternoon."

Darrow pulled himself up slowly in the big brass bed, unable for the moment to believe that the two boys, both sons of millionaires, brilliant students who had been the youngest to be graduated from the Universities of Michigan and Chicago, could have committed the shocking murder. The grief-stricken faces of the four men told him that the story was true. After a long moment of silence he murmured hoarsely, "Then what can I do?"

"Get them a life sentence instead of death. That's all we ask."

"That's all you ask," whispered the sixty-seven-year-old attorney, more to himself than to his intruders. "Millions of people will demand their deaths, and all you ask is that I save their lives."

Loeb fell on his knees beside the bed. "But you will do it!" he cried. "We'll pay anything. Only for God's sake, don't let them hang. You have saved a hundred others. Why won't you save them?"

Darrow sat propped against the brass rungs, his big head sunk on his chest, remembering an incident of a few nights before. He had been lecturing on the inequalities of the law when a young radical had popped out with, "Mr Darrow, since the capitalist law is designed to protect the rich and privileged, don't you think you have wasted your forty-five years in the courts?"

"Why don't you ask the hundred and two men whose lives I have saved?" queried Darrow.

Therein, despite his advancing years, the rheumatism and neuralgia that were harassing him, his fatigue, disillusion and pessimism over mankind's ability ever to raise itself from its animal heritage, lay his compensation: he had kept one hundred and two human beings from being executed by the state.

He had fought for many causes in his day, some more tenable and worthy than others, but his great and permanent crusade had been against capital punishment. Always he had worked with the idea in mind that if he could set a movement on foot which would one day, in some distant century, put an end to legalized killings, his efforts and hardships and sufferings and abuse would have been worth while.

All killings by the state were murder in the first degree. Since one could not reform an offender by executing him they were acts of revenge. His half century in the courts had convinced him that, like all acts of revenge, the executions did not act as a deterrent to further killings, but instead tended to cheapen human life.

It was assumed by many that killers must be executed for fear that they might one day, twenty or thirty years later, be pardoned. So much the better, thought Darrow. When the fear and the hatred and the hysteria engendered by the crime had passed, subsequent doctors, judges and juries might be able to look upon the killer as a man who had acted from a complex set of impulses, over few of which he had any control. Giving the succeeding generations the right of review could only breed mercy.

Could he defend Loeb and Leopold for this murder? Would he not once again be called an anarchist, an enemy of society, a chaos breeder? He knew what a hue and cry would be raised over any defense; the public was too wrought up and frightened by the ghoulishness of the murder to draw the fine distinction between a defense of the crime and a defense of the hapless ones who had perpetrated it. He knew that once again he would be running alone, against the field.

He was getting tired; did he wish to plunge into the midst of another bloody and vituperative maelstrom, one which would rob him of his little energy? Could he again endure the hatreds, the abuse, the ostracism, that must inevitably result? He was rapidly approaching threescore and ten. He had endured the bitterness and revilement of the crowd as much as any public figure of his day. Did he have the strength and courage to take still another beating?

Yet how could he abandon his fight against capital punishment merely because these particular defendants might appear indefensible? How could one set of human beings justify taking another human being's life?

If he could convince the public that Loeb and Leopold were two defective human machines which had somewhere broken down because of heredity or the pressure of external

243

environment, if he could save their lives when all the world wanted them exterminated, might not he deal a deathblow to capital punishment? While the state was trying Loeb and Leopold he could try capital punishment.

Crime, Its Cause and Treatment was the most valuable and revolutionary book he had yet written; in it he had stated the essence of his belief: the machine that is every man is completely formed by the time it slips from its mother's womb, but once its inherent boundaries had been proscribed, the actual fate or pattern of this human machine was determined by the circumstances in which it found itself set up in the external world. Under this philosophy there was no room for free will: a man acted according to the equipment with which he had been endowed and in accordance with the surroundings into which he had been plunged. If, then, there was no free will, there could be no praise or blame; no man was alone responsible for his acts: his ancestors were responsible, and the state of society in which he lived was responsible, and to punish a man for having a brain, a spirit, a character, a set of action impulses that had been determined for him by powers beyond his control, was stupid, wasteful, cruel and barbaric. The papers were screaming that there was absolutely no reason for this fiendish murder by Loeb and Leopold, that it could be traced to no intelligible causes. Yet Darrow knew that there were thousands of tiny and intricate reasons behind the crime, all of them woven into the character and environment of the killers, and that the causes would be intelligible once the world could be made to understand all of the contributing factors that had made these two human machines go haywire.

Darrow wearily dressed, went downstairs with the four men, entered the Loeb limousine and headed for the county jail.

He sat quietly in the back seat while the four men talked explosively at him. He was not listening to them; he was listening to his own voices reminding him that he had always emphasized poverty as the cause of crime.

Nineteen-year-old Nathan F. Leopold, Jr, and Richard A. Loeb, a year yonger, had been raised in the fashionable South Shore section of Chicago. Leopold's father was a retired millionaire box manufacturer, while Loeb's father was the multimillionaire vice-president of Sears, Roebuck and Company. The Loeb estate at Charlevoix, Michigan, was set in the midst of hundreds of acres of magnificently wooded country. The two boys were raised amidst great wealth from their early childhood. Loeb had an allowance of two hundred and fifty dollars a month, with three thousand dollars in the

244

bank under his own name and a standing order from his father to the family secretary that "Dickie" was to be given a check for any sum of money at any time without question. Though Leopold was given only half as large a monthly allowance, he had his own car, charge accounts in the big stores and could have any amount of money for which he asked.

As the car sped through the darkness along the lake and Darrow began listening to the men beside him who were attempting to explain the crime in terms of the boys' backgrounds, he realized that this crime not only sustained his theories of criminology but gave them another dimension. Excessive wealth had been the real protagonist in this murder; had corrupted Loeb and Leopold just as excessive poverty had corrupted the young boys of the Chicago slums who had gone wrong. The Loeb-Leopold murder was the reverse of the shield.

Nathan Leopold, Jr, was the more interesting and brilliant of the two boys; the numerous illnesses in his psyche were largely responsible for the murder of Robert Franks, even though Loeb was the one who desired, planned and executed the killing. Young Leopold was adored by his parents, who called him "Babe." In turn the boy worshiped his mother, whom he called "my sainted mother." From earliest childhood he had been hypersensitive: the barest affront or imagined slight was enough to wound him deeply, cause him mental anguish. Abnormally shy of girls, his parents sought to correct this lack of poise by sending him to a girls' school in charge of his governess, who took him there every morning and brought him home every afternoon. The ignominy of being the only boy in a girl's school turned him the more against the opposite sex, created psychic wounds from which he never fully recovered.

Young Leopold was suffering from glandular irregularities and disorders which were having an effect not only upon his body but upon his mind, that group word for the interfunctions of the brain, the nervous system and the glandular structure that go to make up a complete being. Medical examinations showed that he had had an overactive and diseased thyroid which led to an early sex development. The doctors also found that he had a disorder of the nervous control of the blood vessels, that he suffered from a retrogression of the pineal glands, which had already calcified at the age of nineteen, and that he suffered from an adrenal insufficiency.

This glandular composition inevitably had its effect on Leopold's appearance and consequently on his attitude toward the world. He was small in stature, had prominent eyes, coarse hair, was round-shouldered, flat-footed, with a protuberant abdomen. The glandular disturbances which caused him to suffer from blood disorders, muscular fatigue, low temperature, low blood pressure, low metabolism and anemia depressed him, made him moody as his energy waxed and waned, made him the victim of physical afflictions or inadequacies which determined his personality. These inadequacies, coupled with the fact that he judged himself physically unattractive, gave him a severe inferiority complex, an inferiority complex which made him an easy victim to a superiority complex engendered by his father's great wealth. His father had demonstrated to him that wealth controls the world, that anything he desired could be bought. When he wanted to hunt birds in the park and it was out of season his father's wealth had secured him a special permit; when he was caught fishing out of season his father not only paid the fines but replaced the equipment that had been taken from Leopold and his friends. Neither the father nor the mother made any attempt to teach the boy that his wealth involved responsibilities and obligations to the society that had created it. On the contrary, they showed him by example that through his wealth he was superior to all others, that he was not bound by the same laws that bound the herd. Young Leopold grew up with the idea that he was beyond responsibility because he was beyond the need to earn money, that all his life he could do precisely what he wished because he would always have the money with which to buy that wish.

Thus he suffered constantly from the conflict between his physical heritage and the environment into which he had been born: his physical inheritance brought him pathological inferiority; his environment brought him pathological superiority. From his earliest childhood the boy was a schizophrenic, caught between the blades of his complexes, his conduct pattern never able to be whole or unified because it was constantly cut to shreds by the incessantly working blades of the giant scissors. The youngster did not know why he was constantly churned and torn, why he was so introspective, why he shunned people and preferred to be by himself.

The outstanding characteristic of Nathan Leopold, the one which overshadowed everything else, was his precocity. By the age of eighteen he had completed his course at the University of Chicago, the youngest ever to be graduated from that institution. In addition to the brilliant work he did in class he was widely read in philosophy, methaphysics, literature and science; he read for the pleasure of learning, was able to retain and correlate astounding amounts of these mature and difficult subjects. He was an expert ornithologist, made frequent trips into the country in pursuit of specimens, had a first-rate amateur museum in his home, wrote papers on the subject and was highly thought of by professionals in the field.

This precocity was also a manifestation of the nerve and glandular structure which determined his physical aspect. For the practical purposes of making his life a happy one, his precocity had done him more harm than good: in the lower grades the children had shunned him as teacher's pet, while later in his college years he was too much younger than his fellows to form friendships on the basis of equality. The failure of other young people to like him caused him an agony so intolerable that he decided to defeat it by escape into the realms of the intellect where he could be a master, where he would no longer have feelings, where he would be safe from slights, hurts and emotional pains. The death of his mother increased the intensity of this resolve; further, it turned him against God and religion for taking away so needlessly and senselessly the good woman whom he had loved above all others.

By the time he was fourteen he encountered the superman philosophy of Nietzsche. Equipped to understand this philosophy intellectually, while at the same time too immature to digest or grasp its social implications, young Leopold garnered the idea that there were some few men born who were so much wiser and more gifted than all other men that they could rule the world. Everything they did was right for the reason that they had chosen to do it; the lower breeds of humans had been put upon the earth merely for the superman to lead and do with what he would. This philosophy gave direction to his escape: behind its golden portals he could shut out the manifold agonies of maladjusted youth, conquer his inferiority complex and find surcease from his introversion.

At that moment there was introduced into the Leopold household a governess who committed sexual malpractices on the boy, taught him also to commit sexual malpractices of a cunilingual nature. Several years of exposure to this perversion made any approach to a normal sexual relationship extremely difficult, completed Nathan's maladjustment. Nathan Leopold, Jr, developed an obsession which was the bastard offspring of a coalescing of his father's great wealth, the disturbance of his endocrine glands (one of which may have been pouring an abundance of female secretions into his blood stream), the Nietzschean philosophy and his exposure to the governess. He did not want to become a superman at all; he wanted to become a superwoman, a superwife, the female slave of the superman above him, a voluntary

247

and joyous slave who served out of the overwhelming love which he bore for the superman.

"He became obsessed with the idea of becoming a slave to some big, handsome, powerful king. He would be the abject one who would carry out the orders of the ruler and, if necessary, bear punishment in his stead."

In this state of mind he met Richard Loeb, tall, athletically built, with a beautiful face, alert, sparkling eyes, a brilliant mind, a hard ego and an indomitable will. Young Leopold had found his superman; he fell in love.

In speaking of his worship for Loeb, young Leopold said, "I can illustrate it to you by saying that I felt myself less than the dust beneath his feet. I am jealous of the food and drink that he takes because I cannot come as close to him as does the food and drink."

Babe, who never performed sexual acts with any other boy, implored Dickie Loeb to have relations with him. Loeb, who had been seeking eagerly for several years for a crony who would carry out his orders in committing crimes, decided that he had found the perfect mate in Leopold to help him plan and execute these crimes. He agreed to a homosexual relationship with Leopold, if Leopold would agree to a crime relationship with him. Leopold consented unquestioningly, and the compact was formed.

Richard Loeb was a good-looking boy; the defense physicians had been able to find nothing wrong with him. He too, blamed his downfall upon a governess, under whose control he remained for a number of years. Miss S. was an intelligent woman and a strict disciplinarian who loved young Dickie and wanted to make of him a fine, disciplined and well-educated man. She kept him long hours at his studies, was ever vigilant, made him read books in which he had no interest. Young Dickie liked to read cowboy stories and detective stories, was irked by the routine of duty imposed upon him. A bright and resourceful lad, he soon found that the easiest way to avoid the work was not to come into conflict with his governess over it but to trick her into thinking that the work had been done. He lied; he cheated; he dissembled; he deceived. Always he was clever enough to get away with it. This brought him double pleasure, for now he not only could indulge in his omnivorous reading of crime stories, but he could also congratulate himself on his cleverness. As the years passed he grew to enjoy deception for its own sake, ever sought for newer and more ingenious methods of achieving an object while concealing his intent. The boy had such a beautiful manner, seemed so honest and frank and open and lovable to those who met him, that they would not have believed him capable of duplicity. The youngster got such a thrill out of fooling people that he soon was telling lies, cheating and deceiving solely for the pleasure of the accomplishment.

Dickie, like Leopold, had a brilliant and retentive mind. He was graduated from the University of Michigan at seventeen, the youngest to be graduated. However, by the time he had reached college his psychotic personality was already well developed. One of his fraternity brothers tells of him, "Loeb spoke in a jerky manner, would argue on valueless points, pop into a room instead of walking in, then pop out again. He was regarded as childish. It was my duty to appoint seniors as mentors for freshmen, but I did not appoint Loeb because his judgment and conduct were not considered sufficiently wise to guide a freshman." While at the University of Michigan Loeb amused himself by pilfering from his fraternity brothers; he always enjoyed a theft the more if he could watch the victim's discomfort.

For several years before he met Leopold he had been reading almost nothing but crime stories; he had become obsessed with the idea that he could become a master criminal. This phantasm was in part developed to combat the influence of his suicidal tendencies, but more, was the result of the overwhelming wealth of the Loebs which engendered in Dickie the feeling that he was already a master because a millionaire, that the rules which applied to ordinary people did not apply to him. He believed himself so brilliant that he could never make a mistake in committing a crime, hence could never be caught; even if he were caught, his father's millions could buy him off.

Leopold was fourteen and Loeb thirteen when they entered their pact; for the next four years they contented themselves with such minor crimes as breaking windshields, starting small fires and petty thefts, such as a typewriter from Loeb's fraternity at Ann Arbor. All the while they were reading about crime and laying various plans for the commission of the perfect crime. Their relationship was a stormy one; both boys threatened to kill the other on numerous occasions. Although Leopold looked up to Loeb as the king and superman, he was actually the stronger of the two, just as the adoring wife is often the stronger in a marriage. He was stronger, more brilliant and far more psychotic. Darrow realized the extent of his psychopathy when he read a letter written by Leopold to Loeb when Leopold was only seventeen.

"When you came to my home this afternoon I expected either to break friendship with you or attempt to kill you unless you told me why you acted as you did yesterday. I am going to add a little more in an effort to explain my system of a Nietzschean philosophy with regard to you. It may not have occurred to you why a mere mistake in judgment on your part should be treated as a crime, when on the part of another it should not be so considered. Here are the reasons. In formulating a superman, he is, on account of certain superior qualities inherent in him, exempted from the ordinary laws which govern ordinary men. He is not liable for anything . . . except for the one crime that it is possible for him to commit—to make a mistake. Now obviously any code which conferred upon an individual privileges without also putting on him extraordinary responsibility would be unfair and bad. Therefore, an *Übermensch* is held to have committed a crime every time he errs in judgment—a mistake excusable in others."

In the spring of 1924 Loeb and Leopold were idle and looking for amusement. Leopold had passed his entrance examinations for the law school at Harvard, which he was planning to enter in the fall after he returned from a tour of Europe. Loeb was also planning to enter a law school in the fall. Both boys sensed that they were reaching the end of their relationship. Loeb, dissatisfied with the petty crimes of arson and thievery, longed to commit the great crime of the age, one which would go down in history as the perfect crime. Leopold had no desire to commit a murder, but for four years the boys had been pointing toward their perfect crime, discussing and planning it, day in and day out, until it was too late for him to withdraw.

That was why Bobby Franks lay in the morgue with his head bashed in; that was why Loeb and Leopold were behind prison bars; that was why Clarence Darrow was now speeding through the dark streets of Chicago at three in the morning.

The jailor flatly refused to allow Darrow to see the boys. "I have my orders from State's Attorney Crowe," he said.

All attempts to secure permission from Crowe over the telephone being futile, the five men climbed back into the car and drove to Darrow's office. Here Loeb's uncle wrote out a check for ten thousand dollars, the first act in tragicomedy which was to alienate a large public from Darrow and cause greater misunderstanding of his philosophy than any single factor in his stormy career.

Before nine in the morning Darrow was at State's Attorney Crowe's office, demanding that the two boys be bound over to the sheriff and sent to the county jail, where they would be free to confer with their relatives and attorneys. Up to this time Crowe had been holding them as his personal prisoners in a room in the Hotel La Salle and in the city jail, where his psychiatrists were examining them to secure evidence on their sanity. Crowe refused to release the boys. Darrow haled him before Judge Caverly.

"I realize these boys have rights," said Crowe, "and if the court will give me until two o'clock I will turn them over to their families and attorneys for as long a conference as they want."

"Now there's an extraordinary statement," exclaimed Darrow. "These boys are minors; they have rights."

"A cold-blooded, vicious murder has been committed," retorted Crowe, "and these boys have confessed to it."

"Another most astounding statement," said Darrow. "It matters not how cold-blooded the murder was; there is but one place for them to be held, in the county jail, in the custody of the sheriff. That question is not debatable."

Judge Caverly ordered the boys to the county jail. Within the hour Darrow was closeted with his two young clients, both of whom were immensely pleased and flattered to have defending them America's leading criminal lawyer.

Darrow saw that his first task would be to bring the two boys together again, for no sooner had they been caught than they had begun quarreling. Though the police had seen at once that Leopold was the softer of the two, they had also concluded that Loeb was the weaker. Though both boys had been grilled incessantly for twenty-four hours Leopold had kept up his high spirits and brightness of reply. Loeb had fainted, broken down and confessed. When Leopold learned that his king, his superman, his adored husband, had confessed, he exclaimed in disgust, "Tell Loeb I am surprised he was so weak as to confess in the first place and that I was surprised when he was so weak as to faint under the strain. He's just a weakling after all."

The first real sign that Loeb was breaking down, not merely in confessing, but in his inner spirit, was when he denied having done the actual killing of Bobby Franks. "I drove the car," said Loeb. "Leopold sat in back and hit Bobby over the head with the chisel." When photographers asked him to pose in the back of the murder car he refused, saying that he had driven the car and that he would have his picture taken only at the wheel. This reluctance to admit the actual killing was the only sign of remorse Loeb was ever to show publicly; later he confessed to one of Darrow's psychiatrists that he had struck the blow. To his mother and father he wrote from his jail cell a few days after he was caught:

DEAREST MOMPSIE AND POPSIE: *This thing is all too terrible. I have thought and thought about it, and even now I do* not seem to be able to understand it. I just cannot seem to figure out how it all came about. Of one thing I am certain, tho—and that is that I have no one to blame but myself. I am afraid that you two may try and put the blame upon your own shoulders, and I know that I alone am to blame. I never was frank with you—Mompsie and Popsie dear—and had you suspected anything and came and talked to me I would undoubtedly have denied everything and gone on just the same. Dr Glueck says that I was bent on destroying myself, and I believe he was right. I seem to have discarded all the finer things out of my life! Mompsie and Popsie dear—it may seem terrible, but in one way it is almost providential that I was caught, going on that way, confiding in no one— there is no telling how far I might have gone. This way at best I have a long prison sentence staring at me, but I am hopeful that someday I shall be free again and I really and truly think that I shall be able to do some good and at least live a much better life than I would have . . . otherwise.

I realize that there is always a chance of the death penalty. However, I am not worried and I assure you that although I know I never lived the part—I do know that should I have to pay the penalty, that I at least will die as becomes the son of such a wonderful father and mother as I know now more than ever that I have.

What I wanted to tell you is that I am not really so hard-hearted as I am appearing. Of course, dearest ones, I am afraid that my heart is not what it should be, else how could I have done what I did?

DICK

Although Loeb also had written to his mother, "Mompsie dear, in regard to coming down for the trial, it could not possibly do any good, and altho I should love to see you, I feel that it would only bring more sorrow to you and that we must all think of Dad first and foremost," for Darrow one of the more sorrowful twists of the tragedy was that Loeb's parents never came to visit him in jail. He at last went to the Loeb home and pleaded with the mother, "If you don't show mercy to your own son by at least visiting him in jail, how can you expect the judge to show mercy?" Mrs Loeb then called to see her son, but the father never attended a hearing, never again mentioned his son's name or allowed it to be mentioned in his presence.

When Leopold learned that Loeb had accused him of the slaying he cried bitterly, "Tell Loeb for me that it makes no difference which of us did the actual killing. Tell him that he should not forget that my repugnance to violence is such that I could not have killed Robert. Tell him that my one regret is that I find him so weak as to accuse me and that I know the reason. He thinks that by proving me the actual slayer he will eventually go free. Tell him that I know the law and that I am merely amused by his flourishings. We are both principals in the first degree, and—there is no forgiveness!"

Darrow knew that their further quarreling would seriously injure their defense. He talked to them quietly and earnestly for several hours. At the end of this time Loeb sang out, "We're both in for the same ride, Babe, so we might as well ride together."

Leopold turned around and looked straight into the eyes of Loeb. "Yes, Dickie, we have quarreled before and made up; now we are at the homestretch of the greatest gauntlet we will ever have to run. It is right that we should go along together."

Now that he had the two boys friendly again, Darrow asked them to retrace the crime for him, leaving out not the slightest detail, so that he might be in full possession of the facts that had already been assembled by the prosecution.

The plan to commit a murder had not been sufficient to satisfy Loeb; he also had wanted to commit a kidnaping and collect ransom money. In this way they would be committing the most difficult and complicated of all combinations of crimes, and while the world was searching for the victim, whom it did not know to be already dead, they could be holding the ransom bills and gloating over the success of their accomplishment.

Their first task had been to select a victim. Since neither had any physical courage they planned to kidnap a small boy. They considered in turn abducting Loeb's younger brother, then the grandson of Julius Rosenwald, then a chum by the name of Richard Rubel. They abandoned the idea of killing the brother because in the hour of trouble Dickie would not be able to get away from his family to collect the ransom money; they abandoned the idea of kidnaping Rosenwald's grandson because as Rosenwald was president of Sears, Roebuck and Company, it might hurt the family business; and they abandoned the idea of young Rubel because they had heard his father was a tightwad and in all probability would not come across with the cash.

They decided to set a date for their crime and let circumstances name the victim. Leopold wrote a melodramatic ransom letter on the typewriter they had stolen six months before from Loeb's fraternity house. They opened a bank account under a false name to finance their operations and established credit at a rent-a-car company. Then they began making trips on an Illinois Central train and throwing a package off the observation platform to establish a safe spot for collecting the ransom.

On the twenty-first of May the boys rented a sedan, bought a chisel, a rope and hydrochloric acid. Their plan was to strangle their victim, with each of the boys pulling one end end of the rope so they would be equally responsible. Then they drove to the exclusive Harvard Preparatory School just across the street from the Leopold home. They spied a likely victim in the yard, but when this boy suddenly ran away they settled upon fourteen-year-old Robert Franks, a cousin of Loeb's, whom they enticed into the car under the pretext of discussing a new tennis racket.

In the broad daylight of a well-traveled Chicago street, only a few feet from Leopold's home, Loeb brought his chisel down on the head of the Franks boy. Blood spurted, and he fell unconscious. Loeb pulled the boy onto the floor of the back seat, struck him over the head with the chisel three times more, then wrapped his body in Leopold's lap robe.

Leopold groaned, "O God! I didn't know it would be like this."

They then headed their car through Jackson Park, came out on the Midway and drove for some twenty miles through crowded streets, surrounded on every side by automobiles, streetcars and pedestrians. Knowing that they would have to wait until darkness before they could safely dispose of the body, they stopped at a little restaurant for a sandwich, then drove down the road toward Hammond. At a desolate spot they parked their car, carried the body of young Franks some two hundred feet to a culvert by the side of the Pennsylvania Railroad tracks. They stripped the boy of his clothing, after which Leopold shoved him into the culvert, where they figured he would not be discovered for years. They put young Franks' clothing in the car and started back for town. Not wanting his family to worry about him, Leopold telephoned home to tell them he would be late. The boys stopped at a restaurant for their dinner, then drove to the Loeb house, where they stuffed Franks' clothing into a furnace and burned it. Young Franks' shoes, the buckle from his belt, his jewelry and the bloodstained lap robe they buried in the country, then returned to the Leopold house to wash the bloodstains off the floor of the car.

At midnight Loeb addressed his ransom letter to the Frankses' house while Leopold telephoned to say, "Your boy has been kidnaped. He is safe. Don't worry. Instructions will follow later." They mailed the ransom letter special delivery. The following morning they drove to the Illinois Central depot, where Loeb bought the same ticket he had bought so many times before. He went to the observation car and put into the telegram slot of the stationery desk a letter telling Franks' father the exact spot near the Champion factory where he was to throw his packet of money.

Leopold in the meanwhile telephoned the father, instructing him to take the Yellow Cab that would be at his door and drive to a certain drugstore, where he would receive further orders by telephone. He then ordered a Yellow Cab to go to the Frankses' house. Loeb got off the train, rejoined Leopold in the depot; they next drove slowly uptown, giving Mr Franks sufficient time to reach the designated drugstore. When their watches told them that Mr Franks would have barely enough time to catch the train they telephoned the drugstore to tell him where he must look for further instructions. That task done, they would drive out to the spot near the Champion factory and wait for their ransom money to be thrown from the observation platform. If the train were even one minute late they would drive away, for that would mean that Mr Franks had communicated with the police.

But something had gone wrong: Mr Franks was not at the drugstore when they telephoned. They telephoned twice, three times, until they saw that it was now too late; the father would no longer have time to make the train. Wondering what they must do next to collect their ransom money and thus complete their perfect crime, they stepped out into the street. Staring them in the face were newspaper extras with huge headlines announcing that Bobby Franks' body had been found. A workman on a maintenance crew had seen a bare foot sticking out of the culvert and had summoned the police. Within a very few hours another member of the maintenance crew picket up a pair of horn-rimmed spectacles not far from the culvert. A Chicago optical firm identified the special rims, giving the police the names of three persons who had them. At their first call they found a woman with her glasses on her nose; on the second call they found that the man was in Europe; on their third call Nathan Leopold, Jr, who knew that the officials were in possession of a pair of horn-rimmed spectacles, went to the door to find the police looking for him. Loeb, who had spent the intervening hours feverishly discussing the crime, helping newspapermen locate the drugstore where Mr Franks was to have received his final instructions, was with Leopold when the police arrived. Both boys were taken to the Hotel La Salle where Crowe was waiting. Leopold admitted the glasses were his but maintained that he had frequently gone to the murder spot on his ornithological expeditions and must have lost them there a few Sundays before.

"Do you think you should be released?" he was asked.

"No, it would be criminal on the part of the police to let

me go now, on account of the glasses. I thought all along that the glasses were the best clue . . . to follow, never thinking they were mine. I didn't know I had lost them, but now I am sure I did and was on one of my many bird trips to that vicinity. I think the last time I was there was on the Sunday preceding the Franks murder."

Leopold's alibi, which he and Loeb had agreed upon after the killing, was that on the evening of the kidnaping he and Dickie had taken two girls riding in Lincoln Park in his car.

After Leopold had stuffed young Franks' body into the culvert he had called to Loeb to pick up his coat and bring it to the car. The glasses, which Leopold very seldom used or carried with him, fell out of the pocket when Loeb picked up the coat. At that instant the perfect crime had begun to disintegrate; when the Leopold chauffeur told the police that Nathan's car had been in the garage on the day of the murder and that the next morning he had seen the two boys trying to wash red stains off the floor of a strange car, the perfect crime, and Loeb along with it, collapsed.

By noon, when Darrow took leave of his two clients and went into the warm June sunshine, the extras were already on the street, heralding his entrance into the case. He had known the night before, riding downtown in the Loeb limousine, that people would be resentful, but he was unprepared for the avalanche of protest that broke over his head. Though Chicago has suffered many venal crimes in its turbulent history, the fate of Bobby Franks sickened, frightened and stunned every family. The Franks boy had been so young and small and innocent, so brutally murdered, that nearly every mother and father of Chicago felt they had lost a son under the most heartbreaking of circumstances. Most Chicagoans wanted Loeb and Leopold hanged instantly as object lessons, so that other children would be safe. When they learned that Clarence Darrow was going to defend the two murderers their indignation rose to a blazing intensity that he had never before savored even in the bitterest of his class-war cases. Knowing his reputation, his powers, the city became convulsed with fear that he might get them off. Sweet and gentle elderly ladies were to desecrate Darrow's memory after his death for what they considered his defense of the murder itself.

W. R. Kellogg, a newspaper owner of Nebraska and a dear friend of Darrow's, says, "More of his followers renounced Darrow because of his defense of Loeb and Leopold than for any other case in his entire history. Very few of his stanchest friends stood by. Lawyers said, 'He is disgracing the criminal lawyers of the country,' while criminals said, 'If this Darrow can get Loeb and Leopold off we can commit any crime we like; all we have to do is to get Darrow to defend us, and we'll beat the rap.' The practice of criminal law in America fell into its greatest disfavor and disrepute in decades."

The fact that the country felt Loeb and Leopold should have no defense once they had confessed was only part of the people's objection to Darrow's entering the case; they knew that the combined wealth of the Loeb and Leopold families was between fifteen and twenty million dollars. The country as a whole, including the poorer classes for whom Darrow had given so much of his time without compensation, jumped to the bitter decision that he had taken the case in order to earn the single largest fee in the history of American criminal law.

When reporters stopped Darrow and Loeb's uncle on the steps of the courthouse that afternoon one of them said, "It's true, isn't it, Mr Darrow, that you are to receive a million-dollar fee for defending Loeb and Leopold?" Darrow, hearing this rumor for the first time, simply gaped in astonishment, but Loeb only smiled. The story was broadcast throughout the land that Darrow was to receive a million dollars.

Folks said, "Darrow has sold out. He finally got his price and turned traitor—but who can blame him for a cool million bucks? If those were poor boys they'd be hung on the spot. Darrow is a hypocrite; all his life he's screamed that crime is the result of poverty, but when it's the sons of millionaires that commit a horrible murder he turns his back on his teachings and grabs the chance to defend them for the dough he can get."

The following afternoon when Ruby went to her favorite department store to buy a new dress to wear at the trial and picked out one of her usual inexpensive models, the saleslady said, "Oh, Mrs Darrow, you'll want something better now that your husband is earning a million dollars for one case." Mrs Darrow at last had to trade in places where she was unknown and have the packages sent to the Midway flat in the name of Marie Thompson, her maid.

Realizing at once that this rumor would injure his defense, Darrow issued a flat denial that he was to receive any such sum of money. "No sum has been agreed upon," he stated, "or even discussed. We will have the Bar Association determine the fee at the end of the trial in order that it shall be fair to everyone."

No one believed him.

While the fury was raging about him Darrow was trying to think his way through an almost impossible situation. There was only one thing of which he was certain. These two boys whom he had taken under his wing and for whose lives he alone would be responsible had been mentally ill for a number of years. After their arrest and confession their illness had accelerated.

"The killing was an experiment," Leopold had told him. "It is just as easy to justify such a death as it is to justify an entomologist in killing a beetle on a pin." He had asked for all the newspapers and gloated over his notoriety. "It is unusual for one to see his name adorning the front pages," he observed. "But I suppose that is the only way that I shall ever be able to break into print."

Loeb declared, "This thing will be the making of me. I'll spend a few years in jail and I'll be released. I'll come out to a new life."

Surely anyone could see that these boys were mentally ill, thought Darrow. Then why should the state want to hang them? They would not hang two boys who had committed irrational acts while in an epileptic seizure or the ravages of a physical fever. He must save the lives of these two boys, and he must save Chicago from indulging itself in another of its recurrent blood lusts.

But if he declared them not guilty because insane he would have to try the case before a jury which could not escape the hysteria and pressure which would declare that because the boys had brilliant minds, were able to think fast and talk fast, because they were millionaires' sons who had had every opportunity, they must be sane and hence responsible for their acts and hence executed for the protection of society.

"I know perfectly well," he observed, "that where responsibility is divided by twelve it is easy to say: 'Away with him!' "

No, even he could not risk a jury trial. He could not risk failing to prove the boys insane within the legal framework of that term. He had far better plead them guilty and throw them upon the mercy of the court.

"We did plead guilty before your honor," he was to admit during the trial, "because we were afraid to submit our cause to a jury. I have found that experience with life tempers one's emotions and makes him more understanding of his fellow man. I am aware that as one grows older he is less critical; he is inclined to make some allowance for his fellow man. I am aware that a court has more experience, more judgment and more kindliness than a jury. Your honor, if these boys hang, you must do it. You can never explain that the rest overpowered you. It must be by your own deliberate, cool, premeditated act. It was not a kindness to you. We placed this responsibility on your shoulders because we were mindful of the rights of our clients, and we were mindful of the unhappy families who have done no wrong."

But what right had he to ask for mercy from the court? What defense could he contrive which would persuade a judge to have mercy on killers who had shown no mercy? Well, there was only one possible defense, the inevitable defense: the boys were mentally diseased and hence were not responsible for their acts. He knew that mental illness had never been allowed as a defense in American courts; men were either sane or insane, one hundred per cent or nothing, with no shadings or gradations allowed in between. But this kind of reasoning was barbaric and ignorant, out of line with everything that medical science and psychiatry had evolved. He would have to demonstrate to the court that mental illness was a mitigation, and therein would lie a great opportunity.

From his decades of association and friendship with criminals he knew that a majority of them were either emotionally unbalanced or mentally ill. Over the years he had come to the point of view that the punishment meted out to a miscreant should be based not on the crime itself, but on the degree and curability of the mental illness of the offender. Prisons should become curative institutions for the mentally ill, just as hospitals were curative institutions for the physically ill. If an individual who had committed a major crime could be completely cured by psychiatrical treatment of the illness that had caused the crime, he should be returned to his family and society when it was entirely safe to do so. However, if another man committed only a minor crime but it was found that there was no way to cure his mental illness, even after years of scientific and medical treatment, then that man should be kept away from society all the days of his life. This would be true justice; this would be the civilized way to treat individuals who run afoul of the legal structure.

Not guilty because mentally ill! Mental illness, the halfway house between sanity and insanity, in which transpired so much maladjustment and frustration, so much unhappiness and desperation, in which were committed so many seemingly incomprehensible acts. The world did not blame or punish people who become physically ill; then why should they blame people who became mentally ill when that mental illness was contributed to so largely by physical factors: nerves, glands, secretions, chemical composition. Only two years before he had written a chapter for *Crime, Its Cause and Treatment* called "Responsibility for Crime," which stated his biological attitude with which from his earliest days he had tried to replace the God-religion-moralistic creed of condemnation and punishment. To an astounding degree the chapter applied to and explained the Loeb-Leopold crime.

"It is only lately that we are beginning to find out anything about the origin and nature of man," he had written. "Laws have come down to us from old customs and folkways based on primitive ideas of man's origin, capacity and responsibility. . . .

"The old indictments charged that 'John Smith, being a wicked, malicious and evil-disposed person, not having the fear of God before his eyes but being moved and seduced by the instigation of the devil, etc.' It followed, of course, that John Smith should be punished or made to suffer, for he had purposely brought all the evil on himself. The old idea is still the foundation of the world's judgment of men in court and out. Of course this idea leaves no room for mercy and understanding. Neither does it leave any chance to give the criminal the proper treatment for his defects, which might permit him to lead a normal life. . . .

"That man is the product of heredity and environment and that he acts as his machine responds to outside stimuli and nothing else seem amply proven by the evolution and history of man. Man's every action is caused by motive. Whether his action is wise or unwise the motive was at least strong enough to move him. If two or more motives pulled in opposite directions he could not have acted from the weakest but must have obeyed the strongest. This is not a universe where acts result from chance. Law is everywhere. Every process of nature and life is a continuous sequence of cause and effect. There is a cause for the eternal revolution of the earth around the sun, for the succession of seedtime and harvest, for growth and decay and for the thoughts and actions of man.

"Before any progress can be made in dealing with crime the world must fully realize that . . . all punishment for the purpose of causing suffering or growing out of hatred is cruel and antisocial; that, however much society may feel the need of confining the criminal, it must first of all understand that the act had an all-sufficient cause for which the individual was in no way responsible and must find the cause of his conduct and, so far as possible, remove the cause."

Before the Loeb-Leopold trial Clarence Darrow was modestly famous; through this trial he was to become immeasurably notorious. While his defense could be important for the furthering of the science of criminology, it could not have the far-reaching social implications of his important appeals for labor and civil rights. Because of the weirdness of the crime, the wealth of the participants, the fascination with which people are drawn to the death appeal of a murder, he was to remain best known by the general public for the Loeb-Leopold case. This did not displease him; the gods with one of their occasional kindnesses had given him the opportunity to bring his work against capital punishment into focus.

Keeping his defense plans secret, he made his first moves to quiet the public outcry against the two boys. He sent men to mingle in the crowds in the Loop and ask people whether they thought Loeb and Leopold should hang. Sixty per cent of those questioned said, "Yes." He then had the fathers of Loeb and Leopold issue a letter to the press saying that there would be no attempt to free the boys, only to prove them insane, and that they would agree to have Darrow's fee set by the Bar Association. After the newspapers had printed this letter the men went back to the Loop to ask the same question and found that sixty per cent of the people were now willing to accept life imprisonment for the culprits.

Darrow found himself caught up in a fever of preparation, surrounding himself with books on psychiatry and endocrinology. "During that concentrated stretch of the hot summer," says Ruby, ". . . we were routed out of bed at all hours of the night; they would come ringing and bursting in upon us with fresh rumors, with bright ideas to discuss, with strangers to meet and to talk with, not infrequently remaining until daylight. . . ."

There was a convention of American psychiatrists meeting in Philadelphia at the time. Darrow sent Ben Bachrach there to hire the best men he could find. Bachrach engaged, among a number of others, Dr Benjamin Glueck, former psychiatrist at Sing Sing Prison; Dr William A. White, director of St Elizabeth's Government Hospital at Washington, D.C.; Dr William J. Healy, head of the Judge Baker Foundation for Psychiatric Research in Boston, Massachusetts; Dr Harold S. Hulbert, Chicago neurologist. All of these men had done extensive research and had published authoritative books in their field. They came to Chicago when their convention was over and began to diagnose the young slayers. Loeb and Leopold enjoyed these psychiatrical interviews. Leopold insisted that he didn't care what happened to him during the trial so long as he was allowed to maintain his dignity; that he would not mind going to prison for life, just so long as he could take a complete scrapbook of clippings with him. Loeb recited the gruesome details of the crime matter-of-factly, showing neither remorse, regret nor compassion.

On July 21, 1924, Darrow astounded the state's attorney and the country by pleading his boys guilty. "We dislike to throw this burden upon this court or any court," he said, "but we feel that we must. We ask that the court permit us to offer evidence as to the mental condition of these young men to show the degree of responsibility that they had. We wish to offer evidence in mitigation of the punsihment."

The state's attorney objected on the grounds that since Darrow had pleaded the boys guilty he could not at the same time try to prove their insanity. Judge Caverly declared he would listen to the evidence in mitigation.

Darrow reached the courtroom shortly after ten o'clock on the morning of July twenty-third, to find thousands of people jamming the sidewalk and street trying to get in. When at last he had succeeded in shouldering his way into the courtroom he was pleased to find that with the exception of the young girls who had managed to worm their way in to get a look at handsome Dickie Loeb, most of the spectators were outstanding lawyers and judges attending what they considered would be one of the most interesting and dramatic trials of their age.

Loeb and Leopold were brought in, both fastidiously dressed and barbered. When one of the reporters commented that they had taken a great deal of care regarding their appearance Loeb replied "Of course, this is our show. The public must not be cheated." He flirted with the pretty girls throughout the hearing. Leopold commented, "With our looks and Darrow's brains we'll get along all right." He maintained that he had considerable interest in observing himself as a murderer. Both boys enjoyed themselves so thoroughly that Darrow perceived they had been successful in accomplishing their purpose: they had achieved immortality by committing the perfect crime: a crime so perfectly without motive or justification that their names would never be forgotten. From the expressions on their bright, shining faces Darrow saw that they were neither displeased nor unhappy over their bargain with immortality.

The struggle over the lives of Richard Loeb and Nathan Leopold revolved about two battle cries:

"Mitigation is a defense!" reiterated Darrow.

"The real defense in this case," replied Crowe, "is Clarence Darrow's dangerous philosophy of life!"

In this instance Darrow's dangerous philosophy of life was his belief in psychiatry, the study of man's mental and neurological disturbances and their effect on conduct. Prior to the World War of 1914-18 psychiatry had been both neglected and ridiculed as a curative branch of medicine. Its practitioners had been called "nut doctors." Those suffering from mental and nervous disturbances were sent to insane asylums or sanatoriums or were endured at home by long-suffering families. But when thousands of American soldiers returned shell-shocked and suffering from obscure mental disturbances, when the generation that grew up during the war and post-war hysterias found itself with a high number of disrupted conduct patterns, psychiatry came into its own.

The psychiatrists had done magnificent work; they had achieved thousands of cures; the practice of their craft had at last taken its proper place in the practice of medicine. But the general public still distrusted psychiatrists, or alienists, as they most often were called, when they went into court to testify, for apparently these men managed to find medical justification for whichever side was paying their fee, or at least they were not hired unless they agreed with those who did the hiring.

Darrow had said at the opening of the case that he would not try to prove his boys insane but only mentally diseased. The country asked itself, "What is the real difference between the two?" State's Attorney Crowe bawled, "They denied that their clients are insane and are now spending tens of thousands of dollars to get them off on the grounds of insanity." Over and over the state asked with sarcasm, "Just how insane can a sane man be without being so insane that he needs a jury to determine just how insane he is?"

Darrow now led his defense psychiatrists through their testimony in such a clear and simple fashion that the lay public was able to understand most of what went on in the Chicago courtroom, digesting their first comprehensive course in mental illness as a base for crime.

Dr Bernard Glueck of Sing Sing, whom Loeb maintained was the only psychiatrist who understood him, said about Dickie Loeb, "I was amazed at the absolute absence of any signs of normal feeling. Loeb is suffering from a disordered personality . . . primarily in a profound pathological discord between his intellectual and emotional life. We might designate it as a split personality. This boy, while capable of orienting himself intellectually, is quite incapable of endowing these surroundings with an adequate emotion."

Dr William Healy said of Leopold, "To my mind this crime . . . was possible only because Leopold had these abnormal mental trends with the typical feelings and ideas of a par-anoiac personality. He needed these feelings and ideas sup-plemented by what Loeb could give him. There is no reason why he should not have committed the crime with his diseased notion. Anything he wanted to do was right, even kidnaping and murder. There was no place for sympathy and feeling to play any normal part. He had an established pathological personality before he met Loeb, but probably his activities would have taken other directions except for this chance association. He is right; the world is wrong. . . . Leopold
263

shows little disgust at jail surroundings. His main concern seems to be whether or not reporters say the right thing about him."

Dr W. A. White testified that both Leob and Leopold had an infantile emotional make-up and hence were not normal, that Loeb had confessed that he had lived his life out and had come to its logical conclusion. "I do not believe the Franks homicide can be explained without an understanding of the relation between Loeb and Leopold." He, too, maintained that Leopold would not have entered it alone, because he had no criminalistic tendencies. Loeb would never have gone as far as he did without Leopold to give him that final push."

Speaking somewhat satirically, the New York *Times* characterized Darrow's defense at this point as "a killing in response to an irresistible mandate of two coincidentally insane impulses."

After a number of days of testimony on "diseased motivation," "paranoiac and pathological personalities," "dual life," "abnormal needs," "nervous instability," "subordination of normal feelings and emotions," "profound disorder of judgment," "continuation of childhood fantasies into mature life," "split personality," and "pathological discord between intellectual and emotional life," Darrow led the doctors through their evidence on the endocrine glands, the pathology of internal gland secretions and their effect upon the nervous system. Crowe fought him stubbornly all the way, putting on the stand doctors to testify that "the general status of knowledge concerning the endocrine glands might almost 'be compared to the interior of Africa before Stanley went there.' There are many definite facts known, but they are scattered, disordered, unrelated." Alvin Sellers, in his reportorial book on the case, says, "Dr H. S. Hulbert and Dr Karl M. Bowman submitted a report which covered several thousand typewritten pages. It included physical, neurological, educational, social and mental studies and included researches in the physical chemistry and in the glandular constitution of the defendants." The evidence offered by the other psychiatrists amounted to several thousand pages more.

Each dawn throngs appeared in the street to find places in the courtroom. The more extreme sensation mongers were disappointed, however, when the testimony on the homosexual relations between the boys was taken behind the closed doors of the judge's chamber. The amounts of money wagered on the outcome of the hearing climbed into the millions. Sob sisters poured out their hearts in sticky black ink. Leading jurists throughout the country published their opinions on the legal status of the culprits. Criminologists had a field day lecturing up and down the length of the land. Loeb and Leopold received quantities of fan mail. One open-faced post card, addressed to "Loeb-Leopold murderers, County Jail," read, "Don't worry, boys, money and a slick lawyer can fix anything in America."

There was sitting in a cell in the county jail, waiting to be hanged in only six weeks' time for the murder of a policeman, a nineteen-year-old boy by the name of Bernard Grant, son of a poor man, who had been forced out to work at fourteen. The predicament of young Grant did more to injure Darrow's chances to save the lives of his clients than anything that was to happen in the courtroom. The newspapers and the public at large cried, "Have we one law for the rich and another for the poor? If Grant must hang, why should not Loeb and Leopold hang? Grant's crime was far less vicious and dangerous than Loeb's and Leopold's, for it was unpremeditated." Darrow could only say unofficially, "It would be as wrong to hang Grant as these two young boys. We must save Grant's life. We must save the lives of all minors who commit murders."

As with most of his important trials, this one took place in the intense heat of summer. Cartoons of him "strumming his galluses" appeared in every paper, giving to the country its most clearly limned portrait: a man in shirt sleeves and suspenders, pacing the courtroom, his thumbs holding the suspenders under his armpits, his big round shoulders hunched forward, a now-thinning wisp of hair hanging down over his eyes, his face lined and seamed, his eyes dark and brooding and hurt: the picture of a plain man, a man who knew the sufferings of others, who said, "I may hate the sin but never the sinner."

The prosecution then began its attempt to show aggravation. State's Attorney Crowe based his case on three points: first, the boys were entirely sane; second, their motivation for kidnaping the Franks boy had been the ten thousand dollars in ransom which they needed to pay their gambling debts, and third, that they had abused him homosexually and then had been forced to kill him to cover their attack.

As many alienists took the stand to declare Loeb and Leopold sane and responsible as had testified that the boys were mentally ill and irresponsible. Dr Hugh T. Patrick claimed that he found no evidence of mental disease in the boys, that they were not without emotional reactions. Dr Harold D. Singer stated that a paranoiac personality did not necessarily mean a diseased mind. Dr William O. Krohn testified that the boys had both health and integrity of memory, that they were perfectly oriented as to time, space and social relations. Loeb and Leopold sat with stolid, unchanging faces as they heard the witnesses proclaim them sane. Leopold rested his elbows on a chair arm and cushioned his chin with his hand. Loeb, hands in his lap, stared at the witness. Occasionally they held whispered conversations.

Darrow's outbursts at the testimony were frequent and savage, not only because the accusations of sanity hurt his clients but because he believed these doctors represented a past age of psychiatrical medicine, which considered no one insane unless he were a raving maniac. He spent hours and days cross-examining the prosecution's physicians in an attempt to bring not only to Judge Caverly but to the country at large a conception of the new and crucially important science of psychology, which was revealing hundreds of subtle forms of unbalance which fell short of insanity.

For almost a month the battle raged between expert and cross-examiner, till nerves were frayed. Epithets flew between Crowe and Darrow. Crowe accused Darrow of defending the boys only for the large fee involved. He accused him of preaching doctrines of anarchy, saying that if Judge Caverly put his official seal of approval upon Darrow's anarchy "a greater blow has been struck to our institutions than by a hundred, aye a thousand murders."

Darrow retaliated by calling Crowe a "hanging" state's attorney. When Crowe said the greater part of the defense psychiatrists' testimony made him laugh Darrow countered with, "Yes, you would laugh at anything, except possibly a hanging, and I think maybe you would laugh at the hanging of these boys." Crowe retorted, "We have heard considerable about split personalities in this case. I was somewhat surprised to find that my old friend, who has acted as counsel and nursemaid in this case for two babes who were wandering in dreamland, also was possessed of a split personality. I had heard so much of the milk of human kindness that ran out in streams from his large heart that I was surprised to know he had so much poison in his system also."

As in most American criminal cases, the taking of testimony was only the preliminary to the joining of the issue which would result from the final pleas of counsel and would settle the fate of the boys. Assistant State's Attorneys Thomas Marshall and Joseph P. Savage made the first pleas for the state, offering into evidence cases in which boys, seventeen, eighteen and nineteen, had been hung in Cook County. State's Attorney Crowe made a strong and able plea in which he maintained, "The law says in extreme circumstances death shall be the penalty. If I were in the legislature I might vote against such a law. I don't know. But as a judge I have no right to put aside that law. I have no right to defeat the will of the people, as expressed by the legislature of Illinois. I have no right to be a judicial anarchist, even if Clarence Darrow is an anarchistic advocate." He then went on to say, "Darrow says that hanging does not stop murder. I think he is mistaken," and attempted to prove that public executions had always lessened the number of murders committed in Chicago, just as all punishment deterred others from committing crimes.

He repeated his theory that the Franks boy had been kidnaped for the sake of the ransom money, that the testimony about the glandular structure and secretions was unscientific, that the king-and-slave fantasy was "a pure figment of the imagination of the defense," that the two clever killers had fooled and deluded the psychiatrists, that the psychiatrists were quacks, that the murder was planned logically and sanely by two young boys with criminal instincts, and that "there is nothing the matter with them mentally. The only fault is the trouble with their moral sense, and that is not a defense in a criminal case." He endeavored to show that the age of the boys did not lessen their responsibility. "Mr Darrow is a student of criminology; he has written a book on it and he says the criminal age, the time when crimes are committed, is between the ages of sixteen and twenty-four. Your honor and I know that the average age is twenty-two. If we are going to punish crime and by the punishment stop it, and the criminal age is between seventeen and twenty-four, how can we punish if the age is a defense?"

"Indeed," murmured Darrow. "How can you?"

Crowe caused an explosion by emphasizing certain testimony that had been given to the effect that Leopold had claimed he would get off because the case would be tried before a "friendly judge." Judge Caverly called the "friendly judge" suggestion a "cowardly and dastardly assault upon the integrity of this court. This court will not be intimidated by anybody at any time or place, so long as he occupies this position."

The state's attorney then concluded his plea by charging, as had so many prosecutors before him, that Clarence Darrow was responsible for the crime being tried. He went back to Darrow's speech before the prisoners at Joliet to demonstrate Darrow's anarchism by quoting him as saying, "I do not believe in the least in crime. I do not believe that there is any sort of distinction between the real moral condition in and out of jail. The people here can no more help being here than the people outside can avoid being outside. I do not believe people are in jail because they deserve to be. They

267

are in jail simply because they cannot avoid it on account of circumstances which are entirely beyond their control and for which they are in no way responsible."

He called on Judge Caverly not to succumb to Darrow's anarchism but to do his duty, protect the state and pass upon the boys the death sentence.

On the day Darrow was to make his final plea the New York *Times* reported that "people stormed the courtroom; women fainted in the mob that came to hear him." He spoke for three days; many of those who listened thought it the finest single plea of his life for love, mercy and tolerance, even greater than his appeal before the Anthracite Coal Commission two decades before. After his first day of pleading the newspaper reporters named him the Old Lion, a name he was to retain to the end of his days.

"When the public is interested and demands a punishment it thinks of only one punishment, and that is death. . . . I have seen a court urged almost to the point of threats to hang two boys, in the face of science, in the face of experience and all the better and more humane thought of the age.

"Ninety unfortunate human beings have been hanged by the neck until dead in the city of Chicago in our history. We would not have civilization except for those ninety that were hanged, and if we cannot make it ninety-two we will have to shut up shop. . . . I know that in the last ten years three hundred and forty people have been indicted for murder in the city of Chicago and have pleaded guilty, and only one has been hanged! And my friend who is prosecuting this case deserves the honor of that hanging while he was on the bench. But his victim was forty years old. Of ninety men hanged in Illinois since its beginning, not one person under twenty-three was ever hanged upon a plea of guilty—not one.

"'They say we come here with a preposterous plea for mercy. When did any plea for mercy become preposterous in any tribunal in all the universe? Mr Savage tells this court that if these boys are hanged there will be no more boys like these. Mr Savage is an optimist. If these two boys die on the scaffold, which I can never bring myself to imagine, if they do die on the scaffold the details of this will be spread over the world. Every newspaper in the United States will carry a full account. Every newspaper of Chicago will be filled with the gruesome details. It will enter every home and every family. Will it make men better or make men worse? How many will be colder and crueler for it? How many will enjoy the details? And you cannot enjoy human suffering without being affected for the worse. What influence will it have upon the millions of men who will read it? What influence will it have upon the millions of women who will read it, more sensitive, more impressionable, than men? What influence will it have upon the infinite number of children who will devour its details as Dickie Loeb has enjoyed reading detective stories?. . . .

"I am not pleading so much for these boys as I am for the infinite number of others to follow, those who perhaps cannot be as well defended as these have been, those who may go down in the tempest without aid. It is of them I am thinking and for them I am begging of this court not to turn backward toward the barbarous and cruel past."

Throughout the trial Loeb and Leopold had been calm and composed. Leopold had taken notes as though he were in a classroom; both boys had smiled and laughed frequently during the proceedings. While State's Attorneys Crowe, Savage and Marshall had depicted them as the vilest humans ever to crawl on the face of the earth the boys had kept a perfect composure, regarding their assailants with curiosity. But when Clarence Darrow pictured the tragedy and suffering that had befallen the three families because of their crime Richard Loeb and Nathan Leopold, Jr, became two desperately frightened and sorrowful little boys. The New York *Times* reports, "The appeal proved too much for the self-control of the culprits. . . . Loeb flicked tears from his cheeks and Leopold stumbled from the courtroom with bowed head. So overcome was the latter that he struck blindly against a partition of the narrow entrance to the 'bull pen.' The impact drove him sideways, but he did not raise his head. With extended arms he plowed past the bailiffs and fairly plunged into the elevator that was waiting to convey him to the approach of Cook County's Bridge of Sighs."

On the last day of his plea Darrow's voice faltered frequently, yet every syllable was clear in the terrible silence of the courtroom. Judge Caverly leaned forward, his eyes riveted on the speaker.

"Crime has its cause. Perhaps all crimes do not have the same cause, but they all have some cause. And people today are seeking to find out the cause. Scientists are studying it; criminologists are investigating it, but we lawyers go on . . . punishing and hanging and thinking that by general terror we can stamp out crime.

"If a doctor were called on to treat typhoid fever he would probably try to find out what kind of milk or water the patient drank and perhaps clean out the well so that no one else could get typhoid from the same source. But if a lawyer were called on to treat a typhoid patient he would give him thirty days in jail, and then he would think that nobody else would ever dare to take typhoid. If the patient got well in fifteen days he would be kept until his time was up; if the disease was worse at the end of thirty days the patient would be released because his time was out.

"I do not know how much salvage there is in these two boys. I hate to say it in their presence, but what is there to look forward to? I do not know but what your honor would be merciful if you tied a rope around their necks and let them die; merciful to them, but not merciful to civilization and not merciful to those who would be left behind.

"We placed our fate in the hands of a trained court, thinking that he would be more mindful and considerate than a jury. I cannot say how people feel. I have stood here for three months as one might stand at the ocean, trying to sweep back the tide. I hope the seas are subsiding and the wind is falling, and I believe they are, but I wish to make no false pretense to this court. The easy thing and the popular thing to do is to hang my clients. I know it. Men and women who do not think will applaud. The cruel and thoughtless will approve. It will be easy today, but in Chicago and reaching out over the length and breadth of the land, more and more fathers and mothers, the humane, the kind and the hopeful, who are gaining an understanding and asking questions not only about these poor boys but about their own—these will join in no acclaim at the death of my clients. These would ask that the shedding of blood be stopped and that the normal feelings of man resume their sway.

"But, your honor, what they shall ask may not count. . . . I am pleading for life, understanding, charity, kindness and the infinite mercy that considers all. I am pleading that we overcome cruelty with kindness and hatred with love. I know the future is on my side. You may hang these boys; you may hang them by the neck until they are dead. But in doing it you will turn your face toward the past. In doing it you are making it harder for every other boy who in ignorance and darkness must grope his way through the mazes which only childhood knows."

The Chicago *Herald-Examiner* told that "there was scarcely any telling where his voice had finished and where silence had begun. Silence lasted a minute, two minutes. His own eyes, dimmed by years of serving the accused, the oppressed, the weak, were not the only ones that held tears."

Two weeks were to go by while Judge Caverly studied the testimony and prepared his decision. Two weeks of impatient waiting on the part of the country, of downright agony for Clarence Darrow. He returned to his office, tried to work, but the Loeb-Leopold case had thrown his firm into chaos. For two interminable weeks he lived from hour to hour, breaking out in cold sweats during the day, awakening a dozen times during the night—while Judge Caverly received anonymous letters threatening his life if he did not sentence the boys to hang, and Loeb and Leopold received crank letters telling them that they would be killed on the way to prison if the judge failed to impose the death penalty. When the newspapers editorialized on the need for Judge Caverly to sentence the boys to hang, Darrow cried out in anguish:

"If these boys hang the United States might well vote murder indictments against the unjudicial agencies . . . who are trying to fix public opinion. It is not a question of the sanity or insanity of the two defendants that is at issue. It's a question of the insanity of the methods by which certain forces are seeking to direct public opinion to bloodshed without permitting the world to consider, impartially, the finding of the alienists."

On September tenth, the day upon which Judge Caverly had announced he would read his decision, Darrow closeted himself in his office and began pacing first back and forth, circling the desk in one direction, then in the other. When one of his partners went into the room he found Darrow chain-puffing cigarettes, standing limp and exhausted, with as distraught and stricken a look on his face as though it were his own two sons who stood in imminent danger of hearing themselves condemned to die on the scaffold.

At last word reached him that Judge Caverly was ready. The *Evening American* reported that, "the judge read his decision in a calm, low voice, while the two boys sat motionless in their chairs before him. Clarence Darrow, who made the supreme plea of his life to save them, rocked gently backward and forward in his tilted chair.

"The court is willing to recognize," said the judge, "that the careful analysis made of the life history of the defendants and of their present mental, emotional and ethical condition has been of extreme interest and is a valuable contribution to criminology."

He then read his decision: "The court is willing to meet his responsibilities. It would have been the path of least resistance to impose the extreme penalty of the law. In choosing imprisonment instead of death the court is moved chiefly by the consideration of the age of the defendants. This determination appears to be in accordance with the progress of criminal law all over the world and with the dictates of enlightened humanity. The records of Illinois show only two cases of minors who were put to death by legal process—to which number the court does not feel inclined to make an addition.

"Life imprisonment may not, at the moment, strike the public imagination as forcibly as would death by hanging, but to the offenders, particularly of the type they are, the prolonged suffering of years of confinement may well be the severer form of retribution and expiation."

A reporter for the Chicago *Evening American* gives a touching picture of the finale of this great hearing. "As the judge delivered his sentence Leopold listened unblinkingly. Loeb winked his eyes, and a terrified look crept into them. Judge Caverly finished. Nobody said a word. The courtroom was silent as death. Nobody seemed to know what to do. Then the bailiffs tugged at the boys, and Dickie rose, the puzzled, frightened look still on his face; Nathan, the iron-hearted philosopher, jumped up, and the march from the courtroom, with its social contact to the bleakness of a life-time behind prison walls, began. Before he went he shook hands with Clarence Darrow, a smile of thanks on his face. Dickie just stood still with that pathetic look on his countenance. Then everybody crowded around the defense attorneys and about the relatives of the boys. There were smiles on the faces of all of them—even on the grief-worn face of Nathan Leopold, Sr."

Within a few moments Loeb and Leopold were on their way to Joliet, Loeb to be cut to death after a few years by a fellow prisoner, Leopold to establish a brilliant educational system for incarcerated men.

He tried to pick up the threads of his normal practice. The ten-thousand-dollar retainer fee that Loeb had given him that first hysterical night had been spent on court costs, psychiatrists and office expenses. Since the entire Darrow office had been concentrating on the case, the firm was now several thousand dollars behind in its efforts to save the boys' lives. Neither of the two fathers made any mention of paying Darrow for his services. The weeks went by; several months went by; still no attempt was made to meet the obligation or to ascertain what Darrow's fee might be.

At the end of four months, when he had received no word, Darrow wrote a polite note to Loeb. The letter was ignored. So disgusted with this conduct was Judge Harry Fisher, a friend of Darrow's and an officer of the Bar Association, that he asked Darrow to let the Bar Association both name and collect his fee.

"No," said Clarence, "I don't want to make any trouble. I'll write to Loeb again asking for my money."

At the end of six months he sent another letter to Loeb, suggesting that he come into the office and discuss a settlement. One full month later Dickie Loeb's uncle came into the office and remarked breezily, "You know, Clarence, the world is full of eminent lawyers who would have paid a fortune for the chance to distinguish themselves in this case."

Sick at heart, Clarence could only think, "This is not the same man who fell on his knees by my bedside and begged me to save the boys' lives."

"A hundred thousand dollars is all we can pay in this case, Clarence," continued Loeb. "From that I'll have to deduct the ten thousand dollars I already paid you." He then reached a hand into his pocket, pulled out three checks and handed one to Darrow. "I've broken this up three ways," he said. "A third for each of the Bachrach brothers and a third for you. Here's your check for thirty thousand dollars—now if you will just sign this release."

Ruby reports that "Dee came home feeling pretty bad. He said, 'Rube, I hope you won't disapprove of what I've done.'"

Darrow told her the story, then said, "I took the check and signed the release. What else could I do? I didn't take that case to make money. I hoped to establish a precedent that boys in their teens should not be held accountable for their acts. I can't go and fight for more money or the world will think that's what I took the case for."

Chapter Twelve

"Your Old Man's a Monkey!"

NOW APPROACHING SEVENTY, Clarence Darrow decided that he would slowly ease himself toward retirement. He and Ruby took a trip to Europe. This European vacation had been made possible by the one "gravy" case of his career. Harold McCormick, son of the founder of the McCormick Harvesting Machinery Company, was having difficulties in securing a divorce from Mrs Edith Rockfeller McCormick, third daughter of John D. Rockefeller. "Of the two lawyers handling my case," says McCormick, "John D. Wilson was an aristocrat; the other was a nabob. When I became convinced that these two attorneys were hurting me in the eyes of the public I decided I would call into the case a democrat and a humanitarian. I had always admired Clarence Darrow as one of the great men of his time, with a wonderful soul, and I felt that if he came into the case on my side the public would no longer think it was a contest between millionaire families. When I told Wilson that I wanted Darrow brought into the case he exploded with, 'Why, I wouldn't associate with Clarence Darrow!'

"I finally convinced him that if he knew Darrow he would respect him. Wilson replied, 'All right, Harold, I'll take your word; I'll meet him and we'll talk it over.' Mr Darrow was so kind, sympathetic, patient and gentle with Mrs. McCormick that our complications dissolved and Mrs McCormick settled amiably."

For these few meetings Darrow had received a fee of twenty-five thousand dollars. His face wore a strange and quizzical expression as he fingered the check, an expression similar to the one Ruby was to detect there a year later when the Darrows were entertained on the yacht of Samuel Untermeyer, a New York attorney who had made millions from his practice. Untermeyer had pinned a corsage of orchids onto Ruby's frock as she came aboard from Miami, orchids which he had sent on from his private nurseries every day of the week. As Darrow gazed a little forlornly at Ruby's spray of orchids he muttered, "Hummph, maybe I should have been practicing corporation law all these years. Then I could-a had a yacht and fresh orchids for you every day."

"What would you do with a yacht?" asked Ruby.

As had been true all through his life, he still derived his most constant pleasure from lecturing, debating and writing. Mostly he liked to debate on religion; he enjoyed it so much that his intimates believed him to have deep religious promptings. However, these promptings did not relax his native irreverence. In Palestine an Arabian boatman had offered to take them to the spot where Jesus had walked upon the waters.

"How much will you charge for rowing us over?" he asked.

"Fifteen dollars," replied the boatman.

"No wonder Jesus walked," murmured Darrow.

Despite the fact that he was constantly attacking the intellectual base of organized religion, his friends declared him to be the most religious man they had ever known, one of the few true Christians alive in America. Once when he had completed an evening lecture to the students of Harvard a Congregational minister commented, "No one was ever a greater worker for the good of mankind and for God than Clarence Darrow." Another time, when debating Dr Shirley Case of the University of Chicago on the subject, "Has Christianity Failed?" "Doctor Case said that Clarence Darrow himself was an argument against the failure of Christianity, for he lived as close to the Golden Rule of Jesus as anyone he had ever known."

John Haynes Holmes, minister of the Community Church of New York, wrote more elaborately of him, "Darrow was sharp of tongue, ironic in thought and speech, a pessimist and unbeliever, but he had a heart which could exclude no man from its sympathy. In his own life he demonstrated the reality of the religion which he denied. This world was to him a mad and cruel world. There was no sense nor sanity in it. Especially was there no pity. But men needed pity, just because they were living helplessly in such a world. . . . Darrow's compassion . . . reached everywhere, touched every life. The underdog was his especial friend, the downtrodden and oppressed his brethren, the outcast and wretched and despised his loved ones. Not since Saint Francis walked this earth has the world seen such mercy clad in human flesh. . . . If religion is love, as it surely is, then Clarence Darrow was one of the most religious men who ever lived and his pessimism a purer wellspring of the spirit than all the founts of faith."

Professor A. Eustace Haydon, authority on comparative religions at the University of Chicago, said, "Darrow. . . . would prove that life was not worth living, then he would turn around and prove it was worth living by doing things for people."

He had a tremendous lust for life, yet he came about as close to living according to the Sermon on the Mount as could any man trying to earn his way in a competitive world. He was a man with all the faults, shortcomings and inadequacies of a man, but he was a civilized human being in that he could not endure to see his fellow human beings suffer.

His quarrel had never been with religion itself but with those creeds which turned their backs on education and science; his quarrel with these forms of worship was on the ground that they operated against the welfare of their own people. For forty years now he had been carrying on this fight against those sects which kept knowledge away from their members, which told human beings precisely what they might think and at that point erected unscalable stone walls, sects which battled all findings of science which appeared to controvert their dogma. For the Christian ethic he had love and admiration, but he had only disgust for those branches of religion which circumscribed the human brain, set boundaries to its activities, limited its growth and direction, prescribed what it might think, feel and believe, kept the brain from crying out, "I am free! I am unafraid! I go wherever the truth may lead me." He flayed against those faiths which discouraged the processes of unbiased, vigorous, fearless thinking and which not only cut off part of the brain's potential power but cramped and restricted and enslaved it. He believed with all his heart that if ever man was to become free his brain must be utterly free to lead him to that freedom, for no one could free man but man himself, and he could never accomplish this tremendous task without exerting himself to the utmost through the days and the centuries.

He was a Christian by example and precept, but by intellect he was an agnostic. He was no atheist, as was so commonly charged against him, though he often used the atheist press and pulpit to combat what he judged to be the more baneful influences of rigid dogma. He never became an atheist because he knew it was as difficult to prove "There is no God" as "There is a God."

No man in America was better prepared by background or temperament to meet the challenge of William Jennings Bryan and the Fundamentalists. Just as the Loeb-Leopold case had given him the recapitulatory opportunity against capital punishment, so now the Scopes Evolution Case was to afford him opportunity to bring into international focus his campaign against the oppression, bigotry and ignorance fostered by an intellectually hamstrung church. The newspapers were to call it America's most amazing trial.

The Scopes Evolution Case in Dayton, Tennessee, did not spring up whole and unexpected; the forces had been gathering on either side, the battle swelling for several years. In the early summer of 1923 Bryan and Darrow fought the early skirmishes which were to lead directly to the contest in Dayton which so shocked, amused and revolted the civilized world.

For some time William Jennings Bryan had been quarreling in the press with university professors, offering a hundred dollars in cash to any one of them who would sign an affidavit to the effect that he was personally descended from an ape. He had launched an attack against science which the Chicago *Tribune* published. Darrow had replied in a letter to the *Tribune,* whose editor considered it of sufficient news value to give it the number-two column of the front page.

"I was very much interested in Mr Bryan's letter to the *Tribune* and in your editorial reply," Darrow said. "I have likewise followed Mr Bryan's efforts to shut out the teaching of science from the public schools and his questionnaires to various college professors who believe in evolution and still profess Christianity. Likewise a few questions to Mr Bryan and the Fundamentalists, if fairly answered, might serve the interests of reaching the truth—all of this assuming that the truth is desirable. For this reason I think it would be helpful if Mr Bryan would answer the following questions." He then posed fifty questions at Bryan in an attempt to find out whether Bryan thought the biblical account of the creation of the earth and of life literally true or a poetic allegory.

Bryan replied, "I decline to turn aside to enter into controversy with those who reject the Bible as Mr Darrow does."

Two years later he was to answer all fifty of the questions from the witness stand in the courthouse in Dayton in a shattering scene which proved to be the tragic fulfillment of a tragic career. When the legal aspects of the case had been fought to a temporary conclusion, when both sides had belabored the rights of a sovereign people to pass any legislation it saw fit, when the question of whether the Anti-Evolution Law violated the constitution of Tennessee or the Constitution of the United States had been hopelessly obscured, it was these fifty questions which suddenly flashed the trial into focus, turned defeat into victory, discredited the Anti-Evolution Bill and dealt a deathblow to Fundamentalism.

Strong movements were already under way in fifteen states to enact anti-evolution laws. The state of Kentucky had escaped from such a law by a majority of one vote in its legislature. Darrow feared that if Bryan and his cohorts were permitted to carry on their work unopposed they would soon have the Bible Belt of the Solid South caught in a Fundamentalist dictatorship. Nor had Bryan any intention of stopping at the Mason-Dixon line. His avowed purpose was to carry the fight into the North and the West until he had secured anti-evolution bills in two thirds of the states and could get an anti-evolution amendment added to the United States Constitution. Bills to stop the use of government funds for ethnological research had been drawn and would be introduced at the next session of the Congress. "The purpose of the movement," commented the Chattanooga *Daily Times,* "is to bar the Smithsonian Institute from investigating as to the origin of man and to have Congress accept the Bible theory of the genesis of the human family."

In America there had been effected such a complete separation of Church and State that no religious instruction was allowed in the public schools. The Fundamentalists were now determined to pass laws which would prohibit the teaching in public schools of all subjects which conflicted in any detail with the particulars of their own religion. Did biology and zoology conflict with the biblical story of the creation of the world and man? So much the worse for biology and zoology! Did geology and anthropology conflict? So much the worse for geology and anthropology. Hidden beneath the anti-evolution movement was an attempt to bring the state under the control of the Church, William Jennings Bryan's church.

Nor was Darrow one of those who thought this aim impossible of attainment. Had not these almost identical forces put over prohibition on an unwilling public? Had they not bullied legislators, connived, cried, kicked, yelled, screamed and finally succeeded? He subscribed wholeheartedly to the sentiments of the journalist who wrote, "According to Mr. Bryan,

277

the Fundamentalist party will not be satisfied with writing a defense of the code into state after state; it must be written into the Federal Constitution itself. Journalists laugh. But they are the same journalists who laughed when these same people, not satisfied with capturing state after state for prohibition, began to talk of an Eighteenth Amendment."

He felt that the issue had to be joined, that Bryan and his World's Fundamental Association had to be stopped, not in their own belief or practice of Fundamentalism, but in trying to force their religion upon the rest of the country. Ever since Charles Darwin's earliest promulgation of his theories of evolution certain churches had been fighting them bitterly, ridiculing them, commanding their members to abstain from studying the perfidious doctrines on the pain of excommunication, denying the results of research, calling the scientists and the educators tricksters, dupes, atheists, liars, instruments of evil and destruction. But for the most part, the battle for education and enlightenment in America had been well won. America had thought that the issue was dead; it had forgotten that as long as mankind inhabits this earth, no issue, no matter how cruel, stupid, vicious, or destructive, is ever dead.

And, indeed, in the state of Tennessee an anti-evolution bill had already been drafted, passed through the house and senate, signed by the governor, decreed as the law of their land. John T. Scopes, science teacher and athletic coach of the Rhea Country High Shcool had been arrested for violating the Anti-Evolution Law.

When Darrow entered Dayton on the afternoon of July eighth he found the town decked out as though for a carnival. The road leading in from Chattanooga had been lined with signs which read, "Sweethearts, Come to Jesus," "You Need God in Your Business," "Where Will You Spend Eternity?" Across Main Street were strung colorful banners and flags. Newly constructed hot-dog stands, lemonade stands and sandwich stands lined the sidewalks. Most of the shops had comic posters depicting monkeys and coconuts pasted in their windows. The Anti-Evolution League had taken over a whole building, in front of which they set up bookstalls to sell Bryan's books and their featured volume, *Hell and the High School*. One circus man who had brought two chimpanzees to testify for the prosecution rented a store on Main Street and set them up as a side show. Preachers of a hundred different sects, most of them untutored men who had graduated from some Bible institute of the Deep South, came to Dayton to transform the town into a giant revivalist meeting; they preached on the street corners, set up their tents on the outskirts of town, night and day exhorted the passers-by to repent and come to Jesus. At the more populous street corners "blind, wandering dervishes from the remote hills played their fiddles and chanted gospel hymns through their noses." The Holy Rollers chose Dayton for their annual revival meeting; each night along the riverbank they writhed and rolled on the ground in ecstatic spasms of religious emotionalism. These goings on resulted in the inevitable comment in the newspapers that the people of Dayton were making monkeys of themselves.

By the time Darrow reached Dayton the village already had been overrun by two different groups: on the one hand the hundreds of newspapermen, photographers, editors, radio and telegraph operators, educators, scientists, atheists, liberals, radicals, who thronged there during their summer vacation to see their side win a great victory and whose presence so filled the hotels and boardinghouses that the private homes rented out rooms. On the other, the farmers of the surrounding countryside, the marginal-subsistence families from the hills, the unemployed coal miners, the itinerants and mendicants of all types, most of them Fundamentalists who came to see their side win a great victory and who slept in wagons, rickety cars, in tents and on the ground under the trees. When the trial opened the Daytonians were in a minority in their own town.

He met a number of enlightened and liberal people in the community. There was a progressive Readers' Club, which tried to keep abreast of current thought by reading the new publications and which founded the Dayton Library. At the other extreme he encountered an illiberal group, fanatics who wanted to control the thinking and feeling of the rest of the country. In between were the majority of Daytonians, many of whom had graduated from high school and whose children often went away to college. Dayton was intensely religious; its two thousand residents supported nine churches. Even the most educated would discuss at great length such theological questions as whether Jesus lived to save mankind or died to save mankind. But as far as Darrow could determine, no one in Dayton, intellectual or fanatic, had ever taken a child out of school because he didn't like something that was being taught. Dayton was frankly skeptical about evolution but had done nothing to deserve the ridicule, contempt and contumely that was now to be heaped upon its head when the town was taken over by forces outside its control.

Dayton businessmen originally had encouraged the idea of a trial because they had hoped to put Dayton on the map and capture a permanent tourist trade. They printed a handsome pamphlet called *Why Dayton—Of All Places?* illustrated with pictures of the town and its main industries. Dayton's leading newspaperwoman says, "There was some hope that persons of means might find Dayton attractive enough to cast their lots here. The people seemed to be enthusiastic over the legal and literary talent descending in their midst because of the trial." But the members of the Progressive Dayton Club came to realize that they had a serious trial on their hands and not a highly profitable farce; the monkey posters were taken down, their plans to present "monkey medals" to the participants abandoned.

The chamber of commerce tendered Clarence a banquet at which time he was given the honorary title of Colonel. The same group also had given Bryan a banquet a few days before, at which he had appeared in "a prodigious white pith helmet. . . ." Bryan had announced that the trial would be "a duel to the death." Colonel Darrow retorted, "We will smother Mr Bryan's influence under a mountain of scientific testimony."

Three months before the arrest of Scopes, William Jennings Bryan had delivered a lecture in Nashville called "Is the Bible True?" Though he had not practiced law for thirty-six years, he offered his services to head the prosecution of Scopes, an offer which the hundreds of thousands of people throughout the South who had heard him lecture on the literal verity of the Bible demanded be accepted. At this moment Darrow was also in the South, speaking on "The Sane Treatment of Crime" before the Annual Convention of the American Psychiatric Association in Richmond, Virginia. The occasion was a great honor, for he was the first lawyer to be invited to make the annual address in the eighty years of the association's history. Taking his cue from the religion-versus-science turmoil going on about him, he contested the "divine-inflatus" conception of man's nature by a biological attack best described as a "divine de-flatus." "For an hour or more he kept the audience on its toes. He spoke practically without notes, showed a knowledge of biology, psychology and law, spiced with wonderful bits of humor and sly cynicism."

He enjoyed himself thoroughly; Dr James K. Hall reports, "Darrow's coming to Richmond . . . was a great day for American psychiatry. Clarence Darrow impressed me as an honest, fearless, humble man, passionately anxious to find the truth and to live by it. In spite of his unorthodox speech I thought him deeply religious."

The following day he was taken by Dr Beverly Tucker, together with Dr Hall and the novelist, James Branch Cabell, for a drive through the surrounding country. That morning the newspapers had announced that William Jennings Bryan was going to prosecute John Scopes in Dayton, Tennessee. Clarence was deeply agitated.

Dr Tucker says, "He told us that he was interested in the arrest of Scopes and that he had just heard that Mr Bryan was going to prosecute Scopes. Then in a rather wistful way he said, 'I would like to meet Bryan in this case; I believe I could down him. I would be willing to do it without charging Scopes any fee.' I said, 'Mr Darrow, why don't you offer his attorneys your services on that basis?' He replied, 'I think that would be rather sticking my neck out.' However, when we arrived back in Richmond I told him that there was a telegraph office in the Jefferson Hotel lobby if he wished to offer his services in the Scopes case. 'I believe I shall do it,' he said.

"For the first, the last, the only time in my life," say Darrow, "I volunteered my services in a case. I did this because I really wanted to take part in it."

The week before, in New York, he had discussed the anti-evolution trial with Arthur Garfield Hays and Dudley Field Malone of the Civil Liberties Union; the three men had decided that it would be better for the controversy to be handled by Tennessee attorneys. The entrance of Bryan into the case had shifted its focus from law to religion; if Bryan had not become involved in the prosecution Darrow would never have become counsel for the defense.

He returned immediately to New York to debate with Will Durant on "Progress." Under the caption DARROW SORROWS FOR BRYAN AND ALL IGNORANT BIGOTS, the New York *World* reported him as laying the blame for the Anti-Evolution Bill on the shoulders of William Jennings Bryan. "Mr Bryan's mind was set by his ancestors, and it has remained set. The sorrow is that it was set to believe that man must not think for himself, that he must study only what his ancestors studied, that one may not teach or study what he wishes." When these comments were published in Tennessee the following day State Representative John Washington Butler was deeply offended. "I alone am responsible for the Anti-Evolution Bill," said Mr Butler. "Mr Darrow is wrong in claiming that William Jennings Bryan had anything to do with it."

John Washington Butler was a moderately prosperous farmer. A thickset man with a rugged face and a sincere manner, he had in his youth taught school for five years during the winter. In 1922 a visiting preacher from Nashville had told from the pulpit of Butler's Primitive Baptist Church the story of a young woman who had gone to the university and returned home believing that, instead of God creating man,

281

he was descended from a lower order of animals. This worried Butler; he was a devout man who had raised his five children on the letter of the King James Bible. He knew that evolution was being taught in the Tennessee high schools; it seemed to him neither fair nor just that the public schools, run on the farmers' taxes, should undermine the religion that had been planted in the young while at home.

That year Butler ran for representative of his district; one of the main planks of his platform was the advocacy of a law prohibiting the teaching of evolution in the Tennessee schools. "Ninety-nine people out of a hundred in my district thought just as I did. I say ninety-nine out of a hundred because there may be some hold different, but so far as I know, there isn't a one in the whole district that thinks evolution of man can be the way the scientists tell it. On the morning I was forty-nine I was thinking what to do on my birthday, and I said to myself, 'Well, the first thing, I'll get that law off my mind.' I wrote it out after breakfast at home just like I wanted it. I had the stenographer up at the capitol type it for me, and that's the way the law stands now, just the way I first wrote it."

The Tennessee representatives passed the bill with a seventy-five-to-five vote. The legislators later said that they had passed the buck to the senate, thinking the senate would kill the bill. The senate, however, passed it twenty-four to six. The senators later avowed that they had thought the governor would veto it. The governor signed it on March 21, 1925, remarking that it would never be enforced. The Nashville *Southern Agriculturist* declared, "We should feel ourselves faithless to the children of Tennessee and to the other states in which similar laws are threatened if we did not protest against it." It was the restlessness of the thirty-one-year manager of the Cumberland Coal and Iron Company which brought the act into immediate focus.

George Rappelyea was raised on Third Avenue in New York City; as a boy he sold newspapers at the Times Square entrance to the subway. He studied geology at college for a short time, wandered South on a geological exploring trip, located the main vein of the Cumberland Coal and Iron Company which had disappeared at a fault, a feat for which he was made manager of the mine. "He was an untidy little person with rather ill-tended teeth," writes Mrs Haldeman-Julius. "His dark brown eyes behind horn-rimmed spectacles are fine and alert. His mind is essentially a scientific one, clear, disciplined; his mental integrity and intrinsic sincerity are obvious."

Rappelyea's distaste for Fundamentalism had become acute on the day he went into the mountains to attend the funeral of an eight-year-old boy who had been crushed between two coal cars. "This here boy," said the Fundamentalist preacher, standing by the little coffin, "'cause his pappy and mammy didn't get him baptized, is now awrithin' in the flames of hell." When Rappelyea protested the preacher said with dignity, "Mr Rappelyea, you can boss the men in the mine, but you've got to keep your hands off'n our religion."

"But that isn't religion; that's horrible superstition!"

"Hit's our religion," said the preacher, "and we stick by hit."

"Well, a few days later," said Rappelyea, "I heard that this same bunch, the Fundamentalists, had passed that Anti-Evolution Law, and I made up my mind I'd show them up to the world. Everybody said to calm down and forget it, but I couldn't."

When the Anti-Evolution Bill had been passed John T. Scopes had gone to his principal and shown him that Hunter's *Civic Biology*, which had been the standard textbook in all Tennessee high schools for five years, violated the law. The principal had decided that since school would be out in a few weeks it would be wiser to make no changes or comments but to carry on his teaching as he had before. Scopes reported this scene to his friend Rappelyea, reading to him the pages from *Civic Biology* which taught that man was descended from a lower order of animals. Rappelyea had seen an announcement that the American Civil Liberties Union of New York City had declared itself ready to back any schoolteacher who would test the law. That night he wrote to the Civil Liberties Union asking if they would finance a defense if he could arrange a test case in Dayton. Arthur Garfield Hays, guiding genius of the organization, guaranteed not only the expenses of the defense, but offered a thousand-dollar fee to each of the prosecuting attorneys as well.

Late in the afternoon of May fifth Rappelyea went to Robinson's drugstore, which served as the community center for the town, and had a nickel lemonade with his cronies. Three of Dayton's lawyers dropped in after their day's work. A heated discussion arose over the validity of the Anti-Evolution Law.

"Johnny," said Rappelyea to Scopes as he came in for a soda, "Johnny, you're going to be arrested."

"What for?" asked Johnny mildly. He was a modest boy, one of the best-liked members of the community, particularly among the students, though some of the more rigorous church-goers had been heard to criticize him because he smoked cigarettes and danced.

"For violating the Tennessee Anti-Evolution Bill. The

American Civil Liberties Union has promised to defend you."

"All right," replied Scopes quietly, "I'll stand as a test case."

Rappelyea went for the sheriff, swearing out a warrant for the arrest of John T. Scopes. A deputy came to Robinson's drugstore to arrest him. Four days later the Rhea County grand jury met and indicted him for violating the Anti-Evolution Law.

Rappelyea conceived the romantic idea of reopening The Mansion, an imposing home on the outskirts of Dayton that had been abandoned several years before. It was shaded by huge trees, was far enough out to give seclusion and was the only house in the vicinity large enough to accommodate the group of attorneys and experts who were expected to testify. The fact that the plumbing system did not work, that there was no water in the pipes for washing or shaving, no facilities in the kitchen with which to cook, did not deter Rappelyea. He moved in a few beds, a table and some chairs and awaited the coming of his guests.

Darrow slept only one night in the abandoned mansion. The next day Ruby arrived and, as though by magic, one of the bankers of the town transported his family to the foothills in order that the Darrows might move into their home and be comfortable. Since the town was flooded with strangers, foodstuffs were extremely difficult to buy, particularly milk and butter, and it was next to imposible to secure any ice. That week end the Darrows went to the mountains to escape the lacerating heat; when they returned they found that their neighbor, Mr Wilbur, had filled their icebox "with ice, milk, cream and butter, and even a cantaloupe for breakfast."

"The attitude of the townspeople toward us was especially kindly," says Mrs Darrow, "despite the differences of our beliefs. No one ever displayed the least sign of discourtesy, except perhaps Mr and Mrs Bryan. I was not introduced to them, and I am not aware that they ever had any intention to be rude to me, but they glanced the other way any time we were near each other."

Early on Friday morning of July tenth Clarence and Ruby left their borrowed home and walked to the Rhea County Courthouse, a large brick building with a belfry, surrounded by a neat lawn and half concealed in a grove of elm, oak, poplar and sweet-gum trees. The yard was jammed with vendors of pennants, toy monkeys, hot dogs and lemonade, with barefoot preachers holding prayer meetings and exhorting the milling spectators at the top of their lungs. An observer wrote, "One was hard put to it on the tenth of July to know whether Dayton was holding a camp meeting, a Chautauqua, a street fair, a carnival or a belated Fourth of July celebration. Literally, it was drunk on religious excitement."

Darrow climbed the stairs to the courtroom, which seated more than seven hundred people but which now held another three hundred standees. He pushed his way through the sweltering spectators, past the tables at which were assembled a larger number of journalists than had met and worked on any assignment since the Washington Arms Conference. Microphones had been set up to carry the trial to the nation, the first broadcast of its kind. French, German and English correspondents were present to cable each day's story to their European papers.

Everyone was in shirt sleeves, with the sleeves rolled up and the collar open at the throat; in this crowd Darrow somehow appeared well dressed, for he had replaced his usual black string necktie with a white string necktie which he declined to take off and had on a pair of dashing purple suspenders; it was probably the first time in his forty-five years of practice that he was among the best-dressed members of the court.

At the defense table sat Clarence Darrow, Arthur Garfield Hays, Dudley Field Malone and John Randolph Neal of Tennessee, a former judge and the leading constitutional lawyer of the state, who had represented the American Civil Liberties Union in the past. Neal was in actual charge but preferred to remain in the background to handle the constitutional problems and let his widely publicized colleagues occupy the limelight in the controversy. Malone was a handsome, debonairly dressed, silver-tongued pleader who had no brief for the theory of evolution but who, as Darrow observed of him, "put his allegiance on a higher ground." Arthur Garfield Hays, short, stocky, with a strong face, was an excellent counterbalance to the eloquent Darrow: in addition to his courage and years of devotion to the unpopular cause of civil liberties, he was an expert on the technical aspects of the law.

Opposite, at the prosecution's table sat William Jennings Bryan and his son, former Attorney General Ben McKenzie and his son, Attorney General Stewart and the Hicks brothers of Nashville. The judge was John Raulston, an attorney of Dayton.

Bryan announced, "The trial uncovers an attack for a generation on revealed religion. A successful attack would destroy the Bible and with it revealed religion. If evolution wins Christianity goes." Darrow retorted, "Scopes isn't on trial; civilization is on trial. The prosecution is opening the doors for a reign of bigotry equal to anything in the Middle Ages. No man's belief will be safe. . . ."

Judge Raulston banged his gavel. The monkey trial was on.

The Reverend Mr Cartwright uttered a long prayer which was in effect a judgment for the prosecution, and the first row between the attorneys was symptomatic of the geographic nature of the controversy. Judge Raulston announced, "We are glad to welcome the foreign lawyers for both the state and the defendant." The defense looked at each other quizzically but said nothing until former Attorney General McKenzie claimed the Anti-Evolution Law to be so clear it could be understood by a sixteen-year-old Tennessean, but "if these gentlemen have any laws in the great metropolitan city of New York that conflict with it or in the great white city of the Northwest . . ." Then they objected to geographic distinctions being drawn, since they were present as American citizens. Judge Raulston, who was a courteous man, albeit a trifle bombastic in speech, sought to pour oil on the troubled waters by replying, "I want you gentlemen from New York or any other foreign state to always remember that you are our guests and that we accord you the same privileges and rights and courtesies that we do any other lawyer." The defense subsided resignedly.

Scopes originally having been indicted in unseemly haste, Attorney General Stewart asked that a new indictment be brought against the defendant. The grand jury was summoned. Judge Raulston read to them Section One of the Anti-Evolution Law. "Be it enacted by the general assembly of the state of Tennessee that it shall be unlawful for any teacher in any of the universities, normals and all other public schools of the state, which are supported in whole or in part by the public-school funds of the state, to teach any theory that denies the story of the divine creation of man as taught in the Bible and to teach instead that man has descended from a lower order of animals."

Since the act made it illegal to teach any theory that denied the divine creation of man as taught in the Bible, Judge Raulston picked up his well-worn copy of the Bible, and read the first twenty-three sections of Genesis.

The grand jury returned a new indictment against John T. Scopes.

Since the veniremen thought that service in the jury box would afford them a grandstand seat for the proceedings, few declined to serve. Darrow questioned the prospective jurors only mildly; those selected were middle-aged farmers, eleven of whom were inveterate churchgoers. One juror who admitted he could neither read nor write was accepted by both sides because it was said of him that "he can think and has got quick ears."

After this first session on Friday court was adjourned until Monday to permit the defense attorneys who had assembled from different cities to chart their program of defense. Monday was devoted to the technical aspects of the law, to its constitutionality, for the defense first appealed to Judge Raulston to quash the indictment against John Scopes. The jury was sent out of the courtroom during these arguments. Several days were to elapse before they were allowed back in.

John Neal pleaded that the Anti-Evolution Law was unconstitutional because the title of the law was misleading and did not include everything that was in the body of the law; that it violated the part of the Tennessee constitution which provided that "knowledge, learning and virtue being essential to the preservation of republican institutions . . . it shall be the duty of the general assembly . . . to cherish literature and science"; that it further violated the constitution of Tennessee which provided that "all men have a natural and indefeasible right to worship Almighty God according to the dictates of their own conscience." Arthur Garfield Hays asked that the indictment be thrown out of court because the Anti-Evolution Law unreasonably extended the police powers of the state and was a restriction on the powers of the individual. Dudley Field Malone asked that it be quashed on the grounds that the law imposed upon the people of Tennessee a particular religious opinion from a particular religious book.

When Darrow came into the courtroom to climax the pleading, he told his friends that he was going to take off his gloves and give the enemy the whole works. The New York Times reported, "There was a craning of necks, for Mr Darrow is . . . known as 'the infidel,' and the crowd gazed curiously at the bent figure with the seamed brown face and the great head. He was in his shirt sleeves, his purple suspenders standing out against his shirt, which had a little tear at the left elbow. He would stoop and brood a minute, hunching his shoulders almost up to his ears, and then they would drop; his head would shoot forward and his lower lip protrude as he hurled some bitter word at his opponents. Or he would stand swaying sideways at the hips, balancing himself, while words came slowly from his lips, and then launch himself, a thunderbolt of indignation, words streaming from him in a torrent of denunciation."

In his opening Darrow declared the Anti-Evolution Act to be as "brazen and as bold an attempt to destroy learning as was ever made in the Middle Ages." He turned to William Jennings Bryan, who had thus far sat in humid silence, fanning his face with a palm fan, and declared in unequivocable terms that Bryan was the one responsible for this "foolish, mischievous and wicked act." The spectators gasped to hear their champion labeled foolish, mischievous and wicked: Darrow could feel the familiar wall of resentment rise against him. This resentment became almost tactile when he maintained "The state of Tennessee, under an honest and fair interpretation of the constitution, has no more right to teach the Bible as the divine book than that the Koran is one, or the book of Mormons or the book of Confucius or the Buddha or the Essays of Emerson or any one of the ten thousand books to which human souls have gone for consolation and aid in their troubles.

"I know there are millions of people in the world who derive consolation . . . from the Bible. . . . If anybody finds anything in this life that brings them consolation and health and happiness I think they ought to have it. I haven't any fault to find with them at all. But the Bible is not one book. The Bible is made up of sixty-six books written over a period of about one thousand years, some of them very early and some of them comparatively late. It is a book primarily of religion and morals. It is not a book of science. Never was and was never meant to be."

He believed that the things he had to say in these few hours of pleading might be among the most important of his lifetime. For this reason he was not content to plead merely for the right to heresy; he wanted his argument to be based solidly on the law. He went to great pains to review the legal and technical reasons why the statute was untenable: that the law was so indefinite that no citizen could obey it or court enforce it and that it was entirely possible, since science only illuminated the poetic observations of Genesis, to both violate the law and obey it at the same time; that the constitution of Tennessee, patterned after Thomas Jefferson's, maintained that no act should ever interfere with religious liberty.

"They make it a crime to know more than I know. They publish a law to inhibit learning. This law says that it shall be a criminal offense to teach in the public schools any account of the origin of man that is in conflict with the divine account that is in the Bible. It makes the Bible the yardstick to measure every man's intelligence and to measure every man's learning. Are your mathematics good? Turn to I Elijah ii. Is your philosophy good? See II Samuel iii. Is your chemistry good? See Deuteronomy iii 6, or anything that tells about brimstone. Every bit of knowledge that the mind has must be submitted to a religious test."

As Darrow stood before Judge Raulston, his thumbs locked in his suspenders, the native Tennesseans wondered how a man who looked and acted so much like a farmer could utter such heretical beliefs. "If today you can take a thing like evolution and make it a crime to teach it in the public schools, tomorrow you can make it a crime to teach it in the private schools. And the next year you can make it a crime

288

to teach it in the church. And the next session you may ban books and the newspapers. Soon you may set Catholic against Protestant and Protestant against Protestant and try to foist your own religion upon the mind of man. If you can do one you can do the other. Ignorance and fanaticism is ever busy and needs feeding. Always it is feeding and gloating for more. After a while, your honor, it is setting man against man and creed against creed until with flying banners and beating drums we are marching backward to the glorious ages of the sixteenth century when bigots lighted fagots to burn the man who dared to bring any intelligence and enlightenment and culture to the human mind."

One of the journalists wrote of Darrow at this instant, "In one of his great leisurely shrugs, in which his whole torso participates, he can put more contempt, more combativeness, more of a sense of reserve power, than anyone else can express in a dozen gestures."

"Clarence," said Ruby, pointing at the tear in his shirt through which his elbow was now protruding, "don't you think you'd better put on another shirt?"

"Well, Ruby," smiled Darrow, "don't you think it's too hot today for two shirts?"

As he walked along Main Street toward the Hotel Aqua one Daytonian stepped up to grasp his hand and say, "Mr Darrow, if I could have heard you before I would never have spoken of you as I have in the past."

"That's all right; that's all right," he replied, touched almost to the point of tears. He did not hear the two women behind him mutter, "The damned infidel!"

Ben McKenzie, who had battled hard against the legal arguments of Neal, Hays and Malone, got out of his Ford when Darrow came along, threw an arm affectionately about him and said in a husky voice, "It was the greatest speech I have ever heard in my life on any subject." Darrow returned his embrace so warmly that McKenzie was to say in court the next day that between him and Mr Darrow it had been love at first sight. "It's mighty kind of you to say that," murmured Darrow.

Feeling pleased with themselves, the defense attorneys met for dinner in the dining room of the Hotel Aqua. They had settled down to a serious discussion of the next day's technique when Bryan appeared, the huge pith helmet on his head, his arms laden with bundles of celery, radishes and other vegetables which he had just bought in the local market. Bryan disdained to glance at the defense table but walked to his own, handed the bundles to his waitress and asked her to prepare and serve them along with his dinner.

The following morning, July fourteenth, Darrow exploded a series of bombs in the Dayton courtroom; he objected to the trial being opened each morning with a long prayer by a Fundamentalist preacher. "I don't object to the jury or anyone else praying in secret or in private," he commented. "But I do object to the turning of this courtroom into a meetinghouse in the trial of this case. This case is a conflict between science and religion, and no attempt should be made by means of prayer to influence the deliberation and consideration by the jury of the facts in this case."

A whistling sound of shock swept through the audience; Darrow turned from addressing Judge Raulston to stand facing down his critics.

Though it was not the custom in Tennessee to open court with a prayer, Judge Raulston was a deeply religious man; he had always opened court with a prayer if there were a clergyman present. Darrow's request hurt him even more than it astonished him. He denied Darrow's request but asked the Reverend Dr Charles Francis Potter of the West Side Unitarian Church of New York, a defense witness, to say the prayer the following morning, a compromise which succeeded in satisfying neither side.

The flare had no sooner died down than Darrow lighted another. That morning Attorney General Stewart publicly had labeled him not only an agnostic, but an infidel. Philip Kinsley in the Chicago *Tribune* had reported one of the Dayton prosecutors as saying, "All we have to do is to get the fact that Mr Darrow is an atheist and does not believe in the Bible across to the jury, and his case is lost. . . . They will listen to no one but Bryan." John Scopes had saved the day by rushing to the defense of his defender. "Yes, I consider Mr Darrow an agnostic, but as such that would not prejudice any fair-minded juror. I call myself an agnostic, but I am devoutly religious in my own way."

Darrow now admitted Stewart's right to call him an agnostic: "I do not consider it an insult, but rather a compliment, to be called an agnostic. I do not pretend to know where many ignorant men are sure." However, he was outraged at being called an infidel by an officer of the state of Tennessee. He spent a heated fifteen minutes trying to show the court that to peoples of other religions, in other lands, the good Christians sitting in the Dayton courtroom were regarded as infidels. Judge Raulston reprimanded Attorney General Stewart, ruling that religious criticism should join geographic deprecation in being banned from the prosecution's remarks.

On July fifteenth, almost a week after the opening of the

trial, Judge Raulston read his opinion, refusing to throw the case out of court.

Everyone had known he would refuse to quash the indictment, yet Darrow was made thoroughly and bitterly angry by the decision in a way in which he had never before become angry in a trial. Only the night before he had said to a group of Daytonians, "I have never judged any man. I have had sympathy for all. I have done my best to understand the manifold conditions that surround and control each human life. . . . I do not judge a man; I defend him."

Yet he did not defend Judge Raulston's bias, nor did he consider the background and conditions that had led to the judge's decision: the fact that John Raulston had been born in a little cove in the mountains called Fiery Gizzard, that his mother, a devoutly religious woman, had led him on mule-back over the hills to school each day and read the Bible to him each night, that he had come out of the primitive hill life of Tennessee, a conscientious man who was called "part priest, part judge." Darrow undoubtedly knew that it would have been as congenitally impossible for John Raulston to disavow the Anti-Evolution Law as it would have been for Clarence Darrow to approve it. How could he have expected a small-town trial judge, who agreed wholeheartedly with the law, to set the law aside?

The next morning the jury at last was allowed to take its place in the jury box. The trial of John T. Scopes was to start. Dudley Field Malone first stated that to convict Scopes the prosecution had to prove that Scopes not only taught the theory of evolution but that he at the same time denied the theory of creation as set forth in the Bible. He attempted to convince the jury that there was more than one theory of creation set forth in the Bible and that these were conflicting, that while there was a conflict between evolution and the Old Testament there was no conflict between evolution and Christianity and, lastly, that science did not claim, as the prosecution continued to reiterate, that man had sprung from monkeys. Hays equaled the high standard of pleading set by Darrow and Malone when he discoursed on the history of the Bible, tracing its development from the original manuscripts in Hebrew, Aramaic and Greek and pointing out the difficulties of translation.

Stewart and McKenzie for the prosecution argued spiritedly that the sovereign state of Tennessee had the right to pass any law it wished and to refuse to teach anything in its public schools which it saw fit. Fourteen-year-old Howard Morgan, son of the banker who had given up his home to the Darrows, was put on the stand to testify what he had been taught by

Scopes. Young Morgan said that Scopes had taught him, "The earth was once a hot molten mass, too hot for plant or animal life to exist upon it; in the sea the earth cooled off; there was a little germ of one-cell organism formed, and this organism kept evolving until it got to be a pretty good-sized animal and then came on to be a land animal, and it kept on evolving, and from this was man, and that man was just another mammal."

On this first day that the jury was allowed to be present a number of the spectators rose at the noon hour to go for some lunch but, when they saw the mob of people waiting to take their places, dashed back to their seats and went without food. Again and again the thousand pairs of eyes in the courtroom were turned on William Jennings Bryan, but Bryan sat cooling himself with his fan. The faithful were neither frightened nor impatient; they knew that in his own good time Bryan would speak.

Against the charge that Scopes had taught certain elementals of evolution Darrow had no intention of entering a defense. His defense was to be that although Scopes might have violated the Fundamentalist idea of biblical interpretation he had by no means gone contrary to the biblical theory of creation held by millions of other Christians; that a teacher could demonstrate to his pupils that man had evolved over a period of hundreds of thousands of years, from an infinite variety of lower organisms, without violating the story of Genesis.

The defense had assembled in Dayton an illustrious group of biologists, zoologists, geologists, anthropologists, educators, clergymen and Bible experts who were prepared to relate the story of the birth and growth of the earth and mankind, to testify that this process of evolving was the precise one which the story of Genesis retold in poetic form. For Darrow this was to be the great and important part of the proceedings; with millions of people caught up in the bizarre excitement of the trial, with the press reporting every word from Dayton on its front pages, there would be an opportunity almost unparalleled to illuminate the findings and attitudes of science for those people who had never had an opportunity to encounter these strides forward in man's learning of the truth about himself and his world.

But the prosecution had not the slightest intention of allowing the defense to use the Tennessee courtroom for the purpose of spreading their heresies. The Fundamentalists of Tennessee said that evolution violated the story of creation as told in the Bible; therefore, anything the expert witnesses might have to say about birds and bugs would be immaterial, irrelevant and incompetent. Judge Raulston refused to rule against the admissibility of such evidence until he had heard some of it. Once again the jury was banished, and Darrow put on the stand the first and only defense witness to be called, Dr Maynard M. Metcalf, a zoologist from Johns Hopkins University. Dr Metcalf defined organic evolution as a theory which bound together the findings of the geologists, zoologists and anthropologists; he traced the earliest forms of flora and fauna, sketched briefly the development of man as a primate.

Acrimony once again broke out, for Attorney General Stewart made another personal attack on Darrow. "Mr Darrow is the greatest criminal lawyer in America today. His courtesy is noticeable; his ability is known, and it is a shame in my mind, in the sight of a great God, that a mentality like his has strayed so far from the natural goal that it should follow—great God, the good that a man of his ability could have done if he had aligned himself with the forces of right instead of aligning himself with that which strikes its fangs at the very bosom of Christianity."

Hearty "Amens" came from the spectators.

Darrow wheeled and glared.

The case cut too deeply into his vitals for him to remain calm and judicial, particularly since the greater portion of the trial was being held outside the bounds of law or judicial procedure. No case had ever moved him as did this attack on education. He was terrified at the thought of what would happen to the United States and its people if these Fundamentalists who were fighting his every word and gesture, cheering every sentiment of his opponent, should gain control of the country, the way the Prohibitionists had gained control. In virtually every case of his almost half century of practice he had known that there were two sides; no matter how relentlessly he had fought his opponents, he had been able to understand them and their point of view. This was the first case in his career in which he was profoundly convinced that there were not two sides, but only one; that the Fundamentalists were an insidious potential for destruction; that there was no tolerant word that could be said for their intolerance, not even when he realized that their intolerance and primitive religion had arisen from the devastating poverty growing out of the Civil War, which had left the South little but its belief in God. So passionately did he feel it that there were moments when it threw him.

It was the first case in which Clarence Darrow had proffered his services; it was the first case in which he quarreled with the judge in open court until he was held for contempt; in which he was to lose his temper in the courtroom. In his microscopic dissection of Harry Orchard he had found a moment to say that he did not condemn Orchard, who could not help being what he was; now he was for the first time to

293

be merciless to the point of cruelty to his leading adversary, William Jennings Bryan.

With the jury still banished, Bryan at last rose to his feet; he would permit no more of this "pseudoscientific" material to be interjected into the trial. His shirt collar was tucked under, his sleeves rolled up, his mouth pulled taut and thin, and there was a fighting gleam in his eye. The courtroom became hushed and still; Tennesseans fixed their eyes upon their spokesman with great love and trust. Like Darrow, Bryan, too, considered this a magnificent opportunity for mass education, a God-inspired command to lead a wandering and confused people back to the bosom of the Lord.

Darrow had watched with growing uneasiness how Bryan, stripped of political influence and eased out of the Democratic inner circles, had turned to religion as a career, as a means of re-establishing his power and importance. He did not find it strange that Bryan should devote his full energies to religion as a means of expression. He had always thought that Bryan should have been a preacher; even the "Cross of Gold" speech which had earned him the Democratic nomination in 1896 had been more of a religious harangue than a political or economic one, as the title indicated.

William Jennings Bryan based his Fundamentalism on his oft-repeated statement that "I am more interested in the rock of ages than in the age of rocks." To this mentality and approach to life Clarence Darrow was the complete antithesis; for fifty years he had been fascinated by the ever-ramifying study of evolution, a working theory binding together the factual material that had been unearthed by the sciences.

He felt that Bryan preaching in the Chautauqua Circle on "The Prince of Peace" could do no harm, but Bryan working to organize the Southern states into a solid Fundamentalist anti-evolution block could accomplish an irreparable harm, for in William Jennings Bryan the Fundamentalists had found their perfect leader.

In one respect Clarence Darrow and William Jennings Bryan had achieved a similar greatness. Bryan called himself a commoner; he named his weekly magazine *The Commoner;* he fought always for the poor, the disinherited. Few men fought for the common people; that was why millions of Americans loved him; that was why they had looked up to him for guidance, were confident that he would never betray them because he could never be bought. He had fought for the income tax as a method of leveling wealth when the income tax was being condemned as vicious, radical and destructive. He had worked for international peace; he preached peace on earth, good will to men. So completely had Bryan been for the common people against the money powers of Wall Street that the New York *Tribune* had charged after the 1896 campaign that he belonged to the tradition of Altgeld and Debs.

But Bryan had a sluggish and shallow mind. He was sketchily educated, knew nothing of the arts except that an occasional painting, piece of music or line of literature could be used to illumine a religious principle. He had a native wit, the ability to turn a phrase neatly, but he was too lazy to study, to broaden, deepen or sharpen his mind, to pursue facts and figures with which to put his humanitarian convictions on a solid base. He was possessed by the conviction that he was the most important man of his times, sent to earth directly by the Heavenly Father. "I have always been right," asserted William Jennings Bryan, and he believed it, for how could he be wrong if his every movement was being directed by God? He exclaimed that he did not mind so much with whom he lay down so long as he was clad in the armor of a righteous cause. Never once in his life did he believe that his cause was not righteous. On the lecture platform millions of words poured forth from his enormous mouth, couched in the rolling, majestic prose of the King James Bible, which he read unceasingly, for his outstanding gift lay in his vocal chords; only Henry Ward Beecher had a voice more moving and mesmeric than his.

Though Bryan had failed three times to get himself elected as President of the United States, in 1896, 1900 and 1908, his influence had secured the Democratic nomination for Woodrow Wilson in 1912. Partly out of gratitude, partly because he knew Bryan still had widespread popularity among the Democratic voters, Wilson named him secretary of state. As secretary of state, Bryan displayed such abysmal ignorance of international affairs that he dumfounded the American ambassadors and threw the department into confusion. He set into motion a spoils system for "deserving Democrats" which threatened to disrupt half the governmental service. Of the meaning of legislation, of the economic background and basis of such modernizing of government as the Federal Reserve Act, he could understand nothing. The best men in the administration found that his mind was closed by an iron door behind which nestled only his stock phrases and set speeches.

Colonel House said of him, "I do not believe that anyone ever succeeded in changing his mind. He feels that his ideas are God given and are not susceptible to the mutability of those of the ordinary human being." David Huston remarked, "I discovered that one could drive a prairie schooner through any part of his argument and never scrape against a fact or a sound statement."

Bryan protested against the appointment of Dr Charles W. Eliot as ambassador to China on the grounds that "Eliot was a Unitarian and did not believe in the divinity of Christ, and the new Chinese civilization was founded upon the Christian movement." He spent his hours at his desk sending out autographed cards to Americans, asking them to sign their name above his and thus take the temperance pledge. He further made of his office an object of ridicule throughout the world by insisting upon appearing between vaudeville acts at Chautauqua revival meetings. After a little more than two years he had resigned from his office, to the relief of everyone, because he could not approve President Wilson's policy, which he thought was driving the United States into war. Once war was declared, he offered to enlist in the army as a private— at the age of sixty-five.

A fanatical worker for temperance in the drinking of liquors, he had told President Wilson that he would accept the position of secretary of state, "only if I do not have to serve intoxicating liquors in the course of my duties." However, according to the statement of the man who traveled with him on his presidential campaigns, "few more intemperate men ever lived. Sloan Gordon remembers one huge breakfast eaten by Bryan on a Virginia plantation in 1900. First a large cantaloupe. Then two quail followed by Virginia ham and a half-dozen eggs. After that a full plate of battercakes swimming in butter and a second helping of the same. In addition, there were many cups of coffee and fried potatoes and side dishes of various kinds before he left the table, ready to begin a day of speechmaking on temperance."

An associate commented, "When Bryan attempted to debate he entangled himself and his listeners in a mass of illogical and irrelevant material. His intentions were honest, but he was wrong."

That, thought Darrow, should be Bryan's epitaph: his intentions were honest, but he was wrong.

Bryan had been dealing in Florida real estate and had accumulated over a million dollars. He continued his preaching, particularly to the crowds in the parks at Miami, but both his influence and his powers were waning. He had tried unceasingly to wedge himself into office, to have Florida elect him to the United States Senate, to be elected moderator of the Presbyterian Church, which had just refused his command to pass an anti-evolution resolution. No one wanted to listen to him except the Fundamentalists of the Bible Belt.

Very well then, if God had reduced his vineyard to the Fundamentalists, then God must have meant for him to conquer the world through Fundamentalism. He traveled across mountains and prairies and swamps to harangue, exhort, plead and command that his followers work unceasingly to have their state legislatures pass anti-evolution laws. He hoped to turn Fundamentalism into a political movement of which he would be the head; he was confident that garbed in this righteous cause he could become so powerful that he could dictate the choice of President, congressman, governor; control the school, the university, the press.

He now raised both arms in a pontifical gesture. "My friends——" he said. "I beg your pardon, if the court please, I have been so in the habit of talking to an audience instead of a court that I will sometimes say 'my friends,' although I happen to know not all of them are my friends."

When the laughter subsided he continued. "If the people of Tennessee were to go into a state like New York, the one from which this impulse comes to resist this law, and tried to convince the people that a law they had passed ought not to be enforced, don't you think it would be resented as impertinence? The people of this state knew what they were doing when they passed the law, and they knew the dangers of the doctrine, knew that they did not want it taught to their children. It isn't proper to bring experts in here to try to defeat the purpose of the people of this state by trying to show that what they denounce and outlaw is a beautiful thing that everybody ought to believe in."

The courtroom clapped. Not satisfied with this solid argument, Bryan humorously attacked the evolution testimony of Dr Metcalf. Though his barbs steadily drew laughter, they were based on a tangential reasoning by means of which he avoided the point at issue. His loudest laugh was gained when he lamented satirically that the evolutionists wouldn't even let us descend from American monkeys, only from European monkeys.

The Fundamentalists were delighted with their champion; their confidence rose, for they felt that Bryan was annihilating the evolutionists by making fools of them. They listened with rapt eagerness while he maintained that evolution was not a theory but only a hypothesis, that since the evolutionists could not agree among themselves on the origin of the species, since important changes had been made since Darwin promulgated his findings, evolution was, therefore, an incoherent mass of conjecture and guesswork.

He then delivered the long-awaited sermon on the immutability of revealed religion. "The Bible is the word of God; the Bible is the only expression of man's hope of salvation. . . . That Bible is not going to be driven out of this court by experts who come hundreds of miles to testify that they can reconcile evolution with its ancestor in the jungle, with man made by God in His image, man put here for purposes as a part of the divine plan."

There were loud "Amens" from the back of the courtroom. Darrow cried, "I want those 'Amens' to be put in the record."

Encouraged by the response, Bryan rose to a higher pitch. "Your honor asked me whether evolution has anything to do with the principle of the virgin birth. Yes, because this principle of evolution disputes the miracles, there is no place for the miracles in this train of evolution, and the Old Testament and the New are filled with miracles. If this doctrine is true this logic eliminates every mystery in the Old Testament and the New and eliminates everything supernatural, and that means they eliminate the virgin birth—that means they eliminate the resurrection of the body—that means they eliminate the doctrine of atonement and that they believe man has been rising all the time, that man never fell, that when the Saviour came there was not any reason for His coming; there was no reason why He should not go as soon as He could . . . and when the Christians of this state have tied their hands and said, 'We will not take advantage of our power to teach religion to children by teachers paid by us,' these people come in from the outside of the state and force upon the people of this state and upon the children of the taxpayers of this state a doctrine that refutes not only their belief in God but their belief in a Saviour and belief in heaven and takes from them every moral standard that the Bible gives us."

The crowds swarmed around Bryan, shaking his hand, thumping him on the back, thanking him with tears in their eyes. Darrow turned to Arthur Garfield Hays, "Can it be possible that this trial is taking place in the twentieth century?"

The attorneys for the defense walked out of the courthouse glaze-eyed and bewildered. The only one who cheered them up was Representative Butler, who had written the Anti-Evolution Law. "The Judge ought to give 'em a chance to tell what evolution is," said Butler. "Course we got 'em licked anyhow, but I believe in being fair and square and American. Besides, I'd like to know what evolution is myself." Butler had thought that his Bible was the first and only Bible ever written; when someone had told him that the King James version of the Bible was not the only version the poor man was overcome.

The next morning the court assembled to hear Judge Raulston rule to exclude the experts and their testimony. He based his ruling on the claim that neither religion nor evolution was on trial, that Scopes was on trial for violating a specific Tennessee law.

Robbed of his last shred of defense by what he considered a prejudiced verdict, Darrow went icy with anger. When Judge Raulston attempted to interject humor into his ruling by saying, "I desire to suggest that I believe evolutionists should at least show man the consideration to substitute the word 'ascend' for 'descend,'" his anger exploded.

"The state of Tennessee doesn't rule the world yet," he snapped. "With the hope of enlightening the court as a whole I want to say that the scientists probably will not correct the words 'descent of man,' and I want to explain what descent means as starting with a low form of life and finally reaching man."

"We all have dictionaries," said Attorney General Stewart.

"I don't think the court has one," rejoined Darrow.

When he asked for the rest of the day to draw up certain papers which the defense wished to present to the court and the judge asked why it would take the rest of the day, Darrow replied, "I do not understand why every request of the defense is overruled."

"I hope you do not mean to reflect on the court?" asked Judge Raulston.

"Well," drawled Darrow, "your honor has the right to hope."

"I have a right to do something else," said the judge.

"All right, all right," murmured Darrow.

On Monday Judge Raulston cited him for contempt of court. "Men may become prominent," said Judge Raulston from the bench, "but they should never feel themselves superior to the law or to justice. He who would hurl contempt into the records of my court insults and outrages the good people of one of the greatest states of the Union." He thereupon ordered Darrow to appear before him the following morning to answer the citation and required him to post a lawful bond for five thousand dollars.

"I do not have to put it up this morning?" asked Darrow.

"Not until the papers are served upon you."

"Now I do not know whether I can get anybody, your honor."

Frank Spurlock of Chattanooga went bond. Darrow had placed himself at a disadvantage. Apologizing to the court, he said, "I have been practicing law for forty-seven years, and I have been most of the time in court . . . I never yet have in all my time had any criticism by the court for anything I have done in court. I haven't the slightest fault to find with the court. Personally I don't think it constitutes a contempt, but I am quite certain that the remark should not have been made and the court could not help taking notice of it, and

I am sorry that I made it ever since I got the time to read it, and I want to apologize to the court for it."

He got his biggest hand of the trial on this apology. Judge Raulston forgave him by saying, "My friends, and Colonel Darrow, the Man that I believe came into the world to save man from sin, . . . taught that it was godly to forgive. . . . I believe in that Christ. I believe in these principles. I accept Colonel Darrow's apology. I feel that I am justified in speaking for the people of the great state that I represent when I say to him that we forgive him and we forget it. . . ."

The next morning Judge Raulston ordered the trial to be transferred to the courthouse lawn because the throngs in the courtroom, with their laughter and applause and demonstrations, were weakening the floor, and there was danger of its collapsing. The judge, jury, and counsel were seated on the raised platform used by the preachers of the town, from which Bryan had delivered an address the Sunday before. The rough benches which covered almost the entire lawn were quickly filled with five thousand spectators, sweltering under the midsummer sun.

And once again Darrow caused an uproar; he demanded that the huge sign saying READ YOUR BIBLE, which was attached to the side of the building not more than ten feet from where the jury was to sit, be taken down because it was prejudicial to the interests of the defendant. Ben McKenzie sprang to his feet to voice the sentiments of the Tennesseans in the audience when he said, "It is their defense that they do not deny the Bible, that they expect to introduce proof to make it harmonize. Why should we remove the sign cautioning the people to read the word of God, just to satisfy the others in the case?" His son added, "I have never seen the time in the history of this country when any man should be afraid to be reminded of the fact that he should read his Bible, and if they represent a force that is aligned with the devil and his satellites——"

The accusation that Darrow, Hays and Malone were aligned with the devil caused a furor. Bryan entered the fray to cry, "If their arguments are sound and sincere, that the Bible can be construed so as to recognize evolution, I cannot see why READ YOUR BIBLE would necessarily mean partiality to our side. However . . . if leaving that up there during the trial makes our brother to offend, I would take it down during the trial."

Darrow agreed to let the READ YOUR BIBLE stay where it was, provided the defense could put up a banner of equal size right beside it, which would read, READ YOUR EVOLUTION.

Judge Raulston ordered the sign removed. The jury which again had been excluded during this fracas was brought in hopping mad because they had been sent out to during nine tenths of the trial and had missed the fun. They were ready to acquit Scopes of any and all charges to get even with the court.

It was an old Darrow stratagem of putting the prosecution on the defense, which not only kept the hearing alive but turned the tide of victory. He asked William Jennings Bryan if he would be willing to testify as an expert on the Bible. Bryan assented most happily, and the Scopes monkey trial provided the American people with what the New York *Times* described as the most amazing court scene in Anglo-Saxon history.

Bryan took his seat on the hard, spindle-legged pedestal, began fanning himself and faced his inquisitor. Darrow hesitated for a moment before beginning.

"You have given considerable study to the Bible, haven't you, Mr. Bryan?" he asked quietly.

"Yes, I have," replied Bryan. "I have studied the Bible for about fifty years."

"Do you claim that everything in the Bible should be literally interpreted?"

"I believe everything in the Bible should be accepted as it is given there; some of the Bible is given illustratively. For instance: 'Ye are the salt of the earth.' I would not insist that man was actually salt or that he had flesh of salt, but it is used in the sense of salt as saving God's people."

"Do you believe Joshua made the sun stand still?"

"I believe what the Bible says," answered Bryan doggedly.

"I suppose you mean that the earth stood still?"

"I don't know. I am talking about the Bible now. I accept the Bible absolutely."

"Do you believe at that time the entire sun went around the earth?"

"No, I believe the earth goes around the sun."

"Do you believe that the men who wrote it thought that the day could be lengthened or that the sun could be stopped?"

"I believe what they wrote was inspired by the Almighty, and He may have used language that could be understood at that time—instead of language that could not be understood until Darrow was born."

There was laughter and applause in the courtyard. Bryan beamed. Darrow stood quietly by, expressionless.

"Now, Mr. Bryan, have you ever pondered what would have happened to the earth if it stood still suddenly?"

"No."

"Don't you know it would have been converted into a molten mass of matter?"

301

"You testify to that when you get on the stand; I will give you a chance."

"You believe the story of the flood to be a literal interpretation?" Darrow now asked.

"Yes sir," replied Bryan.

"When was that flood?"

"I would not attempt to fix the day."

"But what do you think that the Bible itself says? Don't you know how it was arrived at?"

"I never made a calculation."

"What do you think?"

"I do not think about things I don't think about."

"Do you think about things you do think about?"

"Well, sometimes."

Once again there was laughter in the courtyard, but this time it was turned against Bryan. He did not like it. He turned to glare at the spectators. When Attorney General Stewart objected to Darrow's cross-examining his own witness Bryan replied, "These gentlemen did not come here to try this case. They came here to try revealed religion. I am here to defend it, and they can ask me any questions they please."

"How long ago was the flood, Mr Bryan?"

"Two thousand three hundred and forty-eight years B.C."

"You believe that all the living things that were not contained in the ark were destroyed?"

"I think the fish may have lived."

"Don't you know there are any number of civilizations that are traced back to more than five thousand years?"

"I am not satisfied by any evidence that I have seen."

"You believe that every civilization on the earth and every living thing, except possibly the fishes, were wiped out by the flood?"

"At that time."

"You have never had any interest in the age of the various races and peoples and civilizations and animals that exist upon the earth today?"

"I have never felt a great deal of interest in the effort that has been made to dispute the Bible by the speculations of men or the investigations of men."

"And you never have investigated to find out how long man has been on the earth?"

"I have never found it necessary."

"Don't you know that the ancient civilizations of China are six thousand or seven thousand years old, at the very least?"

"No, but they would not run back beyond the creation, according to the Bible, six thousand years."

"You don't know how old they are; is that right?"

"I don't know how old they are," answered Byran, "but probably you do. I think you would give the preference to anybody who opposed the Bible."

"Well, you are welcome to your opinion. Have you any idea how old the Egyptian civilization is?"

"No."

"Mr Bryan, you don't know whether any other religion ever gave a similar account of the destruction of the earth by the flood?"

"The Christian religion has satisfied me, and I have never felt it necessary to look up some competing religions."

"Do you know how old the Confucian religion is?"

"I can't give you the exact date of it."

"What about the religion of Confucius or Buddha? Do you regard them as competitive?"

"No, I think they are very inferior. Would you like for me to tell you what I know about it?"

"No. Do you know anything about how many people there were in Egypt thirty-five hundred years ago or how many people there were in China five thousand years ago?"

"No."

"Have you ever tried to find out?"

"No sir; you are the first man I ever heard of that has been interested in it."

"Mr Bryan, am I the first man you ever heard of who has been interested in the age of human societies and primitive man?"

"You are the first man I ever heard speak of the number of people at those different periods."

"You have never in all your life made any attempt to find out about the other peoples of the earth—how old their civilizations are, how long they have existed on the earth—have you?"

"No sir, I have been so well satisfied with the Christian religion that I have spent no time trying to find arguments against it. I have all the information I want to live by and to die by."

Darrow paused for a moment. "Mr Bryan, do you believe that the first woman was Eve?"

"Yes."

"Do you believe she was literally made out of Adam's rib?"

"I do."

"Did you ever discover where Cain got his wife?"

"No sir; I leave the agnostics to hunt for her."

"Do you think the sun was made on the fourth day?"

"Yes."

"And they had evening and morning without the sun?"

"I am simply saying it is a period."

303

"The creation might have been going on for a long time?"

"It might have continued for millions of years."

"Yes. All right." Darrow waited a long moment to allow this admission to sink in. "Do you believe the story of the temptation of Eve by the serpent?" he continued.

"I will believe just what the Bible says. Read the Bible and I will answer."

"All right, I will do that. 'And I will put enmity between thee and the woman and between thy seed and her seed; it shall bruise thy head and thou shalt bruise his heel. Unto the woman he said, "I will greatly multiply thy sorrow and thy conception; in sorrow thou shalt bring forth children; and thy desire shall be to thy husband, and he shall rule over thee." ' That is right, is it?"

"I accept it as it is."

"And God said to the serpent, 'Because thou hast done this, thou art cursed above all cattle, and above every beast of the field; upon thy belly shalt thou go and dust shalt thou eat all the days of thy life.' Do you think that is why the serpent is compelled to crawl upon its belly?"

"I believe that."

"Have you any idea how the snake went before that time?"

"No sir."

"Do you know whether he walked on his tail or not?"

"No sir. I have no way to know."

This answer brought a laugh, one with more derision than humor in it, the kind Bryan did not like. He flushed, turned to the judge. "Your honor, I think I can shorten this testimony. The only purpose Mr Darrow has is to slur at the Bible, but I will answer his questions, I shall answer them at once. I want the world to know that this man, who does not believe in a God, is trying to use a court in Tennessee——"

"I object to your statement," exploded Darrow. "I am exempting you on your fool ideas that no intelligent Christian . . . believes."

Judge Raulston was heartily sick of the rows. He ordered court adjourned before another one could break out. A group gathered about Darrow, shaking his hand and congratulating him. As he left the yard a throng followed him. Looking back, he saw Bryan standing with only one friend by his side. He had taken a terrible licking; the Bible had not suffered, but William Jennings Bryan had. He had been exposed as an ignoramus with a childlike mind. But Darrow felt neither triumphant nor happy; he remembered too well the day he had walked out of the Los Angeles courtroom after pleading the McNamaras guilty, when only one man had stood by him, when the crowd had turned against him as even now it turned against its own champion and spokesman.

In the press of the nation Bryan took an even worse beating, particularly from the columnists.

Bugs Baer released his acidulous humor on the father-and-son combination. " . . . The jury's verdict was that there were two Bryans, with no extenuating circumstances. Junior is a splendid orator of the hip-and-elbow type that mistakes a gesture for an argument and a loud voice for reason."

Will Rogers tried to be humorous but ended in deadly earnest. "Now personally, I like Bill, . . . but now he is going to try to drag something that pertains to the Bible into a political campaign. He can't ever do that. He might make Tennessee the side show of America, but he can't make a street carnival of the whole United States."

The next morning Judge Raulston ruled that Bryan could not go back on the stand, that everything he had said the day before had to be stricken from the evidence. The order to strike Bryan's testimony from the record was a blow to the defense, and yet it was at the same time their only victory. Had Bryan been successful in defending the Fundamentalist conception of the Bible he doubtless would have been permitted to return to the stand; Judge Raulston's ruling could only be an admission of rout, defeat.

The trial was over. The jury was brought in. Darrow asked that they agree on a verdict of guilty in order that the case might be appealed to the Tennessee Supreme Court. Sullenly the jury obeyed Darrow's request and Judge Raulston's instructions; they declared Scopes guilty. The judge fined him a hundred dollars, then made a closing address. "It sometimes takes courage to. . . . declare a truth or stand for an act that is in controvention to the public sentiment. A man who is big enough to search for the truth and find it and declare it in the face of all opposition is a big man."

Darrow thought this a fine and noble sentiment; he wished it had been manifested a little earlier in the trial.

The Darrows left with friends for the Smoky Mountains to cool off and enjoy a rest. Bryan remained in Dayton, preparing for publication the closing speech to the jury which he had not been permitted to make in court, one of the most abstruse, confused and unintelligible documents of its times. On Sunday morning he spoke in a near-by town, telling his audience of his plans for a national campaign to force all schools to teach evolution as a theory instead of a fact and to see that all teachers who taught evolution as a fact were made to resign. On the drive back to Dayton he had a serious discussion with his wife in which he agreed that although he must continue his fight against evolution he must not encroach upon individual religious beliefs, because this would be intolerance.

Back in Dayton, in spite of the intense midday heat, he ate one of his enormous dinners. He then lay down to take a nap and died in his sleep.

Clarence and Ruby were hiking across a summit of the Smoky Mountains when the word of Bryan's death was brought to them. They returned to Dayton. When reporters said to him, "People down here believe that Bryan died of a broken heart because of your questioning," Darrow shrugged his shoulders and murmured in a voice so soft that the reporters could not hear him, "Broken heart nothing; he died of a busted belly." Aloud he said, "His death is a great loss to the American people."

It was almost a year later that the appeal was heard by the Supreme Court of Tennessee. In his argument Darrow recapitulated his philosophy of the freedom of the human mind. Though the hearing in Nashville was more dignified than had been the one in Dayton, the same passions and prejudice were displayed, with audiences thronging the statehouse, jamming the court, indulging in wild bursts of applause.

The Tennessee Supreme Court reversed the decision of the Dayton court on the technicality that Judge Raulston, instead of the jury, had fixed the amount of the fine, a politic evasion. Two of the justices held that the Anti-Evolution Law was constitutional; a third held that it was constitutional but had nothing to do with the Scopes case. One justice declared the law to be unconstitutional.

"Always there is one man!" murmured Darrow. "Amen!"

The Scopes case had won another conquest for freedom: Bryan and his Fundamentalist dogma had been discredited; the literal interpretation of the Bible had been weakened; The high-school students of Tennessee were reading about evolution; the scientific approach to the understanding of man's inheritance had gained impetus; Judge Raulston had agreed to read Darwin's *Origin of the Species* and *Descent of Man*.

Yet for Clarence Darrow the most meaningful aftermath of the trial was that a dance was given in his honor by the young people of Dayton. This tiny uprising seemed to him as though it might be a good omen.

Chapter Thirteen

Road to Glory

HE HAD spent the balance of the summer after the Scopes case lecturing to large crowds in Kansas City, St Louis and Denver. Whatever his announced subject, the experts in that field came to listen; even Al Capone, the liquor racketeer, came to hear him speak on prohibition in a Negro church in Chicago. Shortly after Darrow had returned from Dayton he had been called to the telephone. After listening a while he said, "Why, no. Do you think I would do such a damned-fool thing as that?" and hung up the receiver, exasperated. Asked what the trouble was, he replied, "Why that damned-fool manager over at the vaudeville house has a trained ape, and he wants me to have my picture taken with the ape and he hasn't even got the ape's consent!"

He had been trying to retire from the practice of law since the Pettibone case in Boise in 1907. By 1926 he again had determined to take no more cases in which national conflict, intersectional strife, prejudice and passion played a part; he would watch from the side lines as younger and more vigorous men took up the cudgels. Practically every cause to which he had devoted himself had flashed into focus, giving him the opportunity to state his ultimate case. The sole labor of love which had not yet been afforded him was the chance to recapitulate the plight of the American Negro; he hoped to carry on his work in their behalf through writing and lecturing. Then, because it was an imperative of his life's design to resolve the causes with which he had been identified, in the city of Detroit, Michigan, race riots and mob violence culminated in the arrest of eleven Negroes on a charge of murder. He returned to New York in September, where he was visiting with Arthur Garfield Hays, when a committee from the National Association for the Advancement of Colored People called to urge him to undertake the defense of the family and friends of Dr. Ossian Sweet.

"We found Clarence in bed with all his clothes on," relates Arthur Spingarn. "He had been told that one colored man and two white men would come to see him." Spingarn, who had dark hair and a swarthy complexion, related the facts of the Sweet case to Darrow. When he had finished Darrow said sympathetically:

"Yes, I know full well the difficulties faced by your race."

"I'm sorry, Mr Darrow," replied Spingarn, "but I'm not a Negro."

Darrow turned to Charles Studin, another member of the committee, and said, "Well, you understand what I mean."

"I am not colored either," replied Studin.

Darrow looked at the third man, who had blond hair and blue eyes. "I would not make that mistake with you," he said.

"I am a Negro," replied Walter White, secretary of the National Association for the Advancement of Colored People.

Darrow jumped out of bed. "That settles it," he cried. "I'll take the case."

When Clarence was five years of age John Brown had come to Kinsman to confer with Amirus Darrow about the Underground Railroad. John Brown had put his hand on the boy's head and said, "The Negro has too few friends; you and I must never desert him." Darrow had followed this command. He said, "When it comes to human beings, I am color blind; to me people are not simply white or black; they are all freckled." While refusing to join hundreds of worthwhile organizations that had solicited his membership, he had been a member of the National Association for the Advancement of Colored People since its inception, contributing liberally of his time and money, writing articles for the Negro press, lecturing to their groups, helping them to form trade schools, colleges and labor unions, trying always to secure for them the rights guaranteed by the Federal government but ignored by the individual states. He had defended penniless Negroes in court, attended Negro churches; his friends among the colored people were frequently in his home. Ruby had worked by his side for tolerance and the eradication of racial prejudice.

On the twelfth of October Darrow arrived in Detroit to secure a brief postponement and to assemble the facts in the Sweet case. The expansion of the factories having created a demand for labor which could not be supplied by local markets, the manufacturers set up employment bureaus in various parts of the country, importing workers to Detroit in great numbers. The chief source of supply was the poor white and the Negro of the Southern states, where wages were low, labor mobile. By 1925 the Negro population in Detroit was sixty thousand, yet they were still confined to the three small wards that had been apportioned to six thousand of them in 1910. Rents were exorbitant; most of the buildings violated the health and safety laws. Since the Negro population was earning around seventy-five thousand dollars a day in wages, it was inevitable that there should be a constant immigration of colored doctors, dentists, lawyers, teachers, clergymen, businessmen and entertainers. Many of these could afford to buy good homes. As fewer residences became available in the Negro section, they looked for them outside the colored boundaries.

Many of Detroit's workers had brought with them from the South their anti-Negro prejudice. The police force had taken on a good many Southerners who did not doff their color prejudice when they donned the uniform of the city. During the war there had been a resurgence of the Ku Klux Klan, taking such strong root among the Southerners in Detroit that by 1925 it had gained control over portions of the political machine. When the more affluent colored people began seeking homes outside of their limited neighborhood the Ku Klux Klan organized neighborhood-improvement associations to keep them from either owning or renting property within these districts. Its propaganda campaign spread fear and distrust of the Negro among the native residents. The Detroit police instituted a reign of terror, shooting dead on the streets between forty and fifty colored men. The mayor issued a statement in which he begged the public to see that the riots "do not grow into a condition which will be a lasting stain on the reputation of Detroit as a law-abiding community." No investigation was made of the killings.

In early June of 1925 Dr Ossian Sweet, one of the most brilliant of Detroit's colored population, purchased for eighteen thousand five hundred dollars a two-story brick house in a foreign-born workingman's section. He anticipated no trouble when buying the house, partly because the husband of the white woman who owned it was a Negro (albeit so light in coloring that the neighborhood was never sure of his race) and because the house was only a few blocks from the white district in which Mrs Sweet, the cultivated, well-educated daughter of a Negro musician, had been raised. Yet there were signs on the horizon that portended trouble. Only three months before, a colored woman with a five-weeks-old baby had purchased a home on Merrill Street, in a white neighborhood; a crowd of whites had gathered and stoned it. The next day the woman resolutely had had the windows repaired. The threatening mob again gathered in front of the house. This time she fired over their heads with a shotgun. The crowd ran, but a white neighbor swore out a warrant for her arrest. In April a mob of whites attacked the home of another Negro who had moved a short distance out of the colored section. Dr Turner, highly respected physician and surgeon, was mobbed, his possessions smashed. Negro families who had lived for years in friendliness with their white neighbors

309

were threatened and warned to move back to the colored wards.

During the following weeks Dr Sweet saw three more families driven from their homes. He also knew that a Waterworks Park Improvement Association had been formed in his own neighborhood shortly after he had purchased his home on the corner of Charlevoix and Garland, and that at a meeting of this association held on the school grounds opposite his newly acquired property a crowd of six hundred people gathered to hear a speech by the incendiary who had led the mob which drove Dr Turner from his home. The woman from whom Dr Sweet had purchased his house but who had not yet moved out of it received a telephone call after the meeting of the association, telling her that the assemblage agreed to "co-operate in enforcement of existing property restrictions; that if Doctor Sweet moved in she would be killed, the house blown up." She cried to Sweet, "My God, since the other doctor has allowed them to run him out it looks like they will run everybody out!"

Ossian Sweet knew what these people meant by "co-operation in enforcement." It became obvious that he could not move into his new home without encountering serious trouble. He had already made the down payment of thirty-five hundred dollars, the total of his savings. If he gave up this house, took his loss, what was he to do then? He still had to have a home for himself and his family, and there was no home available in the colored district. If he did not move into this house, which he now owned, where would he move? If he, too, allowed a mob to keep him out of his own home by threats of force and violence, would he not be setting a precedent which would victimize his fellow Negro throughout the land, keep him forever penned within the slums? Could he let himself down? Could he let his people down?

The answer to the problem emerged from the character of the man. Ossian Sweet had been born in Orlando, Florida. He had worked his way through Wilberforce Academy in Ohio and the medical school of Howard University in Washington, D.C. Equipped with a first-rate brain and an indomitable resolution to "rise in the world and make a great deal of money," he paid his tuition by firing furnaces, shoveling snow, waiting on table and serving at parties. In 1921 he opened an office in the colored section of Detroit, where he was immediately successful. The following year he had married Gladys Mitchell. After two years of practice they had put together sufficient savings for a trip to Europe. Ossian worked in the hospitals of Vienna studying gynecology and pediatrics, then went to Paris where he worked under Madame

Curie. Upon returning to Detroit the Sweet family lived with Gladys' parents until the spring of 1925, when Gladys Sweet went looking for a home. "I had in mind only two things," said Mrs. Sweet; "first to find a house that was in itself desirable and, second, to find one that would be within our pocketbook. I wanted a pretty home, and it made no difference to me whether it was in a white neighborhood or a colored neighborhood. Only I couldn't find such a house in the colored neighborhood."

Dr Sweet decided that he must not only move into his new home at all costs but that he must defend it against mob violence. He notified the Detroit police that he was going to move in on September eighth. At ten-thirty in the morning, under police guard, he arrived with two small vans of furniture, a supply of food and a case containing ten guns and almost four hundred rounds of ammunition. Dr and Mrs Sweet, who had left their baby with its grandparents, were joined by two of Ossian's brothers, Dr Otis Sweet, a dentist, and Henry, a student at Wilberforce College. With them went a chauffeur, a chum of Henry's and another friend. Two colored women decorators came in later in the afternoon to assist Mrs Sweet.

Through the neighborhood spread the news that the Negroes had moved in. That evening large numbers of people walked up and down in front of the house. The decorators were too frightened at the aspect of the loiterers to leave. The next day Dr and Mrs Sweet did some shopping downtown, returning home late in the afternoon. They were joined by three friends from the Liberty Life Insurance office. When night fell a crowd began assembling across the street and in the schoolyard. As the laborers came home from work the mob swelled, until it consisted of about four hundred people. Mrs Sweet remained in the kitchen preparing dinner; the men pulled down the blinds, kept the front room dark. Ten policemen walked up and down in front of the Sweet home. Traffic was blocked off by other officers for three blocks around, but cars and taxicabs kept driving up and discharging passengers.

The mob was in a quarrelsome mood. They began throwing stones at the house. "Somebody went to the window," said Dr Sweet, "and I heard him remark, 'People—the people!' I ran out to the kitchen where my wife was. There were several lights burning. I turned them out and opened the door. I heard someone yell, 'Go and raise hell in front! I'm going back!' After getting a gun I ran upstairs. Stones were hitting the house. . . ."

Dr Sweet threw himself on his bed and lay in an agony of fear and uncertainty: Should he surrender, put his family into

311

the protection of the police? . . . flee his new home . . . or should he fight it out? . . . sacrifice the lives of the ten people in the house. . . .

A stone hurtled through the bedroom window, splashing the doctor with broken glass. He jumped up in a paroxysm of terror, ran downstairs. "Pandemonium broke loose," he said. "Everyone was running from room to room. There was a general uproar. Somebody yelled, 'There's someone coming.' They said, 'That's your brother!' A car had pulled up to the curb. My brother and Mr Davis got out. The mob yelled, 'Here's niggers. Get them! Get them!' As they rushed in a mob surged forward. It looked like a human sea. Stones kept coming faster."

Suddenly a shot was fired. Six of the Negroes inside the house fired their guns. One man across the street fell dead. Another was injured. The police instantly thronged into the dark house, turned on the lights, pulled up the shades, arrested the ten Negroes and Mrs Sweet. They were charged with murder. As in the Arthur Person case in Rockford and in the Peter Bianchi, Mary Nardini case of Milwaukee, it was the state against ten men and one woman; the state against Clarence Darrow for the defense.

No set of circumstances in all of his experience moved him to such depths of pity. For a half century now he had been preaching that hatred created hatred, that violence begot violence. Today it was the Negro who was suffering. Who would be tomorrow's victim of this transgression of human rights and dignity? And how was he to prevent mob violence in Detroit from convicting these eleven human beings and sending them to prison? How could he win their freedom when Detroit was determined to convict?

"A kind of hysteria swept over the city," says Mrs Josephine Gomon, a prominent civic leader. "The law-and-order leaders and organizations demanded that these Negroes be made an example. The presiding judge was reluctant to take any action. It was the custom to rotate the office of presiding judge, and it was Frank Murphy's turn next. He told me that no action would be taken until he was presiding. 'Every judge on this bench is afraid to touch the case. They think it's dynamite. They don't realize that this is the opportunity of a lifetime to demonstrate sincere liberalism and judicial integrity at a time when liberalism is coming into its own." As soon as Judge Murphy took his seat he released Mrs Sweet on bail, an act which met with disfavor.

For Darrow it would once again be a case tried in a court of law but in which almost no law would be involved. He learned that the prosecution was formulating its attack on two lines: first, that the fact that the indicted ones were Negroes did not alter the situation; second, that there had been no mob in front of the Sweet home, no violence had been threatened or performed, that the Sweets were in no conceivable danger and hence the shots fired were unjustified and constituted first-degree murder. The only important point of law over which he had to concern himself was, what constituted a "mob"? It was to be his task to prove to the jury that there had been a hostile gathering in front of the Sweet house, in sufficient number to justify the Sweets in believing that they had to protect their home against violence. But from beginning to end it was to be a trial by race prejudice.

He spent three weeks in selecting his jury; he did more than select a jury; he gave the jurors a three weeks' education in the history of the Negro, the only group of people in the country that had been forced into American life. He portrayed feelingly the tragedy of the American Negro imprisoned always in the psychic wilderness of inferiority, relegated to menial and debasing labor, kept in fear, ignorance and poverty. Two Detroit schoolteachers, strangers to Ruby Darrow, telephoned her to ask if, since they wanted to hear Mr Darrow present his viewpoint on race prejudice, she could get them seats in the courtroom. Mrs Darrow gave one of them her own seat and made arrangements for the other. They enjoyed the forenoon session so much, they begged to be allowed to return for the afternoon.

"I explained that I was having James Weldon Johnson, head of the National Association for the Advancement of Colored People, as my guest for luncheon in the basement cafeteria of the courthouse," says Ruby, "and if they cared to join us we could all go back to court together. The two women were speechless; they didn't see how they could allow it to be said that they had sat with a colored person at a meal, the feeling in Detroit being so high and they teachers in the public school. Their very livelihood depended on their preserving their standing. I asked them to meet Mr Johnson and then decide whether they would be my guests with him. They were won by Mr Johnson's personality and his achievements. As a result of this meeting Bernice Powels founded clubs for colored boys and girls and has worked toward making the Detroit schools accept colored students on an equal basis with the whites."

A reporter for the Detroit *Free Press* was to say, "When I was assigned to cover the trial I had the average prejudice against Negroes. Now as I look back over the trial which ended a week ago I am lonesome for some of the Negroes I met. The thought comes to call them up or, better still, go to see them. I want to know them better, go into their homes, meet their children and grandparents. I give Clarence Darrow credit for destroying my race hatred. He opened up a new and interesting vista for me."

His examination was confined to one main tack: "Are you prejudiced against the Negro? Do you consider him as an equal and as a fellow American? Do you like him? Do you believe in him? Do you believe you could give him as fair and square a deal as you would a white man? Will you make every effort to keep prejudice out of your hearts?" After exhausting his panel of two hundred men, he came to the conclusion that he at least had twelve men who, if they were prejudiced against the Negro, carried that prejudice so deep in their minds they did not know it was there. As the jury was taking its oath Darrow turned to Mrs Gomon and said: "The case is won or lost now. The rest is window dressing."

The window dressing proved to be highly dramatic and revealing. The prosecution put on the stand seventy-one witnesses, most of whom lived in the neighborhood of the Sweet house, to testify that although they individually had been close to the Sweet home on the night of the disturbance, they had seen no crowds and had not seen each other. Under Darrow's relentless cross-examination they writhed and stumbled through explanations of having been at the corner of Garland and Charlevoix that evening to locate errant wives, daughters, sons. In spite of the fact that he was able to make the explanation appear ludicrous, to demonstrate their intense racial prejudice, they held fiercely to their story: there had been no unusual gathering in front of the Sweet house on the night of the shooting; the Sweets had been in no danger. The policemen who had been sent to guard the Sweets while they moved into their home testified that although they had blocked off traffic that night, they had seen no unusual crowds across from the Sweet house. In 1941 Prosecutor Toms said,

"There were probably more people around the Sweet house than the people's witnesses testified to and less than the defendant's witnesses testified. At any rate, there were enough to frighten (and justifiably so) a group of nervous, apprehensive Negroes who anticipated trouble. I am sure that the police had the situation well in hand and that there was no immediate danger of the house being stormed or any real riotous conduct. Undoubtedly the situation did not appear that peaceful and harmless to the colored people in the house, and their conduct should probably not be judged from a calm and unimpassioned point of view."

For the defense Darrow called to the stand only a few witnesses. One man revealed the meeting of the Waterworks Park Improvement Association during which violence against

Sweet was urged if he moved into his newly bought home. A newspaper reporter told that, passing close to the Sweet house on the night of the killing, he had had his car routed away from the scene by a police officer, had come back on foot and seen a crowd of between four and five hundred people surrounding the Sweet house. Ray Lorenzo, proprietor of a close-by automobile-accessory shop, estimated that there were at least five hundred people in the schoolyard across from the Sweet house on the night of the shooting. Mrs Mary Spaulding testified that, while driving through the neighborhood on the night of the shooting, she saw people gathered at the corner as if for a meeting and testified that there were at least five hundred.

In spite of the scene of passion that was being described the trial was carried on in an aura of judicial calm, the like of which Darrow had rarely experienced. Prosecutor Robert Toms tells, "I was quite aware of Mr Darrow's capacity for invective and I did not propose to lay myself open by matching barbs with him. Accordingly I treated him throughout the trial with the utmost reverence and deference. After a week of this he said to me, 'God damn it, Toms, I can't get going. I am supposed to be mad at you and I can't even pretend that I am.' He complained throughout the trial that my decent treatment of him was purely strategic and that it was working a great hardship on him."

The second outstanding characteristic of the trial was the startling contrast in the educational and cultural development of the white neighbors of the Sweets, the Poles, Assyrians, Swedes and Germans, and of the Negro witnesses, including the Sweet family, who testified for the defense. The white neighbors were laborers who had had almost no schooling, spoke English badly and were not only unread but uncultivated. The Negroes were largely college graduates, and included doctors, dentists, teachers, clergymen, lawyers, social-service workers, most of whom spoke well and showed evidence of developed minds. For Darrow the irony of the trial was that it was the Sweets who were lowering themselves by moving into a house on the corner of Garland and Charlevoix.

Arthur Garfield Hays, who was associated with Darrow in the case, pleaded superbly and brought every technical point to its logical conclusion. Darrow didn't trouble himself over the technical aspects. Toms relates, "During the course of the trial a rather complex legal point was raised, and all the attorneys retired to the library to look it up. Darrow, however, remained seated in the courtroom. As I passed him he said, 'You go along and talk to Arthur Hays; I can't be annoyed with the goddamn books!'"

The first break in the case he earned for his clients by the intensity of his cross-examination. He cross-examined Alfred H. Andrew, who admitted he had attended a meeting of the Waterworks Park Improvement Association on the grounds of the Howe School before the riot. He also admitted that a visiting member of the Tireman Avenue Improvement Association was among the speakers.

"Did he tell you about any race-riot trouble they had in his neighborhood?" asked Darrow.

"Yes, he told us about a Negro named Doctor Turner, who had bought a house on Spokane Avenue."

"Did he say his organization made Turner leave?"

"Yes. He said that they wouldn't have Negroes in their neighborhood and that they would co-operate with us in keeping them out of ours."

"Did the crowd applaud him?"

"Yes."

"Did you applaud?"

"Yes."

"You feel that way now?"

"Yes, I haven't changed."

"You know a colored man has certain rights?"

"Yes, I was in favor of keeping the Sweets out by legal means."

"Did the speaker talk of legal means?"

"No, he was a radical. I myself do not believe in violence."

"Did anybody in that audience of five hundred or more people protest against the speaker's advocacy of violence?"

"I don't know."

A Mr Monet insisted that there were only a few people in the street on the night of the shooting but under Darrow's cross-examination admitted that he had joined the Waterworks Park Improvement Association to keep out Sweet and his family. The owner of a filling station near the Sweet house, who swore there was no particular crowd there on the fatal night, finally admitted that he had sold an unusual amount of gas during the hours in question. A young boy who admitted that there had been "a large crowd" opposite the Sweet home stopped short in his story, as though he had said something he shouldn't have. The police lieutenant in charge, who had ten officers with him in front of the Sweet house, denied that there had been any congregating or any disturbance, then admitted that he had run for reserves immediately the first shot had been fired. One ominous piece of evidence the prosecution was unable to explain away was the quantity of rocks picked up from the Sweet lawn on the morning after the shooting.

The third outstanding characteristic of the trial was the

changing nature of the spectators. When the trial opened the audience was largely composed of whites; only a few colored people had the courage to attend or were able to find places in the courtroom. However, as the trial progressed, the colored spectators grew in number. By the time Darrow rose to his feet to make his final plea it was a plea he was making to a white jury and a colored world.

In addition to proving that a threatening mob was assembled before the Sweet house, which had already thrown stones and inflicted damage, he set out to prove that the bullet which had killed Leon Breiner could not have been fired from the Sweet house but had been fired by a policeman who admitted having "emptied his gun during the excitement."

He then illuminated the crux of the Sweet murder case. He called Dr Ossian Sweet to the stand to describe his state of mind on the night of September eighth with the milling crowd outside his home. Ossian Sweet told of the race riots he had seen in Washington, when colored men had been hunted through the streets by mobs; of the violence of the Chicago race riots; of the five Negroes who were shot to death in Rosewood when eighteen Negro homes and a Negro church were burned; of the four Johnson brothers of Arkansas, one a physician and another a dentist, who had been taken from a train and lynched; of Dr. A. C. Jackson of Tulsa, whom the Mayo brothers had declared to be a first-rate surgeon and who was murdered by the police to whom he surrendered after trying to protect his home from a mob; of the three thousand Negroes who had been lynched within one generation, of the mobs that had burned, hung, shot and beaten his fellow Negroes to death.

Coming back to Detroit, Dr Sweet told of violence that had been exerted against colored people who had moved into homes in the white sections. Dr Turner had bought a house on Spokane Avenue, had moved in under police guard, but his house had been broken into, the furniture smashed, the windows broken, the interior defaced, his shattered belongings thrown into a van which had been backed up to the front door. Sweet had seen the mob stone the colored couple as they fled. He commented, "Turner always had the greatest confidence in the word of white people; he felt that they belonged to a race superior to his own. Consequently when they wanted to enter his house to rob him it wasn't necessary to break down the door. It was far simpler to deceive him. One of the leaders simply knocked and, when Doctor Turner came to the door, said, 'Open, Turner, I'm your friend.' Turner believed him and opened the door. The next moment he was dough in the hands of the mob."

Referring to the night of the shooting, he said quietly, "When

I opened the door and saw the mob I realized I was facing the same mob that had hounded my people through its entire history. In my mind I was pretty confident of what I was up against. I had my back against the wall. I was filled with a peculiar fear, the fear of one who knows the history of my race. I knew what mobs had done to my people before."

At the end of the seven weeks Darrow made his final appeal. Arthur Garfield Hays reports, "In his address to the jury Darrow showed his master hand. The ordinary lawyer collates facts, analyzes evidence and makes his appeal. There are few who use history, psychology and philosophy in order to show the real underlying facts. Darrow said to those men on the jury that if he had merely to appeal to reason he would have little doubt of the result but that the difficulty lay deeper. It arose from a prejudice which white men take in with their mother's milk. Darrow questioned whether it was possible for twelve white men, however they might try, to give a fair trial to a Negro."

"The Sweets spent their first night in their new home afraid to go to bed," observed Darrow. "The next night they spent in jail. Now the state wants them to spend the rest of their lives in the penitentiary. There are persons in the North and the South who say a black man is inferior to the white and should be controlled by the whites. There are also those who recognize his rights and say he should enjoy them. To me this case is a cross section of human history. It involves the future and the hope of some of us that the future shall be better than the past."

The jury was out for three days and three nights; the quarreling was so violent that it could be heard through the courthouse. Furniture in the jury room was broken; one juror lost twelve pounds. Judge Murphy, convinced that no verdict was possible, declared them a hung jury and ended the trial.

It was rarely vouchsafed to Clarence Darrow to go through an ordeal only once; most of his major cases he had had to try twice. If this pattern of repetition doubled his exhaustion it also doubled his opportunity to campaign for tolerance.

Prosecutor Toms decided to try young Henry Sweet alone, since Henry had admitted firing his gun. Toms went to great pains to gather testimony to the effect that the slain man had been stooping over, lighting his pipe, when the bullet had hit him and that for this reason it would have been entirely possible for the bullet to have come from the Sweet house. When the trial opened Darrow nullified Prosecutor Toms's efforts by admitting that Henry Sweet might have fired the shot, claiming that it was in defense of his life and his home.

The second trial was practically a replica of the first; the outstanding difference lay in Darrow's final plea. "I shall never forget that final plea to the jury," says Mrs. Gomon. "He talked for eight hours. One could have heard a pin drop in the crowded courtroom. Everyone listened breathlessly, crowded so closely together that women fainted and could not fall. He went back through the pages of history and the progress of the human race to trace the development of fear and prejudice in human psychology. Sometimes his resonant, melodious voice sank to a whisper. Sometimes it rose in a roar of indignation. The collars of the jurors wilted. They sat tense, in the grip of contemplation of historic events and tragic happenings which he made real and present before their very eyes.

"As Judge Murphy left the bench I met him just inside the door of his office. I had never seen him so moved. He took my hand and said, 'This is the greatest experience of my life. That was Clarence Darrow at his best. I will never hear anything like it again. He is the most Christlike man I have ever known.'"

His closing words in his last great case of social urgency were more a defense of his own philosophy and of himself as a member of the human race than of Henry Sweet, the accused one, for once again he placed all of humanity in the prisoner's dock.

"I do not believe in the law of hate. I may not be true to my ideals always, but I believe in the law of love, and I believe you can do nothing with hatred. I would like to see a time when a man loves his fellow man and forgets his color or his creed. We will never be civilized until that time comes. I know the Negro race has a long road to go. I believe the life of the Negro race has been a life of tragedy, of injustice, of oppression. The law has made him equal, but man has not. And, after all, the last analysis is, what has man done? and not what has the law done? I know there is a long road ahead of him before he can take the place which I believe he should take. I know that before him there is suffering, sorrow, tribulation and death among the blacks and perhaps the whites. I am sorry. I would do what I could to avert it. I would advise patience; I would advise toleration; I would advise understanding; I would advise all of those things which are necessary for men who live together.

"What do you think is your duty in this case? I have watched day after day these black, tense faces that have crowded this court. These black faces that now are looking to you twelve whites, feeling that the hopes and fears of a race are in your keeping.

"This case is about to end, gentlemen. To them it is life.

Not one of their color sits on this jury. Their fate is in the hands of twelve whites. Their eyes are fixed on you, and their hopes hang on your verdict.

"I ask you, on behalf of this defendant, on behalf of these helpless ones who turn to you, and more than that—on behalf of this great state and this great city which must face this problem and face it fairly—I ask you, in the name of progress and of the human race, to return a verdict of not guilty in this case."

As the jury filed out Darrow indicated one of them and "smiled in that slow, quizzical way he had. 'That is the most stubborn man I have ever run up against. I didn't make any impression on him. His mind is made up, and I don't think anything could have changed him. I wonder if he is for or against us.'"

Later they learned that "when this juror went into the jury room he pulled a box of cigars and a book out of his pocket and announced to his fellow jurors, 'When you get ready to vote not guilty call on me. Until then I am not interested,' and proceeded to light a cigar and settle himself with his book."

At the end of three hours the jury sent word that it had reached a verdict. Judge Murphy took his place upon the bench; the jury filed in. The foreman announced, "Not guilty!" Dr Ossian Sweet thanked Darrow in the name of the twelve million American Negroes for this verdict which freed not only Henry Sweet and the other defendants but, in some small measure, the colored people.

Darrow was unutterably weary from the long and impassioned plea; he sank heavily into his chair. Prosecutor Toms, thinking that he was about to faint, rushed to his side and put both arms around him. Darrow's eyes twinkled as he looked up at Toms.

"Oh, I'm all right," he murmured. "I've heard that verdict before."

At last, following the Henry Sweet case in May of 1926, Clarence Darrow decided that the only way to retire was to retire. He packed up his papers, moved his beautiful black desk and chairs home to the Midway. One of the rear bedrooms had been converted into a study, and here, for the next decade, he devoted the major portion of his time to writing articles for magazines. Continuing in his role as the man on America's conscience, he entered the fray wherever he thought personal liberty and freedom were being invaded.

His articles were sharp, witty, fearless and discerning, but in only one field did his work stand out with a passion and a fury that made him worthy of his master in pamphleteering,

Voltaire. As early as 1909 he had begun writing and lecturing against prohibition. In 1909 in New Bedford, Massachusetts, under the auspices of the New England Union Labor League, he delivered his first scathing talk against the proposed plan to prohibit the sale of liquor. He fought the passage of the Eighteenth Amendment with every weapon at hand; now, seeing the evils it had brought upon the country, he re-entered the struggle to help eradicate it from American life. He published frequent articles in magazines; he lectured and debated in nearly every American city; he published a book in collaboration with Victor S. Yarros called *The Prohibition Mania*, which was widely read and helped considerably in establishing the full case against prohibition by debunking the statistical charts in favor of prohibition published by Professor Irving Fisher.

His argument was not merely that prohibition did not work; that the nature of man being what it is, it could never work; that it increased rather than decreased drinking and drunkenness and was forcing upon people crude and often poisonous liquor; that it was breeding a new class of racketeer, gangster and criminal which was becoming a serious threat to the preservation of law and order. Though these things seemed to him to be of major importance, he based his attack against prohibition on the ground that it was a grievous invasion of personal liberty. He argued that a hundred million persons had had their lives circumscribed on the grounds that a few men and women had drunk to excess, that prohibition was a hang-over of Puritanism and, if tolerated by the American people, would set a precedent for the further encircling of human rights. Because he did not believe that the Eighteenth Amendment ever could be repealed, he advocated that Congress simply refuse to allocate funds for the enforcement of the Volstead Act; it was one of his few errors in social diagnosis.

In 1928 Paul sold the gas plant in Greeley. To Darrow his share seemed a small fortune. He invested the entire sum in remunerative stocks and prepared to live out the rest of his life on his income.

He and Ruby went to Europe, where for a year they had a magnificent time traveling through the countries they loved, visiting with economists, writers, artists, sculptors, with old friends such as John A. Hobson, T. P. O'Connor, H. G. Wells, Charles Edward Russell, Brand Whitlock, Somerset Maugham and Jo Davidson. They toured England, Scotland and Wales by car with W. R. Kellogg; they spent happy months wandering through Switzerland and France as they had on their honeymoon, and again, as on their honeymoon, Clarence began a new book. He felt too old now to tackle the long novel

321

he had been contemplating for twenty years; instead he started work on his autobiography. Ruby worked with him, often typing most of the night so that he might have fresh manuscript to read in the morning. He was to call the book *The Story of My Life,* though it might more accurately have been called *The Story of My Philosophy,* for his almost pathological modesty kept him from telling very much of his own participation in his important cases and causes.

He wrote little else while in Europe, but he continued to send childlike letters to his twelve-year-old granddaughter Mary, as he had through the years. "Dear Mary: Enclosed you will find five dollars. This is sent to you on condition that you shall buy nothing useful with it. Don't spend any of it for stockings or food or tuition. Don't send any of it to foreign missions; the heathens are bad enough as they are. Don't buy any books, at least none that are good and dull. You can buy Esquimaux pie, for that is unhealthy and will make you look sick and interesting. . . . The only thing they use the Parliament Building for is a big clock up in the tower. The clock is mighty handy, for it strikes every fifteen minutes all night, so that when it wakes you up you can tell what time it is without turning on the light and looking at your watch. This is a mighty good plan, because if the clock didn't strike in the night you might go right on sleeping and never know what time it was until you woke up in the morning, and in that way you would lose a lot of time. . . ."

Then in November of 1929 the stock market crashed in New York City. Darrow returned to America to find himself almost penniless at the age of seventy-three, with a living to make. The loss of his money led him to plunge once again into a controversy which kept him both interested and excited and covered another mile along the endless road to brotherhood and unity.

He vowed that he would not try to go back into the law but would earn his living from writing and lecturing. An enterprising young lecture manager by the name of George Whitehead, who worked out of the Redfern Agency in Chicago, conceived the idea of staging four-way debates on religion. In the big cities of the Midwest he arranged with a Protestant clergyman, a prominent Catholic spokesman and a Jewish rabbi to meet with Clarence Darrow, the agnostic, on one platform, to present their varying views. Whitehead was an intelligent, lovable chap whom Darrow enjoyed; sometimes they would be out on the road together for weeks at a stretch. When they were taking the night train out of Chicago Darrow would put on a long white nightgown which he would stuff into his pants; Whitehead would call for him, and they would go down to the station together in a cab. Ruby always prepared two satchels filled with dozens of neat little boxes and envelopes, each labeled, one containing handkerchiefs, another his shoestring ties, another shoelaces, another needles and thread and buttons, another cookies, another fruit, another bottles of medicine. She had a standing arrangement with the Pullman Company to send back all the things he left behind him in the berth and smoking rooms.

He complained to Whitehead that "Ruby takes too good care of me; apparently she believes that eternal vigilance is the price of a husband." Once when he went to New York alone the Spingarns found him greatly disturbed. He took out a shirt and begged Mrs. Spingarn to duplicate it. The doctor had forbidden him to smoke; Ruby had allowed him to make the trip alone on a promise that he would not smoke, and he had burned a hole in the shirt.

"Why not just lose it in the Pullman?" asked Spingarn.

"You don't know Ruby," mourned Darrow.

The four-way debates on religion carried to an even higher pitch the excitement that had been generated by the Scopes case. Outside the Carnegie Music Hall in Pittsburgh a thousand people who were unable to buy tickets tried to break into the auditorium; the police had to be called to control them.

"The only fair way to arrange the order of speaking," said Whitehead, "was to have the four men draw lots from a hat. Since Darrow was always the oldest of the group and, in addition, a visitor in town, the three participants invariably paid him the courtesy of having him draw first. I couldn't have my star open the show, so I always concealed the number-one slip under the hatband before Darrow dove in. I never told him about this little stunt; he would not have permitted me to do it if he had known."

On the morning of each debate Whitehead would arrange a breakfast at which the Protestant, the Catholic, the Jew and the agnostic would meet and discuss the program for that evening, with the photographers and newspapermen present. In Houston they signed a paper for a reporter on which the Protestant clergyman wrote, "God is love." The Catholic wrote, "Religion is love of God and fellow man." The Jew wrote, "I believe that Judaism is the best religion for the Jew, Christianity for the Christian, Mohammedanism for the Mohammedan, agnosticism for the agnostic." Darrow glanced at the three sentences, winked at the reporters and scribbled, "If the above sentiments really represent what religion is, then I shall stop debating." After each debate they gathered at the home of the Catholic or the rabbi to meet the cream of the town's intellects and to enjoy the best of food, drink and conversation. "Almost never did the Protestant clergyman give the party," commented Whitehead, "and almost never would he attend at someone else's home."

For several years they crisscrossed over the face of the nation, lecturing and debating in forums of religion. "We covered the United States," relates Whitehead, "but Mr Darrow steadfastly refrained from intruding himself in California because of the unpleasantness at the ending of the McNamara case."

When he went to Pittsburgh to debate Judge Michael Musmanno on "Does Man Live Again?" the judge asked him, during their get-acquainted meeting at the hotel, "How do you feel about the case in which *you* were the defendant?"

"The sons of bitches," muttered Darrow. "They knew damn well I was innocent, but they knew also damn well that if they accused me there would be somebody to believe the accusation."

"On the platform," says Judge Musmanno, "he was utterly different from the man who had been conversing intimately with me a few minutes before. He was the antagonist, the fighter, the inexorable adversary . . . He questioned the authenticity of my quotation from Voltaire and when I was able to find the quotation in a book on the table and presented it to him he still shrugged his shoulders to dispute the point. Here he was being the intellectual athlete, the consummate actor, the resourceful barrister. Even with the most damaging evidence being presented against his case he still shrugged his shoulders as if to say: 'Oh well, that doesn't amount to much.' Yet if I had failed to authenticate the quotation in question he would have pulverized me with scorn.

"At the conclusion I was surprised at the sincere affection with which he grasped my hand, because I thought he was angry with me."

He received five hundred dollars for each debate, plus fifty dollars for expenses. For one gigantic meeting in Orchestra Hall in Chicago Darrow's cut would have been seventeen hundred and fifty dollars. He insisted that this was too much, that his three opponents be given a bonus and that Professor Hayden be paid for serving as chairman. Says Whitehead, "Mr Darrow always leaned over backward to give men the best part of the deal. With rare exceptions we had capacity audiences. Mr Darrow enjoyed these meetings as much for the association with the local intellectuals as for the compensation."

He got a kick out of matching wits with his adversaries on the platform, but his interest lay in bringing religion into the open air and sunshine of free discussion. There was freedom of religious worship in America, but there was also a tendency on the part of the various religions to suspect, dislike and fear each other. He felt that if every man could be acquainted with every other man's religion, visit his church, understand his point of view, the fear, suspicion and dislike would melt away. Yet of the four men on the platform in each of the cities, the only one who was received with suspicion, fear and dislike was the agnostic among them.

"Eighty per cent of the audiences hated Darrow's point of view," reports Whitehead, "and came to the meeting to hear it demolished. Darrow violated all the rules of oratory, yet he watched his audience like a hawk. He would get under the hide of the religionists, but in the next moment he would say something nice, and they would have to like him. He could tell how far he could carry his audience, and he would spank them half to death, but he knew when he had to give them relief. Many came despising him, thinking him a devil with horns. They went away liking him and feeling sorry for him."

He countered the native ill feeling of his audiences by his humor. One of his opponents told an audience, "I am the master of my fate; I am the captain of my soul." Darrow retorted, "The captain of his soul? Why, he isn't even a deck hand on a raft!" When asked by one of his opponents if, when he died, he didn't want to live eternally, he replied, "When I die all I ask is that there be some friends who will remember my weaknesses and forget my virtues." When debating Albert Edward Wiggam in Cleveland Darrow said, "I am surprised and grieved to hear my friend say that rich men are the most intelligent. Imagine a man with brains spending his time making money! The best way to get money is to marry it." When the subject of marriage came up for discussion and one of his opponents asked, "Mr Darrow, don't you think that marriage could be described as a lottery?" he replied, "Yes, if only there were prizes."

Once when he was debating Professor Scott Nearing on the subject "Is Life Worth Fighting For?" in Symphony Hall in Boston, Nearing, who was arguing for the affirmative, defeated Darrow by a clever maneuver. Professor Nearing enumerated a list of the contributions Clarence Darrow had made to mankind, then, turning to Darrow, said, "What you have done bolsters my argument more than anything else." Darrow received a thunderous ovation.

And so the years passed pleasantly for the Old Lion. His autobiography was well received by both the critics and the public, fulfilling his hope that "someday I shall write a book where the royalties will pay for the copies I give away." When the autobiography was first released a woman journalist of Chicago called Ruby to tell her that Mr Darrow had no right to call his book an autobiography because he had told nothing whatever of his love life. When Clarence returned home that evening Ruby related the conversation to him, adding that the woman had insisted he could have done a whole chapter on his love life. "A whole chapter," grunted Darrow. "Why, I could do a whole library!" Catching Ruby's wifely stare, he apologized with "Well, maybe not a whole library, but at least a couple of best sellers."

Though he considered himself as out of the practice of law, he went back to the courts whenever he thought he could save a human life. He defended Greco and Carrillo, anti-Fascists who were accused of murdering two Italian Fascists parading in New York City. The sole connection between Greco, Carrillo and the killing was that Greco and Carrillo had opposed the Fascist movement in America. When Arthur Garfield Hays and a defense committee asked him to try to save the two boys he said, "I'm tired. I want to rest. I'm past seventy, and it's winter. I want to go away somewhere." Greco's brother burst into tears. Darrow turned to him. "All right, I'll take the case. For God's sake, stop crying." He won an acquittal for his clients.

Once he was discussing with Arthur Spingarn whether or not he should take a certain case which would require a lot of time and in which he would need a good deal of travel and maintenance expense. "What fee can the accused pay?" asked Darrow. "Oh, he has absolutely no money," replied Spingarn. "Well, that settles it," said Darrow. "I'll have to take the case." He paid the disbursements out of his own purse. Yet he could embarrass his friends by debating over a restaurant table whether he and Ruby should order two portions of a dish or share one between them. He had stingy moments, when he tried to save a few cents—and then gave twice the amount to the next mendicant he passed on the street.

Again, at his own expense, he went into Rockford to save the life of seventeen-year-old Russell McWilliams, son of a laboring family who had, while drunk on prohibition liquor, killed a streetcar conductor in a holdup. McWilliams had pleaded guilty and, to everyone's astonishment, since only one minor ever had been executed on a plea of guilty in the history of Illinois, was sentenced to be electrocuted. The streetcar company kept constant pressure on the governor not to commute the sentence. Jessie Binford of Hull House recounts, "The case had a terrific appeal for Darrow because McWilliams had never had a chance; he was a product of poverty, a slender, tragic boy, hardly knowing what it was all about. The poor and the working people of Rockford had come, mute-eyed and mute-tongued, hoping that the boy would be saved." Through Darrow's efforts the boy's sentence was commuted to life.

The only case from which he withdrew, even though he considered an injustice had been done, was that of the five Scottsboro boys, Negroes who were charged with the rape of a white woman. When he agreed to undertake the defense and prepared to leave for the South Arthur Garfield Hays had asked, "Why are you going so early? The trial doesn't start for several months." Darrow had replied, "Oh. I'm not going down for the trial. I'm going down to make friends." He soon withdrew, however, because "the case was controlled by the Communist party, who cared far less for the safety and well-being of those poor Negro boys than the exploitation of their own cause. If I could not be free and completely independent, without political ties, I would have none of it."

He had become a myth during his own time. Few people in America did not know his name and his face. No one of his day was more discussed, more loved and more hated; nor was he unaware of this split in the public affection for him. He had been invited to luncheon at H. L. Mencken's house in Baltimore and was climbing the flights of narrow, steep stairs, when Mencken called down to him, "Be careful, Clarence; if you fall and kill yourself in my house the public will crucify me."

"No, they won't," he sang back. "They'll canonize you."

George Whitehead's twelve-year-old daughter exclaimed after her first trip to Chicago, "I enjoyed Mr Darrow more than I did the Aquarium or the World's Fair." Whitehead comments, "Darrow didn't want anyone to think he had a sentimental side, but he had a hard time being tough. He liked all the attention, but he didn't like people to think he liked it." Frequently he would ask, "Am I as good as I was five years ago? Am I doing it as well?"

He plugged along, hoping that he could do still a little more work for tolerance before he died. H. L. Mencken wrote of him, "The marks of battle are all over his face. He has been through more wars than a whole regiment of Pershings. And most of them have been struggles to the death, without codes or quarter. . . . His cause seems lost among us. Nearly all the imbecilities that he has sought to lay live on. But they are not as safe as they used to be. Someday, let us hope, they will be put down. Whoever at last puts them down will owe half his bays to Clarence Darrow."

He continued to have an answer for everything, one that was nearly always pungent and satiric, but given with such sweetness and good will that the other fellow could not take offense. A young law clerk whom he knew failed to pass his bar examination, taking it a second time six months later. When Darrow again saw the boy he asked, "Well, did you pass?" "Yes sir, I sure did," replied the young chap. Darrow murmured, "And now I suppose you'll want the standards raised." When someone used as an argument in favor of religion that business depressions brought people close to the Church, he replied, "So do funerals." When a lovely blonde who had attended one of his lectures asked distressedly, "Mr Darrow, isn't there anything you believe in?" he replied a trifle wistfully, "Yes, I used to believe in blondes."

At last there emerged an ironic twist to his work for free thought. By the time Clarence reached seventy-five many clergymen and religious students had already passed him by. When he went to speak at the Meadville Theological School, from which his father had been the first student to be graduated, the Unitarian students found him a little old fashioned! "The men always enjoyed his trenchant criticism of religion and the ministry, and their discussions were fierce and hot, with no quarter given; however, I got the impression from their discussion that Mr Darrow did not realize how emancipated Unitarian ministers were of old theology and clericalism. In fact, in comparison with some of our humanists Mr Darrow seemed a bit conservative, and I think this rather annoyed him."

T. V. Smith of the University of Chicago debated him frequently on religion, using against Clarence the most modern and advanced theories of philosophy and metaphysics. "The first time I sprang this on him," says Smith, "he got up and said to the audience, 'If I had three weeks to think this over I might be able to answer it. As it is, I'll have to give my old lecture on free will.' After I had debated Darrow three times on this subject he finally leaned over in the cab one night, put his hand on my knee and said, 'You know, Professor, tonight for the first time I think I understand what you are saying, and there may be something in it after all.' "

In 1932, when Darrow was seventy-five, there was brought to him the last case in which he was to work in the glare of the international spotlight. In the city of Honolulu, Mrs Thalia Massie, wife of a lieutenant in the United States Navy, left a party at the Ala Wai Inn at midnight; the café was hot and smoky; Mrs Massie was upset over a quarrel she had just had with her husband; she decided to walk home alone. She turned onto the John Ena Road, a fairly well-lighted boulevard in the general direction of her home but which at its far end held a row of bungalows which the service men rented when they wanted women brought to them. Mrs Massie had gone only a short way up the road when a car containing two Hawaiians, one Chinaman and two Japanese pulled up at the curb; they were apparently intent upon hijacking one of the native women on her way to the service

328

bungalows, a practice that had been going on for a number of months. One of the Hawaiians and one of the Japanese jumped out and grabbed Mrs Massie. When she struggled with them Kahahawai, a famous Island athlete, slugged her with his fist and broke her jaw. They then threw her into the back seat of the car and drove down the Ala Moana Drive to an abandoned spot where the five men ravished her. Mrs Massie stumbled back to the road, was found by white motorists and taken to her home. She was immediately transferred to the hospital where, the following morning, she identified four of her assailants.

The relations between the mixed-breed population of Honolulu and the whites of the civilian population and army and navy settlements had always been delicate; now the resentment between the various groups flared up. The army and navy men were seriously disturbed; on the Island during the past year there had been some forty cases of attacks on native women that had necessitated hospital treatment. Since the service men had to leave their wives alone while they were at sea, this attack on the wife of an officer shocked and terrorized them. The smoldering ill will the natives felt against the whites manifested itself in large defense funds raised by the Hawaiian population for the two accused Hawaiians, by the Japanese colony for the two accused Japanese, the Chinese colony for the accused Chinaman, in the refusal of the largely native and mixed-breed police force to gather evidence against the five accused men, in the reluctance of the elected district attorney to prosecute, in the insistence that the junior assistant district attorney be assigned to try the case against the two best white attorneys on the Island. A widespread whispering campaign was waged against Mrs Massie in which her character was defamed, her reason for leaving the Ala Wai Inn attacked and a questionable motive attributed to her presence on the John Ena Road.

When the mixed-breed jury disagreed on the verdict and the four accused men were released on bail to engage in Island sports and resume their normal life, the ill feeling between the whites and the natives grew stronger. In an attempt to force a confession from one of the four men Lieutenant Massie severely beat one of the Japanese. He secured his confession, but the Japanese had a photograph taken which revealed the welts from the lashing on his back, and Massie's attorney informed him that such a confession, obtained through force, would be worthless. Lieutenant Massie and his wife's mother, Mrs Fortescue, aided by two sailors who acted out of loyalty to their superior officer, then kidnaped Kahahawai from in front of the courthouse by means of a fradulent affidavit. They took him to Mrs Fortescue's bungalow, where it was claimed by Lieutenant Massie that while he was trying to get the Hawaiian to confess, in the face of a service revolver, he had gone temporarily insane and pulled the trigger, killing Kahahawai instantly when the Hawaiian had mumbled, "Yeah, we done it." The sailors wrapped his body in a piece of canvas which they found in the garage and, after Mrs Fortescue had pulled the blinds in the car, dumped it onto the floor of the back seat. Mrs Fortescue then started driving very fast for the cliffs of Koko Head, where they intended to throw the body into the sea. However, the police already knew about Kahahawai's disappearance; when they saw the drawn blinds of Mrs Fortescue's automobile they gave pursuit, and the four participants in the kidnaping and murder were arrested.

Though the attack upon Mrs Massie had caused consternation in army and navy circles, it had been paid but moderate attention on the mainland. The killing, the arrest and murder charge against Lieutenant Massie, Mrs Fortescue and the two sailors immediately became a *cause célèbre,* was made a major issue in Congress, was heralded on the front pages of newspapers as far away as Budapest. Since it was impossible to secure an all-white jury in Honolulu, the Massie and Fortescue attorneys were fearful of the results of the trial. It was not only that the four indicted ones had an excellent chance of spending the rest of their lives in what the naval commanding officer, Rear Admiral Yates Stirling, described as "a disgusting and revolting Hawaiian prison," but that such a sentence would cause civil war among the varying races, breeds and colors that had to live together.

The friends and relatives of the socially prominent Massie and Fortescue families insisted that the finest criminal lawyer to be found must be retained for their defense. They approached Clarence Darrow. He had been following the unfolding situation with interest but was taken completely by surprise when he was offered a fee of twenty-five thousand dollars to undertake the case.

"I wondered if I could stand the trip," he said, "and I was not certain that I could bear the daily routine beginning in court early each day and watching and catching all that goes on in the trial. I was not even sure that my mind would click with its old-time vigor."

He communicated his doubts to the Massie and Fortescue families; they would not accept his refusal. He went to see his friend Arthur Spingarn, confiding to him that it was not the kind of case he liked, that he felt he ought not to be involved in it.

"I urged him to go for two reasons," relates Spingarn. "One, that he was tired and the trip to Hawaii would do him good and, two, that he needed the money so desperately, he was entitled to take on a case for money, just as other lawyers did, as against the thousands he had tried for nothing."

He accepted the Massie case. When asked after the trial why he had done so he replied, "I had never been to Honolulu and thought I should like to see the country. Besides, they said I was through as a lawyer, and I wanted to show them that a man in his seventies was keener than a younger person. In addition, Mrs Massie, as a psychological study, interested me and appealed to my sympathy." Having decided to undertake the defense, he telephoned to a stranger by the name of George Leisure, a Wall Street lawyer.

George Leisure relates, "One day the telephone rang and a voice said, 'Is this George Leisure?' I said, 'Yes.' He said, 'This is Clarence Darrow speaking.' I thought at first that it was one of my good friends using his name because he knew that I was an admirer of C. D. Since the voice sounded serious, however, I answered, 'Yes sir,' and listened. Mr Darrow then proceeded: 'I am about to try a case in Honolulu, and I have been told that you tried a case in Honolulu a year or so ago. I have never tried a case there and I thought that perhaps you would be willing to talk to me and tell me something of the nature of the procedure in that jurisdiction. If you could have lunch with me today I would appreciate it very much.'

"Some years before, while going to Europe, I had read Ludwig's *Life of Napoleon*. Upon contemplating the book, I thought how interesting it would be to be able to sit down and talk personally with Napoleon about some of his campaigns. My mind then drifted to the great men of my own profession, and I resolved that when I got back from Europe I would one day go to Chicago and have just such a talk with Clarence Darrow. When I got back to New York the regular demands of courtroom practice kept me from going to Chicago as I had planned. I now saw Mr Darrow and spent the entire afternoon with him, during which time I had precisely the kind of talk with him that I had thought it would be interesting to have had with Napoleon. He seemed surprised to know that I was familiar with many of his cases.

"When I left him at the close of the afternoon he said, 'I have been retired from practice . . . and I have not been regularly engaged in courtroom work for several years. I am also getting along in years and I would be very pleased to have a young man accompany me on this trip. I wonder if it would be possible for you to go to Honolulu with me?' Without even checking with my office I assured him that it was entirely possible and that I was prepared to leave at any time. Soon after that Mrs Leisure and I joined Mr and Mrs Darrow in Chicago, and we proceeded to Honolulu together."

In Honolulu Darrow found that most of the legal work already had been done by his associates; he asked the court for a week's postponement in order to interview his clients and witnesses and gain a more complete knowledge of the facts. He found Lieutenant Massie and his wife Thalia to be fine-looking, sensitive young people, under the circumstances quiet and self-possessed, but Thalia's mother, Mrs Fortescue, was a high-strung woman whom some of the Islanders believed responsible for the kidnaping. The navy men, solidly behind Massie, were grimly resolved that their brother officer should not go to prison. Darrow determined once again to plead mental illness, basing his case on an overwhelming provocation. He learned that the prosecution would be headed by the most successful pyrotechnical trial lawyer on the Islands; that Judge Davis, son of an outstanding Island lawyer who had come from New England, could be counted on to remain fair and impartial.

During his four thousand miles of travel Darrow had kept hoping that he would be able to get a majority of white men on the jury. When he finished his examinations and faced the men in the jury box he saw that they were all natives except two. "Even with these natives, however, Mr Darrow always extracted either a laugh or a smile from each juror before he accepted him, although at times the smile was drawn out almost by use of the corkscrew method. Mr Darrow would place his hands in the side pockets of his unpressed coat and, hunching his shoulders forward, make some friendly remark to the prospective juror which would bring forth the desired friendly contact." When he went into action on the first morning of the case Darrow was thrilled to find that his brain was working with its old-time precision and clarity. Though he had expert legal assistance always at his elbow, he tried most of the case himself. "Darrow, his coat hanging loosely about his bony frame, breathed kindliness and sympathy for all," says Rear Admiral Yates Stirling. "The courtroom seemed pervaded with this gentle, old voice. Its soothing effect upon that courtroom was miraculous to see. Slowly his voice was stamping out all bitterness."

He made no attempt to deny the killing, to keep any of the prosecution's material out of evidence, even when the facts were dubitable; neither did he deny that all four of the participants of the kidnaping were equally involved, even though the other three did not know that Lieutenant Massie might kill Kahahawai. The only legal fracas occurred when he attempted to introduce the facts of the rape as mitigation, as a basis for Massie's mental illness. The prosecution fought to keep the story out of the evidence, but Judge Davis ruled the story of the attack to be material and relevant. From the witness stand Mrs Massie recounted the details of the abduction, assault and ravishment, even to the need of having herself curetted because of pregnancy. Lieutenant Massie tried to picture for the jury his state of mind after the attack upon his wife.

Not since the Loeb-Leopold murder had the newspaper readers of the United States been so unified in their concentration on events happening in a courtroom. For the five weeks of the trial they argued the high points of the case, told what they would have done if they had been Lieutenant Massie or Mrs Fortescue or Mrs Massie. With the exception of those lawyers who insisted that the law could not be overthrown, no matter how extenuating the circumstances, the American people were vehement in their demand that the jury in Honolulu declare the four indicted ones not guilty.

If feeling on the mainland was intense, the Islanders were caught in the grip of the most dangerous fever that had seized its people since the American occupation. The feeling of the navy men ran so high that all shore leave had to be denied.

In his summation Darrow spoke to the jury for four hours. He appealed to them in quiet, gentle terms to put an end to this terrible tragedy, which kept multiplying itself with every new development. But even as he spoke he realized that his words were failing. "When I gazed into those dark faces I could see the deep mysteries of the Orient were there. My ideas and words were not registering."

He closed his final argument, which was broadcast by radio to the mainland, by saying, "I would like to think that some time not too far away I might come back here with a consciousness that I had done my small part in bringing peace and justice to an island that today is racked and torn by internal strife. I place this case in your hands and ask you to be kind, understanding and considerate, both to the living and to the dead."

Judge Davis agreed with the attorneys on the mainland; in his instructions to the jury he stressed the implacable fact that no man can take the law into his own hands. In spite of these instructions Darrow and the other defense attorneys, as well as ninety-nine per cent of the people of the United States, were convinced that the jury could bring in nothing but a verdict of not guilty. After two days of anxious and puzzled waiting he was genuinely surprised to hear a verdict of manslaughter, with a recommendation for leniency. Judge Davis sentenced Massie, the two sailors and Mrs Fortescue to ten years' imprisonment.

The backwash of resentment from the mainland was intense. In the United States Senate the verdict was denounced from the floor; the House Territories Committee voted for a sweeping investigation of the government of Hawaii to see if changes weren't necessary. Members of both the House and the Senate demanded that the four convicted ones be pardoned instantly and outright; congressmen publicly condemned Governor Judd, Judge Davis and the jury. Within twenty-four hours the jurors began apologizing for their verdict, explaining that it was the judge's charge which had forced them to bring in a manslaughter decision.

Then something happened that had never before happened to Clarence Darrow in his fifty-four years of practice: the attorney general of Hawaii came to see him at his hotel to say that the prosecution was distressed with its victory! He further told him that any attempt to move Mrs Fortescue, Massie and the two sailors to the Hawaiian prison would cause serious trouble—that Governor Judd wanted to dispose of the case. Darrow convoyed his four clients to the governor's office. Judd commuted their sentence to one hour; the four convicted persons sat with their defense attorney in the Old Palace for the hour, after which they were released. The commutation was roundly condemned in Congress, for without a full pardon, Massie, Mrs Fortescue and the two sailors had lost certain of their citizenship privileges, including the right to vote.

Nothing had been settled. Navy officials in Hawaii and the Congress demanded that the three remaining abductors once again be tried for the Massie outrage. Here Darrow performed the most valuable service of his journey. He persuaded the Massies and the navy men that another trial would only prolong the bitterness, that it would be far better for everyone concerned to drop the matter and let it be forgotten.

They listened to his counsel. A few days later the Darrows boarded ship to return to the mainland, taking with them Mr and Mrs Massie, Mrs Fortescue and the two sailors.

"I felt as we went away," said Darrow, "that we were leaving the Island more peaceful and happy than I had found it, for which I was very glad."

One night in January 1934 he sat up in a Pullman smoking compartment with Lowell B. Mason, an attorney of Washington, D.C., and Senator Gerald Nye of North Dakota, discussing the National Recovery Act, which had been in effect since July of 1933. In 1894, when he had fought in the American Railway Union strike, it had appeared to him that the national government was but another arm of industry and finance; in 1933 the newly elected Democrats appeared to be devoting the major portion of their efforts to getting people back to work at good wages and moderate hours, to the elimination of child labor, to making collective bargaining the law of the land—causes to which Clarence Darrow had given his most fruitful years.

The N.R.A. was in the process of putting two million men back to work; wages had been raised throughout the country; hours had been shortened; children were being taken out of the factories and sent to school; labor unions had been given the backing with which to become an integral part of American life. Yet in the crucial need to rescue the people from the country's shattering depression, in the frantic scurryings of the tens of thousands of businessmen, lawyers, lobbyists and administrators who poured into Washington, in the haste, the hostility, the confusion and the need to compromise, errors were being made. From small businessmen all over the country there arose a cry. In order to peg prices in a falling market so that industry could re-employ men at higher wages, price-fixing clauses had been written into most of the newly created business codes, which were then administered by the industries themselves. This power to fix prices had placed advantages in the hands of the giant corporations and combinations; the small businessman, who did not have the capital to enlarge his plant to deal in volume business, to advertise and promote, could not compete at the higher price levels, nor could he get his share of contracts unless he belonged to the industrial combinations.

The complaints of these smaller businessmen had become so widespread that Senator Nye had demanded an impartial review board be set up to diagnose the injustices of the N.R.A. General Hugh S. Johnson, N.R.A. administrator, and Donald Richberg, chief counsel, insisted that a proven liberal be named to head the board. Remembering the discussion in the Pullman smoking compartment, Senator Nye suggested Darrow as head of the Review Board. President Roosevelt, Senator Borah, General Johnson and Donald Richberg agreed. Darrow undertook what he was quite certain would be a laborious and thankless task because he knew that in order to gain labor-and-wage concessions, the code authorities had permitted such of his old adversaries as the Iron and Steel Institute and the National Coal Association to set their own prices and maintain them at a level which eliminated free trading.

He and Ruby moved to Washington, where he had Lowell B. Mason appointed as his legal adviser, secured the appointment of W. O. Thompson, his former partner from Chicago, and Robert S. Keebler, a Tennessee attorney who had been ostracized by the Nashville Bar Association because he had attacked the anti-evolution bill when it had been passed. He
335

met with the balance of his Review Board, which was popularly to be known as the Darrow Board, to outline what he conceived to be their function in Washington. The board then marched en masse to the offices of General Johnson for instructions. After the amenities had been exchanged Darrow asked Johnson what he thought they ought to do.

"I have provided rooms for you here, right next to time," replied Johnson. "Also clerical help and supplies. You do some investigating and let me know if the codes are all right."

"But if we find the codes not all right?" inquired Darrow.

"Then you report to me. I am the big cheese here."

"I don't think we care to do that," replied Darrow slowly. "I expect we had better go see the President."

There was a moment of strained silence, then Darrow rose and led his troupe to the White House. President Roosevelt received them warmly. He said, "We believe it is a good thing for the country and democracy that we have appointed the N.R.A. Review Board. There are always those who will say that Big Business is ruling this country; you will not find this so under this administration. We believe that the N.R.A. codes have been drafted by men who represent, fairly, all types of business, both big and small."

"Mr President," said Darrow quietly, "before we accept the appointment we want it understood that we will be active and functioning. . . . We are here to protect the interests of the small businessmen, and we do not propose to let them down. Now, Mr President, you are a man of your word. Do we have a free hand?"

"Mr Darrow, you have a free hand," replied the President. "Conduct your hearings, make your findings and give them to me within a specified time, with your recommendations."

Turning to his board Darrow said, "Gentlemen, we will begin work tomorrow morning. And when I said work, I mean work."

The next day President Roosevelt signed an executive order, making the Review Board responsible to him instead of to Johnson. Refusing the adjoining offices offered to him by Johnson on the grounds that he did not want the public or the complainants to feel that he was in any way attached to the administrator, Darrow opened his first hearing in his hotel room at the Willard. Within a few days the Review Board had perforce expanded to four large rooms on the second floor of the Hotel Willard, then to fourteen offices in an uptown office building.

Because of his eagerness to listen to every businessman who thought he had been injured, the seventy-seven-year-old Darrow drove himself and his board mercilessly. Awakened in the middle of the night by a problem that had been presented at the day's hearing, he would think it out to a satisfactory conclusion and, at two or three in the morning, telephone Mason to give him orders. He worked the board for fourteen and sixteen hours a day, including Sundays. Mason comments, "His disregard for the lunch hour became so bad that I finally had to plead with him to adjourn at noon for the sake of the complainants, witnesses and lawyers whose crusading spirits couldn't overcome their hunger. It was comical how some of the other members hid behind Darrow by saying, 'Well, now, gentlemen, I think we should adjourn for a couple of hours; Mr Darrow is in need of a little rest.' Or one of the members who was deaf would say, 'Speak up, Mr Witness, you know Mr Darrow had a mastoid operation years ago, and he can't hear very well out of one ear.'

During the four months that the Darrow Board was in existence it held fifty-seven public hearings, examined thirty-four codes, investigated three thousand complaints. Though Darrow invited the code-authority attorneys and deputy administrators to be present whenever their particular code was being attacked and to cross-examine the witness after he had completed his testimony, the impression got around Washington that he was hostile to the codes. Newspaper stories about a rift between Darrow and Johnson began spreading. On the only occasion that General Johnson ever saw Darrow alone he took him for a ride in his limousine. Sensing that a major battle would be fought in the back seat of the car, reporters assembled twenty-five strong in front of the Hotel Willard to await its return. When Darrow, who had forgotten to take a hat with him, stepped out of the limousine his head was well covered.

"I got the general's hat, boys," he told the reporters with a chuckle. He had also got the general's goat.

On April eighteenth the Darrow Board gave its chief a seventy-seventh birthday party. The Hotel Willard served its regular two-dollar-and-fifty-cent banquet dinner for a dollar and sent Clarence a bouquet of American Beauty roses. In only one way did Clarence show his age. Mason persuaded him to see the moving picture of Greta Garbo as Queen Christina. Just as the queen was climbing into bed with the Spanish ambassador Darrow turned to Mason and said, "Lowell, I think Gerry Nye will be up at the room waiting to see us. I guess we had better go now." Mason complained that he had to go back alone the next day to find out what had happened to the queen.

After three months of hearings and investigations he came to the conclusion that the National Recovery Administration, in its desire to help the workingman, had baited its hook with price protection and that the trusts had proceeded to swallow the bait, the hook, the line and the fisherman. One member of the Review Board says, "Darrow didn't like the spectacle of a regulatory system which seemed to have been seized by large industry with its effects pressed upon small business. He felt it was too large a price to pay for social betterment." Nor did he believe that the country should approve injustices in the codes in the name of labor progress. To his board members he kept saying:

"You can't get to a pleasant place to be at unless you use pleasant methods to get there. When you are dealing with a human society the means is fully as important as the end. This compromise of handing big business a monopoly in order that they may give more work at higher wages will result in destroying all small and independent businesses in the country and will ultimately leave labor and the nation in the hands of a few overwhelming trusts."

At the end of three months Darrow submitted his first report to President Roosevelt. When the report was released to the press two weeks later it was accompanied by a terrific blast from General Johnson, defending the N.R.A. against Darrow's charges. Under the heading of "Tender-Hearted Cynic," Newsweek magazine wrote, " . . . As a foreman of a kind of governmental grand jury to tell the administration how the N.R.A. is working, [Darrow] has brought in a report saying it's doing perfectly terribly. Last week Washington sat forward nervously to see how many holes that particular bomb would tear in New Deal pavements. Meantime Mr Darrow sat back, hitched his fingers in under his gallus straps and looked on with that amazing mixture of cynicism, compassion and incredibly brilliant intelligence that is his character."

In the following month Darrow submitted two more reports to the President in an attempt to outline revisions in the N.R.A. that would protect the small businessman without losing any of labor's gains. These he released to the press at the same time that he sent them to the White House. President Roosevelt read both reports, was convinced by Darrow's evidence, appointed a Senate committee to study the recommendations.

Hugh Johnson was outraged; he "demanded that the President remove its members, declaring them to be ill advised, prejudiced and engaged in special pleading." Both Johnson and Donald Richberg felt that Darrow had betrayed them, that they had made a mistake in thinking him a proven liberal. In spite of Johnson's objections most of the major recommendations of the Darrow Board were put into effect. Price fixing was eliminated from all new codes; the Federal Trade Commission was given the right to examine charges of oppressive practices by monopolies; price fixing was taken out of the service trades; labor controversies were placed in the hands of a special industrial-relations board; the N.R.A. power was taken out of the hands of Johnson, to be distributed through such branches of government as the attorney general's office and the secretary of the interior.

In March 1935 Darrow appeared before the Senate Investigating Committee to give the final conclusions from the investigation.

"I had not been here very long," he told Senators Harrison, George, Barclay, Guffy, Cousins, La Follette and a number of others, "until I rather got the idea that the N.R.A. in effect made it easier for the people who had it all and made it harder for the people who did not have it. The outstanding opinion was that the N.R.A. was gotten up to help 'big business,' and they could not help big business very much unless they took the business away from the small fellows. I know something about big business, more than small business, and my sympathies are all with the small fellow. If there were not so much big business there would be more small business, much more, in my opinion. Big business has all of the advantage, and the N.R.A. very materially increased that advantage. Big business exists because they have got keen men at the head of it; they have got plenty of money, and they can advertise in the leading newspaper, fences and barns. . . . Little business is supposed to pick up the crumbs that are left to fall from the rich man's table. They are made up of people with small capital. The concentration of wealth is going on, and it looks almost as if there were nothing to stop it. If we do not destroy it there will be nothing but masters and slaves left before we get much further along."

He complained against what he called "the economy of scarcity," which created high prices, and attacked the idea that there could be overproduction in a country where half the people were not enjoying a sufficient consumption of goods.

Senator Lonergan asked, "Have you any ideas for improving the system of distribution as to the output of factory and farm?"

"Yes, I have got a lot of them, but nobody listens to them."

"Do you think there is any substitute for economic laws?"

"I am not at all sure about economic laws," rejoined Darrow. "I do not think they are like the laws of gravity. I think we will find that most of them have been made by human beings and pretty human at that. The lords of creation think that the Almighty meant that they should be rich and the great mass of people should be poor. Men have got to do these things themselves, but men are awfully hard-hearted. Kindliness comes from imagination, and very few people have any to waste. When they get so that they can put themselves in other people's places and suffer because they suffer, we will probably get rid of most of these inequalities, but whether they will ever get there, I do not know. I think that something like a socialistic system would be the only thing that would make anything like an equal distribution of wealth. What are all these machines made for if they are not made to help the human race to live a better life and an easier life, to have more pleasure and less pain? . . . I think it is possible that we will have a better situation a few hundred years from now. I hate to wait so long."

He was far from being in top form; he was tired. In addition he was torn by the same lacerating dilemmas that had Washington and the rest of the country sorely perplexed: how to cross nineteenth-century capitalism with twentieth-century socialism so as to retain the best qualities of both, kill off neither parent and breed a healthy, happy, lusty economic child, indigenous to the character of the people and the resources of the land, with a chance for survival in a hostile, changing world. To the majority of Americans the confusion arising from this problem in sociopolitical eugenics was a new kind of headache; to Darrow it was an old, old friend.

The Senate Investigating Committee co-operated in securing the passage of laws which helped to wipe out many of the injustices of the National Recovery Act.

In this last public appearance in which he was to voice a social philosophy for all the nation to hear and read Darrow put the small businessman in the anomalous position of having their champion plead for socialism at the same time that he was pleading for a fair capitalism. William Hard commented in *Survey-Graphic*, "Mr Darrow is in favor of the restoration of competition, and he is in favor of progress into socialization. Walter Lippmann cannot see how Mr Darrow can advocate both capitalistic competition and Russian communism. That is because Mr Lippmann is a logician. Mr Darrow is as wild as life."

Shortly after his appearance before the Senate Investigating Committee he began markedly to fail. Though his heart had been troubling him for a number of years, he paid himself scant attention, figuring that if he had lived to be seventy-eight without taking care of himself it was too late to mend his ways. His interest in the subjects for which he had always worked was of greater importance to him than the conservation of his waning energies. He continued to write his critical articles at the broad black desk he had brought home to his study and went out on the road to lecture under any and all weather conditions.

Julian Street says, "If ever I saw a man whose character showed in his face, that man was Clarence Darrow. He had the face of a prophet. Nobody else looked in the least like him. He must have known that many people didn't understand him, that many regarded him as a devil's advocate, but he didn't care a hang. Placidly, magnificently, he went his way without regard to anything but his own sense of what was right."

He was still in there pitching, but the old arm was getting weak. By the time he reached seventy-eight Ruby had to persuade him to abandon the more arduous lecture tours, to write more sparingly at his desk. He would sit in his wicker chair before the fireplace or at the windows overlooking Jackson Park, the little Japanese bridges and pagodas on Lake Michigan. Opie Reid, author of *The Arkansas Traveler*, lived a few houses down the street; the two men spent amusing hours together, telling each other how the world would go to hell once they had departed from this earth.

He was almost seventy-nine when he wrote one of the most delightful and discerning articles of his journalistic career. Asked by *Esquire* magazine to contribute a piece on jury picking, he minted the accumulated wisdom of his fifty-eight years in the courtroom into a very few paragraphs. Starting off by advising that one should always choose a man who laughs, because a juror who laughs hates to find anyone guilty, and to avoid wealthy men, because rich men will always convict—unless the defendant allegedly had violated the antitrust laws—he then dissected the influence of the various religions upon the character of the prospective juror. He advised that Methodists be accepted as jurymen because "their religious emotions can be transmuted into love and charity," but warned against taking Presbyterians because "they know right from wrong but seldom find anything right," and against Lutherans because "they were almost always sure to convict." After counseling never to accept a prohibitionist under any circumstance, he recommended that the best jurors for the defense were Catholics, Unitarians, Congregationalists, Universalists, Jews and agnostics.

The last words he was to write, which were found in his desk, scribbled in longhand on composition-book paper, were
341

an epitome of his life. "The fact that my father was a heretic always put him on the defensive, and we children thought it was only right and loyal that we should defend his cause. Even in our little shop the neighbors learned that there was something going on and that my father was ever ready to meet all comers on the mysteries of life and death. During my youth I always listened, but my moral support was with my father. I cannot remember that I ever had any doubt that he was right. The fact that most of the community were on the other side made him so much surer of his cause." It also had made Clarence, son of Amirus, surer of his cause.

On his seventy-ninth birthday he made a sentimental trip to Kinsman with George Whitehead, for he sensed that this would be his last chance. He visited his old friends, making pilgrimages to the spots he had loved best as a child. As he sat on the steps of the octagonal-shaped home the reporters gathered around to hear one of his famous blasts at some greed or stupidity current in the news. Clarence wasn't up to it. "The old man didn't have all his buttons," says one of the local Ohio reporters. "But we polished up his quotes. It was that way with Darrow."

He returned to Chicago to enter a hospital for a general diagnosis. There was little that could be done for him. Ruby took him home, put him to bed, called in three male nurses. During the first few weeks of his seventy-ninth year she permitted friends to come and visit with him, but after a time she saw that this exhausted his strength, that he sometimes fell asleep on his guests, that his mind did not always work collectedly. She thereupon shut out all visitors.

In nice weather he had liked to walk for an hour along the Midway or through the University of Chicago campus, but as he grew weaker Ruby would not let him go out. Darrow complained that he would rather go about his normal way, do the things he liked and die a little sooner. When he felt too badly about being confined to the house she would wrap him up warmly and send him across the Midway to visit Professor T. V. Smith at the university. He would chat with Smith about philosophy and religion and the good old days. One day, thinking to amuse the Old Lion, Smith told him that he was going to put up three statuettes in his office: the first of Socrates, his ancient master, high up on the file; the second of Thomas Jefferson, his modern master, on a stand where he could see him face to face, and third, very close to hand, a statuette of the American gadfly, Clarence Darrow. Tears filled Darrow's eyes as he said, "Why, I didn't know you felt that way about me." Smith had been bantering; when he saw the tears in Darrow's eyes he knew that the rock that was Clarence Darrow had been shattered.

Clarence spent a slow, painful and ugly year dying; on his eightieth birthday he could give no interview which his newspaper friends might polish up.

He died on March 13, 1938, from almost eighty-one years of living.

A friend from Woodstock, Illinois, sent a mahogany casket as a gift. The funeral parlor on Sixty-third Street in Chicago was supposed to close at eleven at night but did not shut its doors for forty-eight hours.

At all hours of the day and night people filed past to say their farewells: workingmen from the stockyards and steel mills in their overalls; scrubwomen in their Mother Hubbards; colored men with their lunch baskets under their arms; the cold and frightened ones who had gone to him to warm their hands at his fire; the weak and confused and indeterminate ones who had been strengthened by his boldness and resolution; the harassed, the unhappy, the mentally ill, whose plight he had tried to make intelligible; teachers, whose freedom he had broadened by his struggles; students, whose minds had been stimulated by his iconoclasm; lawyers, to whose trade he had given another dimension; clergymen, to whom he had revealed Christianity at work; those who came from no specific class or section; the labor leaders and union members whose organizations he had preserved under fire; the liberals, for whose middle-of-the-road navigation he had fought unceasingly for half a century; the radical for whose freedom of thought and speech he had endured the spleen of reaction; the long line of men accused of crime for whom he had earned another chance; those who had killed and who lived now only because this dead man had lived; the middle-class folk for whom he had been a rallying point, a debunker, an intellectual spark.

In the dark small hours the creatures of the night, the prostitutes, the bums, the addicts, the thieves, the derelicts, mixed in with those who had come to pray for his soul, with those who had come to remember his friendship and his love; all streamed past his coffin, all those who had needed a friend and had had no friend and to whom Clarence Darrow had been a friend.

Darrow had said, "Let Judge Holly speak at my funeral. He knows everything there is to know about me, and he has sense enough not to tell it."

Funeral services were held in Bond Chapel at the University of Chicago in a torrential downpour. Ruby remained at home, but it seemed as though the rest of Chicago had come.

343

A large crowd that could not be accommodated inside stood outside in the rain to hear whatever they could of the services.

Judge Holly said, "It is a magnificent thing that Clarence Darrow lived. The colored race will long remember him with grateful hearts for his heroic battles in their behalf. The man who toils with his hands, the poor and the unfortunate whom society hunted down, found him ever ready to devote his extraordinary talents in their behalf. He gave up a brilliant legal career, that would have made him one of the rich men of the country, to espouse the cause of labor. In Clarence Darrow's heart was infinite pity and mercy for the poor, the oppressed, the weak and the erring—all races, all colors, all creeds, all humankind. He made the way easier for many. He preached not doctrines, but love and pity, the only virtues that can make this world any better. Thousands of lives were made easier and happier because he lived. . . . His great abilities were given freely to the cause of human liberty and for the succor of the weak and the unfortunate."

Ruby said, "Mr Darrow always maintained that he didn't care whether he went to heaven or hell because he has so many good friends in either place."

Clarence had asked that he be cremated. His son Paul, George Whitehead and the three nurses carried his ashes to the bridge crossing from the mainland of Jackson Park to the Wooded Island, from where they were scattered to the wind, the rain and the water. The owner of the funeral parlor would accept no pay, asking instead for a signed copy of *The Story of My Life*.

From all over the world the tributes poured in. The newspapers said, "What he did for America can never be forgotten." "No one was more reckless of the consequences of what he might say or do in defense of the defenseless."

Judge Frank Murphy called him one of the great spirits of our time. George Jean Nathan said, "One of my greatest and deepest admirations has gone from the world." James Weldon Johnson said, "Clarence Darrow was one of the greatest of Americans, and as time passes the nobility of his character will stand out clearer and clearer in perspective, above misunderstanding, above bitterness, above calumny. . . ."

The *Christian Century* said, "He had a profound concern for men; he pitied them and pitied most the ones most in need of a redress of bitter grievances. He wanted them to have liberty to think and work and live out their little lives in such joy as is possible for men."

Dr Harry Elmer Barnes wrote, "The death of Clarence Darrow brings to an end one of the most colorful and commendable careers in the whole of American biography.

The permanent estimate of his career will probably lay most value upon the fact that he was the outstanding libertarian in American history since the days of Thomas Jefferson. . . ."

One clergyman said, "The three great Americans of our time are Luther Burbank, Thomas Edison and Clarence Darrow: Burbank because he helped release the forces of the earth; Edison because he helped release the forces of nature; Darrow because he helped release the forces of the human spirit."

A young student friend of Darrow's, writing about him as a classroom assignment, carved out the finest epitaph any man could deserve: "Freedom is a favorite word with Darrow. When he wished to express a favorable opinion of someone he would begin by saying, 'He is for freedom.'"

An admirer commented, "I'll bet he's confounding the heavenly courts, just as he did here."

If Darrow could have heard these tributes he would have ducked his head into his big shoulders, raised one eyebrow quizzically and drawled, "I'm the one all this talk's been about. I always thought I was a hell of a fellow, and now I'm sure of it."

And he would have smiled.

BESTSELLERS OF THE YEAR!

An exclusive listing of the Bantam Books America is reading and talking about.

- ☐ F1862 **PIGBOATS**, Theodore Roscoe (50¢)
  The true story of the fighting submariners of World War II.
- ☐ A1848 **LOUISVILLE SATURDAY**, Margaret Long (35¢)
  Powerful and provocative novel of women and soldiers.
- ☐ A1834 **TEMPLE OF GOLD, THE**, William Goldman (35¢)
  A first novel about today's angry, rootless, seeking men and women.
- ☐ F1833 **WAPSHOT CHRONICLE, THE**, John Cheever (50¢)
  Story of a family who refused to let the sap of life run dry.
- ☐ A1831 **PRICE OF SALT, THE**, Claire Morgan (35¢)
  A high voltage novel of two women.
- ☐ A1828 **HARRY BLACK**, David Walter (35¢)
  Dramatic novel filled with high velocity and unbearable tension!
- ☐ A1826 **HELMET FOR MY PILLOW**, Robert Leckie (35¢)
  The real story of Guadalcanal and of the Marines.
- ☐ F1817 **PHILADELPHIAN, THE**, Richard Powell (50¢)
  Vivid and engrossing novel of a man's most profound conflicts.
- ☐ F1807 **HOME BEFORE DARK**, Eileen Bassing (50¢)
  Tender and terrifying novel of a woman's return from a mental institution.
- ☐ 1806 **GIDGET**, Frederick Kohner (25¢)
  Awakening of a young girl who wanted to grow up in a hurry.
- ☐ A1800 **INN OF THE SIXTH HAPPINESS, THE**, Alan Burgess (35¢)
  True story of a courageous English girl in war-torn China.
- ☐ F1791 **RALLY ROUND THE FLAG, BOYS!**, Max Shulman (50¢)
  Hilarious bestseller about sex, guided missiles, real estate, U.S. Army and love.
- ☐ A1785 **THEY FOUGHT FOR THE SKY**, Quentin Reynolds (35¢)
  Breathtaking story of the first men to fight in the air.
- ☐ A1752 **NEVER LOVE A STRANGER**, Harold Robbins (35¢)
  Story of a tough-skinned New York character, never lacks for force or interest.
- ☐ A1721 **BIG NICKELODEON, THE**, Maritta Wolff (35¢)
  Harsh, unsparing novel about the seamy underside of Hollywood.
- ☐ 1737 **LIGHT IN THE FOREST, THE**, Conrad Richter (25¢)
  Vivid and unforgettable story of a white boy raised among savages.
- ☐ A1708 **HELLER, THE**, William E. Henning (35¢)
  Famous novel of a young girl who grew up—*too fast.*
- ☐ F1707 **BIG WAR, THE**, Anton Myrer (50¢)
  Finest novel to come out of World War II! The mighty story of Marines at war.
- ☐ A1677 **BRIDGE OVER THE RIVER KWAI, THE**, Pierre Boulle (35¢)
  An intelligent and thrilling suspense story!
- ☐ F1659 **LAST HURRAH, THE**, Edwin O'Connor (50¢)
  The great big Smash-Hit Bestseller that has taken America by storm.
- ☐ A1641 **SAYONARA**, James A. Michener (35¢)
  Poignant and moving story of an American officer and an exquisite Japanese woman.
- ☐ F1554 **TEN NORTH FREDERICK**, John O'Hara (50¢)
  Profoundly revealing story of life in America today.

BANTAM BOOKS, INC., Dept. J, 657 W. Chicago Ave., Chicago 10, Illinois
Please send me the Bantam Bestsellers which I have checked.

Name..   I am enclosing $...................
(Check or Money Order)

Address..   (NO CURRENCY PLEASE)
Sorry, no C.O.D.'s

City...   NOTE: Please include 10¢ per book for postage and handling
State...   on orders of less than 5 books.

ALLOW TWO TO THREE WEEKS FOR DELIVERY